ↄↄↄↄↄↄↄↄↄↄↄↄↄↄↄↄↄↄↄↄↄↄↄ

Unhappy Valley

Unhappy Valley

Conflict in
Kenya & Africa

Book One: State & Class
Book Two: Violence & Ethnicity

Bruce Berman

Professor of Political Studies
Queen's University, Ontario

&

John Lonsdale

Fellow of Trinity College, Cambridge

James Currey
LONDON

Heinemann Kenya
NAIROBI

Ohio University Press
ATHENS

James Currey Ltd
54b Thornhill Square
Islington
London N1 1BE, England

Heinemann Kenya
Kijabe Street, PO Box 45314
Nairobi, Kenya

Ohio University Press
Scott Quadrangle
Athens, Ohio 45701 USA

British Library Cataloguing in Publication Data
Berman, Bruce
Unhappy valley : conflict in Kenya & Africa
Book One: State & Class
Book Two: Violence & Ethnicity
1. Kenya. Social conditions
I. Title II. Lonsdale, John *1937–*
967.6203

ISBN 0-85255-021-9
ISBN 0-85255-022-7 (pbk Book One)
ISBN 0-85255-099-5 (pbk Book Two)

Library of Congress Cataloging-in-Publication Data
Berman, Bruce (Bruce J.)
Unhappy valley : conflict in Kenya and Africa / Bruce Berman & John Lonsdale.
p. cm. —— (Eastern African studies)
Includes bibliographical references and indexes.
Contents: bk. 1. State and class —— bk. 2. Violence and ethnicity.
ISBN 0-8214-1016-4 (Ohio Univ. Press : cloth)
ISBN 0-8214-1017-2 (Ohio Univ. Press : pbk. : bk. 1). ——
ISBN 0-8214-1025-3 (Ohio Univ. Press : pbk. : bk. 2)
1. Kenya——Politics and government——To 1963. 2. Great Britain——
Colonies——Administration. 3. Kenya——Dependency on Great Britain.
4. Kenya——Economic conditions——To 1963. 5. Kenya——History——To
1963. 6. Clans——Kenya. 7. Mau Mau——History. I. Lonsdale, John.
II. Title. III. Series : Eastern African studies (London, England)
JQ2947.A2B47 1992b
325'.341'096762——dc20 91-48091
CIP

Typeset in 10/11pt Baskerville by Colset Private Limited, Singapore
Printed and bound in Great Britain

Contents

BOOK ONE: State & Class

One
Introduction
An Encounter in Unhappy Valley
BRUCE BERMAN & JOHN LONSDALE

Part I
Conquest

Two
The Conquest State of Kenya, 1895–1905
JOHN LONSDALE

v

Contents

Contents

vii

Contents

Maps

Acknowledgements

Some of the chapters in this book were first published in the journals and collections indicated below. We would like to thank the publishers and editors for permission to reproduce them here.

Cambridge University Press
'Bureaucracy and incumbent violence: colonial administration and the origins of the Mau Mau Emergency in Kenya', *British Journal of Political Science* 6(1) (1976).
'The politics of conquest: the British in Western Kenya, 1894–1908', *The Historical Journal* 20(4) (1977).
'Coping with the contradictions: the development of the colonial state in Kenya, 1895–1914', *Journal of African History* 20(4) (1979).

The Canadian Association of African Studies
'Crises of accumulation, coercion and the colonial state: the development of the labour control system in Kenya, 1919–1929', *Canadian Journal of African Studies* 14(1) (1980).
'The concept of articulation and the political economy of colonialism', *Canadian Journal of African Studies* 18(3) (1984).

Sage Publications
'Structure and process in the bureaucratic states of colonial Africa', *Development and Change* 15(2) 1984.

The Leiden Centre for the History of European Expansion
'The conquest state of Kenya', in J.A. de Moor and H.L. Wesseling (eds), *Imperialism and War: Essays on Colonial Wars in Asia and Africa*, E.J. Brill/Universitaire pers Leiden, Leiden, 1989.

The Centre of African Studies, University of Edinburgh
'African pasts in Africa's future', *African Futures*, Seminar Proceedings No. 28, Edinburgh, 1988.

Preface

In writing these papers over a period of some fifteen years, we have incurred many debts to institutions and individuals that have helped our research and sharpened our thoughts, and which we gratefully acknowledge. Kenya has been fortunate in attracting a remarkable body of scholarship since its independence. The calibre of this work has facilitated and inspired our own. Individual authors and works are cited in our footnotes, but we would like to record some special thanks here. This is a more invidious exercise than most; so much good work has been done; and by an unusually generous group of scholars. But we have particularly important debts, both intellectual and personal, to Dave Anderson, David Cohen, Fred Cooper, Michael Cowen, Tabitha Kanogo, Greet Kershaw, Colin Leys, Godfrey Muriuki, Atieno Odhiambo, John Spencer, David Throup, Richard Waller and Luise White.

Our work has been made possible by the remarkable collections and efficient staff of the Public Record Office, London, and, especially, of the Kenya National Archives in Nairobi and its Chief Archivist, Mr M. Musembi. Professor Ahmed Salim, head of the Department of History at the University of Nairobi, offered us the facilities and hospitality of his department during our most recent visit in July and August 1988. He and Professor Henry Mwaniki, head of the Department of History at Kenyatta University, also enabled us to present some of our findings in seminars of their staff and graduate students.

We would also like to thank the Social Science and Humanities Research Council of Canada, the Smuts Memorial Fund of the University of Cambridge, and the School of Graduate Studies and Advisory Research Committee of Queen's University for grants that over the years have made our research possible. The Master and Fellows of Trinity College, Cambridge, have enabled us to work together during the closing stages of this work.

Preface

To James Currey, long-suffering publisher and friend, we owe the idea for this book. His encouragement and his patience through repeated delays were vital in bringing it to fruition. Roger Thomas provided essential editorial assistance; while Dr Jocelyn Murray efficiently compiled the index and glossary.

Finally, we thank our wives, Elaine Berman and Moya Lonsdale, for their patience and understanding in the face of our repeated absences, especially during summer holidays, and our distracted absorption in the problems of Kenya and colonial Africa. We dedicate this volume to them.

Cambridge and Kingston

Glossary

Note: words in this glossary, unless marked, are Kikuyu. Like Swahili, Kikuyu is a Bantu language, and singular and plural nouns are shown by prefixes. For most nouns of the person class, the singular prefix is mu- or mw-, and the plural is a-.

acenji (mucenji) heathen, savages

ahoi (muhoi) tenant, tenants in friendship

il aigwanak (Maasai) warrior leaders

aimwo good-for-nothings

Akurinu 'growlers', nickname for a sect

anake young men, warriors

anake a forti the unmarried warriors of 1940

andu ago (mundu mugo) medicine man/men; diviners

aramati trustees

arathi prophets

aroti dreamers

aregi 'those who refuse'

athami 'people on the move', migrants

athamaki, (muthamaki) 'those who can speak', 'big men'; Sing. sovereign

athomi readers, = Christian converts

athoni relatives by marriage, in-laws

athoni ahoi friends by marriage

athuuri elders, 'those who choose'

atiriri 'Hear!', 'Listen!'

batuni the 'fighting oath' (from the English 'platoon')

bara (mbaara) fight, battle

buruni country, land

comba (from Sw.) foreigners, Muslims

dini (Sw.) sect, religion

ereriri selfish ones

Gikuyu na Muumbi the Kikuyu 'Adam' and 'Eve'

githaka, (ithaka) land, farms

githukumo waged work

gitonga, (itonga) 'a man of means'; pl. wealth, property

gitungati, (itungati) rearguard

gwika to do

xiii

hinya   power, strength
hongo (Sw.)   road-tolls

ibuku   book
ibuku ria Ngai   Book of God, =
   Bible
ihii   uncircumcised youth
   (insult)
imaramari   hooligans
iregi   'those who refuse', a
   generation name
irungu   'straightener', a
   generation name
ithaka na wiathi   land and
   freedom; self-mastery through
   land
itonga   'men of means'
ituika   generational handover of
   ritual power

kaburu   corporal
karing'a   true, real
kiama   council, society
kiama kia bara   war council
Kiama kia Wiathi   Freedom
   Council (Mau Mau central
   committee)
kibaata   a warriors' dance
kifagio (Sw.)   broom, sweeping
kimaramari, imaramari
   hooligan(s)
kipande   registration certificate,
   carried by adult African males
kirira   silence, secrecy
kiriika   destruction
kirore   thumbprint, 'those who
   have signed'
komerera   bandits
kuna   first clearance of land;
   right derived from this
kuuga   to say

laibon (Maasai)   prophet
'laini'   from English 'line':

labour lines, also town
housing

mai ni maruru   water is bitter
Maina   generation name
mambere   those in front,
   forerunners
mangati (Maasai)   enemy
mashambaini (Sw.)   fields, farms,
   the white highlands
maraya   prostitutes
maskini (Sw.)   the poor
mbari   sub-clan
mikora   'spivs'
miri   roots
mitaro   trenches, terracing
mkunga mbura   rain gatherer,
   rainbow
mucenji   heathen, savage
mugumo   fig tree, site of sacrifices
Muhimu   Nairobi headquarters
   of Mau Mau central
   committee
muhiriga, (mihiriga)   clan, clans
muingi   community
muiritu   circumcised but
   unmarried woman, grown girl
mukuyu   fig tree
Mukuruwe wa Gathanga   Kikuyu
   'Garden of Eden'
muma   oath
mundu, andu   man, person; men,
   people
mundu mugo   medical
   practitioner, diviner
munene   big, chief
muteithia   helper
muthamaki   one who can speak,
   leader, sovereign
muthami, (athami)   one who has
   moved, emigrants
Muthirigu   Song of the big uncut
   girl
Mwangi   generation name

Nabongo (Luyia) chief, chiefly title

ndamathia mythical Kikuyu rainbow dragon

ndege bird, aeroplane

nduiko (Embu, Meru) generation handover of ritual power

ndungata servant, servants

Ngai God

ng'aragu famine

ngerewani vanguard

ngero evil, crime

ngwatio neighbourhood work party

njaguti serfs, good-for-nothings

njiraini by the roadside

nyimbo hymns, political songs

nyoka snake

nyumba house

orkoiyot (Kalenjin) ritual expert

riigi door

riika generation

ruguru the west

ruraya Europe

safari (Sw.) caravan, journey

tene eternity

tha compassion

thabari Kikuyu equivalent of Sw. *safari*, caravan, journey

thahu ritual uncleanness

thaka 'handsome ones'

thama moving, Exodus

thenge he-goat, ram (used in traditional sacrifices)

thingira men's house or dormitory

tuthuuri anti-elders (contemptuous)

ucenji 'heathendom'

uiguano unity

uhuru (Sw.) freedom

Uiguano wa Tha League of Compassion

ukabi Maasai

ukombo slavery

umaramari (Maasai) depravity, lack of self-control

'wabici' (from English) office

wanyahoro 'man of peace'

Watu wa Mungu (Sw.) People of God (a sect)

weru plains, grassland, wilderness

wiathi moral growth, 'freedom', self-control

wira work

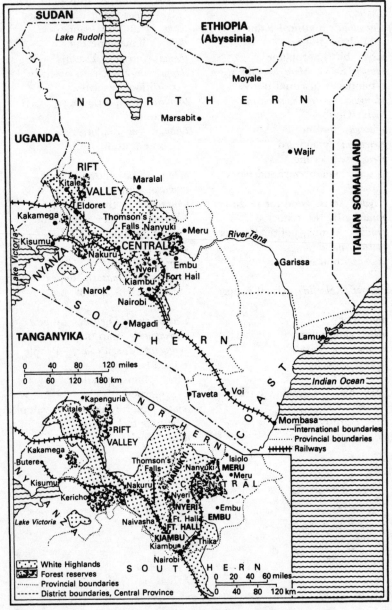

Map 1.1 *General and administrative map of Kenya, 1956–7*

Part V

Unhappy Valley

The State, Mau Mau & the Path to Violence

Ten

𝔇𝔇𝔇𝔇𝔇𝔇𝔇𝔇𝔇𝔇𝔇𝔇𝔇𝔇𝔇𝔇𝔇𝔇𝔇𝔇𝔇𝔇𝔇

Bureaucracy & Incumbent Violence
Colonial Administration & the Origins of the 'Mau Mau' Emergency

BRUCE BERMAN

In the 20-odd years since the declaration of a State of Emergency in Kenya in October 1952, the analysis of the phenomenon known as 'Mau Mau' has undergone a fundamental revision.[1] The initial interpretation, advanced by the colonial authorities and their apologists and by a few (mostly British) scholars, explained 'Mau Mau' as a fanatic, atavistic, savage religious cult consciously created and manipulated by a group of unscrupulous, power-hungry leaders. It was said to be rooted in a mass psychosis affecting an unstable tribe freed from the anchoring constraints of tradition. It was also said to have had no direct links to socio-economic conditions in the colony or to the policies of the Kenya government.[2] This interpretation, popularized by a large and sensational journalistic literature, went virtually unchallenged for more than a decade. During this period 'Mau Mau' and its antecedents were largely ignored by social scientists. As late as 1965, Kushner could report that a search of major anthropological journals had revealed, at best, only peripheral mention of Mau Mau.[3] Where 'Mau Mau' was explicitly considered, the basic premise of the official explanation was generally accepted, and the phenomenon was treated as a nativistic cult or revitalization movement.[4]

Starting in the early 1960s, the official explanation began to be challenged – in memoirs by Kikuyu political figures active in pre-Emergency politics, in books by such non-Kikuyu political figures as Oginga Odinga and Tom Mboya, and in carefully researched historical and anthropological studies by Rosberg and Nottingham, Sorrenson,

Barnett and Buijtenhuijs.[5] These accounts question the official version with regard to both the form of the 'Mau Mau' organization and the factors lying behind it.

While documenting the existence of clandestine mass organization among the Kikuyu, the sporadic outbreaks of terrorism and the ultimately abortive efforts to prepare for violent resistance during the two and a half years preceding October 1952, the recent memoirs and studies have largely denied the existence of any 'Mau Mau' organization. The official explanation had been rejected as a self-serving myth rooted in European misperceptions of Kikuyu society and in a desire to explain away the socio-economic and political inequities of colonial Kenya. The image of 'Mau Mau' as an atavistic and degraded cult is seen as based on the accounts of Kikuyu hostile to the movement or on confessions extorted under duress from detainees. We are asked instead to note that the underground organization known to the Kikuyu primarily as *Uiguano wa Muingi* ('The Unity of the Community') pursued largely secular political goals intended to force major concessions from the colonial authorities by provoking a crisis. The use of oaths was intended to achieve unity and commitment among a divided people subject to increasing social and political stress. Furthermore, the extreme oaths, reliance on supernatural practices, and elements of cultural revitalization were primarily phenomena of the guerrilla groups operating in the forests between 1953 and 1956, and responsibility for them cannot be assigned to the leaders arrested at the start of the Emergency and in prison at the time they occurred.

The factors underlying the increasing militancy of Kikuyu politics in the early postwar period have been identified as the increasing deprivations resulting from rapid socio-economic development in the colony which, among the peoples of Kenya, fell disproportionately on the Kikuyu. These deprivations had three principal geographic foci: the settled districts of the White Highlands, where wages for agricultural laborers remained abysmally low after the Second World War and where an increasing number of Kikuyu squatters and their families were forced off European farms; the Kikuyu reserves, where rapid population growth placed intense pressure on land resources leading to serious soil erosion, a decline in agricultural productivity and an increasingly large group of landless Kikuyu; and the urban areas, notably Nairobi and Mombasa, where a predominantly Kikuyu labour force was squeezed by rapid inflation in the prices of basic consumption items and lived in squalid material circumstances along with a mass of floating unemployed drifting in from the reserves and settled districts. The deterioration of socio-economic conditions came on top of existing grievances relating to the alienation of land to European settlers, attacks on Kikuyu traditions by missionaries (the 'Female Circumcision Crisis' of 1928–31), internal conflicts over the role of appointed chiefs, the increasing accumulation of land and wealth by the chiefs and other members of the tribe's colonial elite, and the harassment and repression of Kikuyu political activity in the 1930s by the colonial authorities.

An important effect of the recent accounts and analyses has been to remove the qualities of strangeness and pathology that made 'Mau Mau', in the official explanation, a singular phenomenon in a tribe incapable of adjusting to change because of idiosyncratic psychological and cultural characteristics. Instead, Kikuyu unrest is now seen in conjunction with patterns of deprivation characteristic of widespread processes of socio-economic growth. Stripped of its status as an historical aberration, Kikuyu political activity becomes explicable within the terms of contemporary theories of revolution and collective violence. Through Gurr's relative deprivation theory, it becomes the reaction of a people whose material conditions worsened as their aspirations increased and as rapid economic growth widened the gap between them and Kenya's increasingly prosperous immigrant communities.[6] In the light of Wolf's analysis of peasant wars, the Kikuyu experience becomes that of a tribal people transformed into a peasantry in relation to an alien white ruling class and subjected to the deterioration of socio-economic circumstances and the increasing internal stratification and conflict characteristic of the incorporation of a traditional society into a capitalist market economy.[7]

The difficulty, however, with both recent accounts of the Emergency period in Kenya and theoretical approaches such as Gurr's and Wolf's is that they are one-sided, analysing the genesis of collective violence almost exclusively from the actions of the insurgents (as is obvious from Gurr's title, *Why Men Rebel*). They can explain the factors that brought the Kikuyu into conflict with the colonial authorities and made them mobilizable for mass action, but not those that shaped the response of the authorities to Kikuyu demands. The importance of this gap is highlighted by the insistence of contemporary scholars, as well as Kenya Africans themselves, that it was the refusal of the Kenya government to increase effective African political participation or implement African demands for socio-economic reforms, and its harassment and repression of African political activity, that directly precipitated Kikuyu militancy, secrecy and violence.[8]

Furthermore, the factors identified as important sources of conflict in Kenya – economic growth, widening distributional inequalities, urbanization, the spread of Western education, rural stagnation and landlessness, and the decline of traditional institutions – are to be found in one combination or another not only in most other colonies in Africa during this period, but also in numerous other societies only some of which have experienced large-scale collective violence. Socio-economic variables can explain the patterns of cleavage and conflict that emerge from major processes of change, and socio-psychological factors can explain the growth of frustrations and predispositions toward violence, but to understand how such tensions and conflicts are worked out in practice we need to analyse the factors shaping the responses of the political authorities. We must understand the bases for repression by incumbents as well as rebellion by insurgents since, as Tilly has pointed out, 'collective violence is a contingent outcome of interactions among contenders and governments, in which the agents of government commonly have the greater discretion and do most of the injury and damage.'[9] Such was the case throughout the colonial period in Kenya, where the resources of coercion and the willingness to use them were both overwhelmingly concentrated in the hands of the British.[10]

However, the response of the colonial authorities to Kikuyu demands cannot be explained by reference to 'structures of domination', or to the inherently repressive qualities of colonial rule, or to the 'interests' of British imperialism. The first two phrases define rather than explain the problem. Nor does it help to treat the issue in terms of a concept such as the 'colonial situation', since it may be that the variables shaping the response of the colonial regime are common to a wider variety of political systems and, as such, are of broader theoretical import. Explanation in terms of British imperial interests is a variant of the 'rational actor' mode of foreign policy analysis and assumes both that there was an identifiable and unitary 'national interest' and that 'if a nation performed a particular action, that nation must have had ends towards which the action constituted an optimal means'.[11] The difficulty here is whose interests do we mean? – the metropolitan government's, British corporate capital's, the local colonial officials', or the Kenya settlers'? Recent studies of these groups in Kenya and other colonies suggest that their interests were far from identical and, at critical junctures, were even in open conflict.[12] The task is therefore to get inside the structures of domination and to identify the factors that lay behind official rigidity and repression. This involves, as Allison has suggested, examining both the sources of institutionalized organizational processes and the outcome of bureaucratic politics involving a variety of individual and organizational actors.[13]

The Kenya Administration: discretion and rigidity

In analysing the factors that shaped the reaction of the Kenya government to African politics, our primary focus must be on the Kenya Administration, the small corps of generalist administrators that staffed the Secretariat in Nairobi and the Provincial Administration in the field.[14] Whatever the socio-economic sources of conflict and cleavage in the colony or the role played by metropolitan or settler interests, the officers of the Administration as the principal agents of imperial control directly confronted and had primary responsibility for dealing with African political activities. Moreover, until the last decade and a half of colonial rule in Kenya the Administration possessed a status and power within the government generally superior to that of the various functional and technical departments. It largely dominated the policy process with regard to the African population in the non-settler districts. The structure of the Administration, the attitudes and values of its personnel, and its position within the distinctive socio-economic and political structures of the colony resulted in organizational processes characterized by rigidity, by an inability to deal with internal or external change except through minor incremental modifications of established practice, by a preoccupation with technique over the substance of policy, and by an absorption in the exigencies of short-run control. These patterns of administrative action, especially in the Provincial Administration in the field, began to emerge before 1914 and crystallized during the inter-war decades, the golden era of colonial administration in Kenya.[15]

Looking broadly at European experience with regard to both the development of centralized states and the extension of colonial rule, prefectural administration has generally been established against a background of political instability in which there were perceived to be threats to the survival of the established regime and/or doubts about the compliance with its directives of significant sectors of the society.[16] The initial purpose and defining commitment of prefectural administration is the conservative one of maintaining the existing regime in power and ensuring compliance with central directives through the exercise of authoritarian control. Prefectural organizations have generally been staffed by an elite cadre of administrators expected to be skilled in the exercise of power and to back up their orders with force if necessary – to 'hold the line', literally, for the regime.[17] As a prefectural organization responsible for the maintenance of 'law, order and good government' and for the general supervision of all other government departments in the field, the Kenya Administration was from the start committed to the maintenance of a status quo in which the continuity and survival of its own power was a critical element.

However, while prefectural administrations are intended to preserve centralized control of the political system, they are subject internally to powerful centripetal pressures growing out of the imperative delegation of discretion to distant and widely dispersed field agents. In colonial Africa this tendency was reinforced by primitive communications and by the heterogeneity of local African societies, which presented a wide variety of circumstances to which policy had to be adjusted. Furthermore, the very breadth and diffuseness of the responsibilities of the colonial field administrator – he had to deal with almost every problem that arose within his jurisdiction – made close central supervision of his activities impossible. In the British system of colonial administration the exercise of a high degree of discretion in the formulation and implementation of policy by subordinate officials in the field was accepted as a matter of course. Each of the more than two-score territorial administrations in the colonial empire exercised considerable autonomy in relation to the Colonial Office in London.[18] A similar pattern marked the relationship between outlying provincial administrations and central administrations in colonial capitals. While the prefectural structure embodied a formal hierarchic chain of command from the colonial governor to the most junior district officer in the field, in practice the relationship between the centre and the periphery was governed by the concept of 'trust the man on the spot'. Field officers were given a wide brief and expected to work out the implementation of any policy in the light of their judgement of local circumstances. In Kenya, communications from the Secretariat 'were guidelines and suggestions, more than definite instructions.'[19]

The discretion of field officers in the implementation of policy gave them considerable influence over its formulation. The Provincial Administration's opportunities for modifying, delaying and generally thwarting any policies that field officers disliked made the governor and senior Secretariat officials seek their general agreement, particularly on issues relating to Africans: 'The District Commissioner or the Provincial Commissioner was perfectly entitled to object to any particular policy being adopted. His views were sought as a rule . . .'[20] Dissent over established central policy was not infrequent, and from the beginning there was a 'protest voice' in the Kenya Administration,[21] especially with regard to what was considered unfair treatment of the African or undue pandering to settler interests by the central government. Such dissent, however, generally stopped short of pursuing the issue beyond the boundaries of the organization (as one field officer put it, 'do be bitterly critical, though only *within* the charmed circle').[22] As a result, decision-making often took the form of a protracted process of bargaining and negotiation, with major issues sometimes circulating for years before a decision was reached. Moreover, given the wide scope of field administrators' responsibilities, there were many areas in which there were no central directives to guide them; they were left to work things out according to their own lights, subject only to post hoc evaluation by their superiors.

The wide discretion permitted to field officers generated, in addition, serious resistance to change. In bureaucratic organizations generally, the wider the discretion of subordinate officials the more they tend to fuse their own goals and purposes with those of the organization. The methods and programmes they carry out, because they have played a major role in their creation, become infused with value in and for themselves. In Selznick's term, they become 'institutionalized' and the focus of vested interests in the organization.[23] The result in the Kenya Administration was that decisions involving fundamental revisions of institutionalized procedures in the field could be made, if at all, only after prolonged internal bargaining or in the face of an external crisis. The Kenya Administration was an organization that could deal flexibly with problems of static adjustment but experienced great difficulty in making a dynamic transformation of its basic purposes in the light of changed circumstances. As Heussler has put it: 'At the start of each colony's association with England policy was important, for there had to be a reason to move forward. At the end of the colonial time, similarly, there was a rationale for going away. In between, the landscape was dominated by a system, not a policy.'[24]

The methods of field administration emerged gradually on an ad hoc basis, partly as the result of previous experience in other colonies but mostly as a series of extrapolations from the experiences and practices of serving officers. Embodied in a series of generalized rules or maxims, these methods formed the conventional wisdom of the Provincial Administration. They were transmitted from one administrative generation to another and eventually reified into a set of hallowed traditional principles.[25] Within the broad confines of this tradition, subordinate officers could exercise a high degree of personalism in the administration of African areas. District commissioners, in particular, were able to run their districts in ways that reflected idiosyncrasies of personal style: 'Each District Commissioner had his own way of running his district and the Provincial Commissioner did not order or direct them. He came to visit and support them . . . You got District Commissioners . . . of considerable caliber and age and they had their own ways of running things and I don't think anyone really bent them in any way.'[26] Inevitably, this meant there were significant variations in the patterns of administration from district to district, even in the same province, and within a single district during the tenure of different district commissioners. Field officers translated policy into action according to their own perceptions and preferences, often pursuing their pet projects to the exclusion of other activities, subject to the general limits of chronic budget austerity, especially during the 1930s, and the knowledge that excessive brutality or other actions that might become 'embarrassing incidents' would bring the swift intervention of the central authorities.

Since widely dispersed field officers could not be controlled directly, the metropolitan authorities attempted as a matter of deliberate policy to staff colonial administrations with men sharing a common background of beliefs and experiences, which would lead them to act in a generally acceptable manner.[27] A necessary corollary of the concept 'trust the man on the spot' was that he had to be the 'right sort of man', capable of being trusted by the authorities at the centre.

In Kenya this policy led to the staffing of the Administration with men of remarkably homogeneous social background and education drawn almost entirely from the middle classes, particularly the older, non-commercial middle class of the Church, the armed forces, the civil service and the learned professions. Even more important, almost all of them had been educated at public schools and at Oxford or Cambridge. As Wilkinson has pointed out, the public schools in particular 'perpetuated the political supremacy of the landed classes by "capturing" talent from the rising bourgeoisie and moulding that talent into "synthetic" gentlemen.'[28] Colonial administrators were consciously selected from among those who had most strongly and unquestioningly accepted this ethos, especially its sense of public service and its easy 'habit of authority'.[29] So uniform and widely accepted were these attitudes and values that they were rarely mentioned or debated in the ordinary course of administration. They formed a set of implicit assumptions behind administrators' patterns of action.

Lying at the core of this ethos was what Moore calls 'Catonism': the anti-rationalist, anti-urban, anti-materialist and anti-bourgeois response of the traditional landed ruling class to the development of modern industrial society.[30] Catonism found a remarkably congenial institutional setting in the prefectural structure of colonial administration, further strengthening the tendencies towards conservatism and rigidity. Central to this system of attitudes and values was an image of society as an integrated organic community characterized by stability and harmony. Change was regarded as disruptive unless it took the form of a gradual organic evolution that preserved essential continuity and order. These ideas were coupled with an emphasis on the value of tradition, a romanticized image of rural society (notably the English country village of some ill-defined golden past) and an insistence on loyalty and a sense of duty toward the community or group ('team spirit'). Colonial administrators deeply distrusted economic individualism, urbanization and industrialization as threats to the organic unity of society.

Central also was the concept of a ruling or 'political' class, linked with a strong emphasis on hierarchy and obedience. According to a former Tory colonial secretary steeped in the ethos, 'You can't have the institutions without a political class, and you can't have the political class without the institutions.'[31] The various segments of society were viewed as hierarchically ordered according to differentials of wealth, status and power, and each had a specific role to play if the organic unity of society were to be sustained. The task of preserving the harmony and continuity of society fell to the ruling class. While this class had great power, it had an equally great moral obligation to use its power on behalf of the common interest. Colonial administrators thus operated with an essentially traditional concept of authority in which the ruler was expected to promote the physical and spiritual well-being of the ruled, in return for the latter's deferential loyalty and obedience.[32] This vision of society had no place for the disruption of social conflict and the squalid pursuit of self-interest of 'the disease of politics', as the chief native commissioner put it in the tense days before the Emergency.[33]

These two elements lay behind the colonial administrators' self-image. They saw themselves as impartial, above politics and guided by a sense of 'fair play' and 'justice'. They understood administration as ameliorative and protective: it corrected the disruption and exploitation introduced by uncontrolled changes and the intrusion of individual selfishness. Their self-image was suffused with moral earnestness and self-righteousness, summed up in the imperial ideals of 'trusteeship' and the 'civilizing mission'. The administrator's job, according to one, was to look after the 'have nots' and to ensure that they received a fair deal, while another, reflecting on the colonial experience, asserted that 'without bureaucracy there can be no social justice'.[34]

The anti-rationalist and anti-intellectual dimensions of Catonism found expression in the cult of the amateur and in a distrust of theories, concepts and the products of abstract thought in general. Thus one provincial commissioner in Kenya asserted that 'we should not allow . . . the results of our work to be undermined by infiltration of the Political Theorists'.[35] Instead, administrators were to be brute empiricists, placing primary value on immediate experience. Determined to treat problems as they arose, concentrating on the 'hard facts' of the case, they tended to treat events in isolation, ignoring the possible linkages between them. Their own theories remained simplistic and largely implicit and were based often on contradictory assumptions. They rejected the use of analytic tools for anticipating necessary changes and were reluctant to look beyond the problem at hand. They distrusted programmatic statements of general policy, tended to deal with policy issues serially only as they reached a magnitude that could no longer be ignored, and then relied upon the traditional administrative maxims. Structural and attitudinal factors thus combined in Kenya to create an administrative style that was a notable example of disjointed incrementalism.[36]

Finally, the administrative process in Kenya was also deeply affected by the presence of immigrant communities, particularly the European settlers. This immigrant population introduced an overt duality into the economy and society of the colony between the world of Nairobi and the settled areas and the world of the rural African districts. This was reflected in a similar duality in the Administration, with the Secretariat in Nairobi preoccupied with settler politics and issues while the

Provincial Administration remained focused on the local concerns of the tribal societies.

The two worlds of colonial society in Kenya were, however, increasingly bound together by settler dependence on African labour and by the increasing incorporation of the African population into the monetary economy as labourers, producers of certain cash crops and consumers of imported manufactured goods. This resulted by the 1920s in a strongly felt need for critical decisions charting the future course of economic and political development in the colony and the consequent relations between the immigrant communities and the African population.[37] As a result of their generally high social status, central position in the existing economy and powerful connections in Britain, the settlers quickly acquired a dominant influence over the middle range of policy, especially that relating to public finances and taxation, public services, immigration, labour and land. Nevertheless, while the settlers could shape policy to meet their immediate interests, they were unable to achieve their most important goal of control of the government on the Southern Rhodesian model. They were blocked by officials of both the Colonial Office and the Kenya Administration, who largely distrusted the settlers' ability to deal fairly with Africans and generally rejected settler self-government as an abrogation of the responsibilities of imperial trusteeship.[38] However, the Colonial Office and the Secretariat in Nairobi could not advance alternative policies without risking a prolonged and bitter conflict. In 1940 Lord Hailey noted that the Kenya Administration demurred from any general statements of policy out of a reluctance to clash with the European community.[39] The governor and senior administrators in the Secretariat could thus not make the decisions necessary to give some definite direction to policy in the colony and hence were largely incapable of supplying effective leadership. The result was a stalemate that left Kenya drifting without coherent direction for more than 30 years and generated a sense of malaise felt by all groups in the political arena even as they blocked each other's efforts to find a solution.[40]

Furthermore, only a small minority of administrative officers accepted the settler goal of self-government as a desirable future for the colony. Such a goal implied the effective destruction of the Administration in its existing form, a prospect few of them accepted with equanimity. Field officers, in particular, felt considerable distaste for the politics of Nairobi and the settled districts and were largely powerless in those areas of policy subject to a dominant settler influence. In addition, in the settled districts and towns their authority and effective power was progressively narrowed during the 1920s and 1930s in favour of settler-dominated local government bodies. As one administrator put it, 'one felt helpless really. Politics were handled at a higher level – one really couldn't deal with them; they were a matter . . . straight between the settlers' leaders and the Governor or senior people in the Government. The DC just had to pass it by.'[41] For administrators the common socio-cultural background and the ties of friendship, school and, in some instances, family that they shared with the settlers were ultimately overridden by their tight sense of group solidarity and their personal and organizational interest in preserving their discretion and freedom from outside interference. The officers of the Provincial Administration struggled to maintain an arena of action free of the settler influence that bound the hands of officials in the central government and isolated from the rancorous political conflicts of Nairobi. This found expression not only in a dislike of Secretariat postings, but also in a strong distaste for administrative posts in the settled districts, despite the more comfortable living conditions and social facilities they offered to officials and their families. Field officers preferred the physical discomfort and isolation of the African districts where 'real administration' remained possible.[42]

The administrator and African politics: protecting the 'man in the blanket' from the 'man in trousers'

Whatever the connection between capitalism and imperialism, colonial administration in Kenya assumed a pattern within the imperial framework that expressed older, precapitalist values and social forms. The characteristic beliefs of colonial administrators in paternalism and social hierarchy, their emphasis on the reciprocal obligations of ruler and ruled, and their preoccupation with order and control reflected a traditional concept of authority and society. There is an archaic, even atavistic quality to colonial administration, as if it represented the last place where the old prerogatives and power of a ruling elite could be exercised. When we look at the orientations of colonial administrators expressed in their attitudes and even in their language of administration, we confront an aspiration to aristocratic, even monarchic, power. Heussler aptly depicts the situation of the British administrator in Africa when he notes that 'year in and year out they lived the lives of little kings in an epoch when their home based brothers had exchanged kingship for bourgeois democracy'.[43] And this was neatly if unconsciously caught in the phrase used by officials and unofficials alike in Kenya to describe the district commissioner: 'the King in his castle'.

At the very periphery of the British imperial system colonial administration preserved the crucial attitudes and prerogatives of the early modern state, with the 'king's men', the field officers, exercising delegated imperial authority within an organizational structure that permitted and even encouraged independent action and traditional, highly personalistic authority. In Kenya two idiosyncratic factors gave local administrators a degree of freedom of action even greater than that of British officials in other African territories. First, the preoccupation of the central authorities with settler issues limited the degree of even general supervision that they exercised over the Provincial Administration. Second, the widespread lack of differentiated political structures and roles among the African societies in Kenya led to a rejection of the more common British practice of 'indirect rule' in favour of direct administration through appointed 'native authorities' with no traditional sanction for their position. The Kenya district commissioner thus possessed an unusual latitude for direct intervention and control over the African population in his area, largely unrestrained by higher authorities or mediated by intervening indigenous institutions.

The world view of colonial administrators led, however, to a fundamental ambivalence in their perception of the African. On the one hand, they saw few cultural achievements of value or worthy of preservation in African society. They regarded the apparently simply structured and mostly stateless societies of Kenya as particularly low on the ladder of social evolution. The African himself they regarded as an ignorant childish savage, more the victim of his society than its creator. The paternalism of administrators found concrete expression in this image of grown-up immaturity, irresponsibility and unpredictability. On the other hand, administrators also tended to see in traditional tribal society precisely the type of organic community they valued and felt was destroyed by the advance of industrial society. As they became increasingly unhappy over the course of development of Western society, particularly after the Second World War and the advent of a Labour government in Britain, they felt a growing desire to preserve the basic fabric of tribal society.[44] This desire was reinforced by the imperatives of control. The destruction of tribal society raised the spectre of a faceless, anomic, 'detribalized' mass, which the Provincial Administration, spread thinly on the ground, regarded with dismay.

Both dimensions of this image of the African shared an assumption of his essential incompetence in dealing with the evils of his own society and the potentially disruptive influence of Western civilization, and his consequent dependence on the strength and benevolence of the Provincial Administration. It was an article of faith among administrators that they alone could identify and act 'in the best interests' of the African: 'I think anyone who was really serious in the Administration regarded our jobs as being sort of a protective screen for the African because there was no one else to look after their interests'.[45] The role of the administrator was to guide the African along the road to a higher civilization, while preserving the organic integrity of society. The field administrators' treatment of the African was consequently a blend of moral exhortation and didactic tutelage, backed up by threats of punishment and coercion. There was no place in this conception for any legitimate African voice in the political process; their role was to obey for their own good.

The Provincial Administration can therefore be seen as a white ruling caste introduced into the fabric of rural tribal society for which the practice of administration gradually became an end in itself. The emphasis on the methods and techniques of administration, carefully recorded and passed down in the conventional wisdom of the organization, expressed the extent to which the exercise of control over a passive and dependent African population was actually the principal satisfaction administrators derived from their work. From this came the intensity with which the field officer defended 'his district' and 'his people' against all outsiders whom he thought might exploit them or disrupt the order of the traditional community. As one district commissioner eloquently put it: 'I didn't like chaps getting between me and my people . . . you must be in charge, there must be no interference, and the settlers were rivals. What's so funny about it is that it was exactly the same attitude we had toward the African politicians.'[46]

It is critically important to note the extent to which this 'guardian' role coincided with the personal and organizational interests of administrators in protecting their freedom of action. Field officers came to regard the preservation of their own discretion as identical to the preservation of the welfare of the African; a threat to one was *ipso facto* a threat to the other. This intertwining of self-interest and paternalism led the Provincial Administration to a distrust of the activities of other groups both inside and outside of the government and to a general hostility to outside criticism.

These structural and ideological factors also led administrators to an intense hostility and suspicion towards any manifestations of organized African opposition and to the development of an established method of dealing with it through a combination of formal co-optation of Africans to largely powerless 'local government' bodies and the harassment and repression of African political associations. This response was shaped not so much by the specific issues raised by these groups as by the mere fact of opposition itself. As one district commissioner put it: 'anyone who stood up and opposed Government policy was naturally suspect by the usual run of administrators'.[47] Given their conception of the protective role of administration and their image of African dependence, field officers tended to see African political associations as unnecessary, premature, even unnatural phenomena. The mere existence of an association claiming to defend African interests implied that the Provincial Administration had failed in its role of benevolent protector and threatened the unchallenged authority and prestige believed to be the basis of effective control. On the same grounds, the associations threatened the personal authority of individual field officers. Such groups constituted rivals for the loyalty of the African masses; the African politicians, the men in trousers, interposed themselves between the administrator and 'his people', the men in blankets. What is especially striking is that this reaction was largely independent of the occurrence of any overt resistance or defiance of authority on the part of the associations.[48]

During the 1919–39 period a rigid stereotype of African politics and politicians emerged in the Provincial Administration. This image was intimately linked to the Kikuyu, particularly through the activities of the Kikuyu Central Association (KCA), the only African political group that evoked serious concern among administrators during that period. The reaction was also rooted in the prevalent colonial stereotype of the Kikuyu as ambitious and intelligent, but also secretive, deceptive and conspiratorial. It also reflected the hostility of colonial officials to the emerging generation of educated Africans. The political associations, particularly the KCA, confirmed administrators' fears that education would create a class of Africans desiring to assume responsibilities for which they were blatantly ill-equipped and which only the Administration could properly handle.[49] This view of the 'semi-educated' and 'detribalized native' made it difficult for administrators to take the associations seriously as expressions of deep-seated African sentiments. Governor Grigg's private secretary used a telling metaphor of the colonial relationship in describing KCA activity as 'groups of young men acting in the same sort of way as first-form boys at school, who make bombs to blow up their form master, and one is disinclined to take them seriously . . . the Kikuyu, still like the first-form boy, loves secret societies'; and he added his belief that 'if the situation is treated with good humour and restraint, that these sillies would give up their conspiracies and . . . be content to go back and work on their shambas [farms]'.[50]

Behind the 'juvenile' activities of the associations, however, administrators detected the ulterior motive of a lust for power and money. The associations were taken seriously as dangerous efforts at personal aggrandisement – a reaction derived from the administrators' view of politics as the irresponsible pursuit of partisan self-interest. On these grounds the associations represented only a tiny minority of 'detribalized' natives detached from and unrepresentative of the masses in the tribal reserves. The activities of the KCA were viewed as irresponsible agitation intended to dupe the ignorant rural African into believing that the association represented their true interests. Visible popular support for the associations tended to be dismissed as manipulated and essentially spurious.[51] To the field administrator the African politician was ultimately another exploiter from whom they had to protect the unsophisticated tribesman in the name of social justice and communal solidarity.

Finally, as a result of its vigorous support of traditional custom during the conflict with the European missionaries over female circumcision in 1929–31, the KCA also came to be seen by the Provincial Administration as a reactionary force supporting an atavistic rejection of Western civilization. This sentiment was reinforced by the administrators' conviction, despite a lack of any direct evidence, that various nativistic or syncretic religious sects that appeared during the interwar years, notably the Watu wa Mungu, were covertly manipulated by African politicians.[52] Furthermore, in 1938 Jomo Kenyatta published his book *Facing Mount Kenya* which asserted both the value of Kikuyu traditional culture and the ability of the African to articulate his interests without the aid of his professional protectors in the Administration. The perceived connection between religious cults and political protest evoked the irrational fanaticism and savage frenzy that were the most unsettling elements of the administrator's image of the African, while the defence of tradition by secular or religious means was interpreted as a total rejection of progressive change. When combined with the tendency of officials to judge a native people's ability and moral worth by their success in conforming to the lines laid down by colonial authority, these views led to the additional understanding of Kikuyu protest as an indication of the tribe's incapacity to adjust to the strains of modernization.[53] This concept became a dominant theme in official explanations of the post-1945 political crisis.

Field administrators thus could not respond positively to the demands of the KCA and other African associations without either limiting the freedom of action they enjoyed or calling into question the whole rationale of colonial administration. Even where Africans were considered to have legitimate grievances, administrators told each other that any change in policy had to appear to be the result of the free and uncoerced action of a benevolent and omnipotent authority and not a concession to outside demands or political agitation.[54] This conviction made it virtually impossible for Africans to get the Provincial Administration to listen to their demands and grievances until they mounted precisely the sort of agitation that threatened to end in disorder and an 'embarrassing incident'. As early as 1926 this was clear to the leaders of the KCA when they wrote: 'There is no [sic] anyone to represent our grievances, there is no faithful person who can speak on our behalf. So if we keep quiet the Government will think we are quite satisfied.'[55] In any event, field officers tended to view the issues raised by such groups as either phoney or fantastically exaggerated. Thus in 1929 the District Commissioner of Kiambu saw the KCA as composed of 'adept liars and past masters at sewing [sic] the seed of false rumours', while Governor Grigg repeated the judgments of his administrators in asserting that 'it is not apparent that the association has any real grievances. It makes all the capital it can out of the apprehensions, genuine or fictitious, of the Kikuyu as to the security of their land'.[56] Moreover, it was impossible for administrators to accept that their own actions, so benevolent in intent, could be construed by Africans as a source of grievance, and they consequently refused to countenance any complaints about the behaviour of individual officers or demands for changes in administrative structures and practice. The associations came to be seen as sources of social disruption creating conflicts that would otherwise not exist or exacerbating grievances that would be dealt with by the Administration itself. Administrators in Kenya came to believe that there was no necessary linkage between African socio-economic problems and political action. The associations engaged in political agitation for their own selfish purposes and did not necessarily express the underlying discontents of the African masses. They were dealt with simply as threats to law and order – a characteristically piecemeal administrative response intended to maintain control on an immediate and short-run basis.

Economic growth and the crisis of colonial administration

During the Second World War two crucial processes of change began to accelerate in Kenya. First, with the war the settler-dominated monetary economy began a process of rapid and sustained growth that lasted for almost two decades. The growth of this sector had been moderate during the interwar decades and had suffered serious setbacks during the depressions of the early 1920s and the 1930s. Between 1940 and 1960, however, the available evidence indicates an average growth rate of 6 per cent per annum, with a staggering rate of 13 per cent per year in the period 1947–54.[57] The monetary economy lurched forward unexpectedly; senior administrators in the Secretariat, expecting another post-war depression, do not appear to have become fully aware of the sustained rapidity of growth until the late 1940s. Second, even as they were unaware of this rapid growth, colonial authorities in the metropole, after more than a decade of discussions with authorities in the colonies and various interested individuals and groups in Britain, made a commitment to the active promotion of the social and economic development of the colonies. This found expression in a series of Colonial Development and Welfare Acts that provided unprecedented metropolitan resources for development programmes after 1945. This led to the rapid growth of the Kenya government and the expansion of its intervention into the society and economy of the colony. The impact of these two changes upon the existing socio-economic and political structure of Kenya generated political and administrative crises in which the Provincial Administration stood at the centre. It was the interaction of these crises that culminated in the Emergency.

As the studies cited earlier have shown, rapid economic growth in the colony both increased the rate of mobilization of Africans into the monetary economy and widened the already yawning gap between them and the immigrant communities. The iniquitous distribution of the benefits of increased investment and production subjected a growing number of Africans, particularly among the Kikuyu, to a series of relative and absolute deprivations on top of earlier grievances. The effect of this process was to increase the scope and intensity of social conflict in the colony. The issues articulated by African political associations, especially the Kenya African Union (founded in 1944), concerning agricultural development, credit facilities, labour conditions and wages, education and the general distribution of both the benefits of development and access to the policy process itself, were matters of colony-wide import incapable of being resolved within the district-level focus of African administration. These issues brought up with renewed urgency the key unresolved problems of the basic direction of Kenya's development and the respective roles of the various racial communities. As early as 1945 Jomo Kenyatta spelled out the essential conflicts with great clarity in a pamphlet published in Britain: 'What we do demand is a fundamental change in the present political, economic, and social relationship between Europeans and Africans . . . the Africans make their claim for justice now, in order that a bloodier and more destructive justice may not be inevitable in time to come.'[58]

This emerging confrontation made the maintenance of the dual political system in the colony, in which the Provincial Administration dealt with the Africans insulated as far as possible from settler politics at the centre, increasingly untenable. The response to African demands involved, in effect, a series of critical decisions either reaffirming the status quo or reorienting the basic objectives and institutions of Kenya's political economy. However, in the years preceding the Emergency the necessary decisions were not made. In the metropole the process of defining the new doctrine of development was not carried very far. No real attempt was made to reshape the existing institutions and methods of colonial administration in light of the anticipated requirements of development: post-1945 'development and welfare' colonialism was simply superimposed on the existing 'law and order' structures,[59] and it was left up to the administration of each individual colony to translate the vague general principles emanating from the Colonial Office into a policy applicable to local conditions. In Kenya, however, the central administration continued to be caught in the political stalemate with the settlers and proved incapable of supplying the necessary leadership to define the direction of the colony's development.

At the same time that it faced the rising demands of significant elements of the African population, the Provincial Administration also found itself involved in a crisis of bureaucratic politics inside the government. This crisis had its origins in the tension between the requirements of socio-economic development programmes and the prefectural system's commitment to the status quo and the maintenance of law and order. Government programmes, directed primarily at the African population, led to a rapid increase in the scale and complexity of the Kenya government, especially in the technical departments. The Provincial Administration was left behind in this growth and little attention was paid to whether the new focus on development required a revision of its structure or a rethinking of its traditional methods. In the districts many of the operational responsibilities formerly handled by field administrators were taken over by technical specialists and the Provincial Administration's control over policy in the African areas was increasingly challenged by the growing size and power of the technical departments. This specialist–generalist conflict and the declining status of the Provincial Administration within the government was exacerbated by the widening of the structural cleavage between the field and the central administration as the Secretariat became almost totally preoccupied with technical issues of economic and fiscal policy and the problems of running a complex bureaucratic machine.

In addition, a series of reforms introduced in 1945, which created a proto-ministerial system by assigning departmental portfolios to official and unofficial members of the governor's Executive Council, ruptured the direct formal line of communications from the Provincial Administration to the Chief Secretary. Executive responsibility for the Provincial Administration at the centre shifted confusingly among senior officials preoccupied with other matters. By 1948 the Provincial Commissioner of Central Province, which included the three largely Kikuyu districts, was complaining of a growing 'blind spot' in his relations with the Secretariat. The Chief Secretary, while openly sympathetic, privately dismissed the problem as the inevitable price of the expansion of government business.[60] Until the last few months before the Emergency, the Governor and senior administrators in the Secretariat remained largely aloof from the issues of African politics, having little direct contact with either African politicians or political organizations. The petitions and resolutions of the Kenya African Union were politely received and just as politely ignored.[61]

The Provincial Administration was thus left on its own to maintain control and to formulate and carry out development programmes in the African districts in conjunction with the increasingly assertive technical departments. Faced with serious internal and external challenges, field administrators suffered a serious loss of direction and confidence in their role. One provincial commissioner noted of his colleagues, 'if they complained about the central administration, it was because they did not know what to do themselves'.[62] Field officers had an increasing sense of being subjected to circumstances largely beyond their control and of being adrift on currents whose origins they only dimly perceived and whose course and destination seemed both capricious and intractable: 'things were always forced on us . . . these problems we had to deal with we didn't go out to meet half way, we had them thrust upon us'.[63] The Provincial Administration, especially in the epicentres of Kikuyu unrest, worked under an intensifying sense of pressure and crisis. Deprived of effective leadership from the centre and almost wholly isolated from sources of innovative ideas and techniques, field administrators formulated 'development' programmes that were essentially reassertions of their established ideas and methods. Fearing the disruptive effects of rapid change, administrators regarded the preservation of the organic community they saw in traditional tribal society as a goal of paramount importance. They approached the idea of 'development' with grave reservations and emphasized the need to maintain social cohesion by introducing change slowly, carefully and under firm control. One district commissioner, for example, cautioned his colleagues that 'patience is needed, a true sense of proportion and a firm hand on the brake', and he added: 'Tradition is what the African needs (just as much as we do) to help him along the right road. We smashed some of his traditions and it is necessary to give him a basis on which to build new traditions'.[64] This preoccupation with using 'development' programmes as a means of halting social disintegration reached its greatest intensity with regard to the Kikuyu. The central thrust of administrative policy in the three Kikuyu districts of Kiambu, Fort Hall and Nyeri became reactionary in the most literal sense; it was intended to reverse existing processes of change the Provincial Administration regarded as destructive.

Kikuyu demands for legally recognized individual land tenure, for agricultural credit and for permission to grow the lucrative cash crops reserved for settler farmers were rejected and the efforts of many Africans to start small businesses regarded coldly by the Provincial Administration out of a fear of 'the tendency of the African to an individualism which was more pronounced than that of the European he tried to imitate'.[65] Administrative policy thus restricted Kikuyu access to the monetary economy as independent farmers and businessmen at a time when the visible prosperity of the European and Asian communities was rapidly increasing. 'Development' programmes in the African districts focused on welfare measures and on an intensive programme of soil conservation to prevent the further erosion and loss of fertility in the Kikuyu reserves – a programme carried out with an unequivocal heavy-handedness involving unpaid 'compulsory communal labour', as well as fines and threats of imprisonment for those who refused to cooperate. In addition, fear of a growing class of 'detribalized' Western-educated Africans led the Provincial Administration also to reject Kikuyu demands for increased facilities for secondary and higher education. It emphasized instead primary and adult education involving vocational and agricultural subjects.[66]

Just as serious as the clash between administrative 'development' policies and Kikuyu aspirations was the fact that the Administration's disjointed incremental style of decision-making led to serious contradictions between the policies carried out in the reserves and the patterns of change taking place in the towns and settled areas. Field administrators in the late 1940s felt that the success of their efforts to preserve the integrity of tribal society in the reserves depended upon forcing 'excess' population off the land, and they assumed that this landless population would be absorbed into the increased employment opportunities created by the growth of the monetary economy.[67] Unfortunately, by this time the absorptive capacity of settler agriculture was declining as European farmers increasingly mechanized and began to push large numbers of Kikuyu squatter labourers off their land.[68] Furthermore, in the urban areas the central government, without coordination with the Provincial Administration, maintained a low-wage policy that prevented African workers from supporting themselves and their families permanently in town and forced them to attempt to maintain a foothold in the reserves. The wage problem was symptomatic of the Administration's continuing neglect of the consequences of change in the urban areas.[69] There is, moreover, no evidence to suggest that administrators were ever aware during this period of the incompatibility between the patterns of change in the immigrant-dominated areas and that being pursued in the African reserves. The end result was to place the Kikuyu in a vicious circle, whether they went to the towns or the settler farms or stayed in the reserves.

While 'development' policies created increasingly sharp conflicts between the Provincial Administration and the Kikuyu, the latter were denied effective access to the political arenas in which these conflicts could legitimately be fought out. During the first post-war decade, the foundation of British policy for African political development was the use of local government as a school for education in democracy, political responsibility and social service. This was supposed to supply the necessary basis for eventual African advancement to self-government. It was also viewed as a means of stimulating local participation in development and as a channel for the safe expression of political opinion.[70] From the arena of local government would emerge a responsible African 'political class' capable of efficiently and honestly guarding the general interest and to which alone power could be safely transferred. In Kenya the basis for this policy was to to be supplied by the Local Native Councils (LNCs) – known after 1950 as African District Councils – which had been operating in African districts since the 1920s.

The LNCs, however, had been established with the conscious intention of coopting African political activity and this objective continued to dominate their operation after 1945. The deliberate political objective of local government development policy was to divert African attention away from participation in central government and undercut the position of the urban-based African politicians.[71] The councils lacked any real legislative or executive power, while the district commissioners who supervised them simply refused to permit 'politics' to be involved in their proceedings. One observer noted that 'as distinct from official descriptions of what the councils have or are doing, they are the 'toys' of the District Commissioners.'[72] When the first post-war elections to the councils returned several members of the Kenya African Union in the Kikuyu districts, the Provincial Administration immediately moved to manipulate the local franchise and electoral procedures 'to prevent political hot-heads, who had no real backing from the majority of the people, from pushing their way into membership of the Local Native Councils by conducting intensive electioneering campaigns.'[73]

While the focus on local government dominated administrative thinking, African access to central government institutions was extremely restricted. A Kikuyu school teacher, Eliud Mathu, was appointed to the Legislative Council in 1944 and a Luo civil servant, B.A. Ohanga, joined him two years later. In 1948 two more African members were appointed to represent the tribes of the Rift Valley and Coast Provinces. These African members were chosen not on the basis of demonstrated leadership or evidence of a widespread following but rather with regard to their possession of the proper education and administrative ability; in short, they had to show both a patina of Western learning and the 'dedication to public service' so highly prized by administrators. Not surprisingly, those selected were usually civil servants. However, the application of administrative criteria for filling ostensibly political positions compromised the effectiveness of the African members of the Legislative Council by transforming them into creatures of the Administration lacking an independent constituency in the African community. African appeals for elected LegCo representatives and for a seat on the Governor's Executive Council were turned down on the grounds that they had not had the experience or demonstrated the ability to exercise so important a 'public trust'.[74]

The Provincial Administration and the KAU: the escalating conflict

The intervention of the colonial regime into increasingly wide areas of African life politicized Kikuyu grievances by bringing the Kikuyu into direct conflict with the agents of the colonial state over a growing range of issues. For an increasing number of them it appeared as if the government's policies were designed to keep the African in a depressed and subservient position and thwart all of their efforts to improve their condition. Kikuyu suspicion of government deepened and they increasingly tended to see nefarious designs behind official programmes, especially those that the authorities insisted were for their benefit.[75] Denied effective expression within the established institutional arenas, these issues were increasingly articulated by the Kenya African Union. Within a few years of the end of the war, it was not only actively opposing administrative 'development' policy but also making increasingly strident demands for fundamental revisions of the socio-economic and political structures of the colony.

The response of the Provincial Administration to the KAU was rooted in the established stereotype of African politics and politicians, pushed to greater intensity by the KAU's opposition to official 'development' programmes. When resistance led by the local and national leaders of the KAU brought many of the programmes in Kikuyu districts to a virtual standstill, administrators reacted with frustrated fury. In their eyes resistance to policies intended to benefit the Kikuyu was utterly irrational. The only possible motive the politicians could have was a simple grab for power by spreading malicious lies about government intentions: 'it was generally anti-government stupidity . . . opposition to anything so as to gain kudos from the people'.[76] The KAU leaders were out to dupe the unsophisticated rural population into supporting them, and by halting development programmes they maintained conditions of poverty that could be exploited by irresponsible agitation. The fact that KAU and other African organizations collected ever larger sums of money to finance their activities reinforced administrators' belief that African politics was essentially duplicitous – a confidence racket battening on the ignorant fears of the rural masses. Moreover, the fact that Nairobi served as the organizational centre for African opposition confirmed their view of the city as a source of subversion and corruption from which flowed a stream of detribalized agitators to disrupt rural tribal society.

Like their predecessors between the wars, field officers reacted to KAU's spirit of opposition and independence and to the threat it presented to their established position in the reserves: 'rival paramount chiefs' was one perceptive officer's phrase.[77] Virtually all statements or acts of opposition to government policies were attributed to the influence or direction of the politicians, while the inability of the Provincial

Administration or the Kenya Police to find conclusive evidence of their complicity in actual subversion was interpreted as an indication of their cleverness in covering their tracks.[78] Field officers increasingly sought violent intentions and covert conspiracies under the surface of African opposition. What is notable is that the less real evidence they had of conspiracy, the more they believed it was taking place. Administrators thus became convinced that the African politicians were beyond reason. There was no point in trying to reach agreement with them on contentious issues since they would only attack the government later over something else. Where African leaders attempted, as Kenyatta did in several instances, to cooperate with the Administration and resolve specific conflicts, administrators rejected these efforts as examples of Kikuyu guile in appearing to cooperate while actually engaging in clandestine subversion.[79]

Administrators in the field continued to believe that the activities of the politicians had no direct linkage with socio-economic factors and they insisted that 'agitation is often a cause of unrest' rather than a symptom of it.[80] By restricting the activities of the agitator they could restore social harmony. This conviction was reflected in their tactics as they sought to isolate Kikuyu politicians from tribes not yet deeply affected by the 'disease of politics', as well as to limit the contact between these agitators and the rural Kikuyu. The Provincial Administration deliberately attempted to prevent the KAU from becoming a national organization by a policy of divide and rule playing upon inter-ethic hostilities. For example, in response to a 1948 KAU petition to the United Nations, administrators found two Nyanza chiefs who 'objected to the way in which this memorandum was presented by a few Kikuyu politicians purporting to represent the peoples of Kenya', and instructed them to stress publicly the implications of the memorandum 'which was the claim of the Kikuyu *to speak for and, therefore, to dominate*, the native peoples of Kenya'.[81]

Meanwhile, field officers in Central Province harassed the officials of KAU and various local Kikuyu associations and placed progressively more severe restrictions on their public meetings and organizational activities, particularly the collection of money. Periodic attempts were also made to control the growing vernacular press and prosecute editors and writers for the most scurrilous articles. In addition, administrators' growing personal hostility to the politicians found expression in bitter attacks on their ability and integrity before official *barazas* and other meetings with Africans in the Kikuyu districts: 'with some care, but considerable directness, the DCs Fort Hall, Nyeri and self have been plastering these boys in public utterances as a counter attack and also to drive a wedge to draw off waverers if possible.'[82]

The inability of the Kenya African Union to effect meaningful changes in policy or resolve specific grievances in the face of the aloofness and rigidity of the Secretariat and the overt hostility and harassment of the Provincial Administration led to a shift in the political initiative towards more militant elements. The conviction among field officers that a violent anti-European conspiracy lay behind the facade of the KAU and other Kikuyu associations became a self-fulfilling prophecy. The critical stage of the crisis began in February 1950 when Kikuyu leaders from the KAU, the Nairobi trade unions and elements of the old KCA that continued to operate within the KAU in the Central Province decided to embark on a campaign of mass oathing to unify the Kikuyu and generate a sustained commitment to the struggle. By early 1952 limited preparations began for armed resistance, although the objective was not full-scale rebellion. Realizing their inability to overthrow the full might of imperial power, the Kikuyu leadership sought instead to create a crisis that would compel the intervention of the metropolitan authorities over the head of the Kenya government.[83]

The information about mass oathings that reached field administrators in 1950 convinced them of the duplicity of the KAU and led to intensified repression. They believed the oathings were carried out by a 'Mau Mau' association dedicated to murder or drive out all of the Europeans in Kenya. Although the origins of the name are obscure, there is little doubt that 'Mau Mau' was intensely real to both government officials and settlers.[84] A series of clashes with African religious sects in 1947–8 and 1950 in which four European officials and several Africans had been killed aroused once more the fear of African fanaticism and the suspicion that these sects were secretly manipulated by African politicians. To many administrators, including Governor Sir Philip Mitchell and several senior Secretariat officials, 'Mau Mau' was apparently a *dini* (sect) controlled by the KCA behind the facade of the KAU. Arrests of Kikuyu for administering illegal oaths began in April 1950 and by the end of the year 120 had been convicted and imprisoned.[85] In August the 'Mau Mau' association was proscribed by the Executive Council.

Administrative officers, meanwhile, struggled to understand the rising Kikuyu unrest. They blamed it on a 'loss of contact' resulting from a bureaucratization of government that tied them to their offices and prevented them from pursuing the traditional methods of administration based on direct personal touch with the African. This meant that the 'human problems' of social disruption due to rapid change were left to fester and that the rural masses were an easy prey for agitators. Continuing to believe that Africans trusted the Provincial Administration and looked to it for guidance and protection, administrators turned to 'closer administration', an intensification of control through 'a welcome return to older methods of administration'.[86] In this strategy their basic values and assumptions – the equation of African welfare with the preservation of the discretion and power of the Provincial Administration, the emphasis on personal authority, the distrust of conflict and change, and the belief that conflict could be eliminated and harmony restored where the will and 'good sense' of the ruling class prevailed – came together in an authoritarian reassertion of their unchallenged control over the African population in the districts.

By 1951 the level of political controversy rose to the point where the metropolitan authorities intervened to mediate in the conflict. In May the Secretary of State for the Colonies, James Griffiths, visited Kenya, and KAU, under Kenyatta's leadership, made one last effort to head off the developing confrontation and work through constitutional channels. The Union asked for 12 elected African members on the Legislative Council. Griffiths, faced with the conflicting demands of the settlers and the Asians, as well as the resistance of the Kenya government to any concessions to African 'agitation', temporized by giving Africans two more appointed members in LegCo and a seat on the Executive Council. He also promised a constitutional conference for late 1952 (never held after the Emergency intervened). An impassioned petition, 'A Prayer for the Restoration of Our Land', seeking redress of Kikuyu socio-economic grievances was ignored. Soon after, Kikuyu extremists completely rejected the politics of petitions and resolutions.[87] Early in 1952 several prominent local leaders of KAU in Fort Hall District were imprisoned for conspiracy. At the same time a wave of arson broke out in Nyeri District directed against official chiefs and other Kikuyu loyal to the colonial regime. By the middle of the year violence had spread to Nairobi and its environs in the form of sporadic acts of terror and assassination against Kikuyu who opposed the secret movement.[88]

During the first half of 1952 field officers in Central and Rift Valley Provinces began to press the central administration for the declaration of a state of emergency.[89] For these men the situation had become extremely threatening and they were convinced that the time had come for definitive action against the politicians whom they believed to be the leaders of an incipient rebellion. To act on their own, without documented proof of a conspiracy, would have exposed them to possible charges of exceeding their authority and using excessive force. However, the declaration of an emergency, which required permission from the Colonial Office, would relieve them of the burden of responsibility and place them in the position of carrying out an established policy. To lend additional weight to their pressures senior field officers enlisted the support of settler politicians, thereby alarming the European community and leading in June and July to heated debates in the Legislative Council and lurid stories in the local press.

Secretariat officials resisted these pressures as involving an isolated element of unrest in an otherwise peaceful and prosperous colony.[90] For them to have approached the Colonial Office for the declaration of a state of emergency would have been an admission of a failure to govern effectively and of the inaccuracy of reports of peace and progress sent to London as late as June. This would invite the active intervention of the metropolitan authorities and possibly blight the careers of the senior officials having to take responsibility for the decision. The situation was further complicated by the fact that, after Governor Mitchell's retirement in June, his successor, Sir Evelyn Baring, was injured in an accident and did not arrive in the colony until the end of September. Instead of the usual three or four weeks, the interregnum between governors stretched to more than three months. During this crucial period the government was headed by the Chief Secretary, assisted by the Chief Native Commissioner and the Attorney General, and these officials were understandably reluctant to make a drastic decision that would commit the new Governor to an emergency even before he arrived. They attempted instead to deal with the situation through incremental legislation extending the existing coercive powers of the Provincial Administration and police. The Colonial Office was not officially informed of a deterioration of law and order in the colony until 17 August.[91]

In September, the Chief Native Commissioner and the Attorney General visited London and received metropolitan approval for further repressive legislation. These measures, however, were never implemented. Baring arrived shortly after and, bypassing the Secretariat, immediately embarked on a personal tour of the Central Province during which field officers directly and forcefully presented their case to him. He returned apparently convinced of the need for a state of emergency. The assassination on 7 October of Senior Chief Waruhiu, one of the government's staunchest supporters in Kiambu, provided a needed precipitating incident. After assent was received from London, more than a week was spent on planning, including arrangements for troop reinforcements. The Emergency was officially declared on 20 October and began with the arrest of Kenyatta and 145 other African political figures, most of them Kikuyu. At this point, the situation in Kenya moved rapidly to a new level of large-scale collective violence.

Incumbent authorities and collective violence

The collective violence of the Kenya Emergency cannot be adequately explained as originating in an armed rebellion by a portion of the African population of the colony. While small numbers of young Kikuyu began to move into the forests on the fringes of the reserves as early as July and August 1952 in response to the demands being made by Europeans for a state of emergency, the underground movement possessed neither coherent plans, organization or training for guerrilla combat nor a significant stockpile of modern arms. Moreover, the arrest of Kikuyu leaders at the beginning of the Emergency largely decapitated the movement, depriving it of virtually all of its educated and experienced top leaders, and left the situation in the hands of local leaders and the rank and file. It was not until the early months of 1953 that the bands in the forests were sufficiently organized to resist the colonial security forces that had invested the Kikuyu reserves. As Rosberg and Nottingham point out, the violence carried out by the Kikuyu 'derived from the conditions of the Emergency itself'.[92]

The Emergency, in reality, was a pre-emptive attack carried out by the incumbent colonial authorities against a significant segment of the African political leadership of Kenya and its supporters. So it was understood both by the administrative officers in the field who had demanded it and by the Kikuyu who believed 'the intent of the white man was to eliminate the whole Kikuyu tribe'.[93] For the Provincial Administration, the Emergency was a means to transcend the internal and external challenges to their control over the African population. First, the Emergency promised a final solution for dealing with the Kikuyu politicians who had vexed and infuriated field officers, capturing from them the loyalty of the rural masses. It was not a sudden and discontinuous outbreak of violence, but rather a logical, if major, escalation of the established organizational processes for dealing with African politics. Second, the Emergency was a powerful weapon of bureaucratic politics with which administrators could attempt to reverse the decline of their prestige and authority in relation to the technical departments and overcome the growing breach with the central administration. The bureaucratic infighting over the declaration of the emergency between the Provincial Administration and the Secretariat officials whose interests it threatened reflected the importance of this aspect of the situation.[94]

The Emergency was thus welcomed by the Provincial Administration as the necessary policy for dealing with an intensifying crisis of long standing. The deterioration in the status and power of field officers visible in the years before October 1952 was apparently reversed and their position restored and even expanded beyond what it had been in the golden era before the Second World War. The contentious politicians and their organizations were removed from the scene and Emergency Regulations gave administrators the punitive powers quickly to eliminate any opposition. Even as the fighting raged, government money began to pour into the affected districts for 'reconstruction and development' programmes. The discretion and power of field administrators in Central Province increased to the point where they could and did act beyond the law to wipe out 'Mau Mau'. A Minister of African Affairs during the Emergency attested to the difficulty of keeping track of what was happening in the field and described it as a return to the style of administration used during the pacification of Kenya 50 years before.[95] Furthermore, despite new and often intense conflicts with the army and police units over emergency pacification, field administrators were also able to reassert their predominant positions over the other departments of government, particularly with regard to crucial socio-economic and welfare policies in the Kikuyu districts. As one district officer noted: 'Emergency regulations you said . . . and you did what you damned well liked'.[96]

This renaissance of the power of the Provincial Administration during the most intense phase of the Emergency between the end of 1952 and mid-1956 had a tonic effect on field officers. Despite the violence and danger, the Emergency became a period of renewed morale, high hopes and intense excitement. The dispirited uncertainty and confusion and the anxious sense of being victims of explosive forces beyond their control disappeared, to be replaced by a buoyant and commanding optimism. A Provincial Commissioner of Central Province during this period remarked: 'We were really beating the Mau Mau. The esprit de corps and general feeling among everyone working in the districts was enormously high. People really felt they were getting somewhere and they were achieving something and they were doing good in every way . . . and they were.'[97] From the eradication of the 'disease of Mau Mau' administrators moved to nothing less than a fundamental reconstruction of Kikuyu society through 'villagization' and land consolidation programmes intended to produce a harmonious society of prosperous villages and sturdy yeoman farmers immune to the appeals of political radicalism. In the end the Emergency became an attempt to re-create their idealized image of the organic community of traditional England.[98] The methods and ethos of field administration remained unchanged.

The importance of the role of incumbent authorities in collective violence must be stressed for two further reasons. First, on the theoretical level, the predominant approach to the analysis of political development and revolution, particularly in the USA, contains a prior commitment to political stability as an overriding value and a preoccupation with the analysis of insurgent challenges to the status quo.[99] Insurgent-centred theories that focus on structural factors tend to emphasize the importance of governmental power capabilities necessary to control social change and conflict. Those that focus on behavioural or social-psychological variables shaping the perceptions and motivations of insurgents risk reducing collective violence to a process of individual frustration, misperception, and psychopathology – the actions of an impatient minority, socially and psychologically marginal.[100] Furthermore, both types of insurgent-centred theory lend collective violence an air of inevitability that obscures the complicity of incumbent authorities in shaping the origins and intensity of conflict: if insurgent violence is an inevitable concomitant of rapid change, then the existing authorities cannot prevent it but only be strong enough to contain and eliminate it when it breaks out. Insurgent-centred theories adopt in effect the perspective of the incumbent authorities themselves and find their policy expression in the socio-political and psychological programmes of counter-insurgency warfare. Such structural and psychological theroies were present in official circles in Kenya during the Emergency, although in far less sophisticated form than contemporary academic analyses, and lay behind the programmes for the reconstruction of Kikuyu society and the elaborate system for the psychological 'rehabilitation' of tens of thousands of Africans held in prisons and detention camps.[101]

Second, on an empirical level, incumbent violence is a matter of critical contemporary importance. As Zolberg pointed out in 1968, 'the most frequent coups in Africa have probably been those initiated by an incumbent government against threatening individuals or groups (real or alleged), and those launched by rulers or dominant factions against their associates'.[102] A crucial factor behind such violence appears to be the reaction of established power groups to the demands of new or previously excluded contenders for power for access to the legitimate political arena and changes in existing value distributions.[103] While the demands of the Kenya African Union in the years before the Emergency were almost entirely within the bounds of legitimacy, even within the restricted confines of the colonial policy, the behaviour of the Provincial Administration clearly displayed the reaction of a group whose established power position was profoundly threatened. In addition, incumbent violence is also affected by the fact that 'although castigated as thoroughly immobilist by critics, pre-revolutionary regimes are to a surprising degree reforming regimes.'[104] However, the changes the regime regards as 'progressive' may actually be experienced by significant sectors of the society as severe deprivations and social instability. In Kenya Governor Mitchell and administrators in the field and in the Secretariat generally believed that the problems of the Kikuyu could only be resolved through socio-economic reforms. But the measures upon which they relied to effect these reforms were, as we have seen, precisely those 'development' programmes that the Kikuyu saw as aggravating their conditions.

At the beginning of this chapter I also suggested that the incidence and rate of socio-economic change was inadequate in itself to account for the occurrence of collective violence. Instead, collective violence can be better understood as contingent upon a variety of political and organizational factors, some idiosyncratic and some of more general incidence, which shape the reactions of incumbents and insurgents to the new patterns of conflict and cleavage generated by change. Just as it is incorrect to assume that under conditions of rapid change insurgents will inevitably rebel, so it is also incorrect to assume that incumbent authorities will inevitably repress. Official repression and violence represent one end of a continuum of possible incumbent responses that also includes numerous options of co-optation, compromise, conciliation, concession and reform. In the case considered here, we cannot assume that repression was the only response possible for the colonial authorities to a challenge from the colonized. I have tried to show that the reactions of the Kenya Administration to African demands were shaped by the internal processes and characteristic ethos of a particular type of bureaucracy set within the idiosyncracies of the colony's political economy. The sources of incumbent reactions can be very mundane indeed and found in seemingly minor details of administrative structure, internal bureaucratic politics between different departments, and the personal interests of individual officials. Without fully exploring its implications for his analysis of peasant wars, Wolf makes this point when he notes that administrators face a choice between 'the operations of a bureaucracy which merely administers rules, and operations which answer the strategic issues of social co-ordination and conflict' and that administrators 'tend to retreat from participation in the existential problems of the population into the protective carapace provided by the administrative machinery.'[105] From this perspective the story of the Emergency in Kenya is not a melodrama but a tragedy involving an intensely dedicated body of men whose individual and organizational interests were so intertwined with their understanding of the welfare of the natives that any compromise with the African politician became a dereliction of their duty to the 'real' African.

Finally, that the Emergency in Kenya was contingent on the character and reactions of the Kenya Administration, rather than inherent in imperialism as such, and that the vested interests of administrators were only one strand in the complex cord of the imperial relationship is strongly suggested by the effect of increasing metropolitan influence after October 1952. The Emergency was exactly the sort of colonial crisis that generated metropolitan repercussions and activated the direct intervention of the London authorities. The continuity of the socio-economic problems of Kenya during the 1950s and the ultimate failure of the Emergency to eliminate African political opposition, which spread rapidly in tribes not subject to the same violent repression as the Kikuyu, shifted the initiative to metropolitan institutions and interests. At first metropolitan intervention was ad hoc and indecisive, attempting to stabilize the situation in Kenya through incremental constitutional adjustments and the financing of counter-insurgency. By the late 1950s, however, metropolitan direction of Kenyan affairs began to take on increasingly coherent direction, reversing in the process all of the pre-Emergency policies of the Provincial Administration through the active stimulation of African cash-crop agriculture, the provision of higher-education facilities, the widening of access to the civil service (including the ranks of the Provincial Administration) and the opening of the central political institutions of the colony to African participation through elected representation on the Legislative Council and the granting of ministerial portfolios. This culminated in 1960 in a programmatic commitment by the metropolitan authorities at the Lancaster House Conference to the independence of Kenya under an African majority government.

During the ensuing four years, the metropolitan authorities, motivated by strategic and economic interests different from those of both the Kenya government and the settlers, carried out what Wasserman has termed 'consensual decolonization', i.e. a process of co-optation and compromise with local African and European political forces that brought Kenya to independence with the structure of the colonial political economy (and major British interests) largely intact.[106] While an analysis of the factors that shaped metropolitan policy is beyond the scope of this chapter, it is important to note how metropolitan reactions to the cleavages and conflicts in the colony were ultimately the reverse of those of the Kenya Administration and dealt with the situation by means short of force. In the process it was the local interests of both the Kenya Administration and the settlers that were sacrificed for a negotiated settlement preserving metropolitan interests. The leader of the 'liberal' wing of the settler community, Michael Blundell, came to this realization after a meeting with Iain Macleod in which he suspected that 'perhaps after all our future was to be decided not so much for our own good, as I had imagined, but for that of Great Britain'; and a few months later at Lancaster House he 'came to the conclusion that the Africans knew from the Colonial Office that they were batting on a wicket specially prepared for them'.[107]

Notes

1. I would like to thank Anthony King, John Lonsdale and Richard Cashmore for their helpful criticism of earlier versions of this chapter. The primary source material cited below comes from archives in London and Nairobi and a series of interviews with former administrators, technical officers and politicians in Britain and Kenya. Archives are identified by the prefixes KNA (Kenya National Archive), KGL (Kenya Government Library) and PRO (Public Record Office, London). The interviews are

identified by number and letter suffix. For administrators, there is a three-digit number, the first digit indicating the officer's rank: 1 for junior officers, 2 for senior officers (provincial commissioners or under secretaries in the Secretariat and up). The suffix indicates the primary area of service in Kenya: field (F) or Secretariat (S) or both (FS). Technical officers are indicated by a two-digit number and the suffix T. Political figures are indicated by a two-digit number and the suffix P with either A (African), B (British) or S (settler).

2. The most complete statement of the official explanation is found in F.D. Corfield. *The Origins and Growth of Mau Mau* (London, Cmd 1030, 1960). Other sources emphasizing one or another of the facets of the official explanation include J.C. Carothers. *The Psychology of Mau Mau* (Nairobi, 1954); Granville Roberts. *The Mau Mau in Kenya* (London, 1954); and L.S.B. Leakey, *Mau Mau and the Kikuyu* (London, 1952) and *Defeating Mau Mau* (London, 1954). An account of the first presentation of the official version at the Kapenguria trials and the evidence used to support it can be found in Montagu Slater. *The Trial of Jomo Kenyatta* (London, 1955).

3. Gilbert Kushner. 'An African revitalization movement: Mau Mau', *Anthropos* 60 (1965), p. 763.

4. See, for example, Kushner. 'African revitalization movement', and Annette Rosenstiel, 'An anthropological approach to the Mau Mau problem', *Political Science Quarterly* 68 (1953), pp. 419-32.

5. J.M. Kariuki, *Mau Mau Detainee* (London, 1964); R. Mugu Gatheru, *Child of Two Worlds* (Garden City, N.Y., 1965); Waruhiu Itote (General China), *Mau Mau General* (Nairobi, 1967); Jomo Kenyatta, *Suffering Without Bitterness* (Nairobi, 1968); Oginga Odinga, *Not Yet Uhuru* (Nairobi and London, 1967); Tom Mboya, *Freedom and After* (London, 1963); Carl Rosberg and John Nottingham. *The Myth of Mau Mau* (New York, 1966); M.P.K. Sorrenson, *Land Reform in the Kikuyu Country* (Nairobi and London, 1967); Donald Barnett and Karari Njama, *Mau Mau from Within* (London, 1968); R. Buijtenhuijs, *Le mouvement 'Mau Mau'* (The Hague, 1971).

6. Ted Gurr, *Why Men Rebel* (Princeton, 1970).

7. Eric Wolf, *Peasant Wars of the Twentieth Century* (New York, 1970).

8. Kariuki, *Mau Mau Detainee*, pp. 50-1; Rosberg and Nottingham, *Myth of Mau Mau*, pp. 220-1, 234, 241-2; Barnett and Njama, *Mau Mau from Within*, pp. 41-2.

9. Charles Tilly, 'Does modernization breed revolution?', *Comparative Politics*, 5 (1972-3), pp. 425-47, p. 439.

10. For a careful analysis of the level of violence during the consolidation of British control in the early years of colonial rule see Chapter 3 above. Disparities in force levels are reflected in the official casualty figures of the Emergency which report 11,503 'terrorists' killed as opposed to the loss of 95 Europeans (35 civilians), 29 Asians (26 civilians) and 1,920 'Loyal Africans' (1,819 civilians), (Corfield, *Origins and Growth of Mau Mau*, p. 316). Unofficial estimates of the number of Africans killed by the security forces are much higher.

11. Graham T. Allison, 'Conceptual models and the Cuban missile crisis', *American Political Science Review* 63 (1969), p. 694.

12. See, for example, Gary B. Wasserman, 'The adaptation of a colonial elite to decolonization' (unpublished Ph.D. thesis, Columbia University, 1973); and Arghiri Emmanuel, 'White settler colonialism and the myth of investment imperialism', *New Left Review*, 73 (1972), pp. 35-57.

13. Allison, 'Conceptual models and the Cuban missile crisis'.

14. The character and political role of the Kenya Administration is explored more fully in my *Control and Crisis in Colonial Kenya* (London, 1990).

15. The fullest analysis of the early decades of the Kenya Administration when many of the patterns discussed here began to take shape is T.H.R. Cashmore, 'Studies in district administration in the East African Protectorate, 1895-1918' (unpublished

Ph.D. dissertation, Cambridge University, 1965).

16. James Fesler, 'The political role of field administration', in F. Heady and S.L. Stokes (eds), *Papers in Comparative Public Administration* (Ann Arbor, Institute of Public Administration, University of Michigan, 1962), pp. 120–3, 129; Brian C. Smith, *Field Administration* (London, 1967), pp. 56–7.

17. James Fesler, 'Approaches to the understanding of decentralization', *Journal of Politics* 27 (1965), pp. 536–66, p. 562.

18. While the metropolitan authorities possessed formal powers to control a colony's internal administration, these were essentially extreme controls clearly intended for use only in exceptional circumstances. They were usually invoked only when the affairs of a colony became a source of political controversy in Britain and a potential embarrassment to the Colonial Office or the government. The London authorities were thus in a position that 'made powers of persuasion more important than powers of command' (M.J. Lee, *Colonial Development and Good Government* (Oxford, 1967), p. 54). The result was a delicate, complex and often protracted process of bargaining in which the individual colonial governments exercised considerable influence on the vague general policy principles enunciated in London.

19. Interview 201FS.

20. Interview 201FS.

21. Cashmore, 'Studies in district administration', *passim.*

22. Personal communication, July 1973.

23. Philip Selznick, *Leadership in Administration* (Evanston, Ill., 1957), p. 17.

24. Robert Heussler, 'British rule in Africa' in P. Gifford and W.R. Louis (eds), *France and Britain in Africa* (New Haven, Conn., 1971), p. 576.

25. Some of the maxims of the Provincial Administration have been recorded by Cashmore: 'When in doubt create a crisis,' 'In each new district one has to have a showdown. Choose your battlefield and win. After that bluff will last to the end of the tour.' 'No officer is any use till he has served at least six months in a district.' 'Remember, one only finds the true reason for any African action months afterward.' ('Studies in district administration', p. 55, n. 3.) In addition, 'All subscribed to that second of the Punjab principles that a shot in time saves nine' (p. 58).

26. Interview 219F.

27. Margery Perham, 'Introduction' to Robert Heussler, *Yesterday's Rulers: The Making of the British Colonial Service* (London, 1963), pp. xx.

28. Rupert Wilkinson, *The Prefects: British Leadership and the Public School Tradition* (London, 1964), p. 4.

29. Sir Ralph Furse, who directed the selection of colonial administrators in the Colonial Office for more than 30 years, recounted his methods of work in *Aucuparius: Memoirs of a Recruiting Officer* (London, 1962).

30. Barrington Moore, *Social Origins of Dictatorship and Democracy* (Boston, 1967), pp. 491–6. See also Cynthia F. Behrmann, 'The mythology of British imperialism' (unpublished Ph.D. dissertation, Boston University, 1965).

31. Interview 04PB.

32. The ideology of traditional authority relationships is analysed in Reinhard Bendix, *Nation-Building and Citizenship* (Garden City, N.Y., 1969), pp. 48–58.

33. KNA, Office of the Chief Secretary 1/1195, Chief Native Commissioner, 'Speech to the United Kenya Club', June 1952.

34. Interview 218F, and R. Tatton-Brown, 'How was colonialism justified: a personal view' (unpublished seminar paper, St Catharine's College, Cambridge, 1968), p. 8.

35. KNA, MAA7/126, P.C., Central Province to Deputy Chief Secretary, 6 December 1948.

36. The principal theorist of incrementalism, Charles Lindblom, incorporated the phrase used by the British to describe their approach into the title of one of his major

papers: 'The science of "muddling through"', *Public Administration Review* 19 (1959), pp. 79–88.

37. It is important to point out that the issues involved critical decisions *within* the imperial relationship about the internal structure of the colonial political economy, i.e. whether Kenya was to be developed on the basis of European settler commercial agriculture or African peasant cash-crop farming. The outcome in either case was a dependent primary-product export economy. For an analysis of the *de facto* growth of settler predominance and its effects in Kenya see E.A. Brett, *Colonialism and Underdevelopment in East Africa* (New York, 1973), especially pp. 165–212.

38. In August 1933, the Tory Secretary of State, Sir Philip Cunliffe-Lister, told the settlers' political leader, Lord Francis Scott, that 'no government in this country would ever agree to the claim on the part of the white settlers to govern on their own'. (PRO, CO533/436/3198/33. 'Note by Sir Samuel Wilson on Discussion between the Secretary of State and Lord Francis Scott, at which Lord Plymouth and Sir S. Wilson were present', 2 August 1933.)

39. KGL, 'Kenya: Report by Lord Hailey Following His Inquiries in April, 1940', p. 40.

40. In 1922 Governor Sir Robert Coryndon exclaimed in a despatch to the Secretary of State, 'Upon my word, it seems as though none of my predecessors had ever thought of the future' (PRO, CO533/280, Despatch of 17 September 1922). The lack of general policy was already in evidence before the First World War and drew several complaints from administrators. (See Cashmore, 'Studies in district administration', pp. 77, 92, 112, 117–20.) In 1929, during discussions of native policy in Kenya, W.C. Bottomley, an Under-Secretary at the Colonial Office, noted that 'It is I think in the possible absence of what I call a definite direction of Administration in Kenya, that the Colonial Government is most open to criticism'. (PRO, CO533/396/16040/1930, Minute of 12 March 1930.) From the unofficial side complaints about the lack of direction came from the missionaries (Roland Oliver, *The Missionary Factor in East Africa* (London, 1954), p. 254) and from settler politicians, one of whom stated, 'Basically, I think the settlers' criticism of the British administration was it never really made up its mind where Kenya was going' (Interview 01PS).

41. Interview 201FS.

42. Interview 103F.

43. Heussler, 'British rule in Africa', p. 578.

44. Thus Governor Sir Philip Mitchell could write in a foreword to a book by one of his district commissioners: 'And what agreeable people what these simple folk are, how like a breath of fresh clean air, in contrast to the fetid wickedness of Western civilization gone putrid in the hands of wicked men': 'Foreword' to R.O. Hennings, *African Morning* (London, 1951), p. 9. While three years later he commented in his memoirs: 'it was, and is, to this day, a picture of simple, ignorant witch- and magic-ridden people at the mercy of many enemies . . . beginning to grope at long last towards escape from behind the Iron Curtain of the black ages of ignorance and terror. A people helpless by themselves': *African Afterthoughts* (London, 1954), p. 26.

45. Interview 210S.

46. Interview 103F.

47. Interview 201FS.

48. Grigg, echoing the opinions of his field officers, wrote during the crisis over female circumcision:

> There is no evidence of any acts or even any propaganda on the part of the association or of individual agitators that could be called definitely seditious . . . what I have to report to your Lordship therefore, is not a series of overt acts of opposition to government or of omission to comply with government's require-ments, but the creation, and, I fear, the spread of an atmosphere of criticism and

mistrust which may have unfortunate effects upon those of the native population who become involved in it.

(PRO, CO533/392/15921, Confidential Despatch no. 130, Grigg to Lord Passfield, 12 October 1929.)

49. PRO, CO533/392/15921, Grigg to Passfield, 12 October 1929.
50. PRO, CO533/384/15540, Sub File A, Major E.A.T. Dutton to W.C. Bottomley, 25 November 1929.
51. According to one former provincial commissioner: 'The politicians were the minority using their superior education or superior wit to persuade the people they lived among to believe whatever they chose to tell them in order to give themselves more political power and authority. Because at that time . . . the great bulk of people, even in Kikuyuland, were extremely ignorant and they could easily be persuaded that almost anything was true' (Interview 214F).
52. The belief is mentioned repeatedly in the papers in KNA, DC/FH1/4.
53. This interpretation was stressed by H.E. Lambert, one of the Provincial Administration's most distinguished amateur anthropologists, in a letter to the PC, Central Province, 15 June 1942 (KNA, DC/FH1/4).
54. For example, during the Taita Hills land dispute the district commissioner insisted policy changes must be made before the leaders of the Taita Hills Association were released from detention 'so that if adjustments are made they cannot in any way be attributed to their return' (KNA, PC/Coast1/108/63, DC Voi to PC Coast, 23 May 1942).
55. KNA, PC/CP8/5/2, Joseph Kang'ethe *et al.*, Letter to Senior Commissioner Nyeri, 10 July 1926.
56. KNA, KBU/1/22, Handing Over Report, M.R.R. Vidal to S.H. Fazan, 21 September 1929 and PRO, CO/533/392/15921, Grigg to Passfield, 12 October 1929.
57. International Bank for Reconstruction and Development, *The Economic Development of Kenya* (Baltimore, 1963), pp. 20–1, 340.
58. Jomo Kenyatta, *Kenya: Land of Conflict* (Manchester: International African Service Bureau no. 3, 1945), p. 22.
59. This distinction is not, of course, absolute. As Brett (*Colonialism and Underdevelopment in East Africa*) and others have shown, individual administrators between the wars did stimulate physical development and sporadically encouraged Africans to enter the monetary economy either as labourers or cash-crop farmers. Nevertheless, administrators between the wars basically conceived of themselves as exercising the less activist guardian role. The post-1945 period involved a change in the intensity, scope and degree of organization and resources applied by the colonial government to 'development', and a concomitant shift in what was demanded and expected of field administrators.
60. KNA, MAA/9/929, PC, Central, E.H. Windley to Chief Secretary J.D. Rankine, 23 November 1948, and Chief Secretary, Memorandum to Deputy Chief Secretary, Chief Native Commissioner and Financial Secretary, 30 November 1948.
61. See the comments about KAU petitions in KNA, MAA/2/5/146, Assistant Secretary, M.N. Evans to Personal Assistant, Chief Native Commissioner, Minute of 17 March 1950.
62. Interview 218F.
63. Interview 219F.
64. KNA, PC/NZA3/1576, H.H. Low, DC Central Kavirondo, 'Memorandum on Native Policy', 8 December 1943.
65. KNA, DC/MKS15/3, 'Minutes of the Provincial Commissioners' Meeting of 10–15 April, 1945'. *The Annual Report of Native Affairs* (Nairobi: Government Printer) for 1946/47 complacently noted that few of the aspiring African entrepreneurs

'had resources in experience and capital commensurate with their ambitions, and gradually the disappointed, who were many, settled down to their former way of life' (p. 3). Oginga Odinga asserts that the Administration actively harassed African efforts, including his own, to establish businesses; that it was impossible for Africans to get loans from banks: and that official trade regulations seemed to exclude Africans. He notes that 'our economic effort was frowned upon not only because it was competition against established trading preserves, but also because it was a demonstration of African initiative and independence'. (*Not Yet Uhuru*, p. 89.)

66. The Report of the Beecher Committee on African education, *African Education in Kenya* (Nairobi, 1949), led to plans for only 16 African secondary schools by 1957. For a detailed analysis of the role of the Administration in educational policy, see John Anderson, *The Struggle for the School* (London and Nairobi, 1970), especially pp. 32–50.

67. KNA, DC/MKS15/3, 'Recommendations made at an informal meeting of Provincial Commissioners, April 28, 1948' and Office of the Chief Secretary 1/1195, Chief Native Commissioner, 'A Talk to the Christian Forum on Some Present Day African Problems', 3 July 1950.

68. Sorrenson, *Land Reform in the Kikuyu Country*, pp. 81–2 and Rosberg and Nottingham. *Myth of Mau Mau*, pp. 248–52.

69. The Municipal African Affairs Officers in Nairobi and Mombasa served in an advisory role to the European dominated City Council and had no executive powers. They also had little influence within the Provincial Administration and felt their colleagues had little understanding or sympathy for the problems they faced in the cities. (Interviews 201FS and 206FS.)

70. KGL, 'Despatch from the Secretary of State to the Governors of the African Territories', 25 February 1947 (bound into the minutes of the African Affairs Committee for 1948). This was the principal Colonial Office statement of political development policy in the immediate post-war period.

71. In his despatch on local government, Creech-Jones warned of the danger of creating a 'class of professional African politicians absorbed in the activities of the centre and out of direct touch with the people themselves', while in his reply Governor Mitchell emphatically asserted the right of the Administration to protect ignorant rural Africans from the wiles of the sophisticated demagogue 'usually inspired by self-interest and . . . a marked lack of concern for truth, honesty, justice or good government' (KGL 'Despatch from the Secretary of State . . .', 25 February 1947: and Sir Philip Mitchell to Arthur Creech-Jones, Confidential Despatch No. 16 of 30 May 1947).

72. Roger Howman, *African Local Government in British East and Central Africa* (Pretoria: Reprint Series of the University of South Africa, No. 4, 1963), Part II, p. 32 (originally published 1952–53).

73. KNA, DC/MKS/15/3, 'Minutes of the Provincial Commissioners' Meeting of 24–26 October 1946' and also 'Minutes of the Provincial Commissioners' Meeting of 26–28 May 1947'.

74. KNA, MAA8/141, P. Wyn-Harris, Chief Native Commissioner to E.W. Mathu, Member of the Legislative Council, 4 June 1948. This statement was repeated verbatim in 1950.

75. In a most revealing and important document of the period, African workers in Mombasa, most of them Kikuyu, expressed their grievances to the Industrial Relations Officer of the Labour Department in October, 1947, a few months after a major strike had paralysed the port. They told him that:

The European wants the African to be poor and come down like dogs . . . African gets too little money for work . . . Because of the low wages they do not get enough and cannot send to the reserve and are compelled to steal . . . The European comes and takes everything belonging to them and then asks for brotherhood . . . When they want to go up government pushes them down . . . They like government but government doesn't like them. Why cannot government assist us so that everyone can be equal . . . The lion and the goat cannot lie down together. Why is government, they asked, not good to the Africans. Everybody in the world is out to put the Africans down.

(KNA, Ministry of Labour/9/372, Report by James Patrick, Industrial Relations Officer, no date [1947].)

76. Interview 227FS.
77. Interview 103F.
78. Corfield. *Origins and Growth of Mau Mau*, pp. 81, 98, 117, 169–70, 221.
79. *Ibid.*, pp. 52–3, 72, 102–3.
80. *Ibid.*, pp. 74–5.
81. KNA, MAA8/25, Secret 'Minutes of a Meeting of the Official Members of the African Affairs Committee', 3 November 1948.
82. KNA, MAA8/65, PC, Central to Chief Native Commissioner, 13 September 1952. A notable example of the image of African politicians can be found in the letters of 1 September and 14 September 1951 from the PC Central Province to the CNC and Chief Secretary respectively commenting on the activities of the Central Province Branch of the KAU (KNA, MAA2/5/146).
83. Rosberg and Nottingham, *Myth of Mau Mau*, pp. 264–5, 269–70.
84. Rosberg and Nottingham, *Myth of Mau Mau*, pp. 331–4; Barnett and Njama, *Mau Mau from Within*, pp. 53–4.
85. Corfield, *Origins and Growth of Mau Mau*, pp. 100–1.
86. KNA, Office of the Chief Secretary 1/1195, Chief Native Commissioner, E.R. Davies, 'Notes on a Speech to Legislative Council', February 1952, Also, CNC 'Notes for a Speech to LegCo', November 1950, and 'Notes for Speech to LegCo Budget Session', November 1950. The Chief Native Commissioner was not the executive head of the Provincial Administration and possessed only advisory powers, serving as the 'friend at court' who articulated the views of the field administration to the central government.
87. KNA, MAA2/5/146, 'A Prayer for the Restoration of Our Land', Kenya African Union to Right Hon. James Griffiths, Secretary of State for the Colonies, 14 May 1951. On 6 June the DC Nyeri prepared a secret report on a KAU mass meeting in Nyeri on 27 May and noted that 'There seems every likelihood of trouble in the near future, if as seems certain, the KAU memorandum on the Kikuyu lands is rejected. The district is hot with rumours of "deeds not words".' (Quoted in Corfield, *Origins and Growth of Mau Mau*, pp. 107.)
88. Corfield, *Origins and Growth of Mau Mau*, p. 136; Rosberg and Nottingham, *Myth of Mau Mau*.
89. Interviews 227FS and 07PS.
90. Reports of unrest from the Provincial Administration were generally considered by the Secretariat to be 'exaggerated' (see Corfield, *Origins and Growth of Mau Mau*, pp. 144–52).
91. *Ibid.*, p. 151.
92. Rosberg and Nottingham, *Myth of Mau Mau*, p. 277.
93. Barnett and Njama, *Mau Mau from Within*, p. 71.
94. The subsequent careers of the Chief Secretary, Attorney General and Chief Native Commissioner were all adversely affected to some degree, especially the last named, by their resistance to the state of emergency and a consequent reputation for being 'soft' in dealing with the situation. The CNC was replaced by E.H. Windley, the

Province Commissioner in Central Province in 1952 and the Secretariat's strongest critic in the Provincial Administration.

95. Interview 227FS.
96. Interview 103F.
97. Interview 214F.
98. Sorrenson, *Land Reform in the Kikuyu Country*, especially pp. 220–36.
99. See Mark Kesselman's critique of Samuel Huntington, *Political Order in Changing Societies* (New Haven, 1968), and Leonard Binder *et al.*, *Crises and Sequences in Political Development* (Princeton, 1971), in 'Order or movement? The literature of political development as ideology', *World Politics* 26 (1973–74), pp. 138–54.
100. Thus, Gurr's interpretation of Mau Mau sees it as a revolt following 'the imposition of restrictions after a period of expansion of political rights' during the 1920s and 1930s when the Kenya government had been 'increasingly responsive' to African political demands! He concludes that 'the frustrations which brought it about were those affecting Westernized Kenyans with intense, modernizing political demands, and it occurred only after a generation of gradual improvement in the political status of the Kenyans most committed to modern politics and its forms' (*Why Men Rebel*, p. 116).
101. The continuity of theory and policy in dealing with peasant rebellions, guerrilla insurgency or 'wars of national liberation' is not accidental. From Malaya to Kenya to Vietnam, etc., the use of 'villagization' or 'strategic hamlet' programs, as well as 'rehabilitation' and various forms of psychological warfare is linked to the emergence of an Anglo-American counter-insurgency community of administrators and scholars. The adoption of the perspective of incumbent authorities in ostensibly neutral academic research thus often has a direct linkage with policy and is implicated in the initiation and escalation of incumbent violence. (Numerous instances of the involvement of social scientists in counter-insurgency programs are discussed in Frances Fitzgerald, *Fire in the Lake: The Vietnamese and the Americans in Vietnam* (Boston, 1972), *passim*. The linkage between theories of revolution and counter-insurgency techniques is discussed at length in Eqbal Ahmad, 'Revolutionary warfare and counter insurgency' in N. Miller and R. Aya (eds), *National Liberation: Revolution in the Third World* (New York, 1971), pp. 137–213.)
102. A.R. Zolberg, 'The structure of political conflict in the new states of Africa', *American Political Science Review*, 62 (1968) p. 77.
103. Tilly, 'Does modernization breed revolution?', pp. 437–47. The model of power contenders and power resources is developed more fully by Charles Anderson in *Politics and Economic Change in Latin America* (New York: Van Nostrand-Reinhold, 1967), pp. 87–114.
104. Mark N. Hagopian, *The Phenomenon of Revolution* (New York: Dodd Mead, 1974), p. 162.
105. Wolf, *Peasant Wars of the Twentieth Century*, p. 287. Wolf's fine study manages to focus on the sources of peasant rebellion without slipping into the perspective of the incumbent authorities.
106. Wasserman, 'The adaptation of a colonial elite to decolonization', and 'The independence bargain: Kenya Europeans and the land issue 1960–62', *Journal of Commonwealth Political Studies*, 11 (1973), pp. 99–120.
107. Sir Michael Blundell, *So Rough a Wind* (London, 1964), pp. 271, 273.

freedom'. He knew, none better, the value of struggle. But as Kenya's first president he could scarcely permit the pangs of its birth to be borne by one heroic minority, the Mau Mau fighters, alone.[6] Kenya had to have a nationalist history that included all Kenyans. But its past does not, at first sight, look like that of a nation. Within frontiers created by European diplomacy and British conquest, it has no common ancestors to worship and many feuds to forget. Were Renan's remark not meant to apply to all states, he might well have had Kenya in mind when he warned that historical research could seem to threaten nationality.[7] The study of Mau Mau puts this insight to the test.

It sometimes looks as if a history is the last thing Kenya wants. It seems too dispiritingly schismatic, studied more in segments than in common. Kenya's scholars know more about the making of the state's many ethnic groups than of its territorial nationalism. They have shown, it is true, that its present-day cultural communities have been continually created by partial permutations from a common fund of diverse ethnic strands, both before the British conquest and since. Nonetheless, tribesmen do not look good Kenyans. And when it comes to modern times it is easy to argue that the post-war African national coalition was broken by Mau Mau's sectarian discipline. The stark opposition between a unified Mau Mau, often seen simply as a guerrilla army, and the allegedly traitorous 'home guards' who fought for their British masters and won the peace, has so deafened this divided Kenya with its slogans that the past is no longer allowed to speak.[8] Mau Mau can seem to be the most divisive element in all Kenya's past, the ugly underside of its pivotal role.

It is understandable that a new state trying to engineer national unity should be averse to intimations of past conflict, but the attitude betrays a narrow view of politics and political history. In Kenya both have been preoccupied with aroused minorities in competitive action. Different perspectives open up if one raises the prior question of how communities became engaged, even created, in thought. To ask that question of Mau Mau is to alert one to its divisions over ends and means, political and military. The movement's presumed unity made it bizarre and threatening. Its internal debates are more tragic and demanding of historical explanation, especially since they were grounded in a moral economy that the insurgents shared with their bitterest enemies, the Kikuyu 'loyalists' who fought on the colonial side. They are a central concern of this essay, which was born of a desire to rescue the study of the rising from its local disfavour and to restore Kenya's recent past to public discussion. In this aim I follow Kenya's leading political scientist, Ali Mazrui. When, many years ago, he pondered the relationship between the future of a new state and its divided past, he concluded that Renan must be reversed. Kenya not only had to have a history; it must get it right. National integration came by facing up to rather than forgetting past feuds. A critical tradition that openly discussed past conflict strengthened the negotiated bond of responsible nationhood; evasion only added silence to the coercive bonds of the state. In Mazrui's view, selective amnesia was no condition for community.[9]

Such a purpose, the reopening of history, obliges us to think yet again about the nature of 'tribes' – a term deplored by social science but used without shame in Kenya. Mau Mau sets Kenyans at odds chiefly because its membership was recruited almost entirely from one ethnic group, Kikuyu-speakers and their closest historical partners – the Embu and Meru peoples – and, to a lesser degree, from their next nearest neighbours – Kamba and Maasai. But it is the Kikuyuness of the rising that is remembered, and the street image of tribe that makes the memory a nightmare to a multicultural state. This vulgar view stresses the tribalism of tribes. These commonsense tribes inherit internal solidarity, guard mutual boundaries, organize competition against rival teams for public goods and reduce contemporary politics to factional conflict. This essay, by contrast, enquires into the past pluralism of tribe and the creative achievement of ethnicity in the course of bitter, unresolved internal competitions to build political community.[10] The inner and outer faces of identity are admittedly inseparable. To illuminate what is 'our own' darkens the shadow of 'the other'. But the relative balance and historical depth of enquiry profoundly affects one's view of the formation of political identity, how unquestioning or critical it may be, how exclusive and unchanging or inclusive, contingent and contractual.

To understand the significance of an historical approach to Kikuyu ethnicity, one must first outline the Kenyan problem of Mau Mau's divisiveness, and the ways in which scholars have faced this logical conclusion to their schemes of explanation. The next two sections show how Mau Mau was jointly constructed by colonial propaganda and Western political science, and how historians have since reconstructed the movement to challenge but not, for the most part, to escape from this earlier model. Only after a guided tour of these Mau Maus of the mind, scarcely short but as brief as possible,[11] can one see the difference between previous readings of the multi-ethnic past and what is attempted here. The rest of the essay probes beneath the movement's cultural and political singularity to explore, if in a preliminary and ignorant way, the ordinary, perplexing human themes which fired its members' cultural imagination and divided their political thought.

My conclusion is best stated at the outset. Tribes, it has been said, 'are not actual social organisations: rather, they are states of mind.'[12] I go further: tribes, like nations – and they are alike in most respects other than in their lack of a state – are changing moral arenas of political debate. Renan thought that nations should be daily plebiscites.[13] Ah yes, but we are here concerned less with utopian hope than with contingent history; and some historical contexts, times of profound change, excite more argument than others. Arguments generate ideas; ideas animate communities; communities require power. In some circumstances, plebiscites can invent nations. Thus Kikuyu nationalism, like any other, was in origin an intellectual response to social process. It was a contest of moral knowledge. Its rival leaders addressed the concerns that face nationalists everywhere. There is some tantalizing evidence that they did so before colonial rule. After British conquest they then had to thrash out again the old issues raised by their society's unequal moral economy, at a time when its distribution of wealth, honour and power was being subverted by external pressure for change. Some tried to subject the new forces to their existing sway, to enlarge old wealth and power. Their rivals had first to persuade themselves, and then their kin, that their novel beliefs and forms of wealth gave authority for new power. Later, yet others, with scant prospect of wealth, tried instead to throw new forms of organization into the competition for honour. To debate civic virtue was to define ethnic identity. While contestants backed their claims with allusions to the uncouth ways of 'the other', black or white, neither ethnic distinction nor tribal rivalry was central to their theme. The vital issue was that of citizenship under an alien regime, what obligations it demanded, what rights it conferred. At the time, citizenship had an ethnic dimension. There were good reasons for this. Three further conclusions need emphasis. First, ethnic identity was the reverse of what it is often said to be, unthinking conformity. A common ethnicity was the arena for the sharpest social and political division. Second, argument over domestic civic virtue tested claims to provide external political leadership. Finally, contests about tribal identity did not exclude and may have kindled a territorial, 'Kenyan' political imagination then. There is no reason why they should not do so now. Much depends on the rules of debate. To rethink tribes may also be to rethink states.

So I end with a query. The memory of Mau Mau's tribally exclusive outer face may well threaten the composure of a young state with a multiple nationality and inhibit Kenyans from discussing their past. This external profile has been drawn by most of the histories that have so far been told, its outline given by the movement's membership, symbols and overt aims. But other histories can be produced by asking different questions of new evidence.[14] And Mau Mau's inner face, imprinted with what I take to be its disputed moral meanings, not only in the minds of its members but also of their most intimate enemies, may well evoke a common sense of self-recognition not just in Kikuyu readers but in all of us who are their 'others'. If both Mau Mau and its Kikuyu resistance were fired in part by domestic debate about citizenship, then these Kikuyu meanings cannot fail to be echoed in other ethnic nationalisms. These have inspired Kenya's many, historically pluralist, communities of civic thought. If the moral pluralism of tribe is explored, like the arguments between Kikuyu, some of whom became Mau Mau, tribal history may cease to be a divisive embarrassment to the state.[15] Thanks to the work of a generation of Kenyan scholars, Kenya's historiography can now move beyond the study of heroic migrations of growing aggregations with collective names, the Luyia, the Meru, and so on. To celebrate what Kenya holds in common, its historians ought not so much to remember its heroes but – reversing Renan again – recall the ideas that divided its separate peoples within; we ought to take Kenya's many political cultures more seriously. Quite apart from any national utility, this would make for richer history. Ethnic nationalisms have longer and more reflective histories than Kenyan nationalism.[16] Kenyan political debate cannot afford to neglect them. All states are made up of diverse nationalities. Short of the barbarous simplifications of genocide, they each have to express their shared, generally disputed, ideas in different regional tongues.[17] It is not a defect peculiar to Africa. It is not a defect.

Did not Kenyatta perhaps intimate all this in his nation-building myth? It could be said that while that master of ambiguity lied for reasons of state, he also hinted at what must always be fought for within a nation. He got one history wrong; he may have been inviting historians to get another one right. Few Kenyans, few who were seen as Mau Mau indeed, took up arms in the 1950s against colonial rule. Fifty years earlier, resistance to British conquest was patchy at best.[18] In that respect he erred. But many, and by no means only among the Kikuyu, have struggled longer if less tragically, in ways that have barely begun to be told, to reform the shape and meaning of their local political communities, in search of freedom.

Problem

Our misunderstandings of Mau Mau have emerged in a series of mutual contradictions. While successive interpretations – colonial, liberal, radical or conservative – have served a different partisan purpose, all share an implicit assumption about the making of modern Africa.[19] We must explore this conventional wisdom in this section and the next. It then has to be exploded in order to reopen the study of Mau Mau.

Africans, it was once thought, had undergone or were still undergoing a modernizing transition. In this, revolutionary leaderships used political anger and then state power to mobilize new nations out of old tribes that had already been compromised by white conquest and social change. This concept coloured the public goals and scholarly analysis of African nationalism. It still sustains the authority of Africa's rulers. The reticence of recent academic comment tacitly admits that it was counterfactual myth. It predicted what did not happen. It did not explain real outcomes, save by the failure of Africans to do what in theory they should have done. This was a dangerous method of explanation. It said more about academic confusion than African conflict. We have been slow to realize that the flaw lay in our model, not in Africans or in their fates.[20] Mau Mau's historiography is an object lesson. The rising was first explained when it had to be fought, in the 1950s, the very time at which the idea of transition was born. British statements of their war aims assisted its birth. They used Mau Mau as a shocking warning against concession to nationalism where Africans had shown themselves unable to master the modern transition. Historical analyses have since 'explained away' this supposed failure, offering excuses and alibis for Mau Mau. We need to ask whether British propaganda and the analytical assumptions by which it was supported were, instead, to blame.

THE DIALECTIC OF NATIONALISM

The cultural abstraction of modernization was thought to have become observed historical process in the fourfold dialectic that African nationalism encountered on its evolutionary pilgrimage through the dichotomies, 'from tribe to nation', and so 'from tradition to modernity'.[21]

Imperialism and nationalism   The first dialectic moulded the rest. In this, modernizing colonialism was midwife to modern nationalism. To profit from Africa, Europeans had to transform it. They subjected the continent to the modern state with the 'three Rs' of rifle, railway and writing. Colonial rule brought mechanical innovation, rational authority and literate enquiry. The yeast of European change was the leaven of educated African ambition.[22] However hostile they may have been to colonial rule, African leaders were bound to mimic Western public doctrine, within a matching set of political structures. They liberated change by domesticating it, removing its stigma of alien control. Beneath the conflicts of self-assertion, their nationalism continued imperialism's world revolution by other means.[23]

Nation and tribe   Nationalism's modernizing compulsion, secondly, was not simply a matter of appealing to the West in a familiar idiom. It was a project of political survival. New nations had to be more than bundles of tribes. They needed a new culture. In its absence, political coalitions would crack, new states collapse, all hope of progress end. If the geographical expressions of conquest were to become contractual arenas of self-government, Africans had to expand their civic imagination. Tribes fostered the wrong culture, suspicious of strangers and change. Tribesmen worshipped only local gods, venerated only their own ancestors. But the new African countries were thronged with mutual strangers; to meet their clamorous needs their states had to invest in change. They had to transcend tribes not merely as political units but also as moral

communities. All this demanded the secularization of the African mind.
Tribe and class Thirdly, old tribal identity was inherited while new
nationhood was created. Persuasive nationalism thus needed rough
colonial economics to bully African society first. Vulgar Marxism lurked
beneath this liberal assumption. Economic base determined social
structure. Tribes faded into 'residual' categories as market society
replaced subsistence community. This social mobilization, as it was
called, created the opportunity for its political equivalent. When men
and women entered voluntary, horizontal associations of class and
vocation, their personal identities were dislodged from the vertical,
involuntary, totally demanding communities of tribe. They had to
explore partial and multiple identities, part inherited, part achieved.
These fractured selfhoods were transitional. Individually confusing, they
must be collectively mobile. They were morally receptive, therefore, to
the creative imprint of a national identity.[24]
Religion and politics Finally, iron necessity forced Africans into
increasingly realistic action under ever more educated leaders who had
passed the personal test of transition and become modern, secular men.
At the beginning, futile armed resistance to white conquest had often
been inspired by tribal religion. Its defeat had caused religious doubt.
Defensive violence had to give way to critical negotiation of social
change. Urban pamphlets replaced tribal spears.[25] This common political experience reinforced economic change in withering the relevance of
tribes. But many analyses of the politics of modernization ended in
doubt. It looked as if religious awe for a charismatic leader might still
be needed to complete the political passage to the nation state.[26]

All this may seem a naively liberal view now. But it was once the
self-serving belief of two Western constructions of Africa. One version
was grudgingly sceptical, held by the dying European imperialisms. The
other was excitedly hopeful, the creed of the vigorous new, largely
American, social sciences. Western self-interest was a poor guide either
to Africans' own selfish dreams or to historical causation, always more
complex than stages of growth. Both views ignored the arbitrary nature
of colonial rule. Each too loftily dismissed ethnicity. Each attributed
undue cultural magnetism to social change. Both expected too much
moral force of territorial nationalism.

THE COLONIAL VIEW

The government of Kenya had its own opinion of this dialectic.
The colony's future was more contested than most. Its officials had
to appraise African politics from within a triangular conflict between
British rule and two local nationalisms, white and black. Any imperial
dream of fulfilment by local self-rule threatened Kenya's white settlers
with a nightmare of nakedness in a strange land.[27] Postwar British

policy papered over this contradiction with the high-sounding prevarication of 'multiracialism'. This denied sovereignty to the white minority now with a promise to withhold it from the African majority in future. Keeping the dominant minority quiet demanded the appearance of holding the majority down and the reality of retaining its advances under state control. British opposition to independent African political organization was also sharpened and yet undermined by the nature of Kenya's tribes. They were stateless societies, not dynastic polities. Weaker buffers against pan-ethnic nationalism than elsewhere, they provided readier platforms for educated elites. Their awkwardness for the state was shown when the British instituted local native councils in the 1920s. These deliberately fragmented African political organization. But they were also, for 20 years, the most democratic form of local government in British Africa.

These two peculiarities in Kenya's national dialectic – its multiracial curb on nationalism and the electoral politics of its tribes – placed an unusual weight of divided white expectation on the educated African elite. Its members were required to show uncommon restraint while bearing unparalleled responsibility. Black leaders were condemned when they fought racial inequality by party means. But they were soon co-opted as individuals into chiefships and other local government offices. Later, they were appointed to the grey-suited official boards that advised on the joint affairs of a farming colony. They were permitted patronage over the supply of public goods but were denied the party manoeuvre that might have enabled them to absorb their clients' envy. Yet service to the state – given settler and Indian domination of the economy – was the best way to get on. Several angry young politicians became powerful old chiefs.[28] Kenyatta thought it well to marry the daughters of two of these government servants.[29] Conversely, government had to trust the educated elite more than in British African colonies that had alternative, if often illusory, dynastic traditions of chiefly authority to fall back on.[30] For the same reason, and with equal reluctance, Kenya was relatively attentive to the third dialectic of progress. From the Second World War a growing number of officials hoped that active encouragement of the formation of African classes would provide successors to tribes as institutions of social control. Plans to help African trade, to convert customary land tenures to freehold property, or to transform bachelor migrant labourers into unionized family men, lacked the political will to overcome white settler objections. The speed with which they were enacted after 1952, to offer a reforming alternative to Mau Mau, confirmed that they were, nonetheless, accepted official goals.[31] For no other colony did pressing on with social transition seem more essential to political stability.

In few other colonies, however, did the modernizing project look so fragile. The dialectic of progress provided an imaginative screen across which flickered both hope and fears. Nobody was much surprised that peripheral pastoral peoples continued to be difficult to govern and unpredictably violent.[32] And among most of the agricultural peoples of Kenya, associational politics and enthusiastic religion were properly separate. Modernization could be seen to work – except at the very centre of Kenya. The Kikuyu – both the largest group of cultivators and the people with the widest diaspora as peasants, traders, clerks and labourers – were of all Kenya's peoples the best known to whites and the objects of their sharpest suspicions. These flared up in the British propaganda that first constructed a Western view of Mau Mau. This has, until recently, dictated the terms of debate. The British controlled the media of communication during the war years; they had liberal wisdom on their side; they were less divided than Africans in their opinion of Mau Mau, though more so than has often been thought. For all that the British unanimity was to some extent contrived, they fought for nearly two years on the premise that their enemy was unthinkingly united, and for a moment feared that the entire Kikuyu people were as one. Mystic unity was instinctive in the tribal mind. This belief was deadly to Kikuyu then and fatal to understanding now.

The official portrait of Mau Mau was drawn in a series of denials that shifted the blame for crisis from the peculiarities of Kenya to the abnormalities of the Kikuyu.[33] Kikuyu politicians led postwar nationalism in part because of their superior learning. Yet their flourishing private school sector, their most efficient response to the West, had been founded largely to defend what whites saw as the barbaric custom of female circumcision. At the opposite, 'enthusiastic' pole of the cultural encounter, Kikuyu spirit churches were peculiarly liable to mistake earthly authority for the powers of darkness; they carried spears as well as Bibles. The great range of modern Kikuyu culture, from white-collared overseas graduates to white-turbanned holy rollers, showed what a fantastic gap remained between airy talk of multiracialism and its possible realization.[34] Few whites of any authority in their own community saw these internal differences as the source of Kikuyu political debate; they seemed, rather, to be evidence of psychic confusion. To many whites the Kikuyu were an 'unfathomable tribe' long before anybody had heard of Mau Mau.[35] The rising merely confirmed what perils there were in political progress when the dichotomies of transition remained unbridged.

Looking, first, for any connection between imperialism and nationalism, the British held that no Kikuyu grievance was sufficient to justify a tribal violence that scorned all moderate nationalist hopes of reform. Mau Mau's main demand was 'land and freedom'. Yet scarcely any of the 'White Highlands' had once been Kikuyu for them now to reclaim; ample land had already been granted in compensation; postwar colonialism was beneficently committed to development. The government was more exasperatedly conscious of pushing forward against white protests than of holding back African desires. Since no burning sense of wrong could be identified, it had to be that Kikuyu were driven to kill by terror.

Secondly, most of Kenya's peoples would not have allowed such fear to fasten its grip. But Kikuyu were 'different'. In colonial lore they had always been a treacherous tribe. It was difficult to deny that they were also the most advanced. That was part of their trouble. In the past 50 years they had received the disruptive benefits of colonialism more rapidly than their weak tribal authorities could assimilate; Kikuyu were thought to be unusually comfortless in the stress of transition.[36] Kenya's black nationalism, appallingly, seemed to be led by a bewildered tribe.

Thirdly, Kikuyu clung, more than other peoples, to their Kikuyuness. Migrant labour did not detribalize them but intensified their old identity. It was infuriating; their conservative tribalism did not lend itself to colonial control any more than did their radical trades unionism.[37] In Nairobi, Kikuyu seemed more a criminal tribe than a working class. As farm-labour tenants or 'squatters', in which role whites best knew them, they were a tribal fifth column within the farm gate. They maintained a peasant economic geography that silently subverted settler claims to Kenya's green highlands.[38]

Finally, their leaders, the elite on whom in Kenya so much depended, had betrayed Western generosity and trust. Jomo Kenyatta and Mbiyu Koinange had both enjoyed overseas higher education. The former had an English wife, the latter was better educated than most whites. If multiracialism had a future, and with it the safety of a white minority no longer protected by metropolitan power, it must lie in the intermediary hands of such modern men. Yet only men as clever as they could have founded a movement as cunning as Mau Mau, whose bestial rituals enthralled so many Kikuyu to murderous violence.

In sum, Mau Mau was certainly not multiracial; it was anti-white. It was thought to be opposed to Christianity which, if no longer much of a white religion, was at least the root of British culture, the only one to which settlers would let a future Kenya aspire.[39] Even if one ignored white sensibilities Mau Mau was still unacceptable. It was clearly not nationalist. It rejected progress and must be tribal. If it enlisted some non-Kikuyu, that was to facilitate Kikuyu domination over Kenya's other peoples, black and white. It recruited workers only to remake them into tribesmen. It replaced pamphlets with pangas, the heavy farm knives that made such clumsy work of killing. Yet Mau Mau was led by men whom one might forgive for their nationalism. Their regressive appeal could only be devilish. One by one, Mau Mau rebutted all the dialectics of progress. Since it betrayed Africans as much as whites, it could be fought with a clear conscience in the nation-building, decolonizing world of the 1950s.[40] This view was most forcefully stated as late as 1960, in the Corfield Report, the official history of Mau Mau. The British had by then promised Kenya majority rule, but some senior officials were determined to use the past to deny that future to Kenyatta.[41] Academic reviewers attacked the report's endorsement of the flimsy prosecution case that he had managed Mau Mau, not its hostile judgment on the movement as a whole.[42]

Scholarly enquiry into Mau Mau started a few years later, in the early 1960s, springtime of the new Africa. It was infused with social science. Of the first three authors one was an American political scientist, another an anthropologist from Canada.[43] Mau Mau, it was clear, had broken settler power; equally, its sectarian violence flouted analytical expectations of nationalism. This need not of itself cause intellectual dismay, since modernization theory had a built-in explanation for fractures in political mobilization. What was disturbing was that Mau Mau did not even conform to the manageable patterns of failure in 'national integration' that were then thought to follow. The first close students of Mau Mau had to calm their colleagues as much as refute propaganda. To establish that key point in the argument one must turn from the sceptical imperial perspective to the cheerfully determinist construction of African nationalism made by political science in the 1950s.

STAGES OF MODERNIZATION

The political scientists of the 1950s saw as inevitable stages of modernization what colonial rulers had set up as tests of responsibility. The dialectic of nationalism made intuitive sense to scholars who still thought of their own United States, 'the first new nation', as a melting pot of peoples.[44] The model was liberal, with Marxian assumptions. It rested on the ethnocentric axiom that creative African politics could mobilize new, wider and more secular, allegiances only where people were first knocked off their social balance by political, economic and cultural change introduced from without. Colonial conquest, after all, had forced on Africans a vast increase in political scale. Each colony was a Babel of little ethnicities. In none was it possible for Africans to build a linguistic nationalism of a more or less invented cultural majority of the subject people, on the 19th-century European pattern. The one unifying principle to hand was territorial, mapped out by conquest. The only possible unifiers were educated African elites, whose national language, literally and metaphorically, was that of the conquerors. The logic was inexorable. To win usable power the political intelligentsia had to lead an 'integrative revolution' in which distinctive tribesmen became common citizens. It was their shining ambition, historic task and self-interested prize.[45] Nationalism was a campaign of mass education in civic values,[46] lighting the path from narrow, tribal conformity to the personal responsibility incumbent upon members of complex societies.

The causal sequence from conquest, through social change, to the political mobilization of mass consciousness was equally direct. White demands for tax and labour, new roads, markets, education and peace, all unwittingly prepared the way. They brought oppression and opportunity. Both evoked change. New exactions drove Africans out of their little tribal ways. New markets pulled them into livelihoods undreamt of before. As they tested out new networks, so men and women depended less on their small community for material and moral refreshment or for political authority. Local patriotism waned as wider loyalties grew.[47] As more people worked for a wage or produced for sale, so kinship ties weakened, household hierarchies of age and gender dissolved, the tutelage of local gods and ancestors decayed and the power of chiefs declined. At this point in the argument societal fate gained a psychic dimension. Transitional men and women were born in painful psychological labour. The cultural particularities of clan and tribe to which they had been born would no longer appeal. Looking for security in the marches between community and society, many took the crucial modernizing step; they chose to join a voluntary association. Whether ethnic, occupational, religious or political in purpose, these offered some control over an uncertain world.[48] To an historian, the next ineluctable stage evoked class consciousness out of economic structure. New townsmen, given to drink and disorder, resembled the 19th-century English working men whom Engels had known before they organized themselves as a self-respecting class, as Africans would do too.[49] A social-democratic certainty then carried the argument to its end. Not so reliant for their needs on tribes, which could still less satisfy their ambitions, Africans became more demanding of states. This was the ruling assumption at the British Colonial Office by the 1940s.[50] It became political science's functional theme. Africans who became the common people were the natural audience for nationalism. This '*inevitable* end product of the impact of Western imperialism and modernity upon African societies'[51] was embodied in the 'organizational end product', the political party.[52]

EXPLANATIONS OF FAILURE

If these stages of political growth were inevitable, why then did their democratic determinism so often falter? All observers accepted this, some with better concealed dismay than others. Pan-ethnic nationalism was a contingency.[53] Successive protest did not always widen the social reach of political action. Nor need a proliferation of personal identities weaken primordial ties. Each identity – ethnic, religious and social – could be exploited in different situations by people who moved between town and country. Only one scholar, Thomas Hodgkin, welcomed this complexity and lumped it together as nationalism. On the radical left, he trusted that presently intricate conflict would forge broader consciousness later.[54] Other scholars saw complexity as threat.[55] Analytical splitters, they held that territorial nationalism was a distinct political form and shared values the only guarantors of stable progress. Yet tribalism often became more strident as independence loomed, not less. Towns were not melting pots. The reason for this lack of linear stages of growth was all too ready to hand in the model, in the defects of its first, formative, dialectic.

Colonial states were tools of change, but it became apparent that they had political and economic flaws. They governed district by district, rather than a whole territory, and fostered uneven development. Some thought them strong enough to push capitalist interests and reward African allies; others that they were weak, with the feeble light of their favour shining only on those who demanded it.[56] The unequal results were much the same. Some peoples were nearer coasts and markets than others or had more rainfall; some chiefs had welcomed rather than barred missionaries; or their young men had gone out first to work on the railway. Such random disparities were converted into self-reinforcing hierarchies of advantage and decline by colonial markets in labour and produce. Political tribalism was the common result.[57] There was a pattern. Ethnic groups more socially mobilized than others produced more of the common people; these escaped ethnicity so as to enjoy, and energize, the state. Groups less affected by change mobilized in tribal counter-marches. The more advanced might then try to defend themselves by retreating into tribe, as in the tragic case of the Igbo of Nigeria. For the easiest way to defend or raise a region's standing on the ladder of improvement was to infuse cultural identity with political fire. Aroused ethnicity was thought to stand for something else, local ambition or relative deprivation.[58] By the 1960s radical scholars went further; they saw tribalism as a mask for class struggle, 'a dependent variable rather than a primordial political force'.[59] It split classes that might otherwise unify their nationalisms, bourgeois or proletarian. This was another African 'failing' for which colonialism was blamed. Foreign capital's jabs at Africa were too puny to enforce that brutal but invigorating break with all past social intricacies which Marx and Engels had welcomed a century before. Most African workers were migrants, merely optional proletarians;[60] class consciousness could not be expected of them.[61]

For all these reasons each colony was a ragged social patchwork. Its ethnic economic hierarchy was bound to find its tribal political voice when constitutional reform created an African market in power, with the prospect, at independence, of a ladder of domination. Nationalists, all observers agreed, had to court strange allies if their parties were to cover the country. Some were stranger than others. Short of the wish-fulfilment of a self-governing democracy disciplined by shared political values, there looked to be four patterns in which African politics faced or reflected the problem of tribe. We can take them in a descending order of hope. Mau Mau seemed to fit only one of them, the last.

PATTERNS OF POLITICS

First, there were a few mass, radical, parties that galvanized transitional men out of tribal frustration by promising a nation fit for their ambition. Kwame Nkrumah's Convention People's Party (CPP) in the Gold Coast was the archetype. By the early 1960s, before the first academic study of Mau Mau, it was already to be doubted that this pattern brought responsible self-government, as distinct from nervously arbitrary rule. Then there were ethnic or regional parties, content to divide power. There need be no harm in them and might be some good, if they arrived at productively self-interested divisions of political labour. They took elite or plebeian forms. Where precolonial structures had been strong, worldly chiefs could make ideal local bosses. They knew their place. They were also on the way out; antique privilege could not much longer survive. As old elites faded away their parties might prove to be midwives of a more pluralist political culture than radicals would stomach.[62] Local parties led by commoners, the third pattern of party and ethnicity, were a tougher proposition. They might look equally tribal and fore-doomed by change, but by the late 1950s there was a growing awareness that tribe was no synonym for tradition. It was often a new process, even an invention by modern men from out of the local disputes or deals that gave districts a livelier existence than colonies. 'Tribelets' among peoples with similar tongues often 'aggregated' under a new identity, to which a political party gave competitive edge.[63] By the 1980s many scholars had come to think this the most common and profound form of social change in modern Africa. It is an insight that informs this essay.

By 1960 these varied relations between culture and politics had acquired an analytical narrative in which political time redefined cultural space. Political mobilization sparred with counter-mobilization. First, a militant mass party like the CPP leapt from the youth wings of moderate elite associations in the urban centres of progress. As it then 'penetrated' upcountry, others less mobile were forced to choose. There were three possibilities. Disaffected commoners might see nationalism as an ally in the overthrow of provincial powers and climb aboard the radical band-wagon. National mobilization then became a broad front of separate local subversions. That response to an initial mobilization looked to be the nearest African approach to the ideal model of national integration. It almost happened in the Gold Coast in the early 1950s.

Two other possibilities generated, at best, processes of devolution.

Provincial chiefs – to take the second link between culture and time – might see nationalism as no more than a mask of public good on the private face of some other region's gain. The adept smothered their commoners' subversion with the patronage and pressure of their local government machines, and retained the power of choice in face of danger. Calculation more often than culture then decided whether they bartered this retrieved control into a national party fief, to resist the centre from within, or built a regional party on a platform of local autonomy.[64] In either case, territorial politics became more a matter of reconciliation, as it was called, than mobilization.

Thirdly, tribal aggregation could often be a plebeian strategy to enlarge political scale beyond the individual competence of chiefs. Portrayals of ambitious commoners changed over time. They were first dismissed as premature school-leavers, 'Standard VII boys'; for a time they were copybook transitionals, the radical mob. They hated chiefs for their privilege, but might return to their local allegiance if the national party dashed their hopes of office.[65] Scholars were slow to see that small businessmen were the more likely political brokers. They had more resources to invest in politics and thus better hopes of a return than the half-educated crowd of veranda-boys. Political latecomers among them could deck out a new regional party as their own 'engine of class formation', just as the national party had been for those who got in first.[66] As independence approached, so the risks of political activity declined, its rewards increased and the prospective price of inactivity soared. Ever more entrepreneurs from yet sleepier peripheries could therefore be expected to crowd the political market, touting new tribes as their wares. They naturally appealed more to tribal 'traditionals' than to modern 'transitionals'. Counter-mobilization threatened to overwhelm mobilization. It was nationalism's common fate to begin as transitional bandwagon and end as primordial circus.[67]

THE DEVIANCE OF MAU MAU

Mau Mau matched none of these patterns. Nobody could reasonably expect it to conform to the evolutionary myth of modernizing integration; but neither did it follow any of the acceptable paths of failure. No Western observer, even of the sympathetic left, saw it as the plea of a nation-in-waiting.[68] But why did it not compare with the varieties of competition that political time had elsewhere evoked from cultural space? Kikuyu occupied, so far as any Africans could, Kenya's core area of progress.[69] They could be expected to produce most of black Kenya's common men. Their representatives certainly dominated the first pan-ethnic congress, the Kenya African Union (KAU), and its radical rival, the African Workers Federation. Members of other groups held office in both. Yet the still more radical body known as Mau Mau, which

279

advanced from mere trades unionism to acts of civil disobedience disciplined by violence, excluded non-Kikuyu from its sworn inner circle; their loyalties could not be trusted under stress.[70] The movement's symbols had nothing 'Kenyan' about them.[71] It was a core militancy which turned, uniquely, against the nation as it grew. Non-Kikuyu African fears and the regional fragmentation of their politics could not be explained by any Mau Mau likeness to the broad-fronted subversions of the CPP or, in Nigeria, of the Zikists. Nor, secondly, was Mau Mau a front for canny Kikuyu chiefs. British inventions, they were the movement's first targets. By no stretch of the imagination, finally, could Kikuyu tribalism be defensive of a sluggard periphery, however much it was sponsored by traders, something that was in any case not well understood at the time.[72]

There remained a fourth possible relationship between national centre and ethnic periphery. It involved religion, which few colonial officials or political scientists understood and most therefore feared. Gods divided where reason united. Traditional belief was tribal; Christian churches and Muslim brotherhoods could be too. Religion was for the anthropologists; it was a thing of the past. For tribal community was believed to have been bound by sacred charter rather than negotiable contract. Traditional, tribal man questioned neither his belief nor the social order and was content. Transitional man questioned both, and was confused. Educated, modern man made rational choices. Political scientists, using Weber's distinction between traditional and rational authority, saw modernization as a war of the psyches. The key experience for the erstwhile tribesman must be the shocked and then confident realization that society was not divinely ordered, inevitably tribal, but subject to men's wills, potentially national.[73] He was learning citizenship. White conquest had begun the lesson; the labour and produce markets had continued it. Religious energy was something that properly belonged to early colonial time or peripheral colonial space. If, therefore, modern nationalists sought local allies among the zealots of whatever faith, they prejudiced their own integrity and the legitimacy of their project. To mobilize the masses through the necromancers of nativism was to tread dangerous ground, far beyond a necessary alliance between two political levels, central and local. It confused two phases of social change, yoked together the contrary categories of pragmatic action and unbending belief, and invited a schizophrenic response to modernity, advance and retreat.[74] Whites were obsessed by the magical powers and religious passion which they believed were invoked by Mau Mau oaths. Tribal in scale and atavistic of mind, the movement seemed to be a double offence to nationalism. It remained only to add a third and the congruence between propaganda and political science was complete.

The optimism of political science had always had its darker side, the

fear that transitional men would want not freedom but authority, not
self-rule but Rousseau's legislator. Charismatic leadership might also be
an analytical necessity, a bridge of transition. Only a power that was
almost divine, some thought, could lead Africans over the moral gulf
between blind obedience to tribal tradition and negotiated consent to a
rational state. The intellectual transition of secularization was not, in the
end, enough; a search for psychic security might, indeed, trample on
rational scruple.[75] Even Hodgkin bowed to the need for a leader at the
key moment when interest groups and talking shops were swept up
into the mass party. A leader could symbolize the nation for 'illiterate
farmers, fishermen, labourers and marketwomen', who might accord
him 'numinous qualities', even 'supernatural powers'. Christians
among them might call him 'the new Moses' and independence the
Promised Land.[76] For the myth of nationalism it was here that a third,
devastating, anomaly was presented by Mau Mau.

Charisma was anti-democratic. This was a tolerable fault in one who
united loyalties to a new state. Moreover, a ruling party might in due
course 'routinize' personal charisma and thus relax the rules of debate.
Kenyatta had charisma in plenty, a 'hypnotic masculinity'. White
settlers and officials who met him felt turned to ash.[77] Among Kikuyu
he enjoyed a command of public oratory, the mystery of long residence
in England and the authority of having published, in English, a book on
his people.[78] He married into two of the most powerful families in
Kikuyuland; he lived well, as a leader should; he was Muigwithania, the
Reconciler, a title given to Christ in the Kikuyu Bible. Adaptations of
Christian hymns and prayers venerated him, as others did Nkrumah.[79]
Unlike Nkrumah, he seemed to use his power not to span the gap between
past tribe and future nation, but to make it unbridgeable. Outside
observers were careful not to call Kenyatta the leader of Mau Mau; it took
a rigged trial, with bought evidence, to find him guilty on that charge.[80]
But nobody doubted that he was and, it appeared, had chosen to be the
leader of the Kikuyu rather than of black Kenyans as a whole. Non-
Kikuyu leaders increasingly mistrusted him. There could be no greater
abuse of personal power, nor deeper betrayal of modernizing nationalism. Hodgkin admitted the failings of nationalist parties, not least their
personality cults, but they were still 'a more constructive method of
canalising African political energies than Mau-Mau.'[81] Quasi-religious
authority was regrettable but perhaps unavoidable in the founder of a
new state. It was deplorable in the rebuilder of tribe. Again, official anger
and scholarly doubt were in close accord.

This uneasy alliance of sword and pen was sealed by James Coleman,
a father of American political science in Africa. He saw Mau Mau as
a complex mixture, a nationalism led by modern men 'with a strong
traditional bias', but also a 'nativism, manipulated by the leaders, on

the part of the masses.' Nativism was the active renewal of inherited culture, the reverse of nationalism's nobler demands. Mau Mau's structure and aims suggested to him 'a higher level of sophistication than sheer nativism',[82] but he did not explore that paradox further. He thought that something like Mau Mau was always possible where colonial rulers did not allow black leaders to hammer popular feeling into political purpose on the anvil of elections. Blighted ambition might then be 'wasted in messianic and puritanical religious movements, or . . . attracted to terrorism as a violent means of breaking the bonds of the plural society'.[83] Coleman cited no sources for this analysis, in two essays which were otherwise well referenced. Mau Mau's nativism appears to have been common knowledge. Transitional men were notoriously volatile; a classic analysis compared them to American juvenile delinquents.[84] Mobilized out of their tribe yet denied political advance, might they not withdraw again into it? Coleman seems to have conceded that as a possible pathology of transition, which exonerated Mau Mau from much of the blame. That was where his explanation ended. It was where the historians began.

Historiography

What historians produce is always a question. Neither scientific proofs nor entire fictions, their texts are torn in three directions by time – future, present and past; and between three moral dimensions – by the demands of power and the limits of perception that simplify history, and the intellectual honesty that recognizes difference and diversity. Instructive pasts and intended futures are cyclically linked by the ambitions stirred in present conflict. Ngugi wa Thiong'o, with Mau Mau also in mind, thought that 'how we look at our yesterday has important bearings on how we look at to-day and how we see possibilities for tomorrow.'[85] But tomorrow can also imprison yesterday in the search for an ideologically useful past, whether servant or solvent of power. The nature of perception is a more deeply seated limitation, for past and future are made visible only by the cultural perspectives of present time and space. We can all agree that the past is another country and then go off to find that it is most clearly charted on the imaginative map with which we navigate our own. Historians take possession of the past by acts of transubstantiation, in which one culture is transformed into and valued by the common currency of another.[86] Nevertheless – and on this proviso the profession of history ultimately rests – past evidence does have its own truth; it imposes the discipline of context on its interpreters; it demands of them an informed imagination and an attentive ear. The past does retain some probity if its actors and witnesses are allowed to tell their own story, in their words, to those who have taken the trouble to get to know them.[87] And, to return to the present world of disputed power, this obstinate past repays respect. It is when the many hesitant voices of history are allowed to speak their own inconvenient thoughts, neither refined by present ideological heroism nor coerced into confession, that they best evoke those alternative futures which allow men and women to visualize the possibility of remaking their lives.[88]

COLONIALS

The study of Mau Mau has a contested archaeology of power, perception and evidence. Its first layer has shaped the rest.[89] The British understood Mau Mau to be a terrorist convulsion rather than a political response to grievance, a tribal frenzy fomented by men of whom better things were expected. Their sense of the fragility of their own power, their perceptions of African society and the nature of their evidence all fed this interpretation. Colonial power justified itself by its gifts of progress and order. The former generally divides people more unequally in power; the latter presupposes at least their acquiescence in such division. They were more difficult to reconcile in Kenya than elsewhere. In early days white settler development, weak in any case, had undermined both tribal order and state authority to the point of crisis, with peremptory demands for scarce black labour.[90] After the Second World War this contradiction in power was no less severe, in the new context of an overabundance of African labour, underemployed and wretchedly paid. White farmers and white and Indian businessmen neither engaged enough workers nor recognized the trades unions within which government was beginning to hope that they might be controlled. Meanwhile African rural life was in legal uproar over disputed rights to lands that were also physically eroding away. An older generation of officials had believed that Africans naturally belonged to tribes, their source of social order. This transubstantiation of African life into Anglo-Saxon myth no longer captivated younger officers impatient for development, many of whom had known marvels of mechanization in the war. They began to see tribes as obstacles to improvement, nurseries of stubborn peasants and rowdy migrant workers. The joint failures of racial domination and tribal discipline to deliver either peace or progress prompted government to look for ways in which to modify both without upsetting either. This called for a reshaping of the legal structures of the state. It was clear that these must do more to promote markets and production; it was better not to decide how far racial or communal distinctions had to be done away with to that end. 'Multiracialism' was the agreeably indeterminate formula for change. By 1952 it had delivered little. White supremacy was dented in the legislative arena but remained entrenched elsewhere. State interventions in African life were no more effective. In rural areas, private tenure and self-governing producer cooperatives had got little further than contentious talk; the provision of cheap housing for workers who had become trades unionists was no better advanced as a reconstitution of urban life.

While government struggled indecisively with the past, Kikuyu oppositions seemed to block all possible roads to peace and progress in the future. Government tended to lump them together. By 1951 officials attributed all obstruction to a tentacular Mau Mau that had insinuated itself into every Kikuyu political body, all operated by 'the same old stiffs working under different guises'.[91] Kikuyu independent schools opposed the orderly expansion of state education, unskilled Kikuyu workers scorned state-sponsored unionism, Kikuyu squatters resisted the capital intensification of white farming, Kikuyu peasants began to refuse to work on soil-conservation measures, Kikuyu businessmen undercut cooperatives; all these activities were egged on by the gutter press. Kikuyu tribal life, it seemed, had lost the imagined solidarity to which officials appealed for help in fostering communal solutions to agrarian stress. But it retained quite enough to respond with enthusiasm to agitators' calls for civil disorder. The British were ready to believe that Kenyatta led a reactionary and, by definition therefore, tribal movement called Mau Mau because of their angry conviction that he had once taken the part of obdurate peasants and excitable women, to oppose progress in its most urgent form of communal labour on works of soil conservation.[92]

While this perception of Mau Mau blew away the last shreds of government's belief in tribes as props of order, it was difficult for Kenya officials to accept Whitehall's construction of African nationalism as an alternative ally in progress.[93] The Colonial Office hoped that unforced reform would instal moderate nationalist alliances in its African dependencies, drawn from chiefs and the middle class. These would, it was envisaged, reproduce on a wider scale and in progressive mode that organic bond between leaders and led which had once made Africa's tribal histories seem as romantic in the official imagination as Britain's island story. This golden future of the past was best served by leaders who modelled themselves on their white officials; these saw their careers as selfless duty, not the vulgar pursuit of power.[94] A criterion by which every nationalism was bound to fail, it was doubly misplaced in Kenya, where the reforms that might have evoked moderation and civic service in Africans were blocked by whites.

The evidence by which the British judged African leaders to have failed the test of national seriousness was, they thought, their own, supplied by men on the spot, the district commissioners. But official knowledge was distorted by racial separation; opaque and partial, it served the interests of their African informants, principally the chiefs, for whom politicians were rivals. This defective intelligence completed the British case against Kenyatta and the nationalism over which he presided in the

KAU. He had every reason to be enlightened but had shown himself reactionary. The unexpected solidity of Mau Mau, first thought to have been an ecstatically religious flash in the pan, suggested that he was something worse. Panic is common in rulers who are shown to be ignorant. Political surprise was blamed on black deception rather than white negligence; the flimsier the evidence, the more cunning the plot. Conspiracy theories implicitly deny division or debate within an opposition cabal; in an open opponent they must therefore suspect guile. Mau Mau conspiracy and Kenyatta's deceit were easy explanations of government unreadiness in face of danger.[95] And KAU's supine subversion by Kikuyu tribalism deprived black nationalism of all claim on the future.

Horrified belief in a conspiratorial link between ungrateful enlightenment and reversionary darkness was not unusual in a threatened colonial regime. It both damned the opposition and proved that the civilizing mission still had much to do. In Kenya the thesis was carried to extremes. For it was also the nightmare of a white minority in Africa. Treason in the African intermediary class seemed to show that there was, after all, no middle road between repression and abdication. Mau Mau brought to waking life that mocking laughter of self-doubt which had already disturbed liberal dreams of a multiracial compromise between hatred and despair. Conservative whites grimly welcomed this endorsement of their earlier warnings against reform; Mau Mau was the best possible argument for the full restoration of white supremacy. The official interpretation reassured settlers only to the extent of agreeing Mau Mau to be savagely tribal rather than justifiably national. For government had no choice but to reopen the path to multiracialism; it had nowhere else to go if it were to retain the support of majority African opinion and of Whitehall. An evasive formula was transformed by political crisis. As an answer to Mau Mau it had to have what it had previously lacked, a political will. This needed the inspiration of a precisely imagined future. Liberal officials, striving for such definition, blamed the rising not on the barbarity of tradition but on the bafflement of transition. To the former there was no answer but war; for the latter there was remedy in reform. This must encompass no less than the re-education of Africans as modern men and (a new emphasis) women.[96] A new determination enthused existing official intentions for propertied farmers and for trades unionists paid a family wage with which to rent a family home. A charged atmosphere of moral crusade spilled over from the vast Mau Mau detention camps, in which detainees earned release by repenting of their tribal oaths and being ready, literally, to work for their personal salvation. Colonial reform was nerved to mobilize transitionals, once and for all, out of their lingering communal solidarities and into the individually responsible, class-divided, electorate of multiracial self-government. But reform could never be admitted to be a response to African terror; it had to be its total contradiction. The urgency of crusade constructed an ever darker mirror, an enemy increasingly backward and unfit for self-rule.[97]

THE FIRST HISTORIANS

The pioneer academic studies of Mau Mau, produced soon after Kenya's independence, were, by deliberate contrast, 'histories for self-government'.[98] The opening line of the first book, the classic liberal study, almost said as much. The last line of the next, the first radical work, said so more plainly.[99] Most of its students have measured Mau Mau retrospectively, by its legacy of African power. By different criteria they have found the postcolonial state, and therefore Mau Mau, to be equally wanting. Liberals were struck by the sheer triumph of majority rule. But, on the assumption that a pan-ethnic sense of moral community was a condition of liberal politics, they also feared lest Mau Mau's sectionalism had frightened national integration away.[100] Radicals, more romantic than Marxian, have seen independence as no more than a neocolonial sleight of hand, by which Mau Mau was robbed of the fruits of its sacrificial courage. They have deplored the absence of some tribute to Mau Mau in a progressive policy of 'land to the (male) tiller', especially to those who fought or were detained.[101] Despite this contrast in their vision of Kenya's future – at the time of their writing its unfolding present – both schools of thought began by using the same general model of modernizing nationalism to structure their accounts of its local failings.

The British had blamed Mau Mau on the Kikuyu. The first historians agreed that the movement fell short of their model, for its ethnic singularity more than its violence. Nor was the mobilization of Kikuyu ethnicity easily passed off as a blameless remaking of cultural space by political time. As explained, Mau Mau was seen as neither a militant nationalism which its enemies had knowingly traduced as tribalism,[102] nor a stand made by traditional chiefs, nor yet a plebeian struggle against regional backwardness.[103] Scholars were reluctant to accept the colonial view that Mau Mau was atavistic religious frenzy, even if they agreed with Coleman that that was a not unlikely outcome of repressive rule. Instead, they shifted the blame on to British rule. As elsewhere, this had brought uneven development. More directly, while white settler oppression had provoked black resistance, white paranoia had cut short its growth. By this reasoning the tribalism of Mau Mau was taken, in conformity with the general myth of nationalism, to stand for something else. It revealed a fractured social structure which had been subjected, in the Kenya case, to unusually violent political process. The Kikuyu people, the argument ran, were fired by an embittered regional ambition that was mobilized by economic geography as much as cultural tradition. This was no insuperable obstacle to their leading a nationalist coalition.

The Problem

The Kikuyu vanguard lost the Kenya nation and turned in on itself only when put under intolerable strain by political events.

Explanation of Mau Mau's 'failure', then, has rested on a causal tripod of uneven social change, a loss of control over their followers by thwarted political leaders and, finally, more or less unplanned black self-defence against white violence. As elsewhere, the first factor had sown regional discord in African politics. The other two soothed away the disturbing thought that what might still have been 'a great nationalist rebellion' nonetheless *degenerated* into tribal revolt'.[104] As in the colonial version, one must ask how far transubstantiation and the nature of the evidence have shaped explanation. On these issues this essay raises doubts and suggests different answers.

The first historians began their argument with a tribute to the cultural artistry of colonialism. The liberals, Rosberg and Nottingham, saw 'rapid social change' as the source of national integration. Those least affected by it, the Somali, were the first to challenge the independent state.[105] The radical Barnett agreed that Kenyans had once lived in 'tribally homogeneous isolates' with 'largely self-sufficient subsistence economies', as was then the conventional anthropological wisdom.[106] Out on the periphery some did so still but, at the centre, markets in produce and labour had caused tribal division to 'give way to broader groupings of an African national character'. Liberal language was higher flown, arguing or perhaps hoping that social change 'challenged the meaning of the tribe as the highest political ideal.'[107] Here then, at the shared base of both accounts, was the transubstantiation demanded by liberal or radical democracy. Colonial rule mobilized Africans out of their vertical tribal isolations; they formed horizontal associations; their common market interests then fired the cultural alchemy that produced the national identity of common men. Mazrui put it succinctly: 'it was the success of colonial governments in creating such cohesion which led to their own downfall.'[108] The supporting evidence lay in the archival record of what Africans had said, in English, in past petitions to whites. It was given colour by the reminiscences of veteran politicians after independence. To scholars eager to trace the lineages of freedom they told how they had cooperated with whom in order to create which political association. What ideas they had floated, which symbols explored, what moral sanctions they had invoked in winning the trust or obedience of others, were not thought to be relevant subjects of enquiry. Nationalism was a self-explanatory moral universe.[109]

Colonialism in Kenya moulded unequal materials with a twisted hand. This was the second agreed step in the argument. Of all African groups the Kikuyu enjoyed the best opportunities and endured the worst oppression.[110] They were naturally endowed with fertile land and regular rains, above the malaria line. Their tribal character, perhaps embarrassing to discuss but, given its demonic prominence in the propaganda, difficult to ignore, was all that self-government required: acquisitive, competitive and democratic.[111] To these blessings of God and the ancestors, colonialism had added the benefits of nearly the best educational provision[112] and the central point on the road and rail network, with easy access to markets in food, fuel and building materials, or to agricultural or urban work. The Kikuyu were well equipped to make the best of colonial rule.

They had also had the worst of it. Of Kenya's cultivators they had lost most land to white settlement. Well over 10 per cent of Kikuyu had perished through privation and epidemic in the First World War, probably more than any other people.[113] Of the peoples whose ecology allowed the cultivation of coffee they were the last to be allowed to plant this most valuable of Kenya's crops, thanks to their proximity to white estates. Lastly, after the Second World War, they had been under uniquely subversive threat on three fronts. They had had more urban poor than any other people, many of them landless, who were forced to break the rules of respectability in the squalor of slum Nairobi.[114] Their 'squatter' or tenant population on the white farms in the Rift Valley, a quarter of all Kikuyu and much of the farm workforce, had been treacherously dispossessed, as they saw it, of the wealth and freedom of labour tenantry. They had been reduced by their landlords to the slavery (*ukombo*) of wage labour or evicted to the degradation of the shanty town.[115] And in the mania for rural regimentation with which the British had badgered postwar Africa in the name of conservation, Kikuyu hill farmers had been the earliest and most forcefully cajoled into the unpaid, communal, largely female labour of terracing their slopes against soil erosion. Under this second colonial occupation a free peasant had become a 'much administered man', ceasing to be his own, or his wife's, master.[116]

It followed, thirdly, that the 'organizational end-product'[117] of Kenya's uneven history was Kikuyu command of the colony's black nationalism. Barnett assured what he clearly feared would be an uneasy readership, taught as much by the modernizing myth as by British propaganda that ethnic inequality had no part in a proper nationalism, that this should come as 'no shock'. Liberals agreed that the Kikuyu were the most mobilized.[118] Here the two accounts began to diverge, but to a revealingly minor extent, in their assessments of how far Kikuyu had become Kenya's common men. Rosberg and Nottingham's vocabulary did not include the term 'class'; Barnett conflated the concept with racial caste.[119] Neither analysis unpacked the social aggregate of tribe. This stage of the argument seems now to be somewhat evasive. Nevertheless, by urging that Kikuyu differences in wealth were insignificant, liberals implied that they were led by common men without class connections.

Chege Kibachia was their chosen hero of social mobilization, something which he had experienced rather than pursued, perhaps at the expense of others. As a boy he had captained the senior missionary school; he then became employer, trader and newspaper editor and, finally, a trade union organizer in the throes of a dock strike.[120] One could not wish for a more classless man.

Barnett could not find a more classless tribe. Given the dearth of other economic openings, he (wrongly) thought, 'labor-exporting peasantries such as the Kikuyu tended to develop as relatively homogeneous aggregates'. They were structurally predisposed to 'unified political action'.[121] An uncomplicated tribe like that apparently had no need for the agency of political inspiration. Furthermore, intertribal links of social mobilization by migrant labour then conferred on them a natural vanguard role. The KAU was Kikuyu-led. This simply meant that it was based, as one would expect, on the capital city and nearest countryside. In this the KAU was like the CPP over in the Gold Coast, of whose triumphs Kenyans read in their vernacular press, their eagerness sharpened by knowing how much the settlers hated Nkrumah.[122]

It was then, fourthly, that things went wrong with the model or, in the phrase most commonly found in the literature, 'out of control' in practice.[123] The proper relationship of captaincy and consent between educated elite and their transitional urban or more traditional rural followers collapsed; but it was a British, not an African, failure.[124] In West Africa, British policy and the absence of settlers had allowed nationalist parties to exercise the power needed to educate and retain mass allegiance, and so play 'a constructive role' while remaining 'within constitutional limits'.[125] In Kenya the KAU was denied authority as a party; its leaders could gain formal recognition only as individuals, by appointment to local government office. This was no way to popular respect; on the contrary, they became the sergeant-majors of rural regimentation or the quartermasters of scarce urban housing and permits to trade.[126] They were granted a share of, not a share in power; they could not shape its policy by public influence, only distribute its costs and benefits by personal intrigue. Governor Mitchell's 'classic blunder', his refusal to nominate Kenyatta to the legislature after the latter's return in 1946, has been taken as the symbolic rebuff to a tragic elite. Disprized by government, they were then jostled off the stair of political development by tougher, more desperate spirits behind them.[127].

The medium of elite political control was also the crux of their failure, the oath of unity. The British had portrayed all Kikuyu political oaths since the Second World War as the intended seed of Mau Mau. Liberal and radical scholars together saw them, rather, as instruments of recruitment, discipline, trust and funding, their form and purpose changing as circumstances required. Their secrecy was necessary for effectiveness among a divided subject people. To Rosberg and Nottingham the first Mau Mau oath, as it was labelled by its opponents, was simply an emotive sign of a rational will to press against white obduracy to the point of civil disobedience; its initiates did no more (and no less) than pledge commitment in dangerous times. So long as the oath remained exclusive, a recognition of trusted lieutenants by the Kikuyu leadership, it was also a curb on precipitate action. But then, in a concurrence of moderates' despair and militants' impatience, it was adapted, by early 1950, as a tool of mass recruitment. Leadership soon faced 'insuperable problems'.[128] These led, step by unanticipated step, to disaster.

The combination of secrecy and inclusiveness demanded the coercion of individual recalcitrants. This intimidation drew a more considered resistance, especially from convinced Christians or faithful traditionalists. These condemned the oaths for their pagan ritual and social impudence respectively. Resistance then provoked 'premature' violence by militants. The state sprang to arms. Government declared an Emergency before militant leaders could implement, as some have claimed they intended, the intertribal scheme of initiation that might have created a national front.[129] Conversely, as repressive measures mounted, so non-Kikuyu initiates found that they did not share the instinctive comradeship that gives stomach for a fight. Barnett agreed with the liberals; the structural collapse of command was sufficient cause of political catastrophe. But Rosberg and Nottingham, with their liberal stress on individual agency, carried the argument further. Mass oathing led to devolved responsibility and made room, therefore, for conflicting definitions of symbol and aim. Outside Kiambu, the home of Kenyatta and the core of the Kikuyu educated elite, the oath fell into the hands of slumland militants; these were readier to contemplate both violence and symbolic departures from customary oaths. Moderates who sought a firmer ethnic base for more effective, but still territorial politics, lost the struggle for mastery to militants ready to risk direct action, at the price of tribal isolation.[130] Mau Mau was a case of mobilization and counter-mobilization in one ethnicity.

Both versions of this closely linked argument concluded that British counter-insurgency, more than Kikuyu conspiracy, created Mau Mau. The Emergency declared on 20 October 1952 was a self-fulfilling prophecy. Neither account paid much heed to Mau Mau before that date. One introduced the movement in a speculative footnote, the other showed that it had no separate existence.[131] Both believed that Mau Mau took on structured form only in self-defence against British violence. Rosberg and Nottingham conceded that in the forests, which were refuges rather than bases, the movement also began to conform to its pejorative British image. In their despair, 'poorly educated' guerrilla fighters naturally looked (backwards, the British had said) to their cultural roots; forest warfare had pushed them to the furthest edge of modernity. Even so, the most horrifying action of the war, the Lari massacre, was the outcome of a specific land dispute and not integral to Mau Mau. Command again failed under stress. Mau Mau's central committee strove in vain to curb a 'reign of terror' in the slums. The forest commander, Dedan Kimathi, himself a usurper, failed to maintain discipline in increasingly ragged and fragmented gangs. An unintended outcome of the elite's loss of control, Mau Mau lost its own fight for order. Barnett took a more positive view; forest organization, free from educated restraint, was for him the essence of the 'Mau Mau revolution', however short-lived it proved to be in the face of military defeat.[132]

These were important revisions of British propaganda. Their chief target was the official colonial history against self-rule, the Corfield Report. Published after the end of the Emergency, this had continued the war by other means. Corfield had restated the case against Kenyatta and Mau Mau as a polemical intervention in the politics of decolonization then in train. He stressed the bewildered volatility of the Kikuyu, the continuities in their subversive politics and their planned mastery over other tribes more upright than themselves.[133] The new histories for self-government showed, to the contrary, that Kikuyu politicians had expressed the rational goals of the most modernized or proletarian of Kenya's people;[134] that political conflict rather than hellish conspiracy had marked the passage from broadly based nationalism to sectarian violence; and that its increasing Kikuyuness, far from proving a tribalist desire to dominate others, had been forced on Mau Mau by the British. The official account and its critics were agreed on one point alone. They all neglected the Kikuyu resistance to Mau Mau. Corfield had seen the so-called 'loyalists' as the lonely few. Their attempts to rally resistance before the emergency were 'rather pathetic'; they were dependent on white missionaries thereafter. Rosberg and Nottingham reiterated this official view with little comment. Barnett said scarcely anything about them at all.[135] The loyalists were a difficulty for Corfield. Their small numbers suggested the wide extent of Kikuyu grievance; their very existence raised questions about the tribally conspiratorial power of Mau Mau. The historians were just as uneasy. The loyalists had been the one indispensable element in suppressing the rising and yet, with Kenyatta, were among the main inheritors of power. They were even more embarrassing to the myth of nationalism than Mau Mau itself.

In spite of themselves, these expatriate scholars were still explaining away tragedy and failure. Kikuyu scholars, or some who were still undergraduates at Makerere College, said, straight out, what that tragedy was. Leaders 'sufficiently educated to think in national, rather than tribal, terms' had lost the initiative to 'the Nairobi thugs'. Mass frustration had led to 'madness', the fighting oath and 'all its horrors'.[136] There could be no link between politicians and lunatics. These young men affirmed what Western scholars were reluctant to concede, that Mau Mau was a terrorist movement. They concluded that tribal identity was irrational and needed control. Education, on the other hand, conferred rationality and the right to rule. Tribal society, black and white, might be dissolving, but that could still spell danger. Since 'ordinary, unsophisticated man' felt at home in small societies, there could well be attempts 'to reassert tribal integrity'. The masses were 'likely to act irrationally'. It was incumbent on the 'sophisticated of all races' to agree calmly on a new political structure.[137] White scholars were disturbed that ineffectual elite nationalism had needed the help of tribal despair to deliver history into the right hands.[138] Black students, more candidly perhaps, showed what dark dangers had still to be mastered in so primordial a circus.

LATER ANALYSES

Still wrestling with this problem, later scholars have drawn apart from each other in five directions. They have broadly accepted the narrative logic of the first accounts: the nation-building potential of colonial rule, the frustration of African attempts to match the territorial imprint of state and market with their own political organization, loss of control by the leadership and, finally, the uprush of political violence through fissures that had been prised open by uneven colonialism. Their analyses have then diverged. Their differences have centred on the social identity of those whom the militants mobilized after the moderates were shouldered aside. These differences require attention, since my own analysis takes issue, to a greater or lesser degree, with all of them. It is the central question about Mau Mau.

Again, the colonial government set the agenda. It saw the movement as a uniquely tribal disease, contagious to non-Kikuyu only where their ethnic immune system had been impaired by linguistic affinity, marriage ties or employment in Nairobi.[139] And all but the tiniest minority of Kikuyu had been infected. The first academic studies had, in reply, blurred the distinction between tribe, class and nation, up to the point when British counter-insurgency made identity a question of life and death. Their successors have been readier to accept these categories as separate identities with self-evidently distinct political projects. But that is to beg the question of how creative the processes of political mobilization can, indeed must, be.

It is a question of some moment. History, it has been said, is largely a record of the oppression of men and women who are either unaware of their miserable condition or who, if they are, have little option but to endure it.[140] From below, the idea of oppression may seem to be a morally frivolous sneer at the only social relations of survival one can imagine. It is not always easy for the weak to reinterpret their fate as another's injustice. It is still more difficult, having done so, to convert the private evasions of misery, the flight or dumb insolence that is the first and easiest response to the intolerable, into a collective will to confront and change it. Active participation in such resistance requires of its militants an entire imaginative reconstruction, not just of present social circumstances but also of future personal possibilities attractive enough to outweigh the costs of conflict. No social structure of inequality can of itself predetermine the strategy of mobilization that seeks to overthrow its privileges and inequities. There is no one mirror of justice; there are too many ways of getting by; and always the temptation to redistribute injustice rather than remove it. Any radical mobilization will need to break the ties of obligation that protect the weak from the worst excesses of the strong. It also needs the remaking of one's nearest competitors, whether for the hire of one's labour or in the market for goods, into trustworthy allies in the physically and morally dangerous business of challenging social facts. Mutual class interest is thus no prefabricated category of trust, certainly not in colonial Africa where concentrations of capital and workers were small, work so varied a sequence of experience in most lifetimes, and workplaces often full of people whose language one did not understand. A joint interest in redressing a specific issue or securing a material resource never solves the problems of authority, discipline or method in the requisite action; it creates them. If a solution to this problem of authority were found by appeal to the supposed antithesis of class, the ethnic solidarity of tribe, that would only complicate the material goals of mobilization. All tribes, like all human societies, were structured by domestic inequalities of power over resources of land and labour. Even in the event that the material objective were commonly agreed, established tribal institutions were in any case hardly likely to furnish the requisite authority for its determined pursuit. Like ethnic identity itself, they were often recently created, certainly in Kenya, by their close association with colonial power. Any mobilization against colonial rule had to reinterpret tribe, just as the construction of colonialism had continually done for the past half century. In search of the right to rebel, any opposition had therefore to invent a past different to that from which the ruling institutions drew their authority. The question of mobilization is by no means answered by the antiphonal chants of 'class' or 'tribe'.

It is inescapable that effective mobilization required imaginative leadership, capable of stirring new political will and cohesion.[141] It was not enough to make protest appear to be, if not rationally hopeful, then at least rationally less pessimistic than submission. But that is probably as far as rational discussion of the issue can ever get. No decisive mobilization was likely to occur until individually possessive morality was fired with public outrage. There seem in general to be two social circumstances in which this electric charge passes through discontent, the more powerfully so when they interact.

One is a sense of unrequited merit. It can be found in the self-conscious emergence of a new class of people who feel that their virtues are not recognized as they ought to be, and are excluded from power while possessing new skills which are themselves a form of political mobilization.[142] In colonial Africa the newly literate were obvious candidates for this role. Mission schools were Africa's 'class'-rooms long before her mineshafts or factory floors. Teachers, clerks, interpreters, printers and telephonists were then installed at the nerve centres of colonial rule. Politics, one could say, was their salaried employment. They dealt daily in its magical coin of communication. There was good reason for their prominence in the evolutionary myth of nationalism. But their social mobilization was misunderstood in the first optimism of political science. Their literacy and association with alien power were not, as assumed, a self-sufficient base for an exemplary new social existence; they were more often a source of scandal. If the educated wished for respect they had to invest external assets in internal authority, to engage in local political conflict. They had to interpret for their own use the canons of civic virtue and deploy them in a manner which their unlettered neighbours recognized to be morally valid.

The other circumstance is a sense of unmerited loss.[143] While customary oppression may be bearable because inevitable and even unremarked, new oppression is immediately visible and by no means inevitable. It takes concrete form in the repudiation from above of reciprocal relations that, however unequal, both made life possible at a material level sanctioned by usage and, more vitally, recognized the moral value of the labour of the weak. A new threat to survival that also affronts self-esteem combines obvious injustice with self-evident remedy, the restoration of past relations. How these are imagined may well be given sharper definition by the literates' reinterpretations of civic virtue. This conjuncture of the rise of a new class and widely feared threats to the status of the weak is a common one in modern history. It is seated in the expansion of the modern state and the rise of capital. The one gives unbounded opportunity to the educated; the other overwhelms most small producers. The definitive experience of Europe in the 19th century, it has been Africa's ordeal in the 20th. It is the seedbed of nationalism.

The sheer complexity of material interest during the bewildering emergence of capitalism, even among the single category of the working poor, means that class coalition, to put it ever so crudely, must be a condition of effective class conflict. Otherwise mobilization can occur only in futile occupational fragments. And the terms of class coalition must refer to a community that appeals to both, or more, of the allies, to some

allegiance therefore other than their class. Ethnicity or nationhood seems
a necessary moral abstraction from the immediacies of material interest
within which such interest can be effectively protected or pursued. And
yet, as already noted, such communities are, even when they do not have
first to be invented, rarely at the immediate disposal of those whose
interest lies in change. The choice of partners in mobilization and its
purposes are rarely plain. Mainly for this reason risings, like revolutions,
are rarely to be attributed to the will of their insurgents.[144] As the first
scholarly accounts showed so well, the Mau Mau war did not take a form
that anybody could be said to have intended. Like most wars, it was
stumbled into. Nevertheless, the costs of fighting and continuing to fight,
as many did, for three years or more, whether for Mau Mau or as part
of its Kikuyu resistance, must clearly have been measurable according
to deeply held civic values, bitterly contested. It was a costly war. Mau
Mau forest fighters' death rates were around 30 per cent for the three
hardest years of fighting, a mortality that no army conscripted by terror
could have sustained.[145] On the other side, barely 10 per cent of Mau
Mau's victims were not themselves Kikuyu. In its bitterest form the
Emergency was a Kikuyu civil war. Kikuyu did not fight because that
was the obvious thing to do, nor because their socially and economically
structured position gave them no alternative, nor yet because the British
forced them to. Indeed, many of them went to considerable lengths not
to kill; there were principled refusals to break the peace all over Kikuyuland. The retrospective division between defeated Mau Mau patriots
and triumphant 'home guard' traitors makes no historical sense. When
Kikuyu did fight, on one side or the other, in a division that could even
split families, it was because, when they were obliged to choose, they
gambled on their contested understanding of how to attain the moral
maturity of working for oneself.[146] This morality of the material under-
lies the ambiguities of all political choice. The straightforward deter-
minations of action offered by the allegedly opposed and unarguable
social categories of class and tribe (or nation) are far too narrow.
'Mobilization' is a persuasive, argued process, creating such categories
rather than being confined by them.

That was not the view of political science in the 1950s and 1960s.
In the 1950s political mobilization was understood to be able to do
little more than give a final edge to the wavering new identity that
social mobilization had impersonally provided. Nationalism was an end-
product rather than a political agency. By the later 1960s Western
political science was beginning to disapprove of any political mobilization in Africa. In the cases of Europe and North America the mobilization of difference around economic issues and social values was held to
be functional for political health. In Africa, as elsewhere in what was
coming to be called the Third World, popular political action was

increasingly seen as a pathogenic disorder. Communal cleavages already existed; anything that stirred them into life was to be avoided; and it was not easy to see what else politics might be about.[147] In its studies of the non-European world political science became increasingly concerned not with democracy but order, not with politics but governance.[148] Mature political science, 10 years on, had acquired the wisdom of Makerere undergraduates. It is not surprising that liberal scholars in Kenya took an increasingly severe view of Mau Mau, nor that their radical opponents therefore should the more exalt it.

LIBERALS

Liberal Kenyan historians, like the Makerere students many of them once were, took the evolutionary myth of nationalism as the reproach of what might have been. Living with continued ethnic tension, they could nonetheless accept the creative potential of colonialism. They emphasized the gulf between the moderate nationalism of educated men able to comprehend the state, and ignorant tribalisms inevitably aroused by mass militancy.[149] The Western education they shared with the politicians was the only available basis for that 'politics of collaboration' which, it was no shame to admit, was the core of any state. Kipkorir argued that only the nationalist elite, younger and better educated than Kenyatta's generation, could have exploited, as they did, the reforms with which the British smothered African sympathy for Mau Mau. Violence may have destroyed colonial power; it could never inspire national authority. Only elected members of parliament could do that. It was their dexterity that dragged Kenya from the 'quagmire' of white and black extremisms. They were articulate and representative; Mau Mau was neither.[150] This conclusion echoed the moderate nationalist Tom Mbotela, translator of Thomas Paine's *The Rights of Man* but opponent and victim of Mau Mau, who in 1950 had criticized strike leaders for not heeding 'people who knew better'.[151] Here was not so much a study in the failure of mobilization as a suggestion, in tune with the disillusioned political science of the later 1960s, that it were better had it not been tried.

If Mau Mau was no political base, nor, in the liberal view, could it serve as cultural inspiration for the new nation. The evidence of what Kikuyu had said to each other, now beginning to be included in the valid record, seemed unequivocal. The doyen of Kenya's historians, Ogot, thought that Mau Mau anthems were too exclusive in their symbolism to be the 'national freedom songs which every Kenyan youth can sing with pride and conviction.'[152] The land issue was more divisive still. Kanogo, herself a Kikuyu squatter's daughter, questioned the squatter claim to have fought as the custodial trustees of the pastoralists who had once controlled most of the White Highlands. It looked more like an apology for tribal expansion, expecting as reward the land that other peoples had proved incapable of defending themselves.[153] Kenya's liberals have thus reinforced Rosberg and Nottingham's fear that Mau Mau's role in putting state power into African hands had thwarted the national integration that alone might make that power legitimate.[154] Ethnic energy was neither a negotiable political currency, nor a source of national culture, nor yet an equitable claim on resources.

This essay questions the first two of these conclusions. They rely too heavily on belief in the first formative dialectic of the liberal myth. Colonial rule was neither culturally creative nor politically inviting enough to give educated elites the authority to mobilize an 'integrative revolution' of common citizens. It has also been persuasively argued that the ambitions of this 'hegemonic project', as the French call it, may have been directly destructive of the only representative politics possible in Africa's new states, responsive to ethnic languages of civic virtue and for that reason thought to be inimical to the state.[155]

RADICALS

Smarting under oppression, Kenya's radicals have denounced the liberals as 'anti-Mau Mau intellectuals', lackeys of the neocolonialism for which formal independence was a mask.[156] Liberals pictured an educated class teaching nationhood to tribal masses. Radicals have produced a mirror transubstantiation. In this, workers were mobilized into a self-aware proletariat by the mute mechanics of economic structure. Tribe, the enemy of class, is in their view an equally smooth capitalist invention. It is an imaginative displacement of injustice from its proper location in economic inequality to the quaint sideshow of cultural difference. The educated class teach tribalism. This 'false consciousness' divides workers and peasants who otherwise share a common, patriotic quarrel with the expropriators of their labour.[157] Tribe masks the unpatriotic class interest of the bourgeoisie, dependent on their foreign puppeteers; it disguises them as communal benefactors. Radicals have pressed Mau Mau into the service of this class analysis of contemporary economic underdevelopment. Unsullied by tribe, it was the forerunner of the only possible Kenyan nation, potentially united by the material class energy of its workers and peasants but constantly betrayed by the educated, in the 1950s and since. Two attitudes to evidence, one narrow, the other cavalier, sustain this radical thesis.

To take an expatriate scholar first, Furedi gathered important new data but interpreted it in the light of two assumptions which persuaded him that Mau Mau could be none other than the militant wing of Kenyan nationalism. The first was that tribes are undivided. Since Mau Mau and its bitterest opponents were both Kikuyu, Mau Mau could not have been a tribal organization.[158] The squatters who gave the movement energy and the urban politicians who, like external class allies in any peasant revolt, gave it direction, were labour tenants and workers before either were Kikuyu. Barnett had allowed that the Kikuyu were tribesmen before they were workers and devoted nine pages to their ethnography. Furedi thought that unnecessary; it 'was the special character of the colonial impact that stimulated the politicization of the Kikuyu and not tribal traditions.'[159] He did not believe that class coalition had to be cemented by some sense of community other than class.

Furedi added much evidence for Barnett's thesis that Mau Mau's Kikuyuness reflected the growing isolation of loyalty under stress. Nonetheless, he also assumed, secondly, that Mau Mau was 'best understood from the vantage point of what happened *afterwards*.'[160] This was to go far beyond the retrospective evaluation implicit in the first scholarly accounts. Indeed, Furedi's criterion denied the common historical premise, found at the centre of Rosberg and Nottingham's work as also of Barnett's, that the uncertainties of conflict tend to produce results that neither opposing party will welcome. Reading his history backwards, Furedi made contested outcomes into intended purposes. After the Emergency, the moderate nationalists, whom British reforms had promoted, blocked Mau Mau's intended gains with tribal objections. By Furedi's reasoning, Mau Mau must therefore have been a militant territorial nationalism.

Kenya's own radicals have rewritten old evidence rather than gathered new. That is the inescapable conclusion of a comparative reading of Maina wa Kinyatti's recent translations of the political songs of the 1950s. The radical utilization today of an earlier generation's sentiments has demanded their ideological refinement, if clumsy Marxification can be so called. In Maina wa Kinyatti's hands 'the people' have become 'revolutionary masses' while Kenyatta has lost his name and been multiplied into 'our national heroes'.[161] Ideological heroism has been most determinedly demanded of the evidence by those who have least studied it, who can indeed sneer at those who bury Mau Mau 'in a heap of footnotes'.[162] Kenyan liberals have protested against this contempt for authorized professional standards, calling it 'intellectual terrorism'.[163] My own response would be to ask the radicals to enquire more closely into the ethnic languages of class.[164] One might then understand the very specific sense of loss experienced by the militants, which mobilized them to recover civic virtues that had been earlier elaborated by moderate politicians, some of whom in fact became 'loyalists'. Without such enquiry the dead will remain just that, lifeless bearers of abstract class forces, not engaged in the moral uncertainties of once living, historically conscious, individually ambitious, human beings.

The Problem

A CONSERVATIVE

Throup, a conservative historian, has overturned both liberal and radical arguments. Observing an independent Kenya ruled for 30 years by ethnic intrigue, he has drawn two inferences for colonial African politics.[165] One is interpretive. He has accepted with equanimity the power of political mobilization within 'the confines of tribe', as shown by Mau Mau.[166] Tribes were the main political teams before independence, as they have been since. Kenyan nationalism, like its Indian forerunner, was a 'ramshackle coalition' within existing society, not the refined end-product of colonial or capitalist social engineering, as it might in future become.[167] Militant Africans, like all effective politicians, simply recognized social facts. Such a comment requires assent to the colonial and liberal transubstantiation by which the 'intricate but fragile' structures that 'contained' tribes were under threat of dissolution by change.[168] It then follows that a primordial circus of still convinced and convincing tribal bosses was not nationalism's fate but its fortune. It was more effective than a wishfully transitional bandwagon like the KAU, which just puffed elite hot air.[169] A circus might not conjure up a future nation. It paraded present power. And that is exactly what Mau Mau delivered.

Throup's second conclusion was methodological, that 'high politics' should hold the explanatory centre ground. This is to argue that competing leaderships can themselves create their political arena by the very acts of the imagination in which they search out their constituencies.[170] With the method, he has brought to Kenyan studies its corollary, that English historiographical tradition which looks for upheaval from below at times when high-political stress gives to normally deferential lower orders the inviting opportunity of distracted masters. This shows a refreshingly unsentimental readiness, untroubled by liberal or radical dreams, to see intrigue and patronage as the labyrinth of power. It is however an approach fraught with conceptual and technical difficulty. It risks reducing the social context of politics to mere faction fights. It also sadly lacks, in Kenya, the intimate evidence for high-political manoeuvre that is found elsewhere in diaries and private letters. Both deficiencies can at least partly be made good by an attempt, as here, to reconstruct the local historical tradition of political debate. This both inspired and, to a contested extent, disciplined the world of high politics, while probing and adjusting the elasticities of tribe.

All three of the above approaches have related what seem to be the obviously contradictory social 'facts' of tribe and class to the problems of creating a territorial nationalism, and have thus left little explanatory room for creative political mobilization. The liberals regretted the failure of the modernizing attempt to mobilize men out of their tribes; radicals argued that abstract class formation was its own subjective mobilization; Throup thought that tribe was political consciousness enough.

ANTHROPOLOGISTS

Anthropologists, less concerned to redeem the analysis of Kenya's nationalism from the shadow of British propaganda, have addressed directly the problem of how constituencies are conjured up by process and persuasion. But they admit to high-political ignorance. Kershaw's exposition of the 'low politics' of gender, age and clan relies not on any exiguous private record but on the copious social documents of daily life. It also offers an entry into the world of 'deep politics', that negotiated arena in which leaders weighed the private rewards of high-political deals against the demands from below that tested their civic virtue.[171] But the nearer the evidence gets to the common experience of the everyday, the less it is able to witness to the relations between Mau Mau and nationalism, or even to the movement's own organization, about which ordinary men and women speculated more than they knew and told less than they guessed. Kershaw has explicitly warned that her village-level data give her no privileged knowledge of 'politics'.[172] This is a most significant ignorance to which I will return.

In his first book Buijtenhuijs, more concerned than Kershaw to link Kikuyu and Kenyan politics, reached what may seem to be a similar conclusion. Equating social structure with political persuasion, he saw Mau Mau as a set of 'popular and anonymous movements', with their successive phases 'dominated by the action of popular Kikuyu classes without the leadership of an educated political elite.'[173] Mau Mau was many movements, rural and urban, traditional and modern, Kikuyu and nationalist, a parochial kaleidoscope of hope and despair, arising rather directly from what academic observers could see as social injustice.[174] Kershaw might agree but would add three provisos: that several local groups were affiliated to Mau Mau only in the minds of their enemies at the time; that the same groups might have been glad to admit to the linkage in retrospect; and that the retrospective view itself was fickle, changing markedly between her two periods of fieldwork in 1956 and 1962.[175] Those provisos are vital; they assert the uncertainty principle in the workings of political authority against Buijtenhuijs' assumption that Kikuyu mobilization was socially predetermined.

Insofar as Mau Mau was unified by inspiration from below, rather than by resistance to British counter-measures from above, Buijtenhuijs believed that it was by a conscious process of 'cultural renewal'. This is anthropology's second, contested, insight.[176] Buijtenhuijs was careful to distinguish renewal from the regressive atavism of British propaganda which, like the nativism of political science, represented a retreat from the complexities of the modern world into the primal simplicity of a tribal golden age. Rather, he believed, Kikuyu were calling up the deep sources of their culture in a creative way, so as to take change under their own subjective control. They did not wish to hide from change but to prevent the British from dictating it to them on discriminatory terms.[177]

These social insights invite development. The first, the household's sense of ignorance about an unauthorized and anonymous power by which it is surrounded, may provide the best approach to terror. Mau Mau terror is something from which scholars have shied away, but must have something to do with the deep uncertainty inherent in any connection between the civic virtue testable in the local community and a power exerted from outside. Power that is not knowably social must always be feared to be unknowably anti-social. This radically unknowable quality will, in colonial conditions, be as true of the state as it may be of its opponents. The second insight, the concept of cultural renewal, misleads if it suggests that there was an unproblematic culture to renew; is weak in its lack of a clear relationship to the civic rights that make a culture a material way of life; and evasive in not addressing the question, so disturbing to Kershaw's informants, of the source of the authority by which culture was mobilized. But these shortcomings fruitfully reinforce the case for studying the local language of political debate.

MARXISTS

In the 1970s, Marxists were not much interested in the historical study of African nationalism. It was of no concern to Kenya's first Marxist social scientist, Njonjo, except as the rhetoric of a rising bourgeoisie in search of class allies. Thus freed from any obligation to counter Corfield, he no longer analysed tribe, class and nation as the discrete dichotomies of liberal or radical historiography. Rather, they were overlapping and mutable constructs that shaped the shifting networks of alliance that men entered, to pursue economic opportunity and to deny it to others.[178] This usefully flexible approach offers two points of departure for the present enquiry.

First, using Cowen's fundamental research into agrarian productive relations,[179] Njonjo showed how class formation is not something that occurs outside the 'confines of tribe' but in its very guts. Its key process was the ideological remodelling of the inclusive productive rights that were embodied in historically expansive lineage relations. Lineage histories came to serve, instead, as charters of exclusive rights in property, refuting the claims of junior kin or non-kin dependants. The language of class among the Kikuyu took its conceptual vocabulary from the language of kinship and its repudiation.[180] For the first time, here was a clear statement that tribes could be divided by class.

Secondly, Njonjo rewrote the political event of elite 'loss of control' in the prehistory of Mau Mau as a social process of 'class struggle'. Until the late 1940s, he argued, African consciousness of such internal division was blunted by shared grievance against white settler capitalism. Black penny-capitalists were as much frustrated by exclusion from opportunity as peasants and workers were frightened by the threat of expropriation from their remaining rights by capitalists both black and white. The growing urgency of African politics fused together their class alliance. Its internal contradictions burst open only under the tightening screw of repression. It was not so much that the smooth men of rural Kiambu lost control to rough Nairobi but that would-be rural capitalists were increasingly separated from the land-poor[181] and landless workers by their property disputes, their hostility as employers to independent trades unionism and by their recruitment to salaried office in the repressive state.[182] Njonjo's main interest, like Furedi's, was in what happened next, the political economy of decolonization. With greater subtlety he focused not on British manipulation but on its essential counterpart, the African search for class coalitions – what Kipkorir had called the politics of collaboration.

Njonjo had a clear eye for the economics of class formation, perhaps too clear. His antagonistic classes were defined too exclusively by tables of employment and wage differentials. They look, for the 1950s, to be too free of their lineage origins. Kershaw's social-survey data on Mau Mau membership which, for all their parochial particularity in two neighbouring villages, are the only such data we have got, show that Mau Mau initiates, however defined, were not readily distinguished from their antagonists in terms of class. What was, in analytical terms, a growing class differentiation between rich, propertied households and poor, landless ones, generally took its highly personal origins in rivalry between wives and between their sons, within the same household.[183] And Mau Mau memoirs show that forest fighters, whom class analysis would deem to be the poor, often took care not to despoil and murder rural businessmen.[184] We need still more flexibility than Njonjo's. It is found in what he called for[185] but did not himself provide, a study of political language in which the moral challenge of class formation was faced and in part declined, with former civic virtues continuing to flourish amid the unfinished construction of new ones.

Listening to the evidence of Kikuyu talking to other Kikuyu, we may hear an emergent middle class seeking to preserve its name and reputation and the new poor responding to the old accusation of civic irresponsibility. Both rich and poor remained caught in the tragic contradiction between the collective solidarities of age or generation and the competitive cares of household.[186]

The Problem
Notes

1. Jomo Kenyatta, *Facing Mount Kenya* (London, 1938), p. 119.
2. Eliud Mutonyi ' "Mau Mau" Chairman', typescript (1970), p. 48.
3. Justin Itotia with James Dougall, 'The voice of Africa: Kikuyu proverbs', *Africa* 1 (1928), p. 486.
4. I have many intellectual debts to acknowledge. My deepest is to Greet Kershaw, who knows the Kikuyu far better than I and who is so generous in her intellectual collegiality. Next to her I owe most to Bruce Berman, for his patience with my constant failure to finish this essay. My undergraduate students asked the right questions. Seminars in Baltimore, Cambridge and Nairobi reminded me how little I still know; I am grateful to my colleagues Tabitha Kanogo, Godfrey Muriuki and Henry Mwaniki for repairing some of the worst defects. I have learned much from muthee Henry Muoria Mwaniki, former editor of *Mumenyereri* and ex-London Transport Underground guard, and from Mungai Mbayah, JP. British and American colleagues have given much needed encouragement, Richard Waller especially. Randall Heather, David Throup and John Spencer have been generous with material. Tom Askwith, Dick Cashmore, J.C. Carothers, Thomas Colchester, Cyril Hooper, Peter Bostock, Terence Gavaghan and Willoughby Thompson have shared their memories of the time. Many of these will dissent from my conclusions and none is responsible for my errors of understanding; these may be grievous, as I later explain.
5. Ernest Renan, 'Qu'est-ce qu'une nation?' (1882), in H. Psichari (ed.) *Oeuvres complètes de Ernest Renan*, vol. 1 (Paris, 1947), pp. 892, 891. Renan set the agenda for one of Kenya's earliest academics, Ali Mazrui, in his review of the first Mau Mau memoir, J.M. Kariuki's *'Mau Mau' Detainee* (Oxford, 1963). This is reprinted in Ali A. Mazrui, *On Heroes and Uhuru-Worship* (London, 1967), pp. 19–34.
6. R. Buijtenhuijs, *Mau Mau Twenty Years After: The Myth and the Survivors* (The Hague, 1973), pp. 50–3.
7. Renan, 'Qu'est-ce qu'une nation?', p. 891.
8. Atieno Odhiambo, 'The production of history in Kenya: the Mau Mau debate', conference paper for Fifth International Roundtable in Anthropology and History (Paris, July 1986).
9. Ali A. Mazrui, *Violence and Thought* (London, 1969), Ch. 5: 'Conflict and the integrative process' (1966); and Ch. 13: 'Political censorship and intellectual creativity' (1966).
10. I use the terms 'tribe', 'ethnic group', 'nationality', etc. equally, without distinction of value. In English parlance 'ethnic' is beginning to acquire the same derogatory overtones as 'tribal', losing its presumed advantage of objectivity; and to renounce the use of all terms with vulgar, misleading connotations would be a severe limitation on vocabulary. More ink has been spilled on the definition of tribe and ethnicity than on any other issue in modern Africa. My own view will appear as the essay proceeds; in general I use 'tribe' to imply the politically conscious dimension, internal and external, of ethnic culture or, in sociological terms, the *Gesellschaft* in the *Gemeinschaft*. Three useful discussions are: Aidan Southall 'The illusion of tribe', *Journal of Asian and African Studies* 5(1–2) (1970), pp. 28–50; Nelson Kasfir, *The Shrinking Political Arena* (Berkeley & Los Angeles, 1976), Ch. 2; and Leroy Vail, 'Introduction: ethnicity in Southern African history', in *idem* (ed.), *The Creation of Tribalism in Southern Africa* (London & Los Angeles, 1989), pp. 1–19.
11. Brevity is required because a longer tour will be forthcoming in association with Bruce Berman in our next project, 'Explaining Mau Mau'; and possible, since the colonial constructions of Mau Mau have been set out in my 'Mau Maus of the mind: making

Mau Mau and remaking Kenya' in *Journal of African History* 31(3) (1990), pp. 393–421.

12. Andrew Roberts, *A History of Zambia* (London, 1976), p. 65.

13. Renan, 'Qu'est-ce qu'une nation?', p. 904.

14. David W. Cohen and E.S. Atieno Odhiambo have taught me much about the production of history, in discussion and now in their book *Siaya: The Historical Anthropology of an African Landscape* (London, 1989).

15. Cohen and Atieno Odhiambo's work (*ibid.*) is an example of what I have in mind. For historians' embarrassment about ethnicity, see Vail's preface to *Creation of Tribalism*, pp. xi, xii, fn. 3.

16. Compare *ibid.*, 'Introduction', p. 2.

17. Renan, 'Qu'est-ce-qu'une nation?', pp. 890f, 896–9, 900. See further, Ernest Gellner, *Nations and Nationalism* (Oxford, 1983); William H. McNeill, *Polyethnicity and National Unity in World History* (Toronto, 1986); Eric J. Hobsbawm, *Nations and Nationalism since 1780* (Cambridge, 1990), p. 157.

18. See Chapters 2 and 3, above.

19. I will also discuss the interpretations offered by social and cultural anthropology and Marxist political science, which are less respectful to the myth of modernization.

20. Political science identified the faults in its model long before historians proposed alternative histories; compare Crawford Young, *The Politics of Cultural Pluralism* (Madison, 1976), with Vail (ed.), *Creation of Tribalism* (1989).

21. The next four paragraphs attempt to summarize the liberal doctrines of the time, found in such standard texts as James S. Coleman, 'Nationalism in tropical Africa', *American Political Science Review* 48(2) (1954), pp. 404–26 [twice reprinted in general readers on Africa: W.J. Hanna (ed.), *Independent Black Africa* (Chicago, 1964) and I.L. Markovitz (ed.), *African Politics and Society* (New York & London, 1970)]; idem, 'The politics of sub-Saharan Africa', Ch. 3 in Gabriel A. Almond and J.S. Coleman (eds), *The Politics of the Developing Areas* (Princeton, 1960, and six reprints in a decade); Karl W. Deutsch, 'Social mobilization and political development', *American Political Science Review* 55(3) (1961), pp. 492–514; Crawford Young, *Politics in the Congo* (Princeton, 1965), esp. Ch. 12, 'The rise of nationalism, from primary resistance to political parties'.

22. F.D. Lugard, *The Dual Mandate in British Tropical Africa* (London, 1922), p. 618; Margery Perham, *The Colonial Reckoning* (London, 1961), p. 22.

23. R.E. Robinson and J. Gallagher, 'The partition of Africa', in F.H. Hinsley (ed.), *The New Cambridge Modern History*, vol. xi (London, 1962), p. 640.

24. A logic stated most clearly in Mazrui, 'Conflict and the integrative process'.

25. It was to challenge this teleology that Terence Ranger wrote his celebrated studies of resistance and rebellion, among which see, *Revolt in Southern Rhodesia 1896–7: A Study in African Resistance* (London, 1967); 'Connexions between "primary resistance" movements and modern mass nationalisms in east and central Africa', *Journal of African History* 9 (1968), pp. 437–53, 631–41; and 'African reactions to the imposition of colonial rule in East and Central Africa', Ch. 9 in L.H. Gann and Peter Duignan (eds), *Colonialism in Africa, 1870–1960*, i: *The History and Politics of Colonialism 1870–1914* (Cambridge, 1969), pp. 293–324.

26. David E. Apter, *The Politics of Modernization* (Chicago & London, 1965), pp. 360–1.

27. This sketch of postwar Kenya is derived from Carl G. Rosberg and John Nottingham, *The Myth of 'Mau Mau': Nationalism in Kenya* (New York & London, 1966), Ch. 6; M.P.K. Sorrenson, *Land Reform in the Kikuyu Country* (Nairobi & London, 1967), Chs 4 and 5; David Throup, *Economic and Social Origins of Mau Mau* (London, 1987); Bruce Berman, *Control and Crisis in Colonial Kenya: The Dialectics of Domination* (London, 1990), Chs 6 and 7; see also Chapter 10, above.

28. For instance, in western Kenya, chiefs Paulo Agoi, Mukudi, Daniel Odindo and

Jonathan Okwirri; and in central Kenya, Parmenas Mukiri Githendu, Koinange wa Mbiyu and Muhoya Kagumba; even a past president of the Kenya African Union, James Gichuru, was thought appropriate for appointment as chief and thought it proper to accept.

29. It is true that one father-in-law, Koinange (whose daughter then died in childbirth), was no longer chief and that both he and chief Muhoho (father of Mama Ngina Kenyatta) were also *aramati* ('trustees') of their subclans; nevertheless, Kenyatta clearly saw state service as no bar to marriage alliance – as I am reminded by Dr Jocelyn Murray.

30. For British hesitation between supporting chiefs and backing elites, see R.D. Pearce, *The Turning Point in Africa: British Colonial Policy 1938-48* (London, 1982); my argument here is the converse of that proposed in Throup, *Origins*, where 'chiefs' are taken to imply 'indirect rule' rather than the growing public sector educated elite. For biographical evidence see, John Spencer, *KAU: the Kenya African Union* (London, 1985), pp. 154-5.

31. Sorrenson, *Land Reform*; Anthony Clayton and Donald C. Savage, *Government and Labour in Kenya 1895-1963* (London, 1974), Chs 8-11; Nicola Swainson, *The Development of Corporate Capitalism in Kenya 1918-1977* (London, 1980), pp. 176-82; Frederick Cooper, *On the African Waterfront* (New Haven & London, 1987).

32. I. Schapera, *Some Problems of Anthropological Research in Kenya Colony* (International African Institute memo. 23, London, 1949), p. 16.

33. Rosberg and Nottingham, *Myth*, Ch. 9; Lonsdale, 'Mau Maus of the mind'.

34. Negley Farson, *Last Chance in Africa* (London, 1949; New York, 1950) gives a privileged and perceptive journalist's view of white attitudes in Kenya.

35. C.T. Stoneham, *Out of Barbarism* (London, 1955), title of Ch. 14.

36. This pejorative view is what is best remembered of J.C. Carothers, *The Psychology of Mau Mau* (Government Printer, Nairobi, 1954), but my 'Mau Maus of the mind' shows this officially sponsored report to have given a more uncomfortable message to whites.

37. F. Cooper, 'Mau Mau and the discourses of decolonization', *Journal of African History* 29 (1988), pp. 313-20.

38. Clayton and Savage, *Government and Labour*, pp. 305-11; Throup, *Origins*, Ch. 5; Tabitha Kanogo, *Squatters and the Roots of Mau Mau 1905-63* (London, 1987); Frank Furedi, *The Mau Mau War in Perspective* (London, 1989), Ch. 2.

39. J.F. Lipscomb, *White Africans* (London, 1955), pp. 37-9.

40. This summary picture is based on two official publications: Colonial Office (CO), *Report to the Secretary of State for the Colonies by the Parliamentary Delegation to Kenya, January 1954* (Cmd 9081, 1954); and CO, *Historical Survey of the Origins and Growth of Mau Mau* (Cmd 1030, 1960), cited henceforth as *Corfield Report*, after its main author.

41. This purpose is most clearly stated in *ibid.*, pp. 284, 285 (the last sentence of the report).

42. Makerere Kikuyu Embu and Meru Students' Association, *Comment on Corfield* (mimeo, Kampala, 1960), cited henceforth as MKEMSA, *Comment*; F.B. Welbourn, 'Comment on Corfield', *Race* 2(2) (1961), pp. 7-27; George Bennett, 'Kenyatta and the Kikuyu', *International Affairs* 37(4) (1961), pp. 477-82.

43. Carl Rosberg and Donald Barnett respectively; the third, John Nottingham, was a former colonial official.

44. S.M. Lipset, *The First New Nation* (New York, 1963).

45. Clifford Geertz (ed.), *Old Societies and New States: The Quest for Modernity in Asia and Africa* (New York & London, 1963); Edward Shils, *Political Development in the New States* (The Hague & Paris, 1964).

46. Thomas Hodgkin, *African Political Parties* (Harmondsworth, 1961), pp. 36-7.

47. Godfrey and Monica Wilson, *The Analysis of Social Change, Based on Observations in*

Central Africa (Cambridge 1945, reprinted 1965), p. 41; the argument of this paragraph is partly based on the first two chapters of this classic work which, as the authors acknowledged (p. vii), drew on the then ruling ideas in sociology.

48. See especially I. Wallerstein, *The Road to Independence: Ghana and the Ivory Coast* (Paris & The Hague, 1964).

49. Thomas Hodgkin, *Nationalism in Colonial Africa* (London, 1956), p. 83.

50. A. Creech Jones (Secretary of State for the Colonies), 'British colonial policy, with particular reference to Africa', *International Affairs* 27(2) (1951), esp. pp. 178-9, 182-3; for the most authoritative account of British African policy at the time, see Ronald Hyam, 'Africa and the Labour Government 1945-1951', *Journal of Imperial and Commonwealth History* 16(3) (1988), pp. 148-72.

51. Coleman, 'Nationalism', p. 426; emphasis added.

52. James Coleman and Carl G. Rosberg, 'Introduction' to their edited collection *Political Parties and National Integration in Africa* (Berkeley & Los Angeles, 1964), p. 3. Anthropologists will recognize the intellectual origins of this functional model of nationalism to be 'the peace in the feud'; see Max Gluckman, *Custom and Conflict in Africa* (Oxford, 1955), Ch. 2.

53. For successive assertions of this subversive truth, see Vincent Harlow, 'Tribalism in Africa', *Journal of African Administration* 7(1) (1955), pp. 17-20; Cranford Pratt, 'East Africa: the pattern of political development', in M. Maclure and D. Anglin (eds), *Africa: The Political Pattern* (Toronto, 1961), p. 111; Aristide A. Zolberg, *Creating Political Order: The Party-states of West Africa* (Chicago, 1966), p. 27; John Iliffe, 'Tanzania under German and British rule', Ch. 14 in B.A. Ogot and J.A. Kieran (eds), *Zamani: A Survey of East African History* (Nairobi, 1968), p. 301.

54. Hodgkin, *Nationalism, passim.*

55. Especially revealing here is Richard L. Sklar, 'Political science and national integration – a radical approach', *Journal of Modern African Studies* 5(1) (1967), pp. 1-2, whose own optimistic belief in the 'inevitability of emancipation through social conflict' was checked by the thought that African and Asian mass movements tended to follow communal rather than class divisions, so that 'the classic social revolution is likely to be intercepted and diverted off course by powerful forces that cast doubt on the inevitability [again!] of social progress'. For my own 'splitting' tendency at the time see John Lonsdale, 'The emergence of African nations', Ch. 18 in T.O. Ranger, (ed.), *Emerging Themes of African History* (Nairobi, 1968).

56. See above, Chapter 7.

57. For another classic study, one should combine a reading of John Iliffe's *Agricultural Change in Modern Tanganyika* (Historical Association of Tanzania Paper no. 10: Nairobi, 1971) with his *A Modern History of Tanganyika* (Cambridge, 1979), pp. 301-41, 487-507.

58. Raymond Apthorpe, 'Does tribalism really matter?' *Transition* 37 (Kampala, Oct 1968), p. 22.

59. Sklar, 'Political science and national integration', p. 6.

60. Giovanni Arrighi and John S. Saul, 'Nationalism and revolution in sub-Saharan Africa' (first published 1969), reprinted in their *Essays on the Political Economy of Africa* (New York & London, 1973), p. 69; but a full theoretical critique still had to wait a few years; see Geoffrey Kay, *Development and Underdevelopment: A Marxist Analysis* (London, 1975), especially Chs 5 and 6.

61. E.P. Thompson's *The Making of the English Working Class* (London, 1965) ought to have reassured Africanists of the historical propriety of regional cultural tradition as a formative element in worker consciousness.

62. The above remarks are a crude summary of the big book that epitomized the political science of the 1950s: Coleman and Rosberg, *Political Parties and National Integration.*

63. Georges Balandier appears to have been the first to analyse this process in his *Sociologie*

actuelle de l'Afrique noire (Paris, 1955), to judge by Hodgkin's reliance on him in *African Political Parties*, pp. 19-20. Carl Rosberg, 'Political conflict and change in Kenya', Ch. 5 in Gwendolen M. Carter and William O. Brown (eds), *Transition in Africa: Studies in Political Adaptation* (Boston, 1958), pp. 113-14, seems to have been the first to do so with reference to Kenya. For the amalgamation of 'tribelets' into tribes: see, George Bennett and Carl Rosberg, *The Kenyatta Election: Kenya 1960-61* (London, 1961), pp. 27-9. The term 'aggregation' I take from D.A. Low, 'Introduction' to his essays on *Buganda in Modern History* (London, 1971), pp. 3-5; developed further in D.A. Low and J.M. Lonsdale, 'Introduction: towards the new order 1945-1963', in D.A. Low and Alison Smith (eds), *History of East Africa*, vol. iii (Oxford, 1976), pp. 24-32. For the fullest, comparatively early, discussion of the process of tribalization in East Africa, see P.H. Gulliver (ed.), *Tradition and Transition in East Africa: Studies of the Tribal Element in the Modern Era* (London, 1969).

64. For the classic example of northern Nigeria, see James S. Coleman, *Nigeria, Background to Nationalism* (Berkeley & Los Angeles, 1963), pp. 358-9.

65. David E. Apter, *The Gold Coast in Transition* (Princeton, 1955), pp. 165-7; idem, 'Ghana', Ch. 7 in Coleman and Rosberg, *Political Parties and National Integration*, pp. 277-8.

66. Richard Rathbone, 'Businessmen in politics: party struggle in Ghana, 1949-57', *Journal of Development Studies* 9(3) (1973), pp. 391-401; but the quotation is from Richard L. Sklar, 'Contradictions in the Nigerian political system', *Journal of Modern African Studies* 3(2) (1965), p. 204.

67. This paragraph paraphrases Zolberg, *Creating Political Order*, Ch. 1, itself a critique of the optimistic analyses of the 1950s.

68. For example, Kingsley Martin's reports from Kenya in *New Statesman and Nation*, 8, 15, 22, 29 Nov., 6 and 13 Dec. 1952; Philip Bolsover, *Kenya: What are the Facts?* (Communist Party, London, May 1953); Fenner Brockway, *Why Mau Mau? An Analysis and a Remedy* (Congress of Peoples against Imperialism, London, 1953); George Padmore, 'Behind the Mau Mau', *Phylon* 14(4) (1954), pp. 355-72.

69. For the statistical proofs, see Edward W. Soja, *The Geography of Modernization in Kenya: A Spatial Analysis of Social, Economic and Political Change* (Syracuse, NY, 1968).

70. This contemporary British opinion has been confirmed by the memoirs of those closest to the Mau Mau leadership in Nairobi: see Mutonyi, 'Mau Mau chairman', p. 67; Mohamed Mathu, *The Urban Guerilla* (Richmond, BC, 1974), pp. 22-3; Bildad Kaggia, *Roots of Freedom 1921-1963* (Nairobi, 1975), p. 82.

71. B.A. Ogot, 'Politics, culture and music in Central Kenya: a study of Mau Mau hymns 1951-1965', *Kenya Historical Review* 5(2) (1977), pp. 275-86.

72. See the list of 139 people arrested on 20 Oct 1952 in Appendix 1 to Gakaara wa Wanjau, *Mau Mau Author in Detention* (Nairobi, 1988), pp. 213-18; among identifiable occupational categories the largest are: independent church priest or schoolteacher: 30; trader or farmer: 18; editor: 11; trades unionist: 11; taxi-driver: 10. None of these would have been mutually exclusive groups.

73. Apter, *Gold Coast*, *passim*; Richard L. Sklar, *Nigerian Political Parties: Power in an Emergent African Nation* (Princeton, 1963), pp. 474-80, especially the footnotes.

74. This composite picture of the priority of secularization is based on the work of four American political scientists: Coleman, 'Nationalism'; idem, *Nigeria*, Part III; Apter, *Gold Coast*; Deutsch, 'Social mobilization and political development'; and Young, *Politics in the Congo*, pp. 281-98. Hodgkin, *Nationalism*, Ch. 3 shared their dismissive view of enthusiastic African sects but later, in *African Political Parties*, p. 16, accepted that the 'telescoping of phases' that in European history had been distinct needed analysis rather than judgment.

75. Apter, *Gold Coast*, *passim*, especially Ch. 14; Rupert Emerson, *From Empire to Nation* (Cambridge, Mass., 1960), Ch. 15, 'The erosion of democracy in the new states'.

76. Hodgkin, *Nationalism*, pp. 162-3.
77. Evidence of Terence Gavaghan, Sir Charles Markham, and Robin Wainwright for 'End of Empire', screened by Granada TV, 1 July 1985.
78. The excitement of one reader converted him from railway guard to newspaper editor: Henry Muoria Mwaniki, who first read *Facing Mount Kenya* (bought in an Eldoret bookshop) under a naked lamp bulb in the rear guards van on the night run from Timboroa (highest railway station in the British empire) to Eldoret in 1939 and founded *Mumenyereri* [*The Guardian*] in 1945; information from H.M. Mwaniki, 27 April 1990.
79. *Ibuku ria Ngai* [*The Bible*] (Nairobi, 1965), *Ahibirania* [*Hebrews*] 12: 24; for the so-called 'KAU hymns', see the translations in L.S.B. Leakey, *Defeating Mau Mau* (London, 1954), pp. 55-73; Leakey's translations can be compared with those in Maina wa Kinyatti (ed.), *Thunder from the Mountains: Mau Mau Patriotic Songs* (London and Nairobi, 1980). The differences between them are discussed below.
80. Suspicions about the conduct of Kenyatta's trials have often been voiced; see, Peter Evans, *Law and Disorder: Scenes of Life in Kenya* (London, 1956), Part IV; Montagu Slater, *The Trial of Jomo Kenyatta* (London, 1955), *passim*; D.N. Pritt (Kenyatta's leading defence counsel), *The Defence Accuses* (London, 1966), Ch. 8. The most recent, and damning, evidence is in Charles Douglas-Home, *Evelyn Baring: The Last Proconsul* (London, 1978), pp. 246-8, where it is also probably rightly implied that no African witness dared to give evidence against Kenyatta unless rewarded by government. For primary evidence suggestive of improper dealings between government and presiding judge, see KNA: Judicial. 1/2097.
81. Hodgkin, *Nationalism*, p. 168.
82. Coleman, 'Nationalism', p. 409.
83. James S. Coleman, 'The emergence of African political parties', in C. Grove Haines (ed.), *Africa Today* (Baltimore, 1955), p. 251.
84. David Riesman, 'Introduction' to Daniel Lerner, *The Passing of Traditional Society: Modernizing the Middle East* (New York, 1958), pp. 5, 10.
85. Ngugi wa Thiong'o, 'Mau Mau is coming back: the revolutionary significance of 20th October 1952 in Kenya today', *J. Afr. Marxists* 4 (1983), pp. 20-21.
86. T.H. von Laue, 'Transubstantiation in the study of African reality', *African Affairs* 74 (1975), pp. 401-19.
87. Bethwell A. Ogot, 'History, ideology and contemporary Kenya', presidential address to the Historical Association of Kenya, mimeographed, Nairobi, 27 August 1981.
88. Cooper, 'Mau Mau and discourses of decolonization', p. 320; see further, Chapter 9, above.
89. For successive reviews of the literature, see O.W. Furley, 'The historiography of Mau Mau', Ch. 6 in B.A. Ogot (ed.), *Hadith 4: Politics and Nationalism in Colonial Kenya* (Nairobi, 1972); Rob Buijtenhuijs, *Essays on Mau Mau: Contributions to Mau Mau Historiography* (Leiden, 1982); Atieno Odhiambo, 'The production of history in Kenya'; John Lonsdale, 'Explanations of the Mau Mau revolt', pp. 168-78 in Tom Lodge (ed.), *Resistance and Ideology in Settler Societies* (Johannesburg, 1986); *idem*, 'Mau Mau through the looking glass', *Index on Censorship* 15(2) (1986), pp. 19-22.
90. See Chapters 4 and 5 above.
91. *Corfield Report*, p. 63, quoting the district commissioner, Nyeri.
92. *Ibid.*, pp. 67-9; Rosberg and Nottingham, *Myth*, pp. 237-9, 322; Spencer, *KAU*, pp. 175-8; Throup, *Origins*, p. 240.
93. R.E. Robinson, 'The moral disarmament of African empire 1919-1947', *Journal of Imperial and Commonwealth History* 8(1) (1979) pp. 86-104.
94. Berman, *Control and Crisis*, well analyses the official view; also Chapter 10, above.
95. The *Corfield Report* referred several times to 'the never-ending struggle between the moderates and extremists' (pp. 49, 51, 63, 267), but never questioned Kenyatta's

The Problem

place among the latter. Corfield also (p. 88) criticized a tendency in the police special branch to 'split' Kikuyu organizations, which should have been 'lumped' under Kenyatta, in whom 'all the Kikuyu organizational strands eventually met' (p. 51). Corfield's conclusions reflected the administrative view rather than that of the police, who knew more about African divisions but to whom government paid less heed (Throup, *Origins*, pp. 225–8).

96. Luise White, 'Separating the men from the boys: constructions of gender, sexuality and terrorism in central Kenya 1939–1959', *Int. J. African Historical Studies* 23(1) (1990), pp. 1–25 (an argument with which I have reservations, as noted in fn. 794, p. 502 below).

97. The argument of the last five paragraphs is a restatement of part of my article 'Mau Maus of the mind', where full references will be found.

98. To adapt Kenneth Dike, the Nigerian historian, writing as early as 1953 and cited in L. Kapteijns, *African Historiography Written by Africans* (Leiden, 1977), pp. 23–34, 80. See also Chapter 9, above.

99. Rosberg and Nottingham, *Myth*, p. xv; Donald Barnett and Karari Njama, *Mau Mau From Within* (London, 1966), p. 492.

100. In the liberal canon I include, in order of publication, George Bennett, *Kenya, A Political History* (London, 1963), pp. 110–34; Rosberg and Nottingham, *Myth*; Sorrenson, *Land Reform*; M. Tamarkin, 'Mau Mau in Nakuru', *Journal of African History* 17(1) (1976), pp. 119–34; Ogot, 'Politics, culture and music'; B.E. Kipkorir, ' "Mau Mau" and the politics of the transfer of power in Kenya 1957–1960', *Kenya Historical Review* 5(2) (1977), pp. 313–28; Spencer, *KAU*; Kanogo, *Squatters*.

101. Among the radicals are to be found Barnett (but not Njama), 'An introduction' in Barnett and Njama, *Within*; F. Furedi, 'The African crowd in Nairobi: popular movements and elite politics', *Journal of African History* 14(2) (1973), pp. 275–90; *idem*, 'The social composition of the Mau Mau movement in the White Highlands', *Journal of Peasant Studies* 1(4) (1974), pp. 486–505; Maina wa Kinyatti, 'Mau Mau: the peak of African political organization in colonial Kenya', *Kenya Historical Review* 5(2) (1977), pp. 287–310; *idem, Thunder; idem*, 'Introduction' to his *Kenya's Freedom Struggle: The Dedan Kimathi Papers* (London, 1987), pp. 1–12; Furedi, *Mau Mau War*. Two more conventional Marxists are A.L. Njonjo, 'The Africanization of the "White Highlands": a study of agrarian class struggles in Kenya 1950–1974' (Princeton University PhD thesis, 1977), pp. 79–128; and D. Mukaru Ngang'a, 'Mau Mau, loyalists and politics in Murang'a 1952–1970', *Kenya Historical Review* 5(2) (1977), pp. 365–84.

102. Maina wa Kinyatti's 'Peak of African political organization' and Furedi's *Mau Mau War* are exceptions, arguing that Mau Mau's tribalism was indeed the polemical construction of the opponents of militant nationalism, whether the British or their alleged creatures, the African moderates.

103. Nobody has pursued St Clair Drake's 1954 suggestion that Kikuyu were conscious of regional deprivation in the pan-African context, in their envious self-comparisons with the Gold Coast; quoted in Robert Buijtenhuijs, *Le mouvement 'Mau Mau': une révolte paysanne et anti-coloniale en Afrique noire* (The Hague, 1971), p. 146.

104. F.B. Welbourn, 'The official history of Mau Mau' [a review of the Corfield Report], *Journal of African History* 2(1) (1961), p. 169; emphasis added. Compare Sorrenson, *Land Reform*, p. 51.

105. Rosberg and Nottingham, *Myth*, p. 3.

106. Fredrik Barth, 'Introduction' to *idem* (ed.) *Ethnic Groups and Boundaries: The Social Organization of Culture Difference* (Bergen, Oslo and London, 1969), pp. 9–10.

107. Barnett, 'Introduction' to Barnett and Njama, *Within*, pp. 28, 31; Rosberg and Nottingham, *Myth*, p. 217.

108. Mazrui, 'Conflict and the integrative process', p. 112.

109. This judgment is based on readings of Rosberg and Nottingham, *Myth*; Barnett and

Njama, *Within*, especially pp. 35–42; and transcripts of the oral sources for Spencer's *KAU*, which he has generously deposited with me. My own work at the time was just as Whig in its assumptions.

110. The 'groupiness' of 'the' Kikuyu in the texts under examination is here reflected in my own language, to disappear later.

111. Rosberg and Nottingham, *Myth*, pp. 145–52; Barnett and Njama, *Within*, pp. 42–9. The most detailed studies of Kikuyu life among students of Mau Mau are in Buijtenhuijs, *Mouvement 'Mau Mau'* and Greet Kershaw, *Mau Mau From Below* (in preparation), but their approach is quite different from those under discussion, as will be explained.

112. The Luo and possibly Luyia peoples had more mission-school places until the 1940s.

113. Donald C. Savage and J. Forbes Munro, 'Carrier corps recruitment in the British East Africa Protectorate 1914–1918', *Journal of African History* 7(2) (1966), p. 339; Anthony Clayton and D.C. Savage, *Government and Labour in Kenya 1895–1963* (London, 1974), p. 87; Kikuyu suffered this disproportionate mortality despite their relative success in avoiding military porterage through medical exemption and farm employment: see Geoffrey Hodges, *The Carrier Corps: Military Labor in the East African Campaign, 1914–1918* (New York, 1986), pp. 207–8.

114. Well described from official evidence in Throup, *Origins*, pp. 172–96; for African views see Luise White's sympathetic study of prostitution, *The Comforts of Home* (Chicago, 1990).

115. Kanogo, *Squatters*, pp. 96–120; Furedi, *Mau Mau War*, pp. 31–7, 47–65, 75–99; Throup, *Origins*, pp. 92–135.

116. Rosberg and Nottingham, *Myth*, pp. 237–8; G. Bennett, 'Revolutionary Kenya: the fifties, a review', *Race* 8(4) (1967), p. 416. D.W. Throup, 'The origins of Mau Mau', *African Affairs* 48(336) (1985), pp. 421–9 and *idem*, *Origins*, pp. 246–61, has latterly stressed the unevenness of enforced agrarian change in the 'second colonial occupation', for which see J.M. Lonsdale, 'Some origins of nationalism in East Africa', *Journal of African History* 9(1) (1968), pp. 141–6, and Low and Lonsdale, 'Introduction: towards the new order', in Low and Smith, *History of East Africa, vol. iii* pp. 12–16. For the 'much administered man' see, Rudyard Kipling, *Departmental Ditties* (Calcutta, 1892), p. 52.

117. Coleman and Rosberg, *Political Parties and National Integration*, p. 3.

118. Barnett and Njama, *Within*, p. 41; Rosberg and Nottingham, *Myth*, pp. 217–20, 348–54.

119. *Ibid.*, p. 242, for the nearest to class analysis; Barnett and Njama, *Within*, pp. 24–6.

120. Rosberg and Nottingham, *Myth*, pp. 208–10.

121. Barnett and Njama, *Within*, p. 35.

122. D.H. Rawcliffe, *The Struggle for Kenya* (London, 1954), p. 96; *Corfield Report*, p. 144; Sir Michael Blundell, *So Rough a Wind* (London, 1964), p. 83.

123. For studies in 'loss of control' see, Rosberg and Nottingham, *Myth*, pp. 220, 232–3, 243, 247–8, 271–5, 301; Barnett and Njama, *Within*, pp. 66–7; Spencer, *KAU*, pp. 172–84, 205–35; Tamarkin, 'Nakuru', pp. 123–8; Throup, *Origins*, pp. 240–1; Furedi, *Mau Mau War*, pp. 6–8, 88–92, 103–15.

124. First argued at any length by Rawcliffe, *Struggle*, and Evans, *Law and Disorder*, this insight was the organizing theme of Rosberg and Nottingham's *Myth*: see their introduction, p. xvii.

125. *Ibid.*, p. 188; compare Throup, *Origins*, p. 240.

126. Throup, *Origins*, pp. 144–62, for the politics of chiefship (but not of rural local government), and pp. 172–8 for the elite and the politics of opportunity in African Nairobi.

127. Sorrenson, *Land Reform*, p. 72; see also, Bennett, *Kenya*, p. 113; Rosberg and Nottingham, *Myth*, p. 216; Spencer, *KAU*, pp. 164–5 (who believed that had Kenyatta been

given a Legislative Council seat the Mau Mau war might not have occurred); but Throup, *Origins*, p. 51, thought that KAU had lost the ear of government before Kenyatta returned.

128. A phrase twice used in Rosberg and Nottingham, *Myth*, pp. 261, 265.

129. *Ibid.*, p. 261; Barnett and Njama, *Within*, pp. 63, 66. David Throup, reviewing Buijtenhuijs, *Essays*, in *Journal of African History* 25(4) (1984), p. 491, doubts that inter-ethnic oathing was being planned; but it must be remembered that Fred Kubai, the author of Mau Mau as much as any individual could be, had a mother from the coast and was brought up outside Kikuyuland: for him even a Kikuyu oath was cross-cultural. Conversely, the existence of an inter-tribal oath managed by the Kikuyu Central Association (KCA), the respectable elders' body against which Mau Mau revolted (see, Kaggia, *Roots*, p. 194) may be a misleading precedent. In 1939 the KCA printed multilingual oath forms, to be attested by signature. This was a ritual of literacy rather than ethnicity, entirely different from Mau Mau oaths: Governor Moore to Secretary of State, 4 August 1940; 'Third report of advisory committee . . .', 26 August 1940, paras 10–11: PRO, CO 533/523/38481.

130. This paragraph summarizes the arguments in Rosberg and Nottingham *Myth*, pp. 241–76; and Barnett and Njama, *Within*, pp. 66–7; for a local study of the same process, see Tamarkin, 'Nakuru'.

131. Rosberg and Nottingham, *Myth*, p. 268; Barnett and Njama, *Within*, pp. 51–5.

132. Rosberg and Nottingham, *Myth*, pp. 272, 286–92, 296–303, 320; Barnett and Njama, *Within*, pp. 71–2, 125–6, 149–56.

133. Corfield's language in explaining why members of other tribes did not join Mau Mau may explain why subsequent scholars have been reluctant to take much account of 'tribal character'. The Kamba, for example, were 'a very conservative race immune to alien influences', liable to 'infection by the Kikuyu virus' only when working in Nairobi; they otherwise preferred 'open expression of their grievances to secrecy, lacking the Kikuyu aptitude for intrigue'. The Maasai, normally 'contemptuous of the Kikuyu' were vulnerable when 'diluted': their 'half-breed' offspring of Kikuyu mothers were inclined to be 'malcontent' or 'disgruntled' and their subversion was overcome only by 'a fresh outburst of vitality' from purer Maasai. Among the Luo and Luyia 'professional agitators' had little influence on 'the stolid and slow thinking masses': *Corfield Report*, pp. 202–4, 208–10, 211.

134. It is reasonable to infer that, in stressing the rationality of Kikuyu politics and in differentiating Mau Mau from religious sects, Rosberg and Nottingham (*Myth*, pp. 324–31) were not only answering British propaganda but reassuring Rosberg's American colleague, Coleman.

135. *Corfield Report*, pp. 274, 284–5; Rosberg and Nottingham, *Myth*, pp. 294–6, 305–6; Barnett and Njama, *Within*, p. 154. The one book that has had much to say on the 'loyalists', Sorrenson's *Land Reform*, did so, one may suggest, precisely because it was not focused on the history of Kenya's nationalism.

136. MKEMSA, *Comment*, pp. 28, 51, 31, 35. The style of this pamphlet suggests that it was chiefly the work of Fred Welbourn, a Makerere lecturer and the author of *East African Rebels* (London, 1961), but the seven Africans (some with distinguished futures) who signed the preface claimed joint authorship. They apparently approved the term 'Nairobi thugs', lifted from the *Corfield Report*, p. 60.

137. MKEMSA, *Comment*, pp. 50, 38; and see Ian Glenn, 'Ngugi wa Thiong'o and the dilemmas of the intellectual elite in Africa: a sociological perspective', *English in Africa* 8(2) (1981), pp. 53–66, or David Maughan-Brown, *Land, Freedom and Fiction: History and Ideology in Kenya* (London, 1965), pp. 206–44, for more or less sympathetic comment on Kenyan novels that express similar elite dismay at leaderless masses. For a recent parallel, in which Professor Johan Heyns of the Dutch Reformed Church

in South Africa contrasted the 'rationality' of liberal multiracial theology with the 'emotionality' of Afrikaner 'religious fanaticism', see *The Independent* (London), 29 June 1990, pp. 11.

138. A discomfort of which Buijtenhuijs complained in *Mouvement 'Mau Mau'*, p. 157.

139. *Corfield Report*, ch. 9.

140. This and most of the other observations of this paragraph are taken from Barrington Moore, *Injustice: The Social Bases of Obedience and Revolt* (London, 1978), chs 1 and 3.

141. It was perhaps because of the felt need to counter the colonial conception of 'agitators' who 'manufactured' grievance that impersonal social rather than creative political mobilization was emphasized in the early studies of Mau Mau. For the nearest approaches to my own stress on the creativity of politics, see Furedi, *Mau Mau War*, p. 5; and Njonjo, 'Africanization', pp. 94–7.

142. To adapt the sources of 'bourgeois' moral outrage suggested in Moore, *Injustice*, p. 128.

143. Again, I am indebted to *ibid.*, ch. 5.

144. Theda Skocpol, *States and Social Revolutions* (Cambridge, 1979), pp. 14–18.

145. There are no reliable figures of Mau Mau fighters; it is probable that there were never more than 15,000 at any one time, which might mean that up to 30,000 had forest experience at some time. On official figures Mau Mau lost over 12,000 dead in action or by hanging; many of these however would not have been in the forests: *Corfield Report*, p. 316.

146. To anticipate the argument of Chapter 12, below.

147. J.P. Nettl, *Political Mobilization: A Sociological Analysis of Methods and Concepts* (London, 1967), ch. 8.

148. As well summarized in Donal Cruise O'Brien, 'Modernization, order and the erosion of a democratic ideal: American political science 1960-70', *Journal of Development Studies* 8(4) (1972), pp. 351–78.

149. This remains the view of what Crawford Young (*Politics of Cultural Pluralism*, p. 213,) has called the 'national mandarinate': see, Kenya High Commissioner to the Editor, *The Times*, 16 July 1990.

150. Kipkorir, ' "Mau Mau" and the transfer of power', pp. 313, 321; see also David F. Gordon, 'Mau Mau and decolonization: Kenya and the defeat of multiracialism in east and central Africa', *Kenya Historical Review* 5(2) (1977), pp. 329–48; M. Tamarkin, 'The loyalists in Nakuru during the Mau Mau revolt and its aftermath', *Asian and African Studies* 12(2) (1978), pp. 247–61. For a survey of British policy for this period, which supports such local-level conclusions, see John Darwin, *Britain and Decolonisation: The Retreat from Empire in the Post-war World* (Basingstoke, 1988), pp. 244–69.

151. As reported in the local press and quoted in Spencer, *KAU*, p. 243, n. 50; for Mbotela's translation of Paine: MKEMSA, *Comment*, p. 21, and E.S. Atieno-Odhiambo, 'Democracy and the ideology of order in Kenya', ch. 9 in Michael G. Schatzberg (ed.), *The Political Economy of Kenya* (New York, 1987), p. 185.

152. Ogot, 'Politics, culture and music', p. 286.

153. Kanogo, *Squatters*, pp. 149–52, 162–75.

154. Rosberg and Nottingham, *Myth*, pp. 350–4.

155. Jean-Francois Bayart, *L'état au Cameroun* (Paris, 2nd edn, 1985); also, Chapter 9, above.

156. Maina wa Kinyatti, *Thunder*, p. x.

157. Maina wa Kinyatti does not use the term 'false consciousness' in his three main analyses of Mau Mau, 'Peak of political organization' (1977); 'Introduction' to *Thunder* (1980); 'Introduction' to *Kenya's Freedom Struggle* (1987), but his reluctance to enter into discussion of cultural identity suggests that any hint of ethnicity may be an analytical embarrassment for him. For similar silent embarrassment, see Ngugi

wa Thiong'o, 'Mau Mau is coming back'; and Shiraz Durrani, *Kimaathi, Mau Mau's First Prime Minister of Kenya* (London, 1986). My criticism of the concept of 'false consciousness' comes later, pp. 350-3, below.

158. Furedi, *Mau Mau War*, pp. 5-6.
159. Barnett and Njama, *Within*, pp. 42-51; Furedi, *Mau Mau War*, p. 5.
160. Furedi, *Mau Mau War*, p. 8; emphasis added.
161. Maina wa Kinyatti's versions of 'Mau Mau patriotic songs' make only three references to Kenyatta: *Thunder*, pp. 47, 56-7. For direct comparisons on the naming of Kenyatta consult Leakey, *Defeating Mau Mau*, p. 69 and Maina wa Kinyatti, *Thunder*, p. 43; or *Thunder*, pp. 106-7 and Barnett and Njama, *Within*, p. 347. I have been unable to find the original texts that would fully resolve the question of the relative fidelity of their translators but, if Kinuthia Mugia has correctly reproduced his 1950s lyrics in his *Urathi wa Cege wa Kibiru* (Nairobi, 1979), pp. 58-73, then Leakey's versions are to be preferred to Maina wa Kinyatti's (but then Leakey also tried to conceal the role of his old friend Mbiyu Koinange in militant politics, nine times referring to him as M . . . in his translations; Leakey's role in the imaginative construction of Mau Mau is the current subject of research by Bruce Berman and myself). See also Buijtenhuijs' critical remarks on the radicals in his *Essays*, pp. 158-61. I am much indebted to Revd John Karanja for help in translation.
162. Ngugi wa Thiong'o, 'Mau Mau is coming back', p. 22.
163. Bethwell A. Ogot, 'History, ideology and contemporary Kenya' (presidential address to the Historical Association of Kenya, 27 August 1981).
164. To adopt the title of and signal a debt to Gareth Stedman Jones, *Languages of Class: Studies in English Working Class History 1832-1982* (Cambridge, 1983).
165. In his *Origins* and 'Moderates, militants and Mau Mau: African politics in Kenya 1944-52' (Northeastern University seminar paper, 1988, prelude to a full-length study that Dr Throup has kindly shown to me in early draft form); some of his approach is also to be found in Spencer, *KAU*.
166. Throup, *Origins*, p. 246.
167. The model was provided by Anil Seal, 'Imperialism and nationalism in India', in John Gallagher, Gordon Johnson and Anil Seal (eds), *Locality, Province and Nation: Essays on Indian Politics 1870 to 1940* (London, 1973), pp. 1-27.
168. Margery Perham, 'The struggle against Mau Mau, ii: seeking the causes and the remedies', *The Times* (London), 23 April 1953.
169. Throup, *Origins*, p. 175.
170. For the theoretical justification of such an approach, see Maurice Cowling, *The Impact of Labour 1920-1924* (Cambridge, 1971), pp. 1-12. For Throup's own fullest discussion see his 'The construction and destruction of the Kenyatta state' in Schatzberg (ed.), *Political Economy*, pp. 33-4.
171. For a wider discussion of high and deep politics see, John Lonsdale, 'Political accountability in African history' in Patrick Chabal (ed.), *Political Domination in Africa: Reflections on the Limits of Power* (Cambridge, 1986), pp. 126-57; this approach has been developed and given precision in Naomi Chazan, Robert Mortimer, John Ravenhill and Donald Rothchild, *Politics and Society in Contemporary Africa* (Basingstoke, 1988), chs 6 and 7.
172. Greet Kershaw, 'Mau Mau from below: fieldwork and experience 1955-57 and 1962' (forthcoming).
173. Buijtenhuijs, *Mouvement 'Mau Mau'*, p. 201.
174. This is Buijtenhuijs' general conclusion, in both his *Mouvement 'Mau Mau'* and his *Essays*.
175. Kershaw, 'Mau Mau from below'; this finding reinforces my methodological criticism of Furedi.

176. Kershaw's interpretation, like my own, emphasizes not cultural renewal but contested history.
177. Buijtenhuijs, *Essays*, p. 166; Coleman, 'Emergence of African political parties', p. 251, had said much the same.
178. Njonjo, 'Africanization'. In the same vein, at the local level, one may cite Mukaru Ng'anga, 'Mau Mau, loyalists and politics'. Both owe much to the data and ideas of the non-Marxist Sorrenson, *Land Reform*.
179. See Michael Cowen's many unpublished works, especially 'Differentiation in a Kenya location' (University of East Africa Social Science Council conference paper, Nairobi, 1972), and 'Capital and household production: the case of wattle in Kenya's Central Province 1903–1964' (Cambridge University PhD, 1979); Cowen's findings are most easily accessible through Gavin Kitching's *Class and Economic Change in Kenya: The Making of an African Petite-bourgeoisie* (New Haven and London, 1980); Njonjo also acknowledged important debts to the non-Marxist Sorrenson's *Land Reform* in his analysis of the 1950s.
180. Njonjo, 'Africanization', pp. 37–78; Kershaw's findings are strikingly similar, despite great differences in the geographical location of her data from Cowen's (eastern Kiambu district rather than northern Nyeri), method and theoretical approach.
181. To borrow a useful term from Professor Kershaw.
182. Njonjo, 'Africanization', pp. 79–128.
183. Kershaw, 'Mau Mau from below'.
184. An observation developed below, p. 453.
185. Njonjo, 'Africanization', pp. 395–400.
186. To recall this essay's preliminary texts.

studying the terms of this debate. What Kikuyu had to argue about is best approached by turning inside out the four dichotomies of modernization theory. We may then begin to see the real, lived, problems that Africans faced in the linked arenas of tribe, class, gender and state. We may also catch a glimpse of the uncertain terror that became horrific reality in the Mau Mau war. This approach may further, by an implicit extension not pursued here, lead to a rethinking of the wider meanings and processes of anti-colonial nationalism in Africa.

My argument starts from the premise, stated earlier, that the dialectic between tradition and modernity at the core of political science's old evolutionary myth was a self-serving construction. Its modernist logic showed why it was both necessary and desirable for African nationalists to model their future on the Western world. That is scarcely a sensational new finding, more a very dead horse. But it still lacks decent burial. A funeral oration – that is, a full revisionist thesis – has yet to be composed.

For Kenya it would read like this, a summary of the rest of this essay. First, empire did not foster the kind of nationalism that political scientists thought they ought to see. Structures that shaped political debate were not territorial but local, some officially recognized, others subversive; there was no coherent doctrine of modernization. Secondly, also contrary to evolution theory, ethnic thought had long addressed issues of civic rights and duties, inseparable from those of gender, with more passion than the extramural class of territorial nationalism could ever have done before independence. Kenya nationalism's chief tactician, Tom Mboya, openly admitted that his secret of success was political inanity. Once his colleagues had rid Africans of any sense of racial inferiority, he advised them to avoid 'discussion groups on policies' which invited 'differences and division.'[1] How to be Kenyan was deliberately made less contentious than how to be, for example, Luo.[2] Yet those ethnic questions became more contentious, not less. For the central stage in my argument is that ethnicity was not reduced to a residual category by the formation of classes. Indeed, tribe was the imagined community against which the morality of new inequality was bound to be tested.[3] The moral language of class could not be freely chosen. What ancestors had taught, or were said to have taught, on the relation between labour and civilization was the only widely known measure of achievement or failure in man- or womanhood. It was a test that male teachers and traders set for themselves and for women between the wars. To argue their case they reshaped ethnic institutions in the mind, enlarged a known vocabulary of reputation in order to dignify self-interest, and created tribal nationalism. At the heart of their new language were the old moral equations of wealth and virtue, poverty and idleness. Manual workers were later to find no better test to pass, having

failed to rewrite its rules. In the forests of Mount Kenya and Nyandarua
Mau Mau fought as much for virtue as for freedom. All this suggests, finally, that the chief fault of evolution theory was its belief that
religious – or at least, moral – projects would give way to merely
material self-interest. It has been persuasively argued more recently that
imagined nationhood has been the necessary modern means of mora-
lizing political economy.[4] The Kikuyu case suggests that, even then,
nationalism can raise terrifying doubts about its own moral authority,
if it is not knowably based on the common means of civic virtue. Nor
do Mboya's warnings suggest that Kenya's nationalism was well able
to calm such fears.

My argument has a conclusion, just as mortuary rites include prayers
for the living. It is that African states might do well to remember the
unquiet ethnic ancestors and their unfinished debates, which provide a
morally critical and locally resonant tradition for discussing a future
nation. What we may call the 'Mboya gap' between argued ethnicity
and undiscussed nation-statehood still needs to be closed.[5] This essay
purports to show that the very uncertainties of the ancestors caused them
to negotiate a political language that responded to social and political
change. But I must first admit how uncertain my own understanding
is of them.

Evidence

I have criticized the Western transubstantiations that have squeezed
African responses to colonial rule into the prefabricated, imported,
moulds of nationhood or class formation. Mau Mau's ethnicity fitted
neither. These misperceptions, as they seem to me, were servants or
critics of present power before they were arbiters of past evidence. My
aim is to use neglected evidence to widen the uses of the past. My sources
suggest that ethnicity was a question of honour within what have become
tribes before it was a weapon of conflict between them. It may be that
this inference can speak to the present formation of Kenya's civil society,
that network of public bodies which in any free country are autonomous
from the state yet enjoy from it protected rights of association and
debate.[6] As scholars once deplored ethnicity, so now the state con-
demns it as a sectarian snare in the path of a critically mature citizenry.
Government looks with suspicion on the institutions of civil society
as potential channels of tribalism. But my reading of history suggests
that ethnicity has been an arena of common moral debate as much as
a vehicle of unquestioning sectional ambition. Its deep political language
has followed an inner logic partly independent of the changing uses to
which its key concepts have been put in high politics. Its values have
fired, but also disciplined, ambition. If that be so, the study of an ethnic

imagination may not be so subversive of modern African states as is generally believed; it may be constructive. That is not for me to say. The immediate question is whether my reading of the past is any more reliable than those I have criticized. It is difficult to reply with confidence, for two reasons: the nature of the sources and my ability to interpret them.

There is no shortage of documentary sources for the study of modern Kikuyu political thought. There are several ethnographies.[7] Three generations of grievance are filed in the archives. Visiting commissions, which attested to British indecision over Kenya's future, printed Kikuyu evidence.[8] I have learned most from three newspapers, or their remnants that survive in translation. From the late 1920s there are a few precious issues of *Muigwithania*, 'The Reconciler' or 'Newsbearer', the monthly journal of the Kikuyu Central Association, whose first editor was Jomo – then Johnstone – Kenyatta.[9] Father Cavicchi has published excerpts from the Catholic *Wathiomo Mukinyu* ('True Friend'), covering two decades from the late 1920s.[10] For the post-war years I have used the weekly *Mumenyereri* ('The Guardian'), probably the most influential Kikuyu newspaper at the time.[11] Then there are memoirs, written with varying degrees of ghosted assistance and political calculation. Among the more helpful are three memories of squatter life on the 'white highlands';[12] five guarded political memoirs; [13] an account of detention and a prison camp diary;[14] eight recollections of the Mau Mau war, three by guerrilla officers, the rest by other ranks;[15] and two churchmen's lives, one a terse autobiography, the other an evocative biography of an early convert by his grandson.[16] Older Kikuyu also edified younger generations by retelling the folklore, customs and personal trials of former times.[17] Their lessons were epitomized in proverbs, of which one collection was made by Italian priests from the turn of the century and completed by newspaper competition in the late 1930s, the other in the 1960s.[18] Finally, and perhaps above all, there is the Bible, *Ibuku ria Ngai* or Book of God, a treasury of stories through which, in ways which I have yet to explore, its Kikuyu translators told their own tales of colonial rule, as in the Egyptian bondage or Babylonian exile, of the struggle for freedom in the wilderness of Exodus, and of battle with the dragon of their old religion.

The availability of source material, then, is not, at first sight, a problem. Its provenance and my critical abilities are. Sources, as scholars know, must be handled with caution. Their authors aim to persuade; wittingly or not, they embroider a tale. They extol their own virtues and blazon their opponents' crimes. They misunderstand or misremember what they report from others. They write from guilt, ambition and fear. They are also bridled by counter-argument, local rules of speech and imaginative traditions. Historians can exercise a critical judgment only when immersion in the sources gives them an easy familiarity with immediate polemical contexts, evolving conventions of argument and the latent springs of common thought, scarcely changing in generations, from which their subjects drew in order to add power to meaning. To Ogot, history is 'a discipline of context';[19] as for Cheney: 'records, like the little children of long ago, only speak when they are spoken to, and they will not talk to strangers'.[20] My attempt to rethink an ethnic past must be judged by such criteria. I must read the meanings of a succession of political texts within their polemical, discursive and moral environments. Such an aim is, to a dismaying degree, absurd.

My problem is simple to state, hard to solve. I can in fact see only that tiny proportion of past Kikuyu thought that was written, either statements made to white officials or missionaries that were thought worthy of record, or the direct thoughts (if often in translation) of literate 'readers' or *athomi*, who were a small minority until the 1950s. I cannot hear the daily clamour of the oral texts in which people conducted their lives. Kikuyu talked politics. Their political culture was oral. I have tried to read its documentary survivals. However adequate a primary bibliography I may seem to have, it is tiny by comparison with what I have not. Kikuyu made thought in writing; their thought was also made in daily life. If I am deaf to most of their intellectual effort, how can I know how dominant or deviant, creative or derived, is the fraction that I can see? The political thought that is available to me was clearly debated by men of power. They argued about sources of civic virtue, the basis of authority. They disputed the means and ends of power. Save for the brief period we know as 'Mau Mau', they also seem to have managed to exclude alternative, as distinct from rival, voices from the record. So far as I can tell, they did so by exercising oral authority and then by privileged access to literacy. Yet neither advantage can be assumed to be a straightforward measure of their intellectual sway in Kikuyu circles of argument, as a few examples will show.

The first white travellers, whose impressions did much to shape the terms of the Anglo-Kikuyu relationship, derived their image of Kikuyu from men who saw to it that theirs was the only received interpretation, who controlled commercial and political exchange by dominating the trade in knowledge. 'The Kikuyu' were first given to a Western public by three men in particular, Waiyaki wa (son of) Hinga, Kinyanjui wa Gatherimu and Karuri wa Gakure. Waiyaki befriended the earliest white visitors and officials;[21] Kinyanjui was the main prop of early colonial rule in southern Kikuyu;[22] Karure's trading network then guided a British sway over central Kikuyu.[23] They were all local spokesman or *athamaki*, the nearest any Kikuyu approached to chiefship. They conveyed an impression of a social order under their control, the asset that made their alliance worth having. Yet, disturbingly for the student of thought, each was to some degree a marginal man. Waiyaki's clan name, Hinga, 'dissembler' or 'hypocrite', was the nickname of the bilingual women who traded between Kikuyu and Maasai. Appropriately he now has two genealogies, one by descent from central Kikuyu, the other from Maasai.[24] Kinyanjui's clan also had Kikuyu and Maasai branches; Karuri was of Dorobo, hunting, extraction.[25] Orderly Kikuyuness was thus constituted by men whose interest, as middlemen, lay in stressing its contrast with their own trans-ethnic ingenuities. A further difficulty is illustrated by the fact that in 1892 British praise for industrious Kikuyu order was subverted by fear of Kikuyu guile, not because whites had met new sources of knowledge but because relations had soured with their chief informant, Waiyaki. Written Kikuyu thought has continued to be constructed in such devious ways. Its authors have had an eye to the reactions of outsiders; many have been of a status that commended them to the British, but not necessarily to Kikuyu, as knowledgeable social actors;[26] and their knowledge has often served intrigue.

The ethnographies are no easier to handle than the travellers' tales. They mostly report the opinions of senior men, rarely the participant observation that might have exposed the intellectual daring by which seniority was passed off as the simple heritage of tradition.[27] For none of these men was simply senior; they were also, however unwilling, junior partners in the colonial enterprise, and not to their own disadvantage. Ambition taught them that white enquirers could also be advocates if played aright. Then Christian *athomi* thought, of which Kenyatta's is best known, was governed by the fear of ostracism. Because many of their ways were both outrageous and externally protected, *athomi* treated local politics with extra care.[28] But I can deduce from this neither how far their romantic conservatism was true to the oral culture that was their judge nor, conversely, how much the systematic nature of their thought was alien to their unlettered kin, a tribute to literacy rather than to their grandparents' folklore. Again, one might take the fact that *athomi* were soon accepted as *aramati*, trustees of property-holding subclans and pillars of civic virtue, as proof of their deference to the elders' sway.[29] But, without access to clan gossip, one could as well argue that their nomination stemmed from a resigned calculation that, however offensive they were, they did at least know how to talk to Europeans. The written form of the Kikuyu thought to which I have access by itself guarantees unrepresentative witness. Naturally, Kikuyu memoirs rarely record the unlettered memories of poor men;[30] poor women have told their story only in response to scholarly enquiry.[31] But it is unclear how far voices that I rarely read were also whispers in that oral world that I cannot hear. The first woman (it seems) who wrote to *Muigwithania*, Wanjiru wa Kinyua, did so with heart in mouth. She had heard the paper read

out but no woman's voice in it. She feared editorial rebuke at a time
when many parents told daughters that school led only to prostitution.[32] But I cannot say if Wanjiru was nervous because she was
a woman or because educated girls had recently acquired a bad name.
It would be unwise to conclude from her anxiety, without other forms
of evidence, that her unlettered mother was also disregarded in the
household decisions that provided a core metaphor for Kikuyu politics.

The analysis that follows, then, gives weight to the words of senior
men, *athamaki*, and then leading Christian *athomi*, many of them eligible
to become clan *aramati*. Kikuyu will be unsurprised by the partiality of
my evidence; they learn that 'the poor man's tongue is always thin.'[33]
Poor men asked 'how can a man who is one goat speak to those who
are a hundred goats?'[34] So 'rich people . . . spoke and the others
listened,' as Kanogo's informants said of farm-squatter society.[35] Any
poor man who presumed to hold forth in public invited the retort, 'he
gives counsel in other people's homes while his own is going to ruin.'[36]
Such aphorisms bespeak a social inequality sharply observed. Yet the
common view of the Kikuyu has for long been one of an egalitarian,
harmonious, society. Some Kikuyu were clearly better than others at
stating their view of their world to strangers. They not only won an
argument about civic virtue, they seem to have silenced their critics. An
early official reported the worries of 50 chiefs and elders as '*the* Kikuyu
point of view'. They complained that wage labour had spoiled young
men who now ignored their seniors and thought only of themselves. It
did not apparently occur to the officer that young men, let alone women
of any age, might also have a view.[37] The essential unity, the 'essen-
tiality', of the native mind dominated official assessments of Kikuyu and
has not been absent from scholarly approaches either. We can more
safely assume that their unanimity was politically construed. But – to
restate my problem – it is one thing to be alert to a polemical context;
it is another to determine how wide was the consensus that made any
argument possible, how consensus was created, what alternative voices
there may have been and how they were suppressed.

I do not speak Kikuyu. I read enough to look up key phrases in the
dictionaries compiled by missionaries and their *athomi* mentors, some
of whom also explored the political uses of the new literacy.[38] I cannot
tell how forced my readings are or those of my translators, one of whom
was an Italian priest whose Kikuyu may have been as imperfect as his
English, and others special branch policemen. A few parallel texts,
Kikuyu and English, helped me to recognize the more persuasive figures
of speech. Kikuyu friends have responded generously to queries.[39] But
I remain haunted by the certainty of misunderstanding. I lack knowledge
of, let alone familiarity with, daily texts and contexts that had nothing
to do with external advocacy. Literate Kikuyu knew that their words

were weighed at this bar of oral opinion. *Muigwithania*, as Wanjiru noted, was read out in public; no newspaper or memoir can be fully understood without reference to its constantly cited oral archive of proverbial wisdom. As will become apparent, authors drew on a limited range of common meanings given by daily life. Some of my doubts about the possibility of reliable insight can therefore be resolved by the assumption that the authority of my fragment of Kikuyu thought was continually renegotiated within its raw material of vulgar speech; the little that I can see was tuned for a rhetorical resonance with what I cannot hear.[40] But that premise only exposes my weakness of method. This common tongue of argument remains for me a submerged medium full of unheard, perhaps dissident voices, with unwritten rules for testing interpretive authority. I cannot prove historically my theoretical assumption, that Kikuyu spokesmen competed for a constantly reformulated intellectual hegemony. I am left to appraise a limited range of texts on their own terms, while knowing that their authors were disciplined by what is to me the invisible grammar of Kikuyu political language as a whole.[41] Anxiety over this unsound procedure was not allayed by the repeated admonitions of *Muigwithania* that Kikuyu should learn English, with allusion to the proverb *gitigunaga muthiomeruo*: 'it is better to speak for yourself' or, more pithily, 'translators, traitors.'[42] Self-doubt has paralysed progress and caused endless delay in publication; the forbearance of my collaborator and publisher has been pushed beyond reasonable limit. This my apology, which one might otherwise be tempted to conceal under the modesty of a footnote, is also an invitation to Kikuyu scholars to speak for themselves in this matter and, meanwhile, a warning to readers. While it may appear that I know what I am saying, nothing that follows is at all certain.

The first stage of the argument, however, requires analysis not so much of Kikuyu thought as of British self-deception, for which I can claim some instinctive understanding. But Kikuyu, too, told a rude joke about the British conquest state. This drew on a rich vein of metaphor about gender and power and illustrated, better than any analysis, the gulf between the theory and practice of modernizing colonialism.

Imperialism and nationalism

Imperialism certainly imposed states on Africa, but historians have emphasized what political scientists left partly out of account, that colonies were conquest states.[43] Evolution theory liked the pedagogy of conquest, its power to persuade Africans to adopt political rather than military forms of protest. Historians are more impressed by the incoherence of conquest, its effect on white rulers. Conquest states wielded force outside daily life rather than persuasive power within. This was not a strength but a weakness.[44] Dominating networks of ethnicity, they lacked the curb of civil society organized in political parties, trades unions, professional associations or churches.[45] Without such political constraints, white rulers were deprived of social purchase. Their political domination could not enjoy moral mastery.[46]

Such empirical deflation at once sinks a silent premise of the modernizing myth. This required that colonialism conform to its officials' self-image as responsible rulers, obedient servants of their subjects. Their self-confident legitimacy rested on belief in themselves as bearers of bureaucratic probity, good government and the rule of law; as guarantors of free access to justice; as handymen of an economic growth that they once feared as a threat to social order but, after the Second World War, welcomed as the prerequisite of self-government; and, finally but above all, as men with a flair for coaxing assent, slow to anger and reluctant to force, as men, in short, within African life rather than above it, more true to the local genius for self-rule than their socially alienated, nationalist, rivals in power.[47] However much it was denied by taboos on inter-racial sexuality,[48] however often unmasked as self-deception at moments of despair and desire,[49] only this assumed inwardness of their presence allowed white officials to believe in the kind of civilizing mission that could be crowned by the cross-cultural gift of their own modernity.

The reality was different. Gentlemanly schooling and strict audit ensured that no officer made a fortune from government. There were no nabobs in the colonial service; a goat bag was poor substitute for the pagoda tree.[50] But the other legitimizing claims were largely false. The British did not rest their rule on legal–rational authority. Their public rituals were Christian, their schools employed missionary teachers. They could scarcely complain if they were frequently judged and generally found wanting by the saving promises of mission Christianity, a faith that fired many Africans and was not always mere pious disguise for self-interest on the part of whites.[51] When officials sought more power to get things done they tried to call up alternative ghostly energy in the ancestral form of clan solidarity.[52] Good government was also more personal than institutional.[53] Its rule of thumb was to trust the man on the spot. District officers did not follow district plans; they rode personal hobbyhorses of improvement, first, perhaps, pit latrines, now afforestation, then famine crops in a dizzying sequence of *wazimu wa mzungu*, white man's madness.[54] African land law grew in graft as prices rose.[55] Planned economic development after 1945 was racially unequal, socially oppressive, vigorously enforced and impatient of African opinion. True to its origins, the state launched a second colonial occupation.[56] It widened the racial division that it had first opened by introducing white settlement.[57] The state looked on expatriate farming and industry as dynamos of growth; officials had little power to soften the consequences for labour. Settlers revoked their squatters' rights, breaking the moral economy of highland manors before Mau Mau retaliated in more violent kind. Businessmen kept down costs with declining real wages, resisted trades unions and, as urban ratepayers, were slow to improve their workers' stinking slums. Until peasant protest forced a change of tack, the improvement of African farming was entrusted to rules and fines, for lack of any faith, from the highest official to the least, in enlightened peasant self-interest.[58] In the inner councils of state the KAU was barely listened to after 1947.

Governing structure, no less than ruling policy, made Kenya an unpromising site of modernizing nationalism. In some respects Kenya was a late-colonial, centralized state. Government answered to an electorate, restricted to whites and Asians until 1957. In others, in which most Africans had their official dealings, it remained an early-colonial, segmentary, authoritarian state. It was not, nor was it intended to be, a single framework of rules and resources that would, through a central representative logic, act as midwife to a unified nationalism. That is the problem with evolution theory's escape clause, that the colonial mould was uneven. It was, but, more important, it was spatchcocked together from different designs. Late colonial states suffered from the very confusions of ideology and structure that were condemned in African nationalism.[59] They had no one set of values to allocate, no one public doctrine for nationalism to adopt. Tribe flourished more on the incoherence than the unevenness of the state.

In Kenya the greatest structural incoherence lay in the law. By 1945 it no longer protected even those rights that the colonial moral economy had earlier established; it more often served those who now expropriated them, white farmers and lineage seniors. Magistrates presided over this conflict between law and custom with the uneasy conscience that made even property owners fear for the future. Settlers were the more determined to shed obligations to their squatters, lineage elders to repudiate kinship with their juniors, lest the customary claims of clients should soon be protected in law.[60] Evolution theory demanded too much enlightenment from social change, forgetting the reaction of institutions. The arbitrary nature of colonial rule gave no assurance that the citizenship of the common man was more rational a goal than that of the tribesman. Whites and blacks both had reason to mistrust the state. The self-help of each, which substituted for political confidence, fed the desperation of the other. The imagination of local resistance was nourished, the aspirations of wider nationhood starved. That was Tom Mboya's problem. He and his colleagues had no single political language by which to discipline their differences.

That is why African politics in Kenya took the forms that it did.

Political structure fostered some political languages and stultified others. Some enlargements of civic imagination were likely, others not. Most politicians sought security, wealth and virtue at the local, district, level. The unsung success story of the postwar years is the Kenyan state's regional accommodation with all its ethnic nationalisms except the white and Kikuyu.[61] White nationalists would not relax their central grip on a state that was so nearly theirs. Kikuyu nationalists and their supporters were too opposed by interest and dispersed outside their homeland for them to be able to patch up working compromises with the meagre material of district politics. Kikuyu politics was more violent than race relations. Since a local concordat with the state was impossible, the local bases of resistance to it grew. They had a lively language of the imagination on which to draw.

The ribald legend of local resistance to the chieftainess Wangu wa Makeri is the best comment on the barbarous structure of the state. It derides the modernizing myth. It is also a story that, in successive versions, has allowed Kikuyu to argue their own political theories in the guise of history. The British made Wangu one of their earliest chiefs in Fort Hall district (now Murang'a) because of her alliance with the local paramount Karuri. She also befriended the nearby Anglican mission; some say she had a baptismal name, Mary.[62] In what may be its earliest and most enduring form, the story goes that the men whom she ruled on behalf of the British, goaded by her tyranny, tricked her into dancing naked the *kibaata*, a dance reserved for male warriors in their finery. Wangu was shamed into resignation. This version was current in the 1940s, during the second colonial occupation.[63] It encoded British rule not as modern promise but, for men at least, as ancient threat. The scabrous tale linked female sexuality and untamed nature to an external force that Kikuyu men could control only by asserting their own civic virtue. It reminded them of an older legend of how, soon after the dawn of time, they were subject to cruel matriarchy.[64] Mau Mau then raised new questions about Wangu. In 1952 the press advertised a seminar about her.[65] In the forest war she became a symbol of women's power. Some guerrillas called the army Wangu's men, to insult the British queen; others named their own women's group Wangu, presumably to praise them.[66] This debatable Wangu emerged in a new fable, a chief still hard but now dignified, who respected the rights and duties of gender, who neither slept with men nor allowed 'loose jokes', yet deferred to male sensibilities by wearing men's clothes when on duty.[67] She may have been a Mau Mau Wangu, a sexually self-disciplined warrior; or, given the missionary source, a loyalist queen who ruled well. In the 1970s she gave her name to land-buying companies in which political ambition solicited the investments of the poor.[68] Another ambiguous Wangu has since appeared in popular drama, a dressy queen, faithful widow and caring mother, resistant to colonial rule but who, when betrayed by a collaborator chief, was prepared to outbid his friendship with the British, dine at the fort, and warn the white man of the wrath (of Mau Mau) to come.[69]

Wangu has been a fascinating magnet for enquiry into the relations between gender and power. Her single story, made and remade, intertwined the inner and outer strands of politics. Her changing image crystallized shifting reflections on how civic virtue or shame could build or destroy fruitful relations with the state. That was what distinguished ethnic nationalisms from territorial nationalism. Political entrepreneurs found that ethnicity furnished an imaginative political vocabulary with much deeper mythical and historical echoes than any joint experience of labour or subjection to the state. Ethnic political imaginations could be unified. As Kenyans, Africans had to use two vocabularies, outer and inner. The former was simple to use, the lexicon of native rights against foreign rule. The latter, the language of political community, was difficult to invent. Wangu was not available to unite them. Mboya was realistic, not cynical, in his recognition that, while tribe was a field of argument, the nation was better served at the time by a chorus of slogans.

Nation and tribe

This chapter will not explain Mau Mau. It hopes to uncover the moral and intellectual context in which explanations may be found. These will have to be as attentive to political imagination as to political calculation. I hope to explain why Sam Thebere, a former guerrilla, answered the question 'Why did you join Mau Mau?' with the twofold reply: 'to regain the stolen lands and to become an adult.'[70] He gave Mau Mau's open purpose and its inner meaning. His political language, like that of colleagues who ruminated on Wangu, linked external power to internal virtue. His personal maturity depended on a public power to win land. A common name for Mau Mau was *ithaka na wiathi*, generally translated as 'lands and freedom'. It is better rendered as 'self-mastery through land', a paraphrase of Thebere's reply. *Wiathi* is moral agency.[71] It was exercised by elders, the *athuuri* or 'those who choose', men who had earned the freedom to judge without fear.[72] So Thebere saw land, *ithaka*, as a challenge to moral growth, *wiathi*. He linked wealth and virtue. These marks of authority were embodied in two Kikuyu institutions. Land was controlled by hundreds of subclans, *mbari*. Moral and political time was incarnate in age and generation sets, *riika*. Together, but in tension, *mbari* and *riika* provided the rules and resources of social standing and moral growth for men and women. And if Sam Thebere wanted to become adult, he had to be a man. In

a human-powered cultivating economy, where most labour was
recruited by marriage and procreation, civic virtue required proper
gender relations. In the 1930s Kenyatta centred his analysis of Kikuyu
society on the successful, polygamous, household. Male mastery in the
home proved ability to manage public affairs. Productive wives nursed
this ambition with hospitality, fruitful mothers gave it a future.[73]
Women's roles in cultivating wealth and reproducing labour earned
them civic virtue, too.[74] When, at a KAU meeting in 1951, Kenyatta
drew the political moral, he fused together the language of gender,
virtue, wealth and power: 'You must rule yourselves in your own lives
if you want to rule the country.'[75] All in all, therefore, Thebere gave
a full reply.

His answer was, nonetheless, incomplete. He left silent the unknowable part which has, since independence, been resolved in the minds of
many former insurgents as a sense of betrayal. *Ithaka na wiathi* was
scarcely a simple statement of purpose and meaning, but it implied a
yet more complex issue of power. Mau Mau raised the question whether
moral maturity was sufficient title to share in the gains of collective
action. Kikuyu gained maturity by pain, the initiation rite of circumcision.[76] Kenyatta had held that circumcision conferred equal rights of
Kikuyu citizenship.[77] That is what a cultural nationalist would think,
or at least say. And Kikuyu implied a faith in such rights when they
asked, 'are you circumcised?' to learn if a friend had been recruited by
Mau Mau.[78] But true, *karing'a*,[79] Kikuyu identity had never been
unquestioned. What it was to be Kikuyu had ever been invented and
disputed; it was yet more so by 1950. Household heads who still had
enough land to endow their grandchildren were no doubt content for
Kikuyu identity to be a propertied confederation of subclans, *mbari*, in
which they had themselves earned seniority. Men who could not hope
to inherit enough land to support even a household of their own, and
whose wage employment had separated their labour from the domestic
moral accumulation of *wiathi*, seem to have put their trust in the tribal
collegiality of age or generation, *riika*. What was terrifying was that
reliance could no longer be put on either concept of community to deliver
adult rights to all, to women still less than to men. Men like Thebere
could not guess what else, beyond their manhood, they had to offer, or
to whom, in order to win a chance of civic virtue by farming the 'stolen
lands' of the white highlands. This unaccountable, amoral, context of
political choice was not new. In the past deference, if not servility, was
the price which many would have to pay in order to survive famine.
But few Kikuyu before the 1940s will have had to reflect quite so bitterly
on the human tragedy of solidarity betrayed that they pictured in the
saying, 'Birds which land together fly up separately' or: 'helpful age-
mates become rival householders.'[80]

327

Kikuyu were not alone in their predicament. All ethnicities are inwardly disputed, not least when they fire outwardly combative tribalism or are taught, as patriotism, by nation states. And ethnicity is universal; it gives the identity that makes social behaviour possible. All socialization is a dual process of example and emulation that teaches relationships, proper ways of doing things. It instructs by moral exclusion; what is 'not done' is separated from what is 'done', what is done by 'others' is not done by 'us'. That much might be generally agreed by students of identity. What divides them is its political history. Evolution theory took the rational view that identity followed a materially enlightened interest in smooth dealing in market and state; it must therefore expand (always expand) as they did. But identity is less predictable than that.[81] People can equally well abandon or restate an identity in order to enter larger arenas of skill and power. Distinctive ethnicities may either give both parties the comparative advantage that protects free trade and mutual respect, or be stirred into the fear and loathing that does not shrink from genocide. Within ethnic groups, one appeal to past identity may defend traditional hierarchy, another demand the equally traditional – or invented – rights of all free-born fellow countrymen. Unsurprisingly, recent work on identity and ethnicity stresses these contingencies. It comes in the wake of the factual disproof – and not only in Africa – of the predictive evolution theory that constructed the ideal model of African nationalism and the deviance of Mau Mau.[82]

The modernist thesis contrasted tribe and nation; the contrast constituted them both. Ethnicity reflected the isolation of closed minds, nationhood a commerce of people and ideas. Tribes were traditional, nations modern. Tribes were bound by kinship and religion, not open to renegotiation. They measured social status by birth rather than merit. They saw no virtue in citizenship.[83] Ethnicity also had an engaging primordial innocence. Tribal law met social need rather than political demand. Colonial rule and markets usurped social function. Tribal structures must collapse and ethnic identity with them. Detribalized people were morally adrift; pan-ethnic nationalism taught them how to think about politics for the first time.[84] If tribes persisted into and against the spirit of the nationalist era, then their ethnicity was no longer innocent; it too was taught. The progressive mind thought nationalist education enlightened, tribal teaching obstinate. The growing study of ethnicity, no less than the plain speaking of Tom Mboya, suggests that we ought to distrust such polarity of judgment.

The relation between ethnicity and politics was nowhere more varied than in precolonial Africa. Contrary to the first claim of evolution theory, ethnicity rarely encased political isolation. In much of eastern Africa, and in all of what became Kenya, ethnicity was wider than politics. Areas of linguistic, economic and social similarity were large, political groups within them small. Daily life took little heed of ethnicity; people could only cope with relations of production and destruction that were much smaller in reach than the ethnic group within which they first looked for wider, but intermittent, support. But, secondly, their world was anything but narrow. When East Africans said, as many did, 'we marry our enemies', they did not speak of the battle of the sexes. They meant that the politics of kinship pursued strategies of trust between strangers. People looked for insurance against hard times by opening, in seasons of plenty, distant networks of marriage and trade. These created mutual obligations within the wider ethnic group. The wealthy could also afford to reinsure themselves by ties with ethnic strangers who followed materially different ways of life in other ecological zones. Drought and disease were feared by all, randomly localized in the event. Indebtedness to outsiders swung this way and that; varying geographies of famine would even it out to a moral reciprocity over time. Ethnicity both marked frontiers and negotiated their transit. People could move from one way of life to another by rites of separation from old social ties and adoption into new.[85] As to goods, barter terms of trade allowed each party to make an arbitrage profit from the different value that was put on, say, stock and grain on either side of an ecological divide. Thirdly, therefore, all ethnicity had about it some creative thought, an eye to the reciprocal bargains of mutually restrictive practice. All groups distinguished between core values and uncouth expedients. Wealthy leaders reinforced the former; the poor often had to resort to the latter, borrowing strange customs to survive. Nonetheless, most powerful men conducted their affairs in several ethnic circles of alliance. Wealth, personal reputation and social insurance came from bridging ethnicity; a narrow ethnic loyalty could invite destitution.[86] European nations were shaped by their competitive state system. East African ethnicities evolved in a world of inter-ethnic relations. There was nothing innocent in their origin, nothing wicked in their modern persistence. Ethnicity is less different from nationality than modernization theory required.

What most distinguishes them are their historical connections with modern states and capitalisms. Once larger than politics, African ethnicity in modern times became an inspiration to local politics and then the divisive symbol of tribal access to the partible goods of the state. This conversion of negotiable ethnicity into competitive tribalism has been a modern phenomenon. It mirrored the growth of the state. Tribe was not so much inherited as invented. Another temple of the old modernist myth lies in ruins. Its historiographical rebuilding rests on three premises. The first is that all politics is local, all experience understood through familiar symbols.[87] Next, as state power has grown, so too have public demands for associations through which either to influence or resist it. Evolution theory noticed only the former goal because political scientists were then less aware of the oppressive nature of colonial states. To influence states civic imaginations had logically to grow; to resist, they might as well develop at more local levels. Finally then, what ensured that such political imaginations and associations would in Africa be more local than 'national' or territorial was that African colonial history was not that of 19th-century Europe. Contrasting capitalisms and the rise of differing states prepared seedbeds for divergent nationalisms. Industrialization created national markets of ambition in Europe; industry then financed states that could reinforce this spur to national identity with the conformities of mass education and conscription for patriotic war.[88] In contrast, Africa's labour markets were often either smaller or much larger than the bounds of individual colonies; its colonial states had little centralizing purpose or power to set against the moral pull of the ethnic diaspora created by labour migration. External and internal incentives to enlarge identity were therefore strongest at levels other than that of states, principally in provincial localities. External ethnicity was the form of the politics of access to the state; it was pursued in tension with an 'interior architecture'[89] of civic virtue. To take first the exterior architecture, tribe became the prevailing metaphor for conflicting strategies of colonial control, and African opportunity and defence.[90]

THE EXTERIOR ARCHITECTURE OF TRIBE

Colonial officials drew local boundaries of control round invented ethnic provinces, tribal districts and, within each district, a dozen or more clannish rural 'locations' under official chiefs. Chiefs collected tax and recruited labour within these smallest circles. At the wider levels provincial and district commissioners codified the law. At all levels the British hoped to profit by the natural conformities that they thought 'tribal custom' ought to provide. Employers then tried to pin down the confusing anonymity of migrant workers by inventing stereotypes that predicted which tribesmen would best perform what job. Missionaries outlined economical geographies of evangelism by standardizing local dialects into sacred languages of print, bound in tribal Bibles. Cattle quarantines and famine regulations reduced interethnic trading contacts. In these and other ways white rulers, wittingly and unwittingly, reconstructed loose African ethnicities as restrictive tribal control.

Africans seized opportunities of state power and market gain. They did so at various levels that, together, structured a political arena. Their conflicts with each other were sharpest in the parochial arenas of the locations. It was here that state power, in the form of chiefship, was most concentrated in African hands and where the ordinary frictions of rural life, therefore, became most politicized. In competitions for chiefship and council seats, clans became factions.[91] Paradoxically, occupational interests were better pursued under the assumed name of tribe. Workers, literates, and farmers all had good uses for the idea of tribe. Far from home, workers exploited employers' stereotypes as a surrogate trades unionism with which to negotiate tribal closed shops and wage differentials. At the regional level Christians used literacy as a medium with which to search the ethnic past for a share in the tribal future, retelling biblical parables in the guise of local folklore. Farmers took to the cash crops that did best in the local ecology. They invented new market identities, 'cotton tribes' or 'coffee tribes' and so on, selling less to their ethnically distinct neighbours and more to foreign buyers or state marketing agencies. Tribes of new worker, clerical and agricultural interest thus formed to exploit advantage in the wider markets for labour and produce. Exterior opportunity helped to inspire ethnic identity; this ethnicity of enterprise also reshaped internal politics when coalitions of interest entered the clannish politics of colonial control. The different layers of opportunity, parochial, regional or territorial, gave a connective context to otherwise local disputes; these began to be seen as successive episodes in a new tribal political tradition.

Defensive strategies also sharpened awareness of ethnicity. People kept a fearful eye on chiefs who used state power to forward private or clan interests. They could load colonial demands on others and exploit public goods for themselves, especially by influencing court decisions on property. In their occupational concerns people found that ethnicity again had its uses, defensive against external threat and protective of internal rights. Workers lowered the external costs and domestic risks of entry into distant labour markets, Christian *athomi* fought off ostracism. Migrant workers looked to an ethnic rather than narrow clan identity to find a wide enough circle of trust with which to face the dangers of travel and their ignorance of town, making friends from this expanded definition of home. They could then use workplace friendships to conduct the clannish politics of the law, to protect land rights that may have been challenged in their absence. *Athomi* similarly combined the defensive politics of ethnicity and kinship. They demanded redress of colonial grievance in the name of tribal associations. They deployed the virtue thereby won in clan politics, pressing fathers not to deny a patrimony to Christians who, though delinquent sons, were tribal patriots.[92]

Tribe imprinted the imagination of Kikuyu as much as anyone else. They were 'the Kikuyu' as never before. This was no relict identity from another age, bound to fade into romantic memory,[93] but a new means of exerting some, by no means illusory, control over the future. The dynamic external architecture of identity is now broadly understood, as sketched above. This essay explores the less familiar interior design. I have claimed that the imaginative architecture of identity arose out of Kikuyu debates about civic virtue in changing times, and that this moral concept disciplined recruitment to and expectations of leadership. One needs to know what they said about politics before colonial rule. The later 19th century was a time of change as dramatic as colonial rule. But Kikuyu were in control. Their senior men profited from change. They monitored what little the first Europeans learned of Kikuyuland. Their successors, colonial chiefs and elders, filled out that knowledge. What follows, again, is based largely on the *athamaki* point of view, and not that of precolonial spokesmen either. The received ethnography on which I have to rely is a self-serving charter by which colonized Kikuyu spokesmen tried to renegotiate their present colonial relations, to secure more say over the future.

This repeated warning is not, however, a surrender to despair at the impossibility of recovering the construction of precolonial political thought. For one can have some sense of the limits of political imagination that Kikuyu spokesmen were able to explore when justifying or criticizing their social order. This flickering critical confidence first came with the discovery of the evocative power of one of their core symbols. Trees, particularly their stumps and roots, exercised a fascination beyond all power of free invention. Their nightmare role in tales of virtue's war with nature seems to indicate, instead, that common meanings governed creative thought, whether conservative or radical. The pervasive imagery suggests a grip on the popular mind, not that Kikuyu were all of one mind. In their polemical allusions to trees and roots Kikuyu leaders showed an awareness that expository discipline might serve intellectual sway. Perhaps they reminded themselves that *muregi gwathwo ndangihota gwathana*: who refuses to obey cannot command.[94]

ROOTS OF VIRTUE

Under police interrogation, the captured Mau Mau fighter Nyagiko was forced to lift a tree stump. It was torture.[95] Her own resistance to the state was an allegory of her people's labours against the wild. Kikuyu police informers were also known as stumps.[96] They obstructed collective politics, as roots hindered the levelling work of agrarian civilization. Mau Mau units that fought in the Kikuyu reserve were named the Kenya Levellation Army: they were to uproot loyalists.[97] Years earlier, Kikuyu had used the evidence of tree stumps turned up by the plough to prove the extent of their cultivation before the white men came.[98] But some trees caused them to admit collective defeat. Popular psychology held that the forest of the soul could be cleared only by the individual afflicted.[99] And one tree was fixed in cosmic terror. An awful curse consigned an enemy to *miri ya mikongoe*, the roots of a mythical tree that reached down into the unknown, entwined with the origins of death.[100] The young journalist Kenyatta enjoyed using it as a figure of speech.[101] As president of KAU he later hurled it against

Mau Mau. The British did not think he meant it. Mau Mau leaders shared his rhetorical tradition, took him at his word and warned him to desist. One of them, Bildad Kaggia, later used the title of his autobiography as a punning riposte to Kenyatta, the only safe criticism of the now president of Kenya. The *Roots of Freedom* or *miri ya wiathi*, the back-breaking source of self-mastery and a metaphor for Mau Mau, represented not death but the fight against it.[102] The British had no comprehension of this division in Kikuyu political thought over the issue of violence, even if they too, like Kikuyu, could read Mau Mau as a symbolic war of the trees. The owner of the Treetops hotel remembered the first Queen Elizabeth under the Hatfield oak when the second Elizabeth became his Queen early in 1952, watching game from up in the *mugumo* fig tree. In a probably republican gesture, Mau Mau burned down the hotel two years later. Some settlers thought the Emergency finally done when their Queen Mother visited the rebuilt Treetops in 1959.[103] A white town council propped up a fig tree whose fall, according to a Kikuyu seer, would signal the end of British rule. And when the policeman Henderson hunted down the Mau Mau general Dedan Kimathi, the general's favourite *mugumo* prayer tree fell.[104]

Hard labour gave this imagery power. A British military handbook gave more space to the problem of clearing trees than to the organization of Mau Mau. It advised soldiers to use hand tools only against smaller trees. Bulldozers could remove trunks up to a half metre wide; explosives cut the time to fell and stump a larger tree to only 40 man-minutes.[105] Without machinery, guncotton or matches, it had taken Kikuyu up to two man-days to fell a single tree; and up to 150 man-days, with fire, axe and crowbar, to clear the three acres of forest land that a mother needed to feed her family. Cleaning fallow land could be even more arduous, as weeds were harder to get rid of than bush.[106] Clinical psychiatry was therefore much misled when asked by the British to advise on counter-insurgency. Dr Carothers thought that the solitary Kikuyu under their trees might have a 'forest psychology', given to 'rumination on more personal lines, to secretiveness, to suspicions and to scheming.'[107] To the contrary, Kikuyu forest-clearing culture rested on the collective exertions of labour, debate about the relations between individual and community, and respect for the sociable ability to cultivate private wealth from the wild.

Kikuyu were aggregations of immigrants whom centuries of toil and argument forged into what they and others recognized to be a people. Ngugi, whose novels breathe earnest *athomi* thought, extols 'man's holy sweat', his 'eternal wrestling with nature'.[108] Ever since agricultural pioneers first hacked a clearing in the Kikuyu forests, early in our era's second millennium,[109] homesteaders had sweated culture from nature. Struggling also for meaning, they evolved a labour theory of value, both material and moral.[110] They acquired property right in two closely linked ways, with a morality to match. The direct investment of human toil gave right of first clearance, *kuna*. Its moral basis was persevering self-discipline. Wamugumo, the herculean folk-hero of Kikuyu labour, could hoe like ten men, kill wild animals single-handed, and gulp five gourds of porridge at a sitting.[111] Property could also be bought. The transfer of domestic livestock compensated a landseller with the capital accumulation of past labour and claims in labour to come. It was said that *mwendi mburi ni murimi*, 'he who farms loves goats'.[112] Livestock were both farm profits and the currency of kinship. Marriage was sealed by transferring some from the man's family to the woman's. Family labour maintained title to land. Purchase by livestock, therefore, was another way of making the equation between land and its deserving people. It was not the law. Kikuyu lacked the rule-making and coercive institutions for that, nor was land a scarce resource. They respected, rather, land relationships between people. These could be entered into under the potentially competitive principles of descent, service and purchase. Where purchase was by a corporation of non-kin, their commitment was strengthened by an *mbari* oath. All land relations were witnessed by kin, protected by beneficial occupation and, in case of dispute, argued by senior elders in their localities.[113] The moral economy of family labour was obedience through time, as stock was labour through time. Fathers, it was said, worked for their sons, earning the next generation's bridewealth.[114] Remembered ancestors were *atiga iri na iriiri*, 'those who left property and upbringing', wealth and virtue.[115] Juniors, children and clients, were expected to give obedience in return. Households had to be ruled; deference brought forth productivity, disobedience shame.[116] It was criminal to stand by while others worked; thieves were 'onlookers'.[117] Peasantry had no room for slackers; there were 'no free things'.[118] Obedience not only taught self-mastery; working one's own land also gave identity, self-respect.[119] 'What would a woman be,' one asked a British officer, 'if she did not work?'[120] Wamugumo practised *ithaka na wiathi* long before Sam Thebere fought for it; and Kikuyu ethnographies used to read like the rules of harmony because that was the elders' dream.

Labour could not by itself create Kikuyu. It gave them something to argue about. They were brought together by the demands and opportunities of forest clearance. Only then did they become *Agikuyu*, less a boast of ancestral descent than a claim to farming skill. They were people who knew how to civilize the land where the *mukuyu* fig trees grow, to which they brought their harvest offerings.[121] It was higher than the malaria and tsetse-fly belts of the encircling pastoral plains whence most of them had come.[122] But within the highland ecological zone nothing was determined, all was open to challenge. Kikuyu had another name

for themselves, *mbari ya atiriri*, 'the clan that is called to order'.[123]
Orators always began with the summons *atiriri Agikuyu*, 'hear, O people
of Kikuyu'. White visitors first heard it in 1887,[124] witnessing the
reiterated rhetorical invention of a people. It is a common phenomenon,
like national anthems. The biblical 'Hear O Israel' had the same
purpose. In the 1940s the several 'Nandi-speaking peoples' began
to recognize a common ethnicity in the same way. Their new name
Kalenjin, 'I say to you', was the opening phrase in wartime radio
talks.[125] Kikuyu were called to a social order by means of debate.

They had much to argue about, the cultural and moral pluralisms of
ethnicity. Cultural complexity arose from migration and a mixed economy. Successive waves of immigrants had had to negotiate the terms
of their superiority or submission to local conventions in order to gain
a footing.[126] These debates – whose existence I infer from ethnographic
confusion in the literature – reduced Kikuyu diversity not to conformity
but to ways of accepting and using difference. Kikuyu had an unusual
number of rival institutions or conflicting social concepts within which
to pursue their competitions in wealth and power. There can be no better
example of the cultural pluralism of ethnicity. They disagreed on their
origins and about their loyalties to kith and kin; they distinguished 'true'
Kikuyu from others; and sneered at each other's barbarities of speech.
Their differences are not to be explained by their mixed origins alone.
In these they were no different from other African peoples. But the
availability of forest land and livestock as reward for labour service meant that the mixture was continually enriched by immigrants,
orphans, pawned women and masterless men who had lost their stock
to drought, disease or war in the plains.[127] Ranged behind usefully different symbols of social order, it seems that Kikuyu debate about social
incorporation and individual autonomy was never done.

Kikuyu held incompatible beliefs about their origins. Some myths
claimed a single descent from Gikuyu and his wife Muumbi, the 'potter'
or moulder of culture, through the 'nine clans' or *mihiriga* mothered by
their daughters. But the contrasts in diet, skills and character popularly
ascribed to these clans were better explained by other myths that held
that each *muhiriga* embodied a different stream of immigration.[128] This
cultural tension may have been little more than a source of political
humour; the next posed a daily conflict of loyalties. Kikuyu say that one
cannot contract out of family or age set,[129] property and time. In other
words, they saw no escape from the contradictions of obedience and
ambition or household autonomy and collective action, which were
probably sharper for women than men. History had given Kikuyu the
rare combination of both strongly conceived subclans and vigorous age
sets, and not only these but the quite different institution of generation
sets too.[130] The *mbari* subclans, notionally segments of the 'nine clans',

were, like pioneering 'houses' of cultivators all over forest or savanna Africa, corporations rather than lineages. Each was a mosaic of patrilineal descent, affinal alliance and unequal patronage. The assimilative but demanding ideology of kin and lineage held them together. Age and generation sets had been adopted from the surrounding pastoral peoples with whom Kikuyu traded, intermarried and from whom in part they came. Chronological age sets, male and female, were normally formed in annual sequence by post- and pre-pubertal initiation respectively. In each male age set there would have been roughly equal numbers of two different generation sets. These were designated by birth in alternating opposition, father and son, but came to political life only at irregular intervals, possibly in response to crisis, when their effective members were already senior elders.[131] Useful on the plains for enlisting the warrior manpower of herders, *riika* could as well rally collective bursts of forest-clearing labour.[132] Kikuyu also seem to have had a welcoming immigration policy. This both incorporated ethnic strangers and enabled Kikuyu down on their luck to make a 'symbolic emigration', becoming therapeutic strangers in order to improve their fortunes. Parallel initiation guilds made this two-way ritual passage possible. The *karing'a* guild for 'pure' Kikuyu was more costly in livestock fees than the *ukabi*, Maasai, guild but it does not appear that *ukabi* membership, whether by ethnic immigrants or therapeutic converts, invited civic disability.[133] Perhaps that degree of toleration was only to be expected in a hybrid people who argued about their borrowed institutions in a mongrel tongue divided by dialect.[134]

Nor did their labour theory inspire Kikuyu with puritan disdain for non-cultivating strangers, rather the reverse. Their most intimate 'others' were Maasai; these spoke a very different, Nilotic, language and led a wholly pastoral life, while the Bantu-speaking Kikuyu practised mixed farming. But they shared the same God, *Ngai*; they intermarried and traded as much as they raided each other; Kikuyu age sets and military doctrine owed much to Maasai; there was also the *ukabi* initiation guild. Kikuyu were ambivalent. They envied Maasai their cattle and thought their pastoral plains, or *weru*, to be profitable markets; but they were also a wilderness of rubbish and disorder.[135] In one breath Kikuyu swore brotherhood with Maasai in order to open trade; in another they called cobras and puff adders, both deadly enemies, *ukabi*.[136] But, at bottom, Kikuyu accepted that Maasai were moral beings subject to the same self-discipline as themselves, for all their refusal to put a hoe to the ground. Indeed, in remarkable witness to a catholicity of culture, Kikuyu borrowed two of their most censorious terms, *ngero* and *umaramari*, from Maasai. The first meant an irrevocable evil caused by failing a moral test, the latter was the depravity expected of naughty children or delinquent adults.[137] So great was the change in ethnicity under colonial rule that failure to meet the standards of Kikuyu labour theory then became a withering reproof to others.

If Kikuyu labour theory did not make them feel superior to others, it was a rod for their own backs, a coercive morality. They have been called a driven people.[138] I have argued that the struggle against the forest was their driver. But how did it shape Kikuyu political thought? Private accumulation, impossible without the social production of labour by marriage and patronage, created cultural space and civil order, triumphs of perseverance.[139] But it also needed leadership. The criteria of power were as much discussed in precolonial times as the question of ethnicity but – or so my evidence suggests – Kikuyu tests of leadership changed much less than their ethnic consciousness during the colonial period. The early evidence is, admittedly, thin; my best comes from a time when radical change had already occurred, when the tradition to which critics appealed had to be invented. This imbalance of evidence makes one suspect the apparent continuity in the dualism of wealthy authority and feckless poverty. But scepticism may be misplaced, for two reasons. First, wealth and poverty were less political than moral concepts, and while colonial political institutions were new, agrarian life and its old moral values continued.[140] Because they continued to be relevant, values could be outraged and thereby sharpened by change; their enemy was cynicism rather than a new moral theory, and out of cynicism they could always be revived. Secondly, the moral lessons of social inequality had in any case never been unquestioned. The wealthy may have been glad of the blessing of God and the ancestors; but the poor were always challenged to think critically about human responsibility.

The best guide to Kikuyu expectations of wealth comes from examination of their political maxim 'say and do', *kuuga na gwika*. By this they declared that public authority came from private achievement, power from virtue. *Athamaki* led opinion because their homes were far from going to ruin. They were their own best exemplars. They welcomed the test of the organic intellectual, whose authority comes from preaching what he commendably practises; they were heirs to a moral as well as political tradition in which private ambition must serve the collective good. Fatness should promise fertility.[141] These remarks seem to apply to a century of Kikuyu leadership. The best evidence for the basis of precolonial power comes from the dictionary. As in other Bantu languages, the Kikuyu lexicon equated wealth and leadership; a line of followers (or ants) was derived from the same root word.[142] But I cannot see how this moral equation was spelt out until the next generation of leaders achieved literacy. Kenyatta did it best. Calling on his readers to 'have done with trifling' and to 'go in for self-help', he scorned those who demanded progress without effort, who said but did not act.

The Moral Economy of Mau Mau

As his ancestors had given him life, so a man's deepest ambition must be for a posterity. Let him set out with self-reliance, being neither beggar nor vagrant. He should then build up his homestead by productive work, while remembering his duty to his parents, bowed with age, who had once toiled for him. Above all, he must neither stand by when there was a job to do nor envy the success of others. Kikuyu must act on behalf of their children's children. '*Atiriri Agikuyu!* Rouse up . . . and shake the couch-grass from the dug earth of your lands.' Otherwise none would respect them. In their shame they would have to dance in the back row of public affairs.[143] His meaning was clear: without individual self-mastery there could be no collective power. I do not in fact know that earlier *athamaki* urged their hearers thus to 'say and do'; it is disconcerting that there seems to be no direct proverbial echo. But it is hard to see how Kenyatta's exhortation would have differed from his grandfather's. In the next generation Mau Mau leaders called themselves the people of 'say and do', an explicit reproach to their elders in Kenyatta's generation, whose newspaper's motto had been the less aggressive 'work and pray'.[144] In their headquarters at Kiburi house, a Nairobi office block, they were however divided between the businessmen whose action had been to buy it and the trades unionists who in its back rooms worked for direct action of a forceful kind.[145] After independence *kuuga na gwika* was revived, unequivocally, as the slogan of rich politicians whose business success commended them as brokers of power.[146] Some called themselves the *Atiriri Bururi* Union, a name that signalled that their enterprise entitled them to 'speak for the country'.[147] The *athamaki* whom Europeans had first heard declaiming *atiriri Agikuyu* a century before would have agreed with them.

It is not easy to hear what those *athamaki* said, still less to explain how they constructed their doctrine in face of popular scepticism and failures of leadership. We can start by refusing to romanticize the moral economy of precapitalist worlds.[148] The morality of agrarian society was calculating. There never was a 'Merrie Africa'. Kikuyu knew that they risked internal conflict, even anarchy, whenever the fickleness of nature incited the moral selfishness of individual survival. Political management was tested by that underlying frailty of existence. Leaders were commended by their actions before their words, by their capacity to mobilize labour and control fertility, and only then by their political theory of harmony or theology of abundance. Plutocratic theory served the partisan interest of powerful polygamous men. Like all public doctrines, it also claimed to promote general wellbeing. It evoked laborious social emulation and self-discipline. That does not mean that the authority of wealth was unbridled or unquestioned. It was bargained with, admonished and resented, just as some felt that the poor merited not scorn but help. People asked deep political questions and high. The poor questioned to what extent leaders should enjoy the profits of power, even in the days before the latter could be diversified out of land and goats. Leaders disputed how far local power could properly enlist external support, long before that meant employment by the colonial state.

To turn first to doing, the Kikuyu market in power and labour was an arena of hard bargains. Rich households enlarged their labour supply by patronage and insured against demographic hazard by plural marriage. Their superior grip on labour power made them enviably but also meritoriously safer than small families against the agrarian stress that even well-watered Kikuyuland sometimes suffered. Over six per cent of proverbs affirmed that leadership and organized cooperation was a public good; it created wealth, cleanliness and satiety. Obedience paid. Conversely, while two per cent deplored greed, only three in a thousand actively condemned the rich as parasites.[149] These axioms were appropriate to a frontier economy. Land was virtually limitless until the 1880s, so landless labour was scarce. The more fortunate prospered further by giving opportunity to the less. Big men were well capitalized in livestock but could always use more warriors or workers. Conversely, men were poor because they lacked stock and, very likely therefore, the close kin through whom stock could be mobilized. They were barred from marriage and a self-respecting manhood. The needs of rich men and poor were complementary, as labour theory said. If the content of remembered proverbs bears any proportional relation to actual political thought, it seems that this moral economy of social inequality was understood and widely, if not uncritically, accepted; there was a Kikuyu language of class. Big men gave out or loaned livestock and areas of land in return for service; poor men got a start in manhood. To lead a successful colonization of the forest meant to multiply the rights of dependants in land.[150] But dependants were by no means equal.

The sliding scale of dependent land relations provides the evidence for bargaining in the labour market. The most servile relationship, *njaguti*, was paid in food and fats. These were consumption goods, not assets, enough to get by but not to get started.[151] *Ndungata*, often herdsmen, had better expectations. Their labour service could earn marriage into an *mbari* partner's family, but any children belonged to the patron's *mbari*, likewise their rights in land. At the middle levels of the labour market there were various forms of tenancy. At the top of the social scale, labour recruitment became transformed into the high politics of *mbari* fertility. This was normally exchanged with other *mbari* by exogamous marriage; daughters were married out and livestock bridewealth received in compensation. An endogamous insurance policy was available, which created an internal source of male partners for the subclan's daughters. This means of keeping control over daughters' fertility is known in the literature as *muhoi* (plural *ahoi*) tenancy. It is misnamed; it was not a dependent relationship but an alliance. Classically, it was initiated by a householder with more *mbari* land than he could use. He invited in as *muhoi* a friend who had more stock than he could graze. It was a deal between men with matching forms of property. The relation was sealed by marriage between the principals' sons and daughters; *ahoi* acquired a female right to land. Host *mbari* thus diversified investments in fertility; stockowners multiplied alliances with land.[152] The unravelling of these relations was one of the bitterest Kikuyu experiences of colonial rule.

It appears, as one would expect, that while the wealthy could demand obedience from the poor and kinless, they had to respect the opportunities open to other men of property. Kikuyu proverbs bear witness to this unequal esteem. A perhaps surprising number, two per cent, advised fortune-seekers to leave home, confirming the existence of a labour market. But the rules of social obligation scorned charity. Most people in this land-rich economy said that only fecklessness excluded the poor from the means of production. Poverty was delinquent. The poor had no heart, no friends and would have no posterity. Their hunger kept nobody else awake. Stockowners – and apparently only they – had it in their power to show compassion, *tha*; but no more than three sayings in a thousand actually commended generosity to the poor. Tenfold more praised the quite different instinct of reciprocity, which expected to be repaid; the rich should give to each other. Altruism in the rich was laughable, the kindness of the poor worthless. As to marriage, Kikuyu, like anybody else, knew that rich youths found courtship easy and that beautiful girls did not call on poor men.[153] While this folk wisdom acknowledged the role of social differentiation in affairs of the heart, its irreverence also accepted an equality in gender relations that ethnography has long recognized.[154]

It is, however, commonly held that Kikuyu women were more than usually subject to patriarchy. This is because sexuality and fertility were conflated with gender as a whole on both sides of the conflict over clitoridectomy or 'female circumcision' between the wars. That is all that most people have heard about in Kikuyu gender relations.[155] But men's preoccupation with fertility made them want to control sexuality, not dominate women. Circumcision and clitoridectomy were like forest clearance; they cut childish nature into adult culture. Women felt the same.[156] The importance of women to the work of cultivation and the hospitality of ambition gave them much sway in domestic politics.[157] Women probably agreed with men that the sexuality of an uncircumcised girl was depraved, and that female promiscuity caused sterility. But Kikuyu respected mothers more than fathers.[158] Sexual relations, they all thought, should be confined to the homestead; they were taboo in the bush. While Kikuyu ogre stories warn only that girls, not boys, get eaten when out in the woods,[159] the discipline that men demanded of women was no more than they imposed on themselves. It was each man's responsibility to close his own hut door (*riigi*) against the wilderness; nobody could do it for him.[160]

This responsibility was at the heart of Kikuyu politics and theology, to turn now from doing to saying. Wealthy Kikuyu, like 17th-century English gentry, advocated a self-regulating society managed by men like themselves. Their pursuit of fertility and production made the alliances that kept the peace. The three-part meaning of the nickname *wanyahoro* summarizes their philosophy. It fitted a man of peace, a man of business and one whose sexual fires had cooled. When, accordingly, a man became a senior elder, a status for which he was eligible only when his eldest children had been circumcised, the sacrificial billy goat's genitals were mutilated, to symbolize redirection of energy to the common good.[161] Big men controlled the politics of kinship by keeping decisions to the lowest level of alliance that could guarantee effective action. One of the earliest British observers described the Kikuyu polity as 'local government run mad';[162] but that was misleading if it implied that Kikuyu also had a central government. There was none; Kikuyu were not politically – or in any other sense – a tribe. At the most there were dynastic alliances of local *mbari*, separated from each other by the steeply corrugated landscape. Neither annual circumcision sets, nor warrior sets, nor even the alternating generation sets, ethnographically 'cross-cutting' though they were, had any Kikuyu-wide authority.[163] Kikuyu politics was much smaller than ethnicity.

There were both deep and high political reasons for this parochialism of politics. In the deep political arena of the labour market, it seems that neither seasons of plenty nor times of dearth were conducive to concentrations of power. The labour market may well have been differentiated but in good farming seasons there were severe limits on how much the powerful could demand of the weak. Patrons, after all, competed for scarce labour. Their clients had to be allowed to enjoy much of their marginal product themselves; they might otherwise transfer their allegiance to a rival. Given the common ambition to found a household, productive assets had to be shared out and warrior service was not easily imposed.[164] The tightness of the labour market seems, as elsewhere in Africa, to have placed a ceiling on the accumulation of force, but there is no sure way of telling how tight the market was. It depends on the unknowable nature and number of the Kikuyu poor. The long-term, structural, poor were probably unemployable, the old and crippled, those who could not contribute labour to a household. More proverbs express weariness with the old than pity or respect.[165] There were probably, therefore, few structural poor. And the temporary, or conjunctural, poor were not the material on which to build firm political followings.[166] They came in two forms, ambitious and despairing. Most of them were probably ambitious young men, beckoned to the forest frontier of opportunity from out of the congested, long-settled *mbari* in the middle of the country which had exhausted their reserves of land. Possibly as many as half the 19th-century Kikuyu frontiersmen were dependent, in some degree, on the *mbari* pioneers in their village fortresses.[167] Early European accounts tell of the large numbers of warriors who could be mobilized on the southern border. But they also attest to the rapid response of Kikuyu agriculture to external market demand.[168] From this one may assume that warriors soon acquired wives. Kikuyu had little to say about war, none of it admiring, since war was not porridge.[169] In good seasons, therefore, the competitive labour market determined that many dependent workers soon achieved the status of junior or affinal kin, no longer so subject to command. Bad seasons could be worse still for political entrepreneurs.

Kikuyu reckoned natural time by famines, as they measured civilized time by *riika*. Famines serious enough to be remembered by name occurred, roughly speaking, every decade.[170] Of these the severest were as much moral panics as material disasters, forcing the strong to disavow the claims of the weak.[171] While, therefore, poor harvests were the other cause of temporary poverty, the very severe famines that look to have recurred every generation could cause dependants to migrate or die. That may partly explain why the poor were despised. A missionary heard that in the terrible famine of the late 1890s 'great numbers of the less well-to-do, chiefly dependants and hangers on of the landowners', had fled in search of food.[172] Chief Kinyanjui thought that those who died were 'nearly all the bad men'.[173] He evaded the guilt of a survivor, it seems, by blaming the victims. The brutality of famine relations was later recalled by Mau Mau detainees when they named one of their camp commandants *ng'aragu*, famine, 'because there could have been none worse than him.'[174] Not a single saying in well over a thousand collected proverbs refers to famine. The selfishness of survival was too dreadful to talk about.[175] Just how dreadful is hinted at in the lexicon of poverty. Some of the poor were admitted to be destitute through no fault of their own. Some, as one might expect, were castigated as filthy rogues, or thriftless. Others, however, were said to have suffered through the hard-heartedness of others; they had been refused what they asked. These last, *aimwo*, were also said to be good-fornothings, but one wonders how far the moral failings imputed to the poor in fact accused their accusers.[176]

Fear of famine, labour shortage and the need to prove mastery over nature drove Kikuyu high politics to compete in consumption rather than arms. A successful life required an outlay of no less than 172 goats for ceremonial slaughter and feasting at rites of passage and other public occasions.[177] Kikuyu history is about those who could pay for a political life. We know almost nothing about those who could not. We can catch glimpses of 'anti-elders' or *tuthuuri* who had not paid their fees and hung around the edges of the council ground, trying to catch the words of the *athuuri*.[178] Many of the latter will have got on as fast as they could, having perhaps paid an aptly named 'goat for climbing' for advanced entry to an elder grade.[179] Rich youths married early and often, partly in order to place their sons later on different rungs of the legal ladder of age-grade councils.[180] Proverbially, small families were defenceless at law. The bitterest complaint against the rich was that they always managed to get hold of the poor man's midden, his most fertile plot.[181] Ceremonial investment may have displayed the virtuous competence of wealth; it also promised political profit. 'Who herds goats eats meat'.[182] But the profits of power visibly accrued to domestic virtue only so long as the political circle was kept small. In the newly settled areas of southern Kikuyu, big men cursed any of their number who stole a march up the graded path of legal power. Some thought to do so by circumcising a son with their parent *mbari* farther north, thus evading the local closed period during which a new southern age-regiment was formed.[183] To call up authority that one had not earned by local reputation was clearly illegitimate. Not only was politics smaller than ethnicity but ethnicity was in this case explicitly denied in the interests of power. History was also seen as a threat then, as it is today. An important ideological resource for elders was their *kirira*, or 'secret knowledge'. Seniors imparted it sparingly to their successors according to their need to know. Knowledge was powerful enough to be explosive. If all was revealed about past intrigue, who would be able to contain the conflicts?[184]

God, similarly, was too powerful to be approached other than by household heads. Kikuyu theology was complex and heterodox. It conceded the power of God or the ancestors but still held that man could master his fate. God was *Ngai*, the divider who allocated his resources between his peoples; Kikuyu were monotheists but their God was not monotribal. He was 'not to be pestered';[185] neither to be coerced nor, like external earthly power, to be called upon to substitute for moral choice. God wanted people to be prosperous but could work only through obedient human hands. Kikuyu were therefore justified by works. Wealth rewarded virtue[186] as poverty punished disobedience. Around 15 per cent of Kikuyu proverbs insisted, in an interminable sermon on discipline, that all could improve themselves. They had only to rise early, sweat, save, persevere and reject feeble excuses. The wealthy expected to enjoy God's favour. A *muthamaki* thought it proper to pray for health not only because he had sacrificed; he was also 'good and rich'.[187] Gratitude for riches was shown in their enjoyment. They proved the love of God and the indulgence of ancestors, both of them dependent on self-discipline and civic virtue.

Kikuyu faced, nonetheless, the universal need to explain how villains could prosper while the virtuous suffered. Occult power was thought to be available to anyone maliciously inclined, but the socially isolated, presumably the poor, were most often charged with its use.[188] Other explanations of misfortune did not blame the poor, even if the remedies favoured the rich. Ancestors were quick to anger, but were as easily appeased by animal sacrifice.[189] *Thahu* or ritual uncleanness was the commonest cause of calamity. Known by the wasting away of people or livestock, it was difficult to avoid, expensive to cure. It could be contracted unwittingly, by transgressing rules that prescribed, in minute detail, how to keep death and blood separate from life and sex; wild game from domestic stock; and the bush out of the homestead. A British official learned more than 60 causes of uncleanness. Kikuyu ran their daily lives with care; they were only too conscious of dangerous disorder in the wild.[190] All sources of misfortune, sorcery, ancestral anger and uncleanness could be diagnosed, for a fee, by a medical practitioner or *mundo mugo*. Doctors were called in middle life by dreams and tribulation, learning their medicine and occult wisdom by apprenticeship. Wealthy novices paid their tuition fees in stock, poor ones were perhaps discouraged by the alternative of long menial service as unqualified assistants. Sacrificial remedy was always expensive. It could be figuratively reinforced by a ritual sweeping away of taint.[191] Households and yards were regularly swept, so Mrs Routledge thought in 1909, 'in a way which shames the camping-ground of most Europeans.'[192] Wealth smelt nicer than poverty. Wealthy old age did not smell at all. In folklore a girl escaped the ogre Wamangeca by disguising herself as poor. Removing her ornaments, she sang 'I who smells shit am not Wamangeca's visitor'. The poor seem to have been undisciplined in more ways than one. The surest way to disgrace one's age set was by disorderly defecation.[193]

Europeans, missionaries especially, thought rich and poor Kikuyu particularly divided in death.[194] Most were led out to die in the bush, where hyenas were efficient if hideously noisy undertakers.[195] Only men and women with at least two circumcised sons – a good definition of wealth – were buried. Kikuyu did not greatly fear death, but dreaded the contagion of corpses. Only adult sons were ritually strong enough to bury their parents; even they needed expensive purification after the funeral. But the differentiated disposal of the dead did not by itself affect their chances in the afterlife. Posterity, not burial, conferred remembrance and reincarnation. Marrying late and often dying young, the poor were at greater risk of oblivion. The rich were assured of both reincarnation in a grandchild and, meanwhile, a shadowy underworld existence where they tended equally shadowy flocks and herds. This last belief featured in the mythical charter of the *ituika*, the transfer of ritual power between the generations that has stirred more ethnographic anxiety, historiographical scepticism and political imagination than any other feature of Kikuyu life.

Ituika was undoubtedly a powerful idea, probably a social process, possibly a ritual event; and it must have had what it has not been given, a political and economic history. If the several accounts are to be credited, and none of them quite agree, then *ituika* was a religious festival to convert private wealth into collective peace and fertility. That is how Kikuyu spokesmen imagined it.[196] *Ituika* formalized the alternating succession of ritual authority between the two generations that were equally represented in all age sets. Authority was transferred only to those who had reached senior elderhood, who were thus already qualified to judge matters of law. It is generally said that this happened every 30 to 40 years. It is hard to imagine that half the elders were content to serve for that length of time as ritual juniors to friends on the same legal bench, and paying higher fees for all ritual observance, simply because demographic chance had put them in the other generation. Nor did they. Men could pay 'an ox of climbing' and move up or down a generation to attain a ritual status equivalent to their legal rank.[197] This was a further costly premium in the political investment that they will have made throughout their adult lives, perhaps including an earlier 'goat of climbing' to gain them legal authority before they were of standing by age. The rules were full of resource for men with resources. Nonetheless, these men of substance, at some point yet to be discussed historically, felt that their ambition should be hallowed and demanded that their postulant generation as a whole be formally promoted. Over a period of years they then paid large livestock fees to the incumbents. They called in their debts and 'purified' the land, possibly, although no source says so, from accumulated accusations of sorcery, a hypothesis to which I will return. One reading of *Mwangi*, one of the alternating generation names, is 'magical protector'.[198] Conspicuous transfer and consumption of wealth culminated in a restricted ritual on a river bank by one of the many waterfalls in lower Kikuyuland. Here, intoxicated as much by the sight of a beautiful maiden as by fumes of honey beer, the rainbow dragon *ndamathia* was said to be lured from his pool so that the officiating elders could pluck his life-giving tail hairs. From the many *ndamathia* legends it appears that the monster embodied the terror of power. When duped rather than propitiated it could restore the dead to life, sustain the daily cycle and make rain. Some stories tell how maidenly courage rescued all the people and livestock it had previously swallowed; they trooped from out of the underworld through the monster's gaping knee. Some say it was the test that gave prince Sun victory over his brother Moon. Others relate how, in its rainbow guise of *mkunga mbura*, the rain gatherer, it gave and withheld rain.[199] The message of *ituika* for Kikuyu was that revivifying power was costly, dangerous, and made demands on daughters; leaders could tame its dragon by cunning, but not without a fortitude tempered by years of self-mastery and virtuous production.

Students of *ituika* have been maddened by the question of time. They have proposed anything between 15- and 40-year cycles for its observance.[200] The competing hypotheses have been based on the ceremony's social structure and function. But neglected evidence suggests that the secret of the *ituika* may be found by asking, as of other upheavals, how its political process related to economic history. The 'ox of climbing' disposes of the need to link *ituika* to biological rhythms. It may be better to look for contingency. Disagreement over timing may be due not to structural confusion but climatic variation. The core symbol of *ituika*, the rainbow dragon *ndamathia*, had power to bring rain and restore life. Yet it has not been noticed that the chronology of the last three supposed *ituika* follows that of famine.[201] More strikingly, in parts of southern Kikuyu the last two remembered *ituika* were as much as 60 years apart, coinciding with the worst famines in recent memory, that of *kiriika*, or destruction, in the late 1830s and of *ruraya*, or Europe, in the late 1890s. Both were largely caused by drought.[202] People who have dared to reminisce about the latter blame its deaths on ill will, sorcery and poisoning. Others say that debt collection, part of *ituika*'s 'straightening-out', hit the poor. So did the steep rise in grain prices caused by famine and accentuated by the sales to British caravans that gave the famine its name, Europe.[203] The question needs research but it may be that what could finally force the issue of *ituika* was the sense that society was disintegrating under famine, that sorcery had to be swept away,[204] and that only a massive expenditure of virtue, financed in part by debt recovery from the dependent poor, could restore both faith in authority and the health of the land. That there may have been as many as five separate *ituika* zones in Kikuyu strengthens this hypothesis, given the localization of power and rain. I know too little to do more than suggest that Kikuyu political and cosmological thought, focused in the idea of *ituika*, shaped responses to economic crisis. But one can start to identify the underlying stresses that may have provoked most thought as the 19th century came to its turbulent, harrowing end.

THE INTERIOR ARCHITECTURE OF CHANGE

Ethnicity needs no further explanation; its changing history does. Modern tribalism is widely regarded as a product of colonial rule. Parts of its inner dynamic nonetheless troubled Kikuyu before the British came. The differences between Kikuyu ethnicity before and after conquest can be restated simply enough; the problem is to explain them. Precolonial politicians called their listeners by a collective name but the audience kept changing. Immigrants became Kikuyu; in hard times failed Kikuyu fled. Kikuyu were continually negotiating rights to their working environment, whether by female pawns, male servants, tenants or allies. Their political thought developed within imported institutions, a multi-ethnic morality and an inclusive theology. Political practice, far from seeking ethnic solidarity, denied its propriety. In contrast, the rhetoric and practice of many colonial Kikuyu politicians came to converge in a competition to construct and lead a unanimous nationality. Their listeners increasingly fought to remain in the audience, whether of clan, age or tribe; their associated rights in property and labour were increasingly at risk but there was nowhere else to go. This involution of ethnicity occurred in part because the colonial architecture of tribal control imposed a new arena. Provincial and district boundaries marshalled resources and set the rules for the possible growth of tribal ethnicity; they did not create it. And smaller boundaries drawn around more accessible resources blocked its growth with the little politics of chiefship, the only formal power that Africans were allowed. There was no power in 'tribe'. It was a resourceful idea, not an office of profit. The idea of tribe had to take hold of the deep political imagination before the wider colonial arena could be turned to high political use.

There are two further problems with any argument that the external tribal architecture simply brought into sharper focus an internal ethnic structure. First, the historical geography of ethnicity was not waiting, already there but half-asleep, needing only a colonial district arena to shock it into life. It was fluid and accidental, without any latent tendency towards a future tribal realization, let alone the one that actually emerged. Secondly, the parallel idea that Africans then entered into alliances of interest to match the structures of rule, only to discover that their partners had unknowingly been fellow tribesmen all the time, is altogether too pragmatic and straightforward. It neither explains the urgency of ethnic nationalism nor identifies its necessarily imaginative creators. To take first the question of the 'fit' between latent ethnicity and conscious tribe, this was as awkward for Kikuyu as for Africans elsewhere in the spheres of language, moral economy and social structure. Literacy gave ethnic nationalism much of its energy. It deepened political imaginations by enabling people to place themselves in a larger framework of space and time. But print did not immediately reveal to Kikuyu their previously hidden identity. Linguistic boundaries were too imprecise. Their dialects were not so much closer to each other than they were to other Thagicu tongues, including those of their neighbours, Embu, Meru and Kamba, that they alone were self-evidently 'Kikuyu' while the others were not. The unstudied politics of Bible translation may have much to offer here.[205] Nor was Kikuyu moral economy peculiarly their own. Embu and Meru were also forest-clearers with the same contempt for poverty;[206] as we have seen, Kikuyu accepted that even the pastoral Maasai knew the meaning of self-discipline. Clan affiliation overlapped all ethnic borders; age-grading was widely shared; other highlanders, Embu and Meru, had a ritual focus like *ituika* in their own *nduiko*.[207] For all these reasons Kikuyu nationalists had to argue the case for unity even when it encompassed only the three core districts of Kikuyu. They called on the people of Nyeri, Fort Hall (Murang'a) and Kiambu districts to cease to think of themselves as, respectively, Gaki, Metume or Kabete. Since each of these identities represented only an amorphous aggregation of immigrant sub-clans, it was not obvious that they belonged together more than with any other set of neighbours. What we now know as 'Kikuyu proper' had first to be imagined as such, not long ago, and its internal jealousies remain. Some ethnic nationalists took this achievement to be a stage on the way to unity with the several Embu and Meru peoples as well. This would extend 'the house of Gikuyu and Muumbi from Ngong to Karimatura [Garba Tula]'.[208] The history of their opposition, the resistance to pan-Kikuyu ethnicity among Embu and Meru, has yet to be told. But that some felt driven to organize it makes the point that there was no ethnic predestination in the present boundaries of 'Kikuyu'.

What inspired Kikuyu nationalists to seize the exterior architecture of tribe was the coarsening of its colonial interior. The values of labour were divided, the relations between civic virtue and power broken. It was like unending famine. Nationalists were recruited from those who were most affected. The earliest, to refer back to the discussion of political mobilization, were 'readers' with an injured sense of unrequited merit. In the next generation they were joined, and opposed, by workers embittered by unmerited loss. Both blamed their plight on injustice rather than fate; they tried to change their lot rather than evade it or take flight. There were three layers of ethnicity to misfortune and its remedy. That Kikuyu were who and where they were was part of the objective cause of grievance; they did indeed suffer more loss than most at British hands. To be Kikuyu also gave them a particular perception of wrong. When Christian 'readers' opposed colonial chiefs their private rivalry was afforced by Kikuyu outrage at the exercise of power without virtue. Workers brought Kikuyu labour theory to bear on their demands for land. Finally, both used, inventively, Kikuyu images of solidarity to enlarge their spheres of political trust. These had been weakened by colonial social change. Precolonial conflicts had already shown how fragile these solidarities had always been. Precolonial ethnicity had no answer to division and uproar; colonial tribal nationalism later claimed that it had. We can better understand the historical process of ethnic involution by examining that contrast more closely.

If latent outer tribal boundaries were not easily discerned in the indistinct marches of precolonial ethnicity, nor were Kikuyu unified within by their experience of colonial conquest, rather the reverse. The random raids that by 1905 had added up to British rule also divided *mbari* against *mbari*, as war had always done.[209] But resistance and accommodation did serve to document for British observers the prior fractures that Kikuyu already knew had opened up in the late 19th century between property in land and livestock, between generations and between kin and client, rich and poor. External markets had strained internal *mbari* alliances ever since the 1860s. Landowners and stockowners fell apart. Uphill agricultural houses cultivated more land, to supply Swahili and then British trade caravans with food. *Ahoi* allies had to graze their cattle farther downhill, at more risk of Maasai raids. Generational friction also grew. The elders' market agreements cramped their warriors' style.[210] The famine that closed the century made matters worse. Disastrous mortality and destitution caused social hatred, especially in southern Kikuyu. Frontier *mbari* patrons rejected the claims of clients who were forced to beg a subsistence elsewhere, whether from Kikuyu *mbari* to the north or from ethnic strangers farther afield. Masterless poor men died; women probably fared better, as pawns. Many *mbari* owners themselves survived only by retreat, claiming from their parent *mbari* a lineage right to survive. *Mbari* thus shed all but their inner core, hanging on to their real rather than fictive kin or, if formed by corporate purchase, then trust in their *mbari* oath. Junior warriors also strengthened individual *riika* loyalties on oath when they decided to disavow their seniors in order to survive themselves. They became bandits, known either as *thabari* because they were as rough as Swahili or British *safari* caravans, or *mau mau*, onomatopoeia for 'greedy eaters'.[211] Kikuyu had many means to endure, flee or to resist their fate. The elders' attempts to do more, to confront the consequent anarchy and restore order, seem merely to have added oppression to hunger; debt collection to meet the costs of *ituika* deprived the poor of what little livestock they had. Twenty years later and 30 years after that, Kikuyu faced similar conflicts within new political and social structures. These still encouraged the rich to invest their wealth in the search for power; they also eventually forced the poor to fight their fate for want of a place to flee.

It was the need to fight, for lack of alternative refuge, that promoted tribal solidarity. Colonial boundaries mapped out how far that solidarity would reach. But, paradoxically, it was mutual conflict that made the modern Kikuyu. They found it ever more difficult to contract out of the conflicts between *riika* and *mbari*, moral growth and property relations. It was a peculiarly Kikuyu conflict; none of their neighbours experienced quite the same problem or in such intensity. Clan and age had never been so strongly at odds among other peoples. Nobody else in colonial times experienced such tension between property and virtue. Existing structures of social knowledge, *mbari* and *riika*, shaped moral perceptions of otherwise incomprehensible flux. Like Wangu, they raised new questions about gender and gave external change a domestic vocabulary. They also took on a mutually more threatening reality of their own, as new interests appropriated their concepts for their own divided purposes. Liberal and Marxist social scientists thought that social mobilization weakened old solidarities by creating new ones. Not so; new interests and associations gave new forms to old loyalties and fresh twists to old arguments. The most *intimate* rivals for virtue and power became seen as fellow tribesmen; there was no getting away from them; Kikuyuland became an oppressively crowded debating hall. The most difficult issues of citizenship were ethnic, not territorial. Ethnic nationalism had no option but to face questions that territorial nationalism did not dare ask. Tribalism was drawn around the most agonized internal debates. Its leaders competed to impose an enlarged form of *kirira*, trying to mask the sharpest domestic disputes behind the boldest external demands. There was a shared solidarity of secret knowledge that, if known, would not only make life still more intolerable but also give external enemies their chance.[212] After the Second World War internal conflict became too bitter to be any longer contained. Mau Mau was no movement of cultural renewal. It used one partisan cultural imagination to resist another. For Kikuyu began to talk ever more openly about the growing gap between their virtue and its reward. By 1950 *mbari* no longer protected but, instead, threatened the rights to land of a large and growing minority of Kikuyu. At the same time, ideas about age, generation and time had never been more disputed. The period was as painful as the 1890s and the issues were strikingly similar. But there was a vital difference. During the 1890s ties of patronage were cut but when the rains returned all knew that the clientage of the survivors could be resumed. Private ambition was then enough to restore the public good. By 1950 inner conflict could no longer be evaded; no external patrons could be relied upon for help. The contradictions of *mbari* and *riika* had come to look like struggles across the unhappy valley of class. Across that new gulf man's holy sweat no longer offered even a subservient means of future return. Private ambition no longer promoted the good of dependants. Nor did legitimate forms of political action.

Tribe and class

The outcome of the modernist myth turned on a clash of champions. 'Culture', dark hero of the past, was to be challenged by 'class', a shining knight of progress whom liberals clothed as white-collared, classless, modern man. This conflict between birth and achievement was the crux of progress; it cross-cut traditional society. The anticipated triumph of class over culture created transitional identities from which new statenationhoods might grow. The future belonged to common people unless, by some trick of uneven development, the fight was inconclusive or the dark hero won. Nationhood would then be baulked by regionalism, true class interests hidden by the false consciousness of cultural pride. This staged duel of the dichotomies in fact condemned all actual politics, not only in Africa, to flounder for ever in transitional limbo. More humane expectations might give the present more hope.

And our understandings are different now, the teleology gone. Like the contrast between tribe and nation, class formation is seen as contingent process. Empirical questions matter; structures of change differ. Modernists forecast that capitalism would shake individuals out of traditional communities and colonial states then pave their way to modern society. Grand theory rested on three errors of perception: about states, capitalism and people. I have argued that colonies were not the coherent structures within which people could argue out a new political contract. More needs to be said on the incoherence of colonial capitalism. This is best done by discussing the social systems within which people met change, which were more resilient than modernist theorists could credit. These theorists believed that closed traditional systems had formerly served functional needs which social change had destroyed. It now seems that in the Kikuyu past (as in those of other peoples) open institutions offered political assets for which informed social actors fought in shifting arenas of interethnic relations.[213] Competition continued under new rules in modern times. Politicians explored the resources of both class and culture in testing the uses of change. I earlier concluded that neither was a ready-made champion of political mobilization. The emergence of class, far from destroying tribe, might call for its invention. This happened in Kikuyuland. Modernist expectations cast this common dynamic of recent African history as political delinquency. History owes more respect to the dead.

Modernists were misled by an error of method, which mistook functional abstraction for human needs. Liberals thought that social change, which radicals called capitalism, simplified the division of labour and that this governed social action. Model productive relations came to look like real political systems. Injustice and its remedies were far too plain. For injustice is as much moral as material fact. Observers may measure economic inequality, but cannot assume that this is mirrored in felt moral inequity.[214] Moral economies are stubbornly distinctive, historical bargains between informed people, not the theoretical construct of a trained mind. Within a local universe of honour people invest their work with what moral agency they can and earn with its fruits as much civic virtue as their neighbours will wear. They judge any new class inequality by the social value which past experience has warned them to put on their labour, the price of their sweat. New patterns of

351

power and property challenge these previously bargained labour values. Material change is a moral issue. Inventively remembered rights show what is at stake. The brute necessities of one age become exemplary myths in the next.[215]

Moral economies are complex. Kenya's settlers competed with Indian traders for the labour of peasantries which endured growing differentiation.[216] Africans therefore had to argue social values at many levels. It was not a simple case of saving community vitality from the greedy maw of external capital. But that was the argument which men threw against each other – and against women – in the competitions of their own rural capitalism. All had good reason to extol the past moral economy. However unequally, its protagonists will have bargained, as in Kikuyu, the vital contrast between reciprocal duty and one-sided oppression. In the new context of colonial class formation, winners sought virtue by performing wider protective duties for the community, losers fought oppression by calling them to account. Old social bargains, invented memories hallowing with time, were the most intimate image of unequal equity in new struggles for self-mastery, still the proper reward of labour, however much the political economy had changed. All modes of production have these local genealogies of dispute. They bring forth varied degrees of exploitation, moral and material. Equally, it is only within communities for whom some common history may be claimed that class formation can occur. Only communities of time can be told how they have changed. In 1950 a better past was more readily imagined by a Kikuyu than by a Kenyan working class. All class consciousness is to some extent colloquial or ethnic and therefore 'false'.[217]

Far from implying that class struggle must be struck from the canon of causality, these reflections suggest that it is more pervasive than formal analyses of productive relations or class ideologies might accept. Class is the universal moral issue between the social and material values of labour. Found in all economic relations, conflicts over class rarely assume the simple adversarial form we have been taught to expect. The real class issue is citizenship; how, within the most pressing community of reputation, civic rights and distributive justice, one may gain or retain the status of moral agent, neither an anti-social swindler on the make nor slavish instrument of stronger men's wills.[218]

People compete not in one community of esteem but in several, which interact within a wider arena. Kikuyu knew this in the pull of *mbari* and *riika*, the privacy of property and community of time. They chased reputation in other communities too, guild and gender, in an ethnic arena. British rule added churches, urban villages and new occupations to the range of belonging. No theory can predict to which of these communities people will turn to defend their labour's social value; how, in so doing, they will change them and their mutual relations; nor if a political arena will become a moral community. There are only historical answers after the event. I earlier argued that the most demanding community of esteem was predestined neither by ethnic inheritance nor by economic change. Desire for a community other than class seemed necessary to inspire class struggle; more than that one could not say. Neither tribe nor state-nationhood – what have proved to be the most alluring images of community and potent constituencies of power – lay ready to hand for either Kikuyu penny-capitalists or workers. Creative political leaders conceived them as they went, improvising an audience from day to day. High politics has its explanatory place, once one has found its imaginative coin.

Communities of interest are arenas of dissent about power. The modernist myth forgot that. It had to stage the clash of champions because each contrary abstraction of tribe and class was so inwardly harmonious that they were mutually exclusive. They could be connected only by those, typically migrant workers, who wore their twin identities in the course of mobile lives. This was a misconception. Separate identities, deployed in appropriate situations, could not connect contrasting communities. They were intended to keep them apart, personal evasions of rival demands. No doubt many did try to fence off their different lives. Common experience suggests that most will have failed. To resolve the tension, people needed new social imaginations. For Kikuyu readers the problem was, how could they, *maraya*, prostituted by external influence, become instead *mambere*, domestic forerunners?[219] To grasp the dynamics of such connection we need to weigh less the cross-cutting loyalties of modernization that weakened one another, and more the cross-referenced arguments of survival that confirmed each other. New conflicts often drum up partisans from either side of existing divides. Familiarity breeds contempt as well as alliance. Kikuyu already had a language of disagreement, of moral authority and cynical dissent, in their labour theory of value. The question to ask of the relation between class and ethnicity is whether the contradictions of colonial capitalism lacked moral purchase on these familiar quarrels or if, to the contrary, they divided Kikuyu more deeply. The modernist myth worked on the first hypothesis; the latter is nearer the mark. That is the difference between dichotomy and dynamic.

THE LANGUAGE OF DISAGREEMENT

Kikuyu arguments about virtue and power, property and labour reinforced each other in three dimensions. Their invented past, first, governed their views, secondly, of colonial rule and, finally, of Christianity. From these sources Kikuyu thought authorized Christian improvement, disparaged wage labour, and invented a tribe. First, the hard bargains of the past were transmuted into a myth of equal opportunity, even as rural capitalism revalued property at the expense of labour. As conflict within *mbari* squeezed the rights of the poor, so rich men claimed fertile responsibility on a wider plane. Patrons moved out of providing land and into the mediation of state power. Less able to prove wealth's virtue by rewarding personal service, they argued that their patriotic production gave wider opportunity to all deserving Kikuyu. Their critics invoked democratic, then populist, ideas of *riika*. Age sets or generations were freed from wealthy sponsors, more easily in print than practice, and spanned a whole new tribe. These preoccupations, secondly, cried out for British claims to legitimacy to be turned against their authors. The dual colonial mandate of accumulation and control, profit and peace, was an abstraction made visible in the boundary trench between white and black land. The state banked its civilizing mission on white farmers who would teach idle natives the value of work in taming the bush, a moral and material project justifying conquest. African land was reserved for the reproduction of placid labour.[220] Kikuyu soon grasped that this was poor protection. Fired by their own labour theory, they claimed a civilizing mission themselves. Purposeful labour on private property became polemically Kikuyu. They had an external moral boundary as never before, to which the migrant labour of their own poor and the idleness of outsiders, whether in Maasai pastoralism or the under-use of white farmland, were equally offensive.[221] Lastly, Christianity and the Bible gave the Kikuyu God, *Ngai*, a past which was longer and more precise than the mists of *tene na agu*, or perhaps it was *ndemi na mathathi*, but in any case time out of mind.[222] *Ngai* became a Jehovah, a tribal and interventionist God, father of a people whom he repeatedly rescued from the hand of their enemies. In the minds of Kikuyu people the Bible fostered a Kikuyu tribe.[223]

New wrangles over old arguments made modern Kikuyu. They began when young men bought freedom from parents by investing the wages of external service in marriage. *Mbari* seniors, uneasily allied to *riika* juniors, then challenged colonial chiefs. *Riika* spokesmen spent their foreign income of clerical office and urban contacts in local intrigue. These cross-border forays revealed a larger political arena in the mind. The arena became a tribe, a community far from traditional and almost entirely new. People did not remain but became Kikuyu. Tribe became a body of defence against and demand upon the state, a formerly unimaginable role. Two generations modelled tribe out of ethnicity, penny-capitalists in the Kikuyu Central Association (KCA) between the wars and then trades unionists in the 1940s. While the KCA and then Nairobi workers tried to shape a community which saw class interest as common virtue they also sought state favour for their sectional needs. Tribe and state were not divergent paths to power, nor class and tribe exclusive communities of thought. Their internal disagreements spoke to each other. Leaders always had to test the size of the arena in which their actions gave them the right to speak and their thought was echoed in action. They interpreted experience whose confusion they shared. Most Kikuyu lived in several communities. The successful invested the gains of one in the opportunities of another, *maraya* aspiring to be *mambere*. The unfortunate tried to defend their local rights by selling their labour elsewhere. These entwined spirals of success and failure reflected the complex encounter between Kikuyu and colonial capitalisms and governed the new agenda for Kikuyu thought.

This agenda is generally said to have been set by the loss of the 'stolen lands', alienated to white settlers in the years 1902 to 1906 in southern Kikuyu and a decade or more later in the north. About 6 per cent of Kikuyu land was lost, much of it pasture.[224] Other issues have been examined: the divisive state power enjoyed by chiefs, their tax and labour exactions, cultural imperialism against clitoridectomy, forced labour to terrace hills against soil erosion and, lastly, the plight of the Kikuyu diaspora after the Second World War, deprived of squatter rights on white farms and degraded by the stratagems of survival in Nairobi's slums.[225] This conventional priority given to land in a galaxy of complaint needs to be rephrased, for all grievances were more closely connected than previous accounts have allowed. They all attacked one body of political thought, the labour theory of value. At bottom, Kikuyu argued with each other and complained to the British about the loss of calculable relation between obedient labour, civic virtue and rights in land and power. Labour bargains had once made Kikuyu people; labour disputes now drove them into the Kikuyu tribe. Men who could no longer offer or expect reciprocal relations at the productive level of household sought them at the political level of tribe. Evidence for this thesis is most plentiful in two separate postwar decades. The first saw the rise of the readers, fired by their unrequited merit; in the second they faced rivals whom they despised as spivs and hooligans, *mikora* and *imaramari*, who were goaded by unmerited loss. Political competition generated fresh thought about wealth and poverty, virtue and power. Between the wars politicians had such modest external expectations that they did not press their main point of internal disagreement. By 1950 the need for power was so urgent that the price of *kirira*, silence about domestic dispute in the face of external threat, had become internal terror.

HOUSEHOLD, EMPLOYMENT AND IDENTITY

To sketch in the material context first, one could say that Kikuyu pursued labour's value through the labyrinth of articulated relations of production.[226] More simply, their lives straddled[227] domestic tillage, trade and employment. Wage work varied. It could be local, stable and powerful, in school or chief's office; seasonal, a few hours' walk away on white farms; or migrant, often brief manual or long-term clerical labour in distant towns. Kikuyu wove complex job networks while guarding their stake in the competitive field of kin relations. Capitalism entered this field. It did not sweep it away by dividing the few who owned property from the many who could only sell labour. Most wage-workers held on to land rights. They had many situational identities: sons who expected productive rights at home; tribesmen helped by new friends to find urban housing; labourers, clerks or traders with collective interests in field, office or shop. Life was complicated, subject to the wills of others. Ingenuity secured survival. Survival was a victory. It did not earn civic virtue. A syllabus of stratagems explains neither why people hoped for, nor how they were mobilized to demand, that greater control over their labour's social value which is *wiathi*.

What inspired the ingenuity of survival and made most wage-labour migrants from Kikuyu the more determined to become Kikuyu? Kaleidoscopic working lives made this a real question. Wage labour looks to have been essential to all men at some time in their lives. Some took up profitable residence in towns, perhaps fewer men than women. Townspeople developed their own civic culture. There was, then, competition to redefine virtue in new times; not all who were officially designated as Kikuyu were in agreement that was what, however inventedly, they wished to be.

Young people, women among them,[228] wanted work for many reasons. Many had lost kin and stock in the great hunger; some had lost land to settlers; all had to pay tax. But the incentive for young men is best seen in the paradox that Kikuyu farm exports grew steadily, checked only by drought and disease, throughout the colonial era.[229] To farm was household work. Men controlled no land before marriage; bachelor labour profited fathers. Elders invested livestock in their own next marriage or their sons'. Formerly, young men had been able to raid stock for their own bridewealth. Male competition for capital now forced young men out to work. The evidence is thin, but of ten Kikuyu workers asked by a commission of enquiry in 1912, seven said that they were working in order to buy goats and marry. Three had been driven out. One was sent by his parents to earn their tax; another, Makumi wa Mohia, was simply poor, with a mother to support; the third was forced out by his chief and now feared for the safety of his two wives.[230] In short, most youths wanted wages so as to earn the civic virtue of domestic production sooner than their fathers might have allowed. Wages financed entry to the married business of farming.

This common link between wage and household became a mutually reinforcing matrix of need and power, to judge by the only hard evidence there is, from the 1950s. An urban budget survey then showed that unskilled workers were subsidized by poor rural kin while clerical or skilled workers invested part of their pay in land purchase.[231] All were straddlers. The poorest failed to make ends meet in both sides of life. The rich schooled rural privilege for urban profit, coming home to rise still more. They were really spiralists, the poor descending, the richer climbing the winding stair of class formation between household and employment.[232] Each needed both twists in the stair. Wage labour helped the poor to fend off proletarianization; without the cash to mitigate harvest failure they might have had to sell off land the sooner. Wages could delay disinvestment. The rich added value to their labour with clerical work and trade; salaries accelerated investment. Anonymous accumulation in town drew off some of the poison of rural envy. Many situational identities were thus tied by a single thread of anxiety or hope to the civilizing farm household, still the source of labour's value.

Rural Kikuyu defended this household sway by teaching that towns sapped self-mastery. Elders complained of spoilt young men. By the 1920s some felt that 'Nairobi Kikuyu' had forfeited any say in rural affairs. Kenyatta, writing from experience and perhaps with remorse, castigated shabby city pleasures. Opinion of townsmen had not improved 20 years later. Political songs or *nyimbo* had no time for them; they were too smart – *thaka*, 'handsome ones' who might die childless – or too feckless to work either for their people or on the land.[233] Some managed to resist this moral pressure. Prostitutes bought town houses, rejecting the marriage strategies of country kin. Kikuyu landlords, men and women, owned half the lodgings in African Nairobi in the 1930s. Most were Muslim, committed to town. They complained about the loss of rural land rights but did little to reclaim them.[234] Worker action tells a similar story. Strikes overflowed the disputed workplace. Workers acted as fellow townsmen, not as tribesmen or even workmates, simply as neighbours with common hardships.[235] By 1945 officials reckoned that more than half the African population of Nairobi had been resident for five years or more and that Kikuyu were more likely than other named groups to become townspeople.[236]

In town, 'Kikuyu' was one of several classes and was itself three ways divided. One cannot be sure of so slippery a matter, but recorded behaviour gives some clues. There were two urban classes to which some Kikuyu assimilated, one respectable, the other not. The first were the Muslim landlords. While some found in Islam merely a refuge from pass laws, Kikuyu Muslim believers could seem so estranged that Mau Mau took them to be traitors.[237] The second class was the poor. The poorest were an underclass, unable to afford circumcision.[238] Despite the chairman's fear that they were too poor to be patriotic, by 1950 Mau Mau was recruiting hooligans for their criminal skills. But their undisciplined whoring, drinking and smoking breached security; their impatience menaced the lives of even radical leaders.[239] Hard-bitten townsmen also profiteered by supplying Mau Mau. One, Mohamed Mathu, later exonerated himself by deploring its Kikuyuness.[240] Yet the first urban Kikuyu identity was unavoidable, however irksome it may have been to men like Mathu. Tribe-naming was part of the outer architecture of life, built by official passes, employer stereotypes and chain migrations of workers. It created a grudging solidarity and latent prejudice which politicians distrusted but tried to exploit. Urban middle-class Kikuyuness was very different. It announced success with hospitality, allayed anxiety with officious concern. Traders and clerks in the Kikuyu General Union sponsored traditional dance troupes, denounced Western frivolity, and tried to detain uncircumcised men, repatriate women prostitutes and fine their customers.[241] By word and deed the middle class created a tribe with a civic code. They despised those who did not make the effort, perhaps the very people whose land-clientage their fathers had repudiated at home. Their anxious class pride filled the so-called Mau Mau hymns or *nyimbo* with praise for wealth and scorn for vagrancy. Finally, there was an aspirant ethnic identity of junior townsmen who strove to pay the rising dues of tribal membership, whose ambition the *nyimbo* fanned. The pull on their moral thread is well shown by the collapse of the Anti-Dowry Association the moment its soldier-founders disembarked from the Second World War. Looking for wives, they found fathers-in-law.[242] Kikuyu virtue, this fiasco suggests, would have had little drawing power had it not been tied to the private concerns of property and gender or, in short, to class.

Workers responded to the household's moral pull because it was a far from imaginary asset. No statistical series exist, but all evidence agrees that land and marriage costs rose continually. Land prices, measured in soured friendship, legal fees and then on the market, were pushed up by land alienation, produce sales and population growth. The labours of women rose in value too. The monetization of bridewealth in the 1940s inflated this passport to production and posterity yet faster, a staple of press complaint.[243] Rural capitalism concentrated power by raising costs. Unskilled wages failed to keep pace from the 1930s.[244] The best means to a respectable living, with its ceremonial expense, remained rights in land and fit family labour. Poor households had neither the extra land nor the hired hands with which wealthy neighbours produced a surplus to household needs; they could not therefore enjoy rising export opportunities. But at least the landed poor might feed themselves and keep a man in work, where his wages outweighed the marginal product of his labour on a small plot of increasingly tired soil. Land was a foothold on the spiral stair.

That was what mattered. If external capitalism offered them little, rural capitalism threatened the poor with the loss of their all. The growing risk of exclusion from rights in land imperilled manhood. The dependent relationships that characterized the land-abundant, labour-scarce economy of the past were tested by patron lineages when land became dearer at labour's expense.[245] To keep cultivation rights one had to keep cultivating. Although it was no guarantee that he would retain his land, a wage-worker at least had to have a wife with a hoe to have any prospect of so doing. There is as yet no history of Kikuyu marriage, but rural capitalism appears to have added two new forms of household. In homes neither rich nor poor, men and women maintained conventional spheres of economic autonomy and mutual respect. Above this now middle range, wives of the wealthy few found their food-crop domain devalued by male control over produce sales and salaried office, even if rich women also earned civic influence outside the home. Below, poor men depended on wives whose labour both fed and protected their household.[246] Mutual gender relations became more demanding for the poor. That is the measure of most workers' determination to meet the mounting cost of being Kikuyu. If that was a 'false' ambition it was not an easy option. Its price was high – rising bridewealth, female mastery in the home, and eventually exorbitant fees to unknowable political patrons. The risks in non-payment were higher still.

The poor fought a Kikuyu class struggle, first for adult rights in the community and then for a community that accepted them as adult. Sam Thebere spoke for many. It was costly but all knew that there were no free things. In political strategy as in labouring lives, household and workplace remained tightly entwined. Kikuyu subclan rights became increasingly attenuated; workers had scarcely any rights at all. To build a new tribe was thus as sensible – or as daring – as inventing the claims of workers. The poor did both. Many took strike action to extract from employers the increased resources with which to become tribesmen. The contrasts between external and rural capitalisms, not least the armed protection which the state gave to the former, made that entirely rational. In a complicated world singleness of aim, moral agency, required a multiplicity of means.

LABOUR, LAND, LINEAGE AND OFFICE

I can now suggest how the changing terms of moral agency were argued out. I cannot prove that anybody pursued them in quite the way set out below. The issues are in the evidence, the logic is mine. I believe what follows to be a plausible Kikuyu language of class. But oral and printed argument do not follow the same rules. My account is also one-sided. How the lettered explored the idea of tribe as their authority for gain is fairly clear. Poor men's struggles for an ethnic insurance policy are seen in the scorn of their critics. Women scarcely appear except as objects of male anxiety. From internal dispute and external complaint one can nonetheless pick out a quarrel between land and labour through, and in the language of, time. *Mbari* were the ubiquitous cockpits of conflict. As rural capitalism gripped their institutions, so men developed opposing ideologies, landlord paternalism within *mbari*, community of age or generation without. Propertied space became stratified; moral time made room for manoeuvre. Successful politicians exploited both. Readers were recruited on every side. *Athomi* needed to be Kikuyu; facing clannish division, they helped to define what, in general, a tribe might mean.[247] They proved their worth by shaping personal disputes over property, labour and office. They then used the Bible as a library of instructive stories of united national struggle behind inspired leadership. Tales of civic virtue now echoed Exodus as well as *ituika*.

The new language of clan, class and tribe developed as a means to articulate difference in seven circles of dispute. Two of these were at the centre of life, between generations and genders. The former soon surfaced, the latter flared only after other issues had come to a head. In sequence, then, the changing balance of labour and property caused domestic strife between fathers and sons, set rich over poor, strengthened the rights of descent against the claims of service and alliance, opposed lineage to state office, informed the ideology of conflict between Kikuyu and British and then, reverting to the heart of the matter, estranged old believers from readers and made all men worry about women.

To turn to the first circle of dispute colonial Kikuyu argued between themselves about labour almost before they protested to the British about land. Since labour gave property the two issues were one. Conflict between fathers and sons over stock and women used to be eased by filial defence of family herds. Warriors had also helped mothers to weed fields against reconquest by bush.[248] Wage-migration now drained labour from households, made young men neglect their duties and yet earned them self-mastery. Elders tried to restore discipline in a moral contest, with undertones of class, over trousers, blankets and skins. Young men soon learnt to wear trousers, the uniform of Western decency, when job-hunting; employers paid them more than 'a boy in a blanket only'. But their theatre of deference had two audiences. At home, trousers were the uniform of power; returning migrants therefore, unwilling to offend elders, took off trousers and threw on the blankets thought proper for 'common men'. Elders still wore the sheep- or monkey-skin cloaks which so elegantly flaunted both agrarian wealth and commercial grip over hunting.[249] Almost overnight, fashion in dress, a cloak and blanket affair, came to symbolize the gulf between domestic production for self-mastery and delinquent labour migration. Waged work, *githukumo*, subject to another, was not *wira*, purposeful toil within a web of obligation. Unlike parents or patrons, employers had no relation to workers beyond the wage. Migrants therefore, elders complained, wasted their

Wealth, Poverty & Civic Virtue in Kikuyu Political Thought

pay in daily consumption, a frivolous loss of virtue from the circuit of household production.[250]

Such views coloured relations, secondly, between rich and poor. Whites suspected that Kikuyu chiefs, like others, picked on the poor to supply demands for labour.[251] Makumi wa Mohia blamed poverty for driving him out; chief Muraru thought that wholly proper, implying that the rich were busy enough at home.[252] Officials exploited this labour calculus. In 1919 chiefs called for a record of *mbari* land, *githaka*. In reply, the British pressed them to register migrant workers. These were clearly seen as complementary procedures, one to protect the propertied, the other to control the poor. The same use of social differentiation as a tool of government is seen in the recruitment of chiefs' retainers, the *kapiteni*, from the rich. They had a self-interest in one of their duties, preventing stock theft from whites. If they failed their own large herds would bear the brunt of any collective fine.[253] They also recruited labour for public works or outside employers. The exercise of state power by the wealthy over the poor was a precondition of rural capitalism.

To establish unencumbered property right was another. There were two legacies of the past abundance of land and shortage of labour to overcome. One was the labour strategy of pioneer *mbari*, which had buttressed the reproduction of labour by endowing immigrant clients with dependent rights. *Mbari* land was a mosaic of obligations. The other was redeemable sale, by which a land transfer could be revoked by repaying however many livestock had bought its use, no matter how long ago. Now land was becoming not so much scarce as valuable and labourers not more numerous but more mobile. Loss of land to whites was probably less significant than the addition of market value to its product. Farmers wanted to make improvements too: to build the stone houses which signified progress;[254] and to plant wattle trees, which in the 1930s were the most profitable export but slow to mature.[255] They had to protect investments as never before, against malicious kin, ambitious dependants or redemption at unimproved values. They went to law to turn land into property. They proved the right of descent against allies and clients, then of senior against junior descendants, and commuted redemption rights. As to labour, even before population growth increased its supply, money wages made it more easily available, and more freely disposable, as a market commodity.

This redefinition of *mbari* as descent groups increasingly shorn of clients, the third arena of conflict, now looks to be the most brutal exposure of the dangers to the poor inherent in Kikuyu thought. It was not resisted as such until the 1940s. Initially the process had the familiar look of fission and expansion. Exclusionary effects were slow to appear; piecemeal and personal, they could be resisted only by disputing family history.[256] Moreover, the first affected were *ahoi* stockowners; *mbari*

361

reconstitution called for a limitation on rich men's herds before the repudiation of poor men's labour. There were two patterns, south and north. Southern Kikuyu farmers banked their export earnings in imported livestock.[257] Uphill hoe tillage, afforced by ploughs, competed for land with downhill pasture, much of it alienated to whites under its owners' feet. Contentious since the 1860s, the herders' cause was lost, cut off from their *mbari* seniors by British rather than Kikuyu decision. It was not a harsh fate at the time; the social closure they faced from arable expansion within reduced boundaries was compensated by a vast opening of mobility elsewhere. The history of *mbari* revision is inseparable from that of emigrant labour tenancy or 'squatting' on white farms. Whole households, with dependants, left the Kiambu reserve and its recently alienated border farms to colonize the Maasai pastures now under white ownership in the Rift Valley.[258] The exodus continued through the 1920s. Kikuyu called the Rift *weru*, grassland, or *ruguru*, 'the west', to which, like Americans, high expectations led them out.[259] They went in two streams, adventurers and refugees.[260] Like his colleagues, chief Mairuri saw them both as a threat. Emigrants chose their own destinations 'as profitable places in which to live [and] if all went, there would be no one remaining over whom he could exercise authority.' Chiefs tried both to patronize the upstart profits of adventurers by sponsoring their clientage to known white farmers and to block the escape of refugees. Without opponents to victimize on behalf of the state, chiefs' friends might find that they had to build roads themselves or carry the commissioner's safari gear.[261] Big men first harmed the weak by retaining their services, not by denying their rights.

White settlement came a decade later in the north. Kikuyu herds thus grazed former Maasai land before it was parcelled out to whites. After 1918 white ranchers threw back the Kikuyu pastoral frontier; it became internal, heavier on weak *mbari* claims than in Kiambu. Closest allies were hardest hit. The pastures of *athoni ahoi*, friends with daughters' rights, were so large they had to be repossessed.[262] The fall of *athoni ahoi*, not only in Nyeri, has been matched in thought. Ethnography is rich in old terms for affiliation; modern terms are few and scornful. All clients have become simply *ahoi*, and they in turn 'tenants' or 'beggars'.[263] The Kikuyu Association (KA) of Kiambu chiefs who were also seniors in their *mbari* gave the cue for this moral devaluation, this new language of class, in the early 1920s. Wanting land registers, to stop white expansion, they first prescribed an undifferentiated list of 'githaka owners', then of both 'owners' and 'tenants' and, finally, asked that owners be specified as a minority, distinct from 'the much larger body' who were 'only tenants'.[264] No proverb had moralized the difference between owner and tenant, only rich and poor. This disparity is slim evidence for changing attitudes but if one adds the political history of the time[265] and the further circles of argument below, one may hazard that elders were rethinking social inequality in three ways. First, it might pay to seek an exceptional status at a time when all Africans were legally mere 'tenants-at-will of the Crown'. Then, land was a measurable basis of exception; breadth of patronage was not. They wanted title deeds. While patrilineal descent, lastly, had always had first claim on disputed rights, descent was always debatable; if the KA got its way, lineage property would be safe from amendment by partisan memory. A gazetted gentry was in view, a new class definition of true, *karing'a*, Kikuyu.[266] Land disputes did not begin to crowd the courts until the 1930s. It seems, however, that a silent choice of to whom to deny *mbari* rights had already been made, should the need arise. It would be the majority.

A similar equation of lineage with legitimacy came to colour the politics of chiefship, the fourth circle of dispute. Colonial chiefs have been roughly treated by historians.[267] Everything about them was contradictory, even their critics. But Kikuyu knew what they meant by an arbitrary state; it separated power from virtue. Kikuyu leaders used to emerge; authority was parochial. The British imposed chiefs, delegating power to as few as possible. Hundreds of independent *mbari* were lumped into 60 locations, each a pyramid of subclans, ruling and ruled. *Athamaki* had adjusted claims when all men bore arms. Chiefs announced rules; their retainers monopolized force. *Athamaki* had won repute by 'long and laborious process';[268] the British liked vigorous young chiefs. Wealth had endowed labour with land; chiefs supplied it to the lands of strangers. Big men traded favours in a market of power; the British expected impartial agents on paltry pay. In Kikuyu theory wealth was accountable to selfish human nature; open goat transfers represented known people; they confirmed or challenged known alliances. Wealth earned power; fertile power fed clients. British chiefship baffled such Kikuyu calculation. Competition risked being called subversion, the new sorcery; hidden bribe could ruin open investment; cash was not people. Office bought wealth; police could make good a lack of supporters. But the state's power made its favour vital to all. It conferred divisible benefits which enabled people to live well, like roads, schools, distribution of improved seeds or exemption from forced labour; it imposed partible costs which caused privation, especially the press gang. Nor was the state an institution, however much the British tried to separate executive and judiciary; it was a chief with an eye to keeping allies and isolating enemies. The price of influence and the profits of office flourished on the contrasts, as also boozy abdications by chiefs from the tensions of their role. Chiefs rarely gained the respect of both Kikuyu and British. But if state power outraged small society, it was not easy to mount a coherent critique in stateless Kikuyu thought.

Chiefs were criticized on three grounds which elaborated on the separation of power and virtue. They were thought opportunist, immune to generational discipline and lacking in pedigree. This opposition was confused from the start; more clarity later showed how much its images of political community conflicted. First, colonial records and Kikuyu memory contain much complaint, well aired by historians, that early chiefs were mere camp followers of conquest, men of no standing but known to the British, on the spot. Some used their unprecedented power to claim *ithaka* at the expense of people who had more right to land but were less alert to opportunity. Kinyanjui's career, from porter to paramount chief of Kiambu, is the exemplar.[269] It is hard to know how wide the resentment was. Northern Kikuyu scoffed at the idea that a young if important chief should be honoured in death by burial.[270] But three cautions are in order. First, accusations of lowly origin came oddly from people whose proverbs of equal opportunity taught that all could prosper. Secondly, abnormal times needed rare qualities; some chiefs had proved themselves by bringing followers through famine. Labour for the state was a new way to clear space for civilization; a modern folktale tells how a family scattered by famine was reunited by sons who had grown up to be policemen.[271] Lastly, our sources are suspect. Critics were often from *mbari* other than those of chiefs. To sneer at chiefs who exploited force rather than earned virtue was an easy resort for envious minds.

The complaint that chiefs flouted generational rules was no better founded. The few official references to *ituika* suggest its utility to district commissioners eager to replace conservative elders with enlightened younger men. The turnover of chiefs, under pressure, after the First World War, with young readers often supplanting the remaining veterans of conquest, looked very like the passing of a generation; it was the same story after the next war. Yet Kikuyu often complained that the British had banned the *ituika* allegedly due between the wars, to protect irresponsible chiefs. This was an imaginatively evasive view. Few chiefs lasted anything like 30 years in office; they wielded an executive power which *ituika* had never addressed; there had never been one sole *ituika* anyway. British officials were happy to watch the generational handover proceed; Kikuyu were increasingly divided over its theology. The British did not ban *ituika*; Kikuyu transformed it. Once, perhaps, a process, it became a powerful idea, constantly available as a symbol of opposition to the state.[272]

The third critique of chiefship had more weight. Like the institution it attacked, it contradicted ideas both of equally accessible virtue and of communal *ituika*. The accusation of opportunism levelled at some (by no means all) of the first chiefs grew from a taunt into a theory. Politicians, chiefs included, tried to construct a less exacting colonialism by reminding the British of their debt to the leaders who had first welcomed them and whose sons now served church and state. British mythology and practice had shown the way. A white adventurer's memoirs boasted that his Kikuyu trading partners had eased the path of rule; officials then appended the legitimacy of future dynasty to past alliance by pressing chiefs to send their sons to school.[273] By an act of political judo[274] Kikuyu recaptured the initiative. They elaborated a dynastic political theory which relieved them of dependence on the British by asserting patriarchal alliance with them. They discovered a past which joined dynastic rights, tribe-wide diplomacy and Anglo-Kikuyu treaties to the greatest dynast of all, Queen Victoria. Waiyaki in the south, blood-brother to the man who had become Lord Lugard, was said to have advised Wang'ombe in the north, by courtesy of Karure in the centre. All three frontier barons had welcomed the first white officials. Waiyaki's son Munyua sponsored the Scots mission, Karuri had died a Catholic and Wang'ombe's son Nderi became the senior Nyeri chief, praised by Kenyatta and then murdered by Mau Mau.[275] That was in 1952. Until the 1930s it had seemed that dynastic theory held political promise. It told a history of tribal rather than mere *mbari* authority, no more implausible than that of its alternative, *ituika*. It recalled an older colonialism when the good Queen ruled, Kikuyu land rights had been respected and patriarchs had pushed improvement. Upstart settlers had revoked the treaties of Waiyaki's era once Victoria and Wang'ombe were dead; it was up to government to undo their treachery.[276] And at a time when dynasts were becoming landlords, Kikuyu might establish still greater moral sway over the British if they could present white land alienation as a further betrayal, of relations between patron and *ahoi*.

This is to reach the outermost circle of dispute, reserving the domestic issues of belief and gender to the next section. For whites and blacks production was propaganda. Settlers justified themselves by Kenya's export growth; they feared the observation that they had neither the numbers, the capital nor the skill to farm more than a tiny proportion of their land.[277] Chief Koinange accused them of ostentatiously ploughing hitherto neglected acres to impress visiting commissions of enquiry.[278] Later, in the Mau Mau war, general Kimbo turned the tables. He frightened a Captain Thorpe off his farm on the forest edge. In a political war, white morale depended on the owner's return. Each unoccupied farm was 'a visible Mau Mau success'. 'The enemy's moral victory' continued as long as Thorpe's remained unfarmed,[279] perhaps even more so in Kikuyu eyes because of the general's *nom de guerre*. Kimbo was the brand name of a local cooking fat. Kikuyu power was fat; fatness promised fertility.[280] Under Mau Mau threat, infertile white farms lost power. This equation may seem far-fetched. But Kikuyu had lived with it a long time. They were well warned, too.

The Moral Economy of Mau Mau

In 1911 their senior commissioner advised Kikuyu to use their land if they wished to keep it, a formula they understood.[281] But they complained that the racial battle of the plough was unequal. From their calculus of labour, land and office, the district commissioner of Kiambu inferred that white prosperity must therefore depend on the grant of Kikuyu land titles. Without such protection chiefs saw their duty to export labour as economic treachery, helping white estates to flourish at Kikuyu expense. They knew black labour was essential to settlers, that cultivation expanded with the labour supplied, and feared that such increase would prompt white demands for more land.[282] By 1954 Kimbo had found a violent remedy; before then Kikuyu relied on argument. We must add this outer causal layer to the generational dispute in the cloak and blanket affair; to chief Muraru's unconcern with the migration of the poor who cultivated little anyway; to farmers' displacement of herdsmen from *ithaka* truncated by land alienation; and to the rise in stature of the dynastic heads of *mbari*, clearers of land, against appointed chiefs, exporters of sweat. Labour theory drove these disputes; racial production propaganda sharpened them. Landlord theory was pursued in two further directions, internal and external.

The cultivation contest started in 1899, when frontier *mbari* rushed to claim all vacant land up to the new line of rail.[283] It then induced Kiambu subclan trustees to release grazing reserves for readers to farm, under a 1919 tenancy agreement witnessed by missionaries.[284] It probably influenced their decision to allow *mbari* householders to receive immigrant northern *ahoi* who wanted to live near Nairobi. This gave Kiambu the fastest population growth in Kikuyu,[285] eroding *aramati* control over the emergent land market sooner than in Nyeri or Murang'a.[286] Patriotic landlord theory, thus carried to extremes, turned lords over land into mere landowners, large owners still but no longer *mbari* trustees. By 1950 Kiambu *aramati* had relinquished to their fellow *mbari* owners full discretion over the disposal of family land. Landlord theory was no more effective externally. Demanding the repeal of later land legislation, Kikuyu argued that whites had originally been a category of *ahoi*. Waiyaki had given land for Lugard's fort on that basis. *Ahoi* could never gain control over their hosts' land and labour. But settlers had done so, trampling on the rights of their Kikuyu patrons in defiance of the wishes of their own late Queen. Kenyatta's fable of animal white treachery against Kikuyu man romanticized a common view.[287] Landlord theory may have impressed Kikuyu but, despite chief Koinange's constant reminder, it did not move the British.[288] That was but one of its failings. Its roots in *mbari* rivalry gave chiefs cliques of supporters, allowing them to perform and profit by the business of the state. The same rivalry kept opposition to the level of factional intrigue. Dynastic theory also portrayed past leaders as failures, duped by their

generosity, yet thwarted alternative mobilization in the idiom of *riika*.
Kikuyu readers faced these difficulties. They began to think their way
through them.

Religion and politics

The modernization myth separated religion from politics, yet judged it
by political criteria. Religion was hostile, apathetic or prior to politics.
Nativism was the worst. Fanatic old belief had caused futile deaths in
colonial wars; it turned the frenzied face of Mau Mau against nationalist
reason. Christian enthusiasm could be equally turbulent in millenarian form. But charismatic faith more often caused quietism; prayer at
local Zions was an otherworldly flight from this world's injustice, not an
answer to it. There remained the sober 'Ethiopian' churches, which
valued African leadership more than spiritual gifts. Political science was
more comfortable with these. They were schools of politics in the days
before colonial rulers conceded political rights. The first accounts of
Kikuyu Christianity followed these distinctions. They were reinforced
by the view that the religious clash between Kikuyu and British was
wrapped in culture. But 'cultural resistance' was too easy an explanation
of politics.[289] Our hypotheses have since changed in three ways. We
can accept that there were continuities between Kikuyu and biblical
belief deeper than the differences of culture, that theology and politics
can rationally inform each other and that, nonetheless, matters of faith
can have their own autonomy.

Disagreements within Kikuyu and Christian belief interlocked in the
same way as their political thought and colonial experience. The missionary and Kikuyu encounter was mutual; it brought doubt to both.
There was less of the heroic confrontation between them than mission
or nationalist hagiographies imagine. Kikuyu religion, we may recall,
separated powers, God, ancestors, sorcery and *thahu*; and authorities, priestly elders and prophetic *andu ago*. People emigrated ritually over
ethnic frontiers and between initiation guilds. In *ituika* Kikuyu speculated on the link between wealth, age, ritual payment, witchcraft cleansing and fertility. The battery of replies to misfortune suggests room for
scepticism and enquiry. Christianity extended the range of religious
explanation; few readers found it a self-sufficient substitute. There
were many Christianities to choose from; wandering schooldays made
choice between these very Kikuyu sectarianisms a real one.[290] Catholics
opened fewer windows on the soul than Protestants. These differed over
fundamental matters like the literal truth of the Bible, and secondary
ones, such as readers' abstention from drink, *riika* payments, bridewealth or clitoridectomy. The conservative American Africa Inland Mission (AIM) wanted no social gospel other than soap with salvation; the

Scots and Anglican missions were agents of health and education as much as revelation. Christianity could also give and receive different messages. Whites preached salvation and translated the New Testament before the Old; *athomi* searched out stories of the worldly power of Jehovah and his prophets, Moses especially, in the Swahili Bible. Missionaries urged repentance and improvement; most readers desired disciplined progress, wealthy *wiathi* in this world as much as heaven hereafter. The deepest account of conversion associates Christianity with cultivation; a wealthy Christian's farm was named Paradise.[291] Kikuyu Christianity could be as materialist as any other. Equally, some young Kikuyu felt called because Christianity condemned their own society and its beliefs, while also challenging racial domination. Religious opposition to social or political convention reflected Kikuyu choice as much as missionary demand.[292]

There was no clear social pattern to Christian adhesion or conversion. Some pioneer readers were poor; some orphans, like Kenyatta, with none to stop them going to school. 'I was an orphan now . . . I therefore turned to God', his brother-in-law Bishop Kariuki also remembered. The first women readers were reluctant brides or runaway wives.[293] Youths who explored the new world as workers went as independently to school, hoping to understand it; conversely, ambitious chiefs sent their sons.[294] Increasingly, readers were young men of any origin who saw that literacy paid; some went to the Anglican night school in Nairobi after work. Readers entered all kinds of conflict, accordingly, in this sixth circle of dispute. They disobeyed fathers, becoming 'loose like the English', broke family ritual solidarity, threatened to undergo mission circumcision if parents did not initiate them early.[295] They menaced *mbari* control of property by going off as *ahoi* to a mission estate or coming to an *mbari* other than their own to open an outschool.[296] Mission protection allowed them to refuse chiefs' calls to perform state labour, road-building or porterage. Some officials tolerated clerical exemption from these misnamed 'tribal obligations' as a working theory of modernization.[297] Many *athomi*, Kenyatta and his early political hero Harry Thuku included, broke age-set ranks by mission-supervised initiation, with Christian circumcision fathers. In a later access of piety, Kenyatta blamed the loss of *riika* discipline for promiscuity among the young, 'foreign fondling' as it was called.[298] Many saw change as decay. Young readers subverted elders' control of knowledge. They wore trousers. They attacked ritual objects and deliberately invited uncleanness or *thahu*, breaking dietary rules and handling corpses. This last is remembered most, a matter of disgust or pride.[299]

But readers had many social uses and all but the closest of mission intimates needed their non-Christian community. Compromise was found everywhere, first in households. Parents wanted heirs to understand the new power. *Athomi* sons needed fathers' support and the approval of fathers-in-law to marry; Christian brides were few.[300] Polygyny remained the mark of male success; as in Buganda adult church membership therefore became largely excommunicate.[301] *Athomi* really flourished in parochial politics. Chiefs had clerks. They counted huts, tallied the tax collected on them, recorded migrant workers and legal decisions, banked fines. Their enormous power could be curbed only with the same literacy. Familiarity with the skills of office and a salaried income pushed *athomi* to the fore in every dispute. They mapped *mbari*, drawing up land claims against neighbouring subclans. Success earned a share of the winnings. They listed *mbari* genealogies to advance descent against clientage, then threw genealogy at upstart chiefs. Kenyatta's first public service, and political failure, was as legal spokesman for his patron, chief Kioi, whom others accused of land-grabbing second only to Kinyanjui. *Mbari* soon scrambled for access to the state. Their *aramati* gave land and labour to build mission outschools. Rapid mission expansion in the 1920s owed as much to corporate competition for power as to private spiritual hunger.[302] *Mbari* politics scarcely made for *athomi* solidarity. Intimations of that came in the alternative idioms of age and generation and in an appropriate context – war.

HARRY AND THE DRAGON

State power and the emergence of property hardened *mbari* divisions but subverted *riika* solidarities. Mission initiation, the end of collective raids and rise of individual migrant labour, conflict between chiefs' retainers and those whom they put to work, all fractured age sets. Unceremonious initiation 'by the roadside' or *njiriani*, always the recourse of poor youths who could not find a sponsor, was thought to increase.[303] Warrior sets faded out; there were no breaks in annual initiations after 1912, needed to give room for either a new regiment or a generation hand-over.[304] The trauma of the First World War then revived *riika* in new forms. Chiefs recruited porters for the Carrier Corps who supplied the campaign in German East Africa, now Tanzania. Conscription was soon seen as a death sentence; twice as many Kikuyu carriers died serving the empire as Mau Mau insurgents did fighting it. Chiefs demanded ten sheep to turn a blind eye.[305] Until 1917 mission students were exempt. Warned that the state would have to call them up too, missionaries raised the Kikuyu Mission Volunteers, 1,800 strong, and led them off to war. Almost all returned. Total carrier mortality was nearly one quarter, mostly from dysentery or pneumonia; the KMV lost fewer than 6 per cent. All had been issued with Swahili Bibles. One can see why veterans remembered that 'religion was mostly learned in the war'. So was independence; teachers carried on while missionaries were away.[306]

War, epidemic and postwar recession created two Kikuyu parties, establishment and critics. Political division crossed racial lines. Settlers made Africans pay for the slump with more tax, pass controls and wage cuts. They feared Indian demographic and economic pressure more than African protest. This racial conflict widened Kikuyu division. Chiefs and their retainers were the first to mobilize, calling on the state to relax demands which humiliated them and angered their people. They had missionary friends and the ear of district commissioners. Their alliances were ready-made; they did not wish to enlarge them. The calculations of patronage set their face against any body outside their personal control; it might open the rifts beneath them. Their politics was smaller than ethnicity, knots of state power and *mbari* faction. It could not be attacked on its own terms; narrow rivalry needed wider support. *Athomi* who suffered by exclusion from power had to find allies. The KMV gave a shared inspirational past; they had school networks and urban contacts; access to the Nairobi Indian press sharpened their conflict with chiefs and missions. Intrigues became ideologies. Chiefs took on dynastic authority; their opponents explored a range of dissident thought.

Harry Thuku led the opposition. Ambiguous first hero of nationalism, he pioneered the mass meeting and later became a leading 'loyalist' in the fight against Mau Mau. His movement was a mosaic. It coalesced in the Nairobi village of Pangani in early 1921 and ended in a police fusillade, with 25 dead, a year later. Rarely can such motley militants have acknowledged a single leader, in foretaste of Kenyatta's problem. 'Thukuism' followed the discordant banners of clan and pan-ethnic education, exodus and *ituika*. Thuku's subclan, Gathirimu, were fighting a rural battle of chiefship, resisting the appointment of his classmate Waruhiu, the then chief's clerk. They used sorcery to raise money, asserted that the current chief was the seventh in their 'royal' line and, in an early repudiation of *athoni ahoi*, of which Waruhiu's father was one, denied that the chief presumptive had any relation 'of any kind whatsoever' with their *mbari*.[307] Thuku told London nothing about royal families. Telegraphing wider African grievances, he demanded the vote for all educated British subjects. Literacy transcended ethnicity and race; missionaries should no longer represent African interests. He issued manifestoes in Swahili and used an Indian's car.[308] But by what authority did he speak to fellow Kikuyu who were not Gathirimu?

Thuku's Murang'a supporters in the Anglican Church Missionary Society (CMS) found biblical support. He was called to lead them from slavery, as '*our* living God' Jehovah had chosen Moses in Egypt or David to fight Goliath.[309] Kiambu enthusiasts compared him with Christ; they angered chiefs, even old believers, by calling them Judas.[310] Readers initiated during the influenza epidemic of 1919 had taken the name *Kimiri* or 'flu, believing that God had spared them for some great task.[311] Such sense of moral time, part Kikuyu, part biblical, seems to have led Thuku to liken himself to the old symbol of power, *ndamathia*. The evidence fuels speculation, it does not provide proof; but a generational analogy was as apt as the messianic. In July 1921 Kinyanjui called chiefs to the Chania falls near Thika, one of the rainbow-dragon's haunts, to discuss Thuku. Thuku came uninvited. Some say Kinyanjui tried to throw him in the river, the fate of sacrificial virgins.[312] In reply, Thuku toured Murang'a, beyond Kinyanjui's reach. He excited his audiences, unlettered crowds outnumbering readers, by forbidding them to work for the state. He had broken its power. 'Tell all the Europeans that I am truly a snake,' he said, 'Do they wish to mix milk with blood?'[313] Was this his answer to Kinyanjui, that he was no sacrifice to power but its life-renewing reality?[314] The British reclaimed power over Thuku through their chiefs' sworn statements that he endangered peace; arrested him; shot supporters who tried to release him from his Nairobi police cell; and sent him into internal exile. His ideas, not the pallidly pan-ethnic but the thrillingly tribal, were taken up by the survivors who founded the Kikuyu Central Association in 1924.

GENERATING NATIONALISM

The KCA were the first generation of Kikuyu nationalists. They invented a nation, as others have done elsewhere, at a time of rapid social change and new state demands. Existing power was discredited; there was no political community. New men, they aspired to make their private interest the public good. Having to invent a public they conjured up a tribe, not so much an impatient constituency as a contested idea. It loomed in their language of disagreement, from cloaks and blankets to the threatened drowning of Thuku – or was it Moses? – in *ndamathia*'s pool. Contrary tribal images, dynastic and collective, then shaped and linked disputes. Chiefs tried to confine politics to their locations. The KCA, a middle class[315] in formation, moralized inequality in an age of social closure by opening politics up. Readers strove not to be a separate class like the prostitute, *maraya*, who consorts with strangers. They aimed to meet old tests of leadership in a new moral community, to be a vanguard, *mambere*. Using external opportunity they could not do without internal trust. The first modern oaths of solidarity, it seems, were forced on allegedly untrustworthy *athomi* by unlettered militants during the Thuku crisis.[316] Readers therefore paid heed to the spiralist parable of the prodigal son. Filled with the husks of strangers, they must make their peace at home.[317] To naturalize their nonconformity they tried to remake their rural community of esteem. They had to convert the pollution of grave-digging and the smell of soap into the oiled and ochred cleanliness of wealth. The KCA announced that intention and welcomed wealth's burdens in the name they gave themselves – the League of Compassion, *uiguano wa tha*.[318]

The politically active, establishment and critics, were, as they had always been, the materially successful. Often employed by whites, they cultivated domestic resources. Not wholly dependent on missions or state, they were their own masters. They exercised *wiathi*, said and did, practised what they preached. They owned shops, carts and, soon, lorries; farmed, milled and exported grain. The most dissident were out-school teachers who owed more to their *mbari* than to missionary support.[319] Politicians were divided by official favour and personal enmity. Chiefs could be the larger capitalists.[320] Ins and outs were one political class, often related to each other, if only by lineage rivalry, and with the same ambitions. The narrow structure of power satisfied few. Power and its frustration fostered polemical political thought. Formerly dissident dynastic theory became the official line, as *mbari* politics assumed a larger role in appointment to chiefships by a better-informed regime. Chiefs straddled society and the state, some with growing ease. For as long as they were excluded from power their rivals tried to remake both, linking alternative constituency, theology and political thought.

Chiefs began to master not only *mbari* politics but *riika* legitimacy too, paying, if need be, an ox-of-climbing to join the ritually senior *Mwangi* generation.[321] Opposition to them was necessarily ambivalent, especially in the shared fears for Kikuyu land. The state was a similarly awkward target. White fears of urban politics and government's need for more African revenue had induced reform. Local Native Councils (LNCs) were inaugurated in each Kikuyu district in 1925. Chiefs were in official majorities; KCA men were among the elected councillors. If chiefs and critics had not been parties then LNC debates made them so. Councils spent their rates, which were levied on all, on services like roads, schools, clinics and markets, which rich peasants, some of them KCA members, disproportionately used or supplied.[322] By using public goods, not least to check Indian commercial supremacy, the KCA gave tacit consent to the state while opposing its agents. The party had to find some critical distance from the state, denying any hand in its demands while lending a hand for progress. The question was how to make the LNC, a state body, into a friendly 'helper' or *muteithia*, a wishful name given to the age set initiated when councils were announced.[323] Some KCA members told of this more pliant state in dynastic *mbari* narratives, only to see them appropriated by chiefs. Another past was available. Age and generation *riika* began to acquire, in competition with dynastic theory, the equally invented tribal image of democracy.

Southern and northern readers acted differently here. The Kiambu opposition seems to have mobilized only in age sets. In Murang'a and Nyeri politics took generational forms too, a contrast which later shaped Mau Mau. Famine had taught age sets secrecy if needed; generations had to display wealth. Strong Kiambu chiefship forced its sternest critics underground; weak northern chiefs could not quash open conflict. But Kiambu was not all cabals. Male initiates, delighting in the gender at the heart of politics, shocked elders by denouncing marriage while teasing their Christian age-mates with polygynous dreams. *Athomi* used age sets as openly but to more purpose, as school teams and old-boy networks. For years the KCA, a club for married men, full adults, ruled that no member could be younger than the influenza age set, on whose readers so much duty had been laid. But the party in Kiambu had a narrow base in small, secret, age-set societies with specific land fears.[324] While Kiambu pioneered new age-set organizations, new ideas seem to have crystallized first in Murang'a, the KCA's district of origin and the most extravagant in paying for *ituika*.

Northern Protestant *athomi* – Catholics played small part in politics – were more divided over taking part in ritual practice than in Kiambu. Kiambu missions were uniformly hostile to pagan rites; northern ones were not. The CMS at Kahuhia, Murang'a, was unusually tolerant. Age-set fees caused few problems; generation fees raised theological strife. The dragon of *ituika* focused the conflict between the new message of salvation and the old theology of abundance. *Athomi* who refused to pay *riika* goats saw them as sacrifices that blasphemed the Saviour. Accommodators thought them payment for the services of the wealthy, who already had God's blessing. Liberal missionaries watched that the goats were eaten, not put aside for *Ngai*; their readers urged more usefully but in vain that the stock values be credited to a schools fund.[325] Rival theologies had political effects. KCA thought distanced itself from its clerical mentors independently of the notorious clash over clitoridectomy. But arguments about *ituika* and female sexuality were connected, again, through the labour theory of value.

Missionaries set the polemical context. The first CMS priest in Murang'a thought *ituika* a fraudulent cult, its shrines 'vile dens of infamy'. Others followed him.[326] Their problem was to find a properly Kikuyu distinction between Old and New Testaments. Missionaries were happy to turn Jehovah into *Ngai*. To equate Christ and *ndamathia* was unthinkable. But the verb by which the proud redeemed the country at *ituika* best conveyed his saving of the meek.[327] The theological debt was tolerable only if its source were damned. The Kikuyu New Testament came out in 1926, during Murang'a's *ituika*. In its Swahili predecessor the dragon of the apocalypse had been a snake, *joka*, like the serpent of Eden but larger. Reading Revelation in their own tongue, however, Kikuyu found that the dragon was no longer a snake, but *ndamathia*. And *ndamathia*, cast out of heaven, was now the devil.[328] Two Bible scholars, Stephen Kinuthia and Mathew Njoroge, had helped to found the Kikuyu Association. Insulted as they were by Thuku,[329] was the damnation of *ndamathia* not only essential theology but also happy politics?[330] Kenyatta knew his Bible as well and came to *ndamathia*'s rescue. To him it was a 'sacred monster', his 'national totem',[331] a democratic dragon to tame the state.

I cannot trace *ndamathia*'s path to democracy in detail, but the KCA clearly saw itself as the generation next due to master the monster, power. Kenyatta, as general secretary, started the monthly *Muigwithania* in 1928. Its readers called themselves *irungu* or 'straighteners', the apprentice name for the next *riika* which, duly installed, would be called *Maina*. Kenyatta described how the KCA *irungu* responded in the mid-1920s to 'the spirit of *ituika*'.[332] The exiled Thuku was remembered each 16 March, the day of the Nairobi shootings, for ending the oppression and hunger of forced labour after the war.[333] If past transfers of *riika* wealth removed the taint of oppression from the starvation of clients, that had always been *ituika*'s theme. It was central to its postwar myths, the first of which a visionary white forester heard in the early 1920s. His 'secrets of the council' included a version of the central African tale of the cosmic tower, like the Tower of Babel. The Kikuyu story differed from most others in two respects. Their forebears had built the tower not in hope of immortality but in fear of their king. It fell, not by God's anger but by worker resistance to the privations of forced labour.[334] The KCA's stories also told of oppression, hunger and rebellion. Different versions were given by the two men it sent to London in 1931, Parmenas Githendu Mukiri, head teacher at CMS Kahuhia, and Kenyatta. Mukiri told how starving conscripts, weary of war, deposed their King Gikuyu and restored cultivation. All later generations were 'revolutionary movements' of circumcised men and women to protect democracy.[335] Kenyatta, who cited Aristotle, not Mukiri, as his authority, added the taming of *ndamathia* to the tale, altered the sequence of *riika* and disputed the property right seized at *ituika*. Mukiri thought it communal. But that was to grant the British case for not buying out evicted Kikuyu landholders, which was that vacant 'communal land' could be found elsewhere. More carefully, Kenyatta contrasted common citizenship in circumcision with 'family ownership' of land, *riika* with *mbari*. The *iregi* or refusers, his revolutionary generation, had created dynastic landlord right. KCA opposition theory had captured, at a stroke, the official view, perhaps at the expense of opposition.[336]

The myth of tyranny overthrown gave Kikuyu a collective past, the KCA a constituency, and its demand for a democratically elected paramount chief the authority of past precedent. Kenyatta's democratic dragon promoted possessive individualism in the service of community. His three differences with Mukiri said more about actual politics. His addition of *ndamathia* to the myth showed the gulf between more and less convinced Christians. Anglican *athomi* from Kahuhia, like Mukiri, furnished much KCA thought; members of the most liberal of missions, they still valued white approval. The KCA was torn between two respectabilities.[337] But, secondly, readers on both sides wrote history; the prodigal's shame was the root of cultural nationalism. Whatever their theology, literates could not abide the easy eclecticism of an unlettered past; they argued it out. Mukiri and Kenyatta's difference over past generation lists could not be slurred in subsequent speech. To reduce nationalism to class interest or a political structure to match the state is to miss such intellectual challenge. Readers disputed how to build a nation in a standardized print language which they helped to create.[338] Like all historians the KCA found that controversy stimulated research. Mukiri probably got his *ituika* story from the folklore society he founded in 1928. Kenyatta posed editorial questions on custom. His half-brother James Muigai, who later photographed idyllic scenes for *Facing Mount Kenya*, wanted patriotic history; if *athomi* despised their people, so too would whites.[339] Kikuyu wrote at least five histories between the wars.[340] Arguments about unity produced composite answers; historical controversy was reconciled by creating more distant pasts. The best-informed missionary believed that the tribal Adam, Gikuyu, was a product of this era. *Mwene-nyaga*, the 'owner of whiteness', an old name for God, was also revived; he was more firmly seated on the sacred Mount Kenya than the missionary-adopted *Ngai*.[341]

The production of history may have united KCA readers whom the dragon divided. But the third issue between Mukiri and Kenyatta, which reflected a split social constituency, was ultimately fatal for the party. They disputed the land right won by *ituika*, communal or 'family'. In his book Kenyatta, whose father had 15 *ahoi*, later stifled discussion of dependent tenures by waffling on about Merrie Africa.[342] The British also prevaricated in the face of capitalism's attack on the supposed equilibrium of the old '*githaka* system'. Under this the subclan trustees, *aramati*, were thought to have balanced 'seigniory and usufruct', or overall *mbari* control and the user rights of its full members or 'right holders' and clients. A 1929 land tenure enquiry reported that *mbari* redefinition was taking opposite paths within the growing ascendancy of right-holding descent over discretionary clientage. Northern *aramati* were becoming livestock barons; smallholders were emerging in the south. Both looked ominous. Barons excited class conflict, independent peasants were notoriously obdurate. Nervous of any decision on African tenure and anxious to preserve 'tribal control', the British did not know what to do.[343] Nor did the KCA. Chiefs did, committed now to the dynastic rights of 'seigniory' over tenants. *Muigwithania* reported that many of them hated the KCA.[344] In reply, one might expect the KCA to espouse individual occupier rights. They did do so, but ambiguously. They wanted individual rather than subclan title, but not universal freehold. They wished to reserve a customary discretion for *mbari* elders. In London Kenyatta sounded as dynastic as any chief, foreshowing his book's myth of *ituika*.³⁴⁵ Moreover, while chiefs exploited British discord to blast individual tenure, the KCA missed the same chance to defend it. The 1929 committee favoured legal inaction but, in his minority report, Kenya's cleverest district commissioner, Sidney Fazan, urged that smallholdings be registered, with limits on the right of elders to evict improving tenants.³⁴⁶ The chiefs of the KA, now the Kikuyu Loyal Patriots (KLP), were aghast. Misrepresenting Fazan, but knowing wealth and virtue from poverty and delinquency, they condemned his 'communism' for proposing to give 'the things of a rich man or the property of a hard worker' to 'be divided amongst all people who are staying idle in their homes'.³⁴⁷ The KCA welcomed the report and passed over in silence the opportunity to support Fazan.³⁴⁸

Why then did the KCA call for individual title but with so little apparent enthusiasm, or Mukiri and Kenyatta draw different lessons from *ituika*? The answer will help to explain both the connection of class to tribal consciousness between the wars and the later terror of Mau Mau. First, it must be said that any definition of property was politically dangerous and conceptually crude. The idea of past communal property blamed the British for present Kikuyu conflict but left each household naked in the face of land alienation. Kenyatta's 'family ownership', my landlord or dynastic theory, defended Kikuyu in general but set right holders, thought to be a minority, against their dependants. Individual title was the surest defence against settlers – if it also prohibited inter-racial sale. But to establish title would, finally, divide right holders between improving farmers who wanted property and cultivating herdsmen who needed agreements. To secure the necessary *mbari* support would be a costly and disruptive gamble. In any case, all definition was dubious. It transformed people into a thing. Kikuyu property was relationship. Land was people, not the product of a contract enforced by law. All in all, it paid to be vague on principle, particularly for a representative body.

No scholar has yet analysed the KCA by landed status. Without full knowledge of kin and connection it is foolish to try. But the evidence of thought and action suggests that KCA leaders were right holders – householders in *mbari* core lineages – and that members were often *ahoi* or other clients. Right-holder interest is plain to see. KCA political action was mainly concerned to defend *mbari* land, in a generalization of individual readers' spokesman role in litigation. Political conflict began to suggest the need for appropriate property law in four contexts. The first came from KCA protests against chiefs who afforced land claims with a strong arm or a packed bench of elders. Equally commonly, *mbari* also invoked KCA help to protect their authority over the local outschool from the central mission station. *Aramati* had scrambled for schools so that their *mbari* could learn white power; some feared that their outschool had become a tool of white power over them. Fear could turn petition into direct action; in Nyeri's 'war of the gardens' in the late 1920s, KCA-backed *mbari* uprooted CSM school vegetable plots lest their new agricultural curriculum encourage white land seizure. KCA opposition to the AIM in Murang'a sprang from a conjuncture of conflict over both chief and school.[349] Thirdly, some politicians took up patriotic production to defend a reserve boundary. James Beauttah, later KCA leader in Murang'a, was summoned from his job in Mombasa to buy land on the border 'to stop the advance of the European Settlers'. Once a runaway orphan, his *mbari* connection with the land he was defending is unclear. In two other cases high lineage standing looks to have been essential. The historian Stanley Kiama Gathigira, of the Progressive Kikuyu Party, promoted himself sole claimant to an area of excised forest land after squaring all neighbouring *mbari*. Job Muchuchu, a KCA leader on another border, best explained their role. His *mbari* was 'like a tongue between the teeth' and his the tongue to stop the teeth of white settlement from closing.[350]

The fourth context was the most contentious, showing how a desire for progress, as the readers' party, could at first clash and then mesh with the KCA's need, as spiralists, to make peace with their kin. It concerned death and burial. The British had tried before the First World War to get Kikuyu to bury at least those who died on the roads, in full European view; *athomi* later mounted a general campaign, with equally little effect; by 1925 the KCA were so impatient with Kikuyu obduracy that they asked the governor to arrange 'decent burials' and two years later were ready to collude with government in making them compulsory.[351] Christianity and public health changed Kikuyu burial practice more than any other aspect of life. At least three missions were built on sites left empty as 'a place of the dead', hyena country.[352] Converts took some persuading that all dead should be interred, not just the wealthy old; deaths in mission hospitals then loaded a growing grave-digging burden on them. One of the LNCs' first public health enactments required all dead to be buried by their relatives. Some paid *athomi* to do so; most took no notice. Graves were dug anywhere; KA members of the Kiambu LNC protested at this 'waste of cultivable land', since farmers dared not disturb them. Each *mbari* then had to set aside a grave-yard; this meant breaking another taboo, on the carriage of bodies. Healers profited; they cleansed bereaved old believers, getting them to 'vomit all impurities imposed on you by these cursed readers.'[353] But, with history being scanned for intimations of property, there were clear correlations between burial and memory, exposure and oblivion. When chief Koinange – who had buried his father Christian-style in 1916 with large stones on top – appealed for restitution of his *mbari* land, he named 14 ancestors lying under what was now European coffee; he did not mention the others 'as they were thrown out to the wild beasts.'[354] It looked as if burial might pay; its enthusiasts on the Kiambu council were all landed dynasts. The climax of Christian burial in the service of *mbari* came in February 1933. To prove to the doubting Kenya Land Commission his claim to white land, Koinange allowed his grandfather to be exhumed, a terrible desecration. *Athomi* uncovered the remains, which were then 'reverently removed to a coffin' and reburied by Canon Leakey of the CMS.[355] The cursed readers had a point, after all. It was the one on which KCA and chiefs were most agreed. That is perhaps the most decisive proof for which one could wish that KCA leaders were right holders, dissident dynasts, and that the 30 per cent of *mbari* representatives who in 1932 were Christian were indeed *aramati*.[356] Chiefs would not otherwise have cooperated with KCA councillors to compel burial; only if right holders controlled the graveyard would *ahoi* stay submissive even underground.

The question can now be put more crisply. Why did the KCA not follow chiefs and simply call for dynastic titles to distinguish '*githaka* owner' or right holder from tenant, according to what was spuriously called 'custom'? That would meet the need of all who defined custom as the rights of descent and protect *mbari* seniors against chiefs, missions and buried *ahoi*. But the KCA wanted individual title within a flexible custom which did not explicitly separate owner and tenant. Two answers suggest themselves. First, individual title benefited only a few people sufficiently to repay the cost of marshalling *mbari* witness. These were right holders in powerful, supportive lineages, whose capital investment in stone houses, paddocks or tree crops made them fear litigation for land redemption at the paltry values that had prevailed a generation or more before. Rich *athomi* are indicated, especially those who had helped to expand *mbari* boundaries in the courts or whose frontier farming waged the racial battle of the plough. The KCA demand for individual title may also reflect its relative strength in Murang'a and Nyeri, since redeemability had almost disappeared in Kiambu by the 1920s, if indeed it had ever existed on this recently colonized frontier. Capital made land redemption an issue; Christianity helped to combat the sorcery with which it might be prosecuted.[357] But if its leaders were served by individual title, the KCA refusal to define custom as a conflict between owner and tenant is best explained by its party interest. *Mbari* could not fight alone. They needed a form of association. The *mihiriga* or 'nine clans of Kikuyu' were too insubstantial to provide a common front. If the apprentice generation could be said to have a secretariat it was the KCA. The KCA's own bureaucracy was the network of mission outschools. This was the nub. Many readers, teachers who served away from home, were *ahoi* at increasing risk of eviction. They paid their incremental age-set fees as an insurance. Equally, as Kenyatta and others said, missions were like the cattle kraals which protected Kikuyu from hyenas.[358] In other words, well-connected *ahoi*, clients-in-friendship, were as useful as ever. Ambitious right-holding elders, like KCA members, were well advised to treat them with a flexible discretion. The question was for how long that could be exercised with compassion, *tha*.

Thus divided, the KCA developed two agrarian patriotisms. The first was the virtuous pursuit of middle-class interest. To make private Kikuyu property fruitful was for Kikuyuland's good. At a time of danger, when settlers seemed about to win self-rule within a projected East African Federation, the Kikuyu civilizing mission deprived white encroachment of its excuse of black idleness.[359] Right holders could mobilize patriotic production once they had freed their land from history's encumbrances. *Ahoi* could not safely do the same before a land market was generalized; but their interest, I have argued, was nursed by their right-holding leaders. Canon Leakey's son, Louis, believed that it was the *ahoi* membership who, seeking to reopen social mobility, pressed the KCA to add to its platform the demand for return of the 'stolen lands'. The Leakey family's ties with chief Koinange – who condemned Kenyatta's conceit in going to London – makes this partisan evidence, but it has the ring of truth.[360] It is the best there is without KCA minutes. The KCA demand for the return of all alienated land came late, not until 1929, and temperately, invoking the principle of redeemable sale. It was coupled with the middle-class request that Africans be permitted to buy in the white land market which would remain.[361] Educated *mbari* right holders thus responded to their *ahoi* needs, but without urgency. Defence of existing Kikuyu land was their main concern. Their internal authority was as yet scarcely questioned by external despair. For Kikuyu farm production was expanding. Peasant emigration as 'white highland' squatters remained open, since the 1930s depression halted the capitalization of settler farming. The social closure of *mbari* redefinition had barely begun. Conflict of interest between right holder and client was not yet a source of terror, although chief Waruhiu, foretelling his own fate, warned that land disputes would shortly be settled in blood.[362]

The opposition's political divisions nonetheless ran deep. *Athomi* theology was at odds over generation and *ituika*. Perhaps this best explains why Murang'a's huge investment in prospective virtue in the mid-1920s was not crowned with a formal transfer of authority by the *Mwangi* generation; the imagination of 'tribe' had imposed on *ituika* a hurdle of uniformity it had never had before. *Irungu* remained a generation-in-waiting, despite the prosperity which its members enjoyed in these well-watered years.[363] In any case, the livestock fees for earning age-grade seniority or supplanting the older generation could be realized only in judicial authority over *mbari* property. Collective opposition continually dissolved itself in segmented satisfaction. Young men sought their fortune together; when it came they parted company. The KCA generation learned this from experience as well as by recording their parents' proverbs.[364] The Kikuyu were not, as they claimed, 'a solid compact tribe' whose 'tribal customs' sanctioned rule under 'one educated paramount chief'.[365] The class interest of married men of property was another matter. It was not an ethnic institution which divided but a tribal aspiration under which all readers could unite.

CLASS, GENDER AND CLAN

Harry Thuku returned from exile early in 1931, a political hero.[366] His first thought was for virtue and authority; for these he needed an improved farm and a stone house. He evicted the tenants who had farmed in his absence, compensating them for their banana patch. Dividing the property with his elder brother, the *muramati*, 'so that there would be no arguments later with [their] children', he formally sued him for possession, to reinforce agreement with law. The local elders witnessed the boundary, doubtless thinking their fee of one fat sheep easily earned. While Thuku saw to his property and posterity, he searched old men's memory for a pamphlet on his *mbari* history. In the language of Genesis and Exodus, he showed how his kin were both 'very rich people' and stepbrothers to the prophet clan of the Maasai.[367] Wealthy *athamaki* still expanded their authority with inter-ethnic alliance.

This is nothing less than a parable of an emergent middle class, a narrative of responsibly possessive individualism, telling how some men won the property of self-mastery, 'Paradise' as it was called in Thuku's case, later to be Sam Thebere's dream. They did so at the expense of the weak, by insider mastery of the law. They drew up clan charters in a sacred, tribal, print language, dynastic title-deeds for those whose ancestry they chose to record. Thuku showed (as all *mbari* could if they tried) both his exclusively Kikuyu descent from the local Garden of Eden, *Mukuruwe wa Gathanga*, and his affinity to neighbouring peoples. All this was a preface to re-entering the politics of defending his people. He no longer confused the interest of lineage with the language of generation, as in 1922; a senior householder now, his private inequality could be converted directly into public cares. *Athomi* spiralists were determined not to be seen, by themselves or others, as 'selfish or self-regarding' men.[368] But nor would they allow their manhood itself to be challenged.

Muigwithania and the Catholic *Wathiomo Mukinyu* were the middle-class voice. They called their readers to private wealth, to give a public example of defence against the encircling wilderness of colonial oppression. 'Prostitutes' aspiring to be 'forerunners', they deplored the degradation and disease of migrant labour and hymned domestic production and trade; these would remove the stigma of *ucenji* or 'heathendom' pinned on Kikuyu by Muslim townsmen and white farmers alike.[369] Legend told how the ancestors had rebelled against the waste of their labour in warfare or folly-building on behalf of their tyrant king. Domestic cultivation now, whether in Kikuyuland or in squatter villages on white farms, would similarly defeat the debilitating slavery of working for whites. Husbandmen needed productive wives, 'earth softeners';[370] but female, urban Kenya threatened this vista of masculine ethnicity. And by 1934 the dynastic base on which propertied male hopes had rested was smashed by the British. The years of the 'female circumcision crisis' and the Kenya (or Carter) Land Commission were even more fateful for Kikuyu nationalism than has been generally realized.

At a time when the cursed readers of the KCA were advocating both compulsory burial and the rebuilding of all insanitary huts – which their district commissioner feared would make all Kikuyu homeless[371] – they praised stone or brick houses, square, windowed and iron-roofed. These were not, they pleaded, alien monstrosities but the best defence against the yet more fearful diseases of foreign rule. Jiggers had come – sand-fleas which laid their eggs in toes and crippled people – and plague increased with the strange invasion. It was easier to clear jiggers and rats out of airy houses than gloomy huts. White-imported mealy-bug and blackscale also attacked sturdy Kikuyu crops; but then better granaries could be made from imported chicken wire.[372] For people with a proverbial nose for the stench of poverty, the politics of the new-fangled cleanliness of wealth – soaped, close-cropped, trousered, frocked, with orderly defecation in pit latrines – was crucial. Chief Koinange capped his case against Federation by reflecting that if a mere Governor thought Africans too dirty to visit, a federal High Commissioner would be quite out of reach. Conversely, Louis Leakey cited his stone house and flower garden to predict the evanescence of white supremacy.[373] Joseph Kang'ethe, the KCA president, was as much concerned by the sneers of Swahili townsmen; Kikuyu must trade profitably, to disprove their nickname of *mucenji* or heathen. Readers should also teach parents the things of youth.[374] Education was the first of these. Many elders thought school a waste of juvenile labour. In reply, readers compared it with stock-herding and raiding. Literacy created and defended family property; readers were the warriors of today.[375] Kikuyu of all persuasions voted much of their LNC revenue for government secondary schools. The missionary schools of their youth were inadequate; if school was to be *muteithia*, a helper, it must be, like square houses, as near as possible their own creation.[376]

Reassuring themselves of their fitness to lead, KCA members did not forget policy. Their goal was patriotic production. To rebut the settler jibe of native idleness and keep foreign pests at bay, profitable farming must bring migrant workers home. Better farming raised issues of gender and class which at the time were suppressed by continuing belief in equality of opportunity and the virtue of wealth, ideally embodied in the polygynous household. Signing himself *muteithia wa bururi*, the country's helper, Henry Gichuiri saw the KCA as husband of the Kikuyu. The party was a shepherd; it was his wife's duty to protect his land by cultivating. He praised contract ploughing as an aid to production but failed to consider how that might damage women's status.[377] Job Muchuchu was proud that his *mbari* had saved women work by employing a European plough team for the incredible sum of £650, raised by selling stock.[378] Kenyatta commended agricultural officers' advice (given to men, not women); he was tired of hearing that Kikuyu merely scratched the ground like partridges.[379] But farming must pay. Africans were still forbidden to grow coffee, the most profitable of Kenya's crops. Kikuyu wanted it on grounds of public health and fertility. Coffee would kill rats by financing stone houses; and syphilis, by persuading migrant workers to leave loose women and come home.[380] The social closures of rural capitalism would serve the whole community. And those whose labour weakened Kikuyu and strengthened whites must play their part. Kenyatta, with a gift for metaphor, dreamed up in London a homesick exile's image of a nation. All absent workers, he thought, should make a model of the shelter from which people guarded their crops. This would remind them of home; a bird out looking for food remembered its nest. But it was better to return; circumcision among strangers looked like cowardice and did not heal. Workers must remember Moses. He refused the sinful luxury of becoming the son of Pharoah's daughter; they must leave trivial jobs which caused disobedience, return to their people and accept the discipline of school. 'Poor Kikuyu' damaged the Kikuyu cause, as 'poor whites' were thought to hurt settlers. They weakened communal virtue.[381] Household labour was becoming more explicitly required of 'Kikuyu', for oneself or for a Kikuyu patron. School and migrancy gave orphans too much freedom. The past was better ordered, when men without strength of their own could find it by serving the rich.[382] Failing their return, chief Koinange wanted to levy from migrants, at their place of work, the two-shilling LNC rate; this financed the rural roads and bridges which carried domestic produce to market.[383] Evidently, workers must make good the alienation of their labour by subsidizing rural capitalism, the patriotic production of a middle class who, more virtuously, kept wealth in circulation at home.[384]

Labour theory had wider application. It shaped Kikuyu views of their squatter diaspora in the Rift Valley and the squatters' own sense of superiority to farmworkers of diffferent ethnic origin. The KCA feared that squatters, getting on for a quarter of all Kikuyu, would become, in Kenyatta's words, 'lost tribesmen' who 'disorganized the tribe'. Their sons did not know where Kikuyu was; they mistakenly believed it was where they lived, on a white farm.[385] But that was precisely the connection which the squatter political imagination was making. In conceiving a right to inherit settler land, squatters told their own dynastic history, backing it with labour theory and, possibly, echoes of Exodus. The area had been Maasailand. Maasai had ceded it by treaty. Lord Delamere, head of the white clan, *mbari ya nyakeru*, and *munene wa mathetera* or chief of the settlers, then invited Kikuyu to colonize these 'white highlands'.[386] Squatters had not looked for work; he had sent for them, fetching their families and flocks by train.[387] Patrons ought thus to initiate *ahoi* relations, for *ahoi* were not mere servants, *ndungata*. Settlers then allowed squatters to cultivate and graze stock on their own account in return for waged labour, sometimes rent and, often, a landlord commission on tenant produce sales. Labour service buttressed alliance with the right of *kuna* or first clearance of the wilderness which the Maasai had left untamed, as Kikuyu saw it no less than settlers.[388] Squatters 'nourished the White Highlands with their sweat.'[389] The old labour hero, Wamugumo, became their own (when, I cannot say). He was a giant, covered in scales, uncannily like *ndamathia* and indispensable to whites. Able to hold Delamere's herds single-handedly, he downed a month's porridge in two days, garnished with calf. Whites grumbled at his appetite but, unable to do without him, gave him a plot of building land on which fellow Kikuyu put up his house. He had earned the strongest tenant right, that of *muthami*, one who has moved.[390]

Much squatter labour was household work. Settlers farmed few of their acres until the 1940s. The white highlands were really 'black'. Squatters probably worked longer 'in their gardens' than 'slaving' for their landlord.[391] Their children's blood soaked the soil at circumcision; they buried their dead on white farms.[392] They controlled domestic space in villages hidden in corners of white estates. Monthly contract workers, single men, almost always of other ethnic origin, were *maskini*, the poor. Their private space was public, regimented in labour lines or *laini*.[393] Without mastery over their lives they had no property in their labour, nor in the land they worked. Dynastic history, sweat and ritual sway over the land all told squatters that they, by contrast, were earning property right – which is why settlers were later so anxious to be rid of them. It is tempting to think that squatters found biblical support for their dreams. Exodus or *Thama*, house-moving, was the exemplary text. Squatters called each other *athami*, people on the move but entitled to stay.³⁹⁴ Kikuyu Old Testament books were available separately long before their joint publication in 1951; an early school primer had material on Egypt.³⁹⁵ Squatter and Jewish histories had obvious parallels. Pharoah had sent for Joseph; Delamere called in Kikuyu. Egypt was the house of bondage, *nyumba ya ukombo*; Kikuyu talked of *ukombo ya ruguru*, the slavery of the highlands. The Rift Valley was *weru*, both pasture and a wilderness such as had tested the wandering Israelites. Other biblical echoes may also have prompted wishful word-play. The Rift was *ruguru*, the west; so was Kikuyu high ground, *iguru*, which became Heaven in the Bible. The terms had no colloquial con-nection but their root was the same,³⁹⁶ and Kikuyu proverbs loved puns. Egyptian taskmasters sounded like Boer farmers, said to be hard employers.³⁹⁷ A taskmaster was *kaburu*, or 'corporal'; Boers were *maburu*.³⁹⁸ Is it impossible that squatter imagination mapped a com-pressed historical geography of Exodus in the Rift: house of bon-dage, testing wilderness and promised land all in one?³⁹⁹ Mission schools which might have imparted that sacred landscape were rare on white farms. But, perhaps for this very reason, some squatters took up a charismatic Christianity which developed an urgent sense of similarity between Kikuyu and biblical notions of pollution (taught to the Israelites in the wilderness) and of the power of God on earth.⁴⁰⁰

The first squatter crisis politicized different views of squatterdom and introduced language which was to return with added force in the Mau Mau conflict. Squatters called the late 1920s *kifagio* or broom. Settlers swept up their wealth by making them fix their thumbprints, *kirore*, to new contracts which cut their livestock allowance to a few head per household. Many resisted by moving to easier employers or back to the reserves. Chiefs and KCA responded to this sudden social closure in opposite ways. Kiambu chiefs were appalled by the prospect of refugee squatters agitating swarms of dormant disputes to regain land they or their fathers had left. They toured the Rift in their own and the settler interest, advising squatters to accept the terms. Chiefs assured squatters, in Koinange's words, that they would not forfeit 'their property and . . . their freedom' – the first recorded use of the political couplet of *ithaka na wiathi*, later adopted by Mau Mau.⁴⁰¹ The KCA accused him of condemning squatters to become servants, *ndungata*. He retorted that the KCA took fees from distressed squatters, promised support when they repatriated their labour, and then delivered nothing. Too idle to grow their own maize, they harvested other people's shillings – an accusation later made against Mau Mau.⁴⁰²

The harsh words do not reveal the underlying issue, but it looks as if conflict between chiefs and KCA over squatter futures was, like much else, shaped by tension between *mbari* and *riika*. Chiefs tried to save their agreements with settlers. Squatter assent to new contracts would meet white labour needs, confirm this new form of *mbari* fission and migration, and keep the peace in Kikuyuland. Koinange seems to have pushed this dynastic theory as far as the squatters themselves: labour service for Delamere's *aramati* ought in time to earn them rights in the white highlands. KCA agents in the Rift, on the other hand, were seen as members of a notoriously dissident age set, *Njane*.[403] Squatters may have seen KCA subscriptions as age-set fees which any threatened *ahoi* would maintain in order to keep friends at court.[404] It may also be that the squatter withdrawal of labour was what first alerted the KCA to the possibility of getting back the 'stolen lands'. The timing was propitious. *Mbari* elders were even then preparing for *ituika* by ritually beating the bounds of their *ithaka*, including any part now under white ownership.[405] And *ituika* stories, whether of towers or dragons, showed how strike action could defeat slavery and instal household production. The interests of the apprentice *irungu* generation, *ahoi* members of the KCA and the squatters were one, to win legitimate control of land. *Ituika* had 'redeemed the land' from sorcery; settler abuse of *ahoi* rights, first their own and then their squatters', was no less serious. Chiefs may have been content to gamble the squatter future on continued landlord compacts, white and black. The KCA understood, earlier than either chiefs or squatters, that settler agriculture must soon foreclose on dependent tenures, perhaps because they were beginning to force such capitalist closures of relations themselves. But if the men of the Kikuyu political class were divided over the fate of alienated squatter labour, they were united by the growing conflict between male and female Kikuyu concepts of Kenya, to come now to the final, central, circle of dispute.

As in all societies, Kikuyu men and women bargained their mutual roles. In the past they had been by no means unequal.[406] Social change under colonial rule had given each sex new resources. But many more men than women now went to school; they earned more money and power in employment; they owned the capital goods, such as carts and then lorries, which carried produce to market; they had the ear of the state when making the 'customary law' which strove to restore juniors' obedience in a world full of new paths of migrant delinquency; their apt metaphor for indiscipline was 'by the roadside'.[407] All these male advantages were mobilized in the great political drama of 1928 for *Muigwithania*'s readers, the visit of Edward, Prince of Wales. In a year in which KCA leaders had given their views on land to the Governor and Legislative Council, the royal visit appeared to pour dynastic blessing on the politics of generation and patriotic production. Joseph Kang'ethe paraded with the ex-soldiers; Henry Gichuiri, shortly to become editor, attended as a local councillor; Kenyatta seems to have gatecrashed the Governor's garden party. All three compared the festivities to *ituika*. Kang'ethe imagined he was dancing a preparatory *kibaata*; the others called the housing for chiefs and councillors 'the lodges of the *irungu*', as if Africans from all over Kenya had met for a generation succession.[408] The KCA could visualize an inter-ethnic male Kenya, federated by masculine ceremony and the dynastic allegiance of official chiefs. There was money in it, too. Petro Kigondu, pillar of the CMS in Murang'a, clerk to the district commissioner, KCA leader, local councillor, officer of traders' and cart-owners' associations, first African bus-owner, spiralist-in-chief, had the contract to feed the gathering.[409] After Kenyatta went to London, people said that he was advised to do so by the Prince, since his father the King could do more than he to right Kikuyu wrongs.[410] Rural capitalism, inter-ethnic themes of generation succession and an expanded dynastic myth of a compassionate king promised men some control over a larger world.

They needed that reassurance, menaced as they were by another, female, Kenya which extinguished rather than celebrated ethnicity. Men of the *irungu* generation, the KCA, appointed themselves guardians of Kikuyu 'seed', alarmed that women in Nairobi were breaking what seems to have been an entirely new expectation of patriotic Kikuyu motherhood. Their prostitution caused sterility. Men of other tribes sang of supping with merry Kikuyu wives made giddy by motorcars. 'WE ARE BEING EXTERMINATED AT A BLOW', George Ndegwa protested in capital letters. Money, too, tempted women to burn 'their MODESTY LIKE FIREWOOD.'[411] Clearly, women exploited new resources as well as men. Men condemned a wide range of gender competition as the road to prostitution. Women who went to school, stayed overnight in rural trading centres or, worst of all, sold vegetables in Nairobi, all risked that fate. There were indeed Kikuyu prostitutes in Nairobi and, like others, they found clients from other groups more profitable, especially the uncircumcised Luo.[412] But Kikuyu men's fears were more pervasive. Ndegwa's outburst against giddy women was entitled 'the beginnings of insubordination', not of immorality. Disciplined reproduction and labour were at stake – the whole civilizing world of the household and by now, therefore, of 'Kikuyu'. Linguistically, the word *hinya* bound male anxieties together. In the abstract it meant power; bodily it was semen; the causative form of the verb could indicate both the thrashing out of argument and the final weeding of a field.[413] The behaviour of Nairobi women threatened male power and Kikuyu posterity, politics and production.

Delinquent women shamed Kikuyu men. Men who could not control women were heathen, *acenji*. Kang'ethe wanted to repudiate the insult with masculine trade. Kenyatta also demanded more male authority. Famous nations were those which honoured and protected their women; his readers must not drop theirs like millet stalks by the roadside, by which he meant allowing them to hawk potatoes in Nairobi. Gichuiri, like Ndegwa, blamed money. Men used to value girls in livestock; girls now sold themselves for cash. Men might soon be forced to follow Moses and strike any who insulted Kikuyu for letting strangers enslave their women.[414] Inter-ethnic shame originated in male gender insecurities at home; readers would have felt them most keenly. There were four areas of competition: between generations, husbands and wives, KCA men and women, and male and female traders. Men's generational conflict over migrant labour had moved on from cloaks and blankets to issues of capital. A returning son, it was said, had more regard for a mother from whom he would most directly inherit land than for a father; he did not add his earnings to the household's bridewealth reserve but bought his own plough instead. A father would then refuse to help his son to marry, since 'that plough is now his wife.'[415] Capital killed kin, more especially the kin of readers, who were most likely to invest. Job Muchuchu boasted that the *mambere*, those in the forefront of education, also led in cultivation, 'for it is the breast which we all suck'. Despite his metaphor, *athomi* kin relations were often strained enough already. Mukiri's parents feared that they would be refused membership of senior councils if he were not properly initiated. For girls to take Christian names was particularly subversive. They could no longer be called 'so and so's daughter'. Nor did they respect husbands.[416] The marital household was the next sphere of uncertainty. Again, readers had a particular problem. Polygyny was the best investment in productive capacity, especially for men who worked away from home. Franchesko Gechohi admitted that it was tempting for wealthy Christians. How credible, one wonders, was his counter-argument that children were the main purpose of marriage and wives an expense? A monogamist could afford a bicycle or car and was clean; polygamists had goats and mice in their huts. But, lest any reader should think monogamy solved all problems of gender, there was a terrible warning in the tale of a nurse who bought a better bed than her husband could afford and then turned him out of it: 'a woman's wealth makes no sense; . . . like stinging nettles which have not been mashed.'[417] Mashed nettles made good soup; and it appears, thirdly, that women resented being treated as cooks rather than colleagues by the KCA. In 1930 they formed their own group, the Muumbi Central Association (after the Kikuyu Eve), to jolt men into accepting them as full KCA members.[418] For women, too, 'tribe' was now available as a prop to status. But it was the fourth sphere of competition, in production and trade, which frightened men most.

Men, I have suggested, ploughed without regard for wives. And Kenyatta advised that fields be divided into trade and food crops, male and female.[419] But economic spheres could no longer be kept separate. Food was a commodity; women competed in trade. Cart-owners offered to lift their burdens;[420] but women hawkers captured much of the Nairobi vegetable market. So Kenyatta approved the Kiambu LNC's ban on the women's trade and its warning to all women not to go to town immodestly dressed; if women sold potatoes on the streets the Kikuyu nation would go down to the roots of the dreaded *mikongoe* tree. Men's worries overcame their political divisions. Kenyatta praised the Kiambu chiefs' bye-law. He also told how Thuku's old enemy, paramount chief Kinyanjui, had on his deathbed deplored government's refusal to ratify the council ban.[421] What then was to be done about the woman question? From Kahuhia, Gideon Mugo offered an Anglican compromise. He defended Christian names that promised racial equality, but called on government to forbid Kikuyu women to marry 'foreigners' or *comba*, by which he meant Muslims; if not, the Kikuyu nation would decrease. Others thought that it was up to men to be more careful. It was no good trying to reform prostitutes by marriage. Enemies, not wives, they disobeyed fathers and might castrate husbands.[422] Men could also appeal to precedent to curb female ambition. In the issue of *Muigwithania* that reported the royal visit as an *ituika*, readers were reminded that women were excluded from those *ituika* ceremonies that blessed war medicines, lest warriors be enfeebled by sexual activity. More practically, Kenyatta implied that women should be kept busy at home. He appealed to chiefs and councillors 'to wield the turning pole' which cleared cut bush away. A popular work song claimed that women found this male exertion sexually seductive; it also enabled them to dig. There should also be a market just outside Nairobi, to keep women from further mischief.[423] It was in this mood of moral panic[424] that readers found themselves having to face the issue of clitoridectomy or female circumcision.

The female circumcision crisis of 1928–30 is generally seen as a clash of cultures – evangelical Christianity opposed to a core Kikuyu value. But that was only one of the ways in which Kikuyu saw it: a refusal to allow ignorant 'religious fanatics' to force them to be 'corrupted by detribalisation'.[425] For initiation was mainly a drama of disputed genders. Kikuyu would immediately recognize the analytical terms of academic argument about puberty rites. Three broad approaches are current. Female (like male) initiation is seen as a means to resolve psychosexual conflict; as a drama of the male competition to control women's reproductive powers; or as a rite in which social seniors use an anxious private transition to school people in the public values of responsible adulthood.[426] Protestant missionaries (almost all of them men, the older ones probably uncircumcised) saw clitoridectomy more simply, as sexually repressive genital mutilation surrounded by orgiastic ritual. Kikuyu resistance forced them to Christianize rather than ban male circumcision, which had in any case by now become fashionable among the British middle classes.[427] But clitoridectomy was different,

altogether more invasive, especially as it often included labial as well
as clitoral excision. It sometimes caused later difficulties in childbirth.
Scots mission doctors, after a brief trial which revolted them, refused to
guide clitoridectomy down the same road of mission-sponsored surgi-
cal modernization as male circumcision, purged of all public lessons
in sexuality. Thus for women, unlike men, there was no middle road
between Christian abolition and continuing convention, possibly now
with a heightened emotional charge. From early days most Protestant
missionaries, but never all, taught that church members must not cir-
cumcise their daughters. Americans were as adamant as Scots. The
CMS wavered. In Kiambu Leakey supported his Scots neighbours and
threatened to punish church members who broke the ban; in Murang'a,
Kahuhia left the decision to private Kikuyu conscience. Catholics, more
numerous than Protestants, saw initiation as a social issue, outside their
spiritual concern. Whites, then, were divided. Kikuyu men were divided
too. Had all defended female initiation, there would have been no crisis.
Missionaries would not have felt able to oppose it so vigorously, in
the belief that they had influential Kikuyu opinion with them.[428] But
why did a gender issue became one of class and ethnicity? In retrospect
it seems inevitable. Domestic labour theory fired the mounting racial
competition in cultivation; disciplined women reproduced labour or,
as Kikuyu men put it, seed. But, meanwhile, there was much to argue
about.

The first Kikuyu approach to initiation, then, was Freudian. To differentiate sexualities by circumcising boys and excising a girl's 'male'
member, the clitoris, removed male fear and female aggression as obstacles to fruitful coition. Otherwise men might as well be women and
women men; they would not be able to give birth.[429] Initiation also
made male bargains possible within a competitive society. Disciplined
daughters allowed fathers to negotiate terms for granting their virginal
reproductive powers to approved sons-in-law. Making a second psychosexual assumption opposed to their first, Kikuyu feared that uncut girls
would sell or marry their fertility to strangers, perhaps enemies. Tabitha Wangui thought that to ban circumcision would increase harlotry,
since mothers-in-law would drive out uninitiated brides with the lash
of contempt.[430] For women supported, more strongly than some men,
the third view, that initiation taught adult responsibility. In June 1929,
during heated *athomi* debate on clitoridectomy within the church, Anglican men in Kiambu agreed to its abolition. Their wives refused,
not wishing 'their girls to remain children for ever in the eyes of the
tribe.'[431] The first Kikuyu accounts of initiation took the women's side.
The untrained Gathigira and then the trained anthropologist Kenyatta
described transition rites in the classic tripartite form of separation
from childhood, then a transition period of ritual seclusion and, finally,

incorporation in society as a full, adult, member. It was a crucial moment of social and religious education.[432] The physical operation was an intrinsic part; women say it bought maturity with pain.[433] Kenyatta the cultural nationalist found the language of structural functionalism well suited to his needs. He assured his British readers that initiation taught 'the moral code of the tribe' and symbolically unified 'the whole tribal organisation.' It was certainly not a horrible practice suited 'only to barbarians'.[434]

In Kikuyu, Kenyatta's barbarians were *acenji*, the dismissive ethnic epithet his *athomi* friends hated. Their personal struggle with heathendom was the arena in which clitoridectomy moved from a gender issue to one of tribe. *Athomi* were anxious about gender and improvement in three spheres: property, theology and reproduction. Property, an increasingly apt shorthand for kin and neighbourhood relations, was a daily concern. Kikuyu remained a fee-paying, investing, insurance-seeking world. Readers wanted new-style cleanliness. Square houses abolished *ucenji*, heathendom; black Muslims built them, as well as white Christians. But to be men of property they had to be properly men; the patriotic production which paid for progress needed understandings with unlettered kin. These required age-set fee payments, bridewealth agreements and, in due course, the initiation of churchgoing daughters. Only a tiny minority of Christian families were so wrapped in mission-station life that all this no longer mattered. Most readers lived in their *mbari*. They could not build improvement on rotten fondations; as *athomi* prodigals, they returned home to look for a heroic, not a savage. past. Longing to be forerunners, not prostitutes, they needed an uncorrupt tribe if their seniors were not to see them as corrupted by progress. Kenyatta, accordingly, compared Kikuyu medicine with upper class London's; circumcisers worked with 'the dexterity of a Harley Street surgeon'. And initiation had 'from time immemorial' taught age-sets the politics of the KCA, the 'spirit of collectivism and national solidarity'.[435]

In any case, as Wanjiru wa Kinyua, the nervous first woman contributor to *Muigwithania*, pointed out, the choice between uncut civilization and heathen circumcision was false. Atttibuting to Christ a dictum of St Paul's, that 'circumcision is nothing and uncircumcision is nothing', she called on readers to stop arguing about it; salvation came from faith, not from circumcision or its lack.[436] Biblical circumcision was the Kikuyu *irua*, which applied to both sexes. In the Old Testament it was a constant reminder of God's promises to Abraham the tribal patriarch. In the New, which came out in Kikuyu two years before the crisis, St Paul used it as a metaphor of salvation and the denial, as Kikuyu would have agreed, of one's lower nature. The Virgin Mary was translated as *muiritu*, unmarried but circumcised.[437] Not even the Son of God could be born to an uninitiated woman.

Two opposed male sexualities brought the argument to a head in this sphere of reproductive discipline. White clergy believed that sexuality was fulfilled in monogamous unions of private souls. Their own cultures admonished people less and less by physical means, increasingly by moral constraints. Kikuyu men's sexuality was learnt in public and as publicly prized in polygyny; social roles were bodily incised, punishment was often corporal.[438] This conflict of sexualities made the crisis more anxious than our unsexed 'cultural' approach previously allowed us to see. The key polemical source for the crisis is the Scots mission's Memorandum, produced soon after the event. Scholars have been too dependent on its thesis, not alert enough to its evidence. The CSM accused the KCA of fomenting the conflict by its decision to oppose the trend of opinion against clitoridectomy among readers. Historians have thought it enough, in reverse, to accept the political legitimacy of cultural resistance. They have forgotten the CSM's motive in writing, which was to answer government's complaint that the church had caused the uproar by its 'sudden attack' on Kikuyu custom.[439] In response, the mission blamed the KCA's decision to pander to pagan prejudice in the Nyeri local election campaign of 1928.[440] Historians have since clinched their argument for a cultural explanation of the crisis with the pained question put to whites by Joseph Kang'ethe in August 1929. Believing, with reason, that missionaries wanted to abolish the practice altogether, he asked if, 'circumcision being the custom of the Kikuyu Christian, he is to be a heathen simply because he is a Kikuyu.'[441] That looks like a question of 'tribal culture', but only because the idea of an ordered masculine tribe was under threat from unruly women. It is not enough to sympathize with a political party under clerical attack; we must also see its members as men, which missionaries took for granted. In an unnoticed letter Kang'ethe put it to the missions that, if clitoridectomy was to be ended, it would be best, first, 'to remove the things we see taking place in Nairobi, because there are many kinds of people there that do many things [implied meaning: many offensive things]. . .'[442] In this early show of anxious middle-class male ethnicity, he accused whites of failing to control the urban wilderness of social change. There, many kinds of people did offensive things with Kikuyu women. This feminine delinquency, not the intended discipline of female initiation, was what made Kikuyu men 'heathen'. If prostitution were banned, as KCA members wanted, then their president was quite willing to discuss clitoridectomy. Until whites cleaned up Nairobi their attack on female initiation could only encourage the heathendom they affected to despise.

This debate on what it was to be a man or a woman defined, perhaps more than any other issue, what it was to be Kikuyu. It marked the boundaries of a mutually intelligible ethnic language of class, gender and virtue. And, by contrast with their nearest cultural neighbours, the Meru and Embu, Kikuyu found that they had no overarching institutions which could be reinvented to control the debate. Kikuyu were thus set apart as *mbari ya atiriri*, still a people called together and competed over by rhetoric, not one obedient to common authorities.[443] Kikuyu ethnicity was now more or less established, but not, politically, the Kikuyu tribe. For all the public discourse on tribal custom and unifying rites of transition, whether sexual or generational, the crisis grew, and was later resolved, at the different level of *mbari* and in another sphere, the politics of kinship.[444]

The formal debates on circumcision which we know about occurred in specific church conferences and LNC meetings. The informal debate, which we can divine only from the scurrilous songs and violent clashes over school property in late 1929, went on all the time in hundreds of *mbari*. From 1916, senior *athomi* were partners in the mission discussions on clitoridectomy; according to the CSM, they took the lead in proposing sanctions for readers who practised it. We may doubt that many obeyed church teaching; it was not until the later 1920s that many readers had to face the issue in any case, with daughters reaching puberty. Almost all early Christian brides had been initiated before baptism. Of the 328 women who petitioned for the protection of non-circumcisers in late 1929, only 67 were uninitiated; of these none was married.[445] They appealed in fear, the climax of some years of growing argument about the future of *mbari* autonomy in the politics of reproduction. This was menaced from two sources, state and church. First, district commissioners pushed through LNC rules which regulated the timing and severity of circumcision, male and female. One motive was to prevent surgery and convalescence from clashing with the peaks of white planters' labour needs.[446] There was little compliance with the rules but still much resentment. The clerical threat was greater still, channelled through the outschools, the rural crossroads of *mbari* power-seeking and mission sway. The growth of girls' education in the 1920s made many parents nervous. Their daughters' adolescent transition to full sexuality occurred in the ritual seclusion of school, subject to foreigners. Some teachers were strangers, living locally as *ahoi*. Initiation rites, while they gave entry to age-sets, were always organized by *mbari* elders. Externally directed schools usurped this *mbari* management of reproductive resources and led, or so it was widely believed, to promiscuity, if not prostitution.

Save for relatively calm Kiambu, outschool conflict had been sharpest where the clerical anti-circumcision stand was firmest, in the AIM schools in Murang'a and the CSM sphere in Nyeri. Parents here, mothers no less than fathers, had to weigh a daughter's learning against the risk of losing both control over her fertility and their own hopes of promotion in community councils.[447] *Athomi* first divided into clear parties over the issue in Nyeri. The CSM sponsored its own people, the Progressive Kikuyu Party, to compete with the KCA in the Nyeri LNC elections. The groups were based on different *mbari*.[448] Their argument was projected to the district level by the exterior architecture of local government. Missionary division then helped to mobilize the all-Kikuyu arena. Having the hesitant CMS station at Kahuhia for its intellectual base, the KCA in Nyeri saw no need to toe the tough Scots line.[449] But it was a family dispute in Kiambu that brought the matter to a head. An unwanted excision was forced on a Christian girl because of her stepmother's hopes for a reversion of property. Angered by the light fine imposed on the girl's assailants, Dr Arthur, head of the CSM, demanded legal clarification. Kang'ethe mobilized the KCA, resisting Arthur's curtailment of Kikuyu debate as much as his attack on circumcision itself.[450] Readers had been deciding and evading decision for years. Now, in a competitive crescendo of demands for loyalty on either side of the divide, 'true' or *karing'a* Kikuyu mocked the *kirore*, the 'thumbprints' who signed the petition of protection and then successive clerical denunciations of circumcision and the KCA.

The crisis of clitoridectomy coincided with that of *kifagio*. Both were collisions in the common but fragmented struggle to control the reproduction of labour and then labour's production of property. Squatters who accepted new labour contracts were said to be selling themselves into slavery; *kirore* Christians were accused of bribing the district commissioner with uninitiated girls 'so that the land may go'. This was one of many insults in the *muthirigu*, 'the song of the big uncut girl', which swept through Kikuyu late in 1929, gathering profanities as it went. Its anonymous authors imagined nightmares of anarchy – sexual and agrarian. The disciplines of reproduction and production were indivisible; without initiation, fertility went out of control and civilization collapsed. Uninitiated girls were thus said to be social outcasts, to smell bad, wet their beds and cost only seven dogs to marry in church. They would have their front six teeth knocked out like the uncircumcised Luo. Even in-laws, *athoni*, would be like bitches. Christian married couples would both give birth; none would cook for them. Trains would sweep away young cows; but tinned milk was exorbitant. Singers themselves admitted to sleeping out in the bush like wild dogs. The churches would also be reduced to preaching to baboons in the forest. Dr Arthur had caused the trouble. Once there were ten commandments; when he came 'they multiplied like gourds'. But Kenyatta would return with Thuku, 'king of the Kikuyu'. Koinange – who scorned 'natives' and sent his son to be educated overseas – would then, together with other leading chiefs, be buried or be made to wear women's clothes.[451]

This last taunt linked men, women, property and the state, the heart of the matter. Chiefs were more worried than government by the KCA.

The Moral Economy of Mau Mau

In late 1928, the district commissioner of Fort Hall had contemplated co-opting a KCA legally constituted and financially audited; early that year Kenyatta had been received by the Governor and the party had been consulted by the provincial commissioner.[452] The British thought the KCA a sectional party of the literate minority who might, with tutelage, do some good. Most chiefs saw it as a patchwork of *mbari* faction-fighters; they took oaths, ate sheep fees after dark, and should be suppressed.[453] In the crisis of the following year chiefs stood by the missions. It was not that they wanted to ban clitoridectomy; their district commissioners assured them that government would do no such thing. But they did want to quash any official thought of KCA recognition. The party's opposition to the missions gave chiefs the chance to destroy its base in the mission outschools, the formal link between party, progress and *mbari* property.[454] For chiefs, as for the KCA, the crisis continued dynastic diplomacy by other means. The *kirore* Christians whom chiefs supported had no more wish than the KCA to surrender control of daughters. They gave three arguments against clitoridectomy. It was not found in the Bible; its absence ensured safer childbirth; and, decisively, it was easier to tell if an uncut woman had been 'defiled by force' and, therefore, to take the man responsible to court.[455]

By early 1930 government had banned the *muthirigu*, forbidden the KCA to collect subscriptions and encouraged chiefs to suppress public meetings. Perhaps this repression is what is remembered as the banning of *ituika*. Dissident readers, after all, called themselves not only *karing'a*, 'true Kikuyu' but also *aregi*, both 'refusers' and the revolutionary generation who had once wrenched household cultivation from the grip of tyranny. But to believe that the *irungu* were prevented from coming to power by a church-and-state alliance against 'custom' is to be deluded about the nature of Kikuyu politics. For the *irungu* did indeed come to power. That does not mean that they took control of a tribe by means of generation succession. That central idea could never overcome untidy local reality. They rose, instead, to control their myriad *mbari* by reason of advancing age, wealth and virtue. The late 1920s are remembered as a period of wholesale turnover in Kiambu's community council, or *kiama*, elders; the incomers were KCA men, sympathetic to the property interests of the young.[456] The crisis had given the party an entry to Kiambu for the first time; it gained members ridge by ridge, *mbari* by *mbari*. By the same means the party consolidated itself elsewhere.[457] But the conditions that built the party up almost immediately started to dissolve it. The public solidarities of *riika* had no defence against the propertied privacies of *mbari*.

For some months in late 1929 and early 1930 there was bitter dissension, even violence, in some parts of Kikuyuland. The Scots and American missions lost most of their students and many of their full members by insisting that church members and teachers declare against clitoridectomy. The CMS lost adherents only where it took the same hard line. But the violence was neither political, racial nor religious.[458] It centred on school property, disputed between local *kirore* and *karing'a* factions. These were often of the same denomination, sometimes of the same *mbari*, and had usually given land or labour and materials.[459] Some compromises were patched up, with alternating uses timed by the church bell.[460] Some schools stood empty; Kenya's education director, already under pressure from LNCs to give more secular education, sympathized with local school committees who wanted to provide their own.[461] Two groups of independent schools emerged. The out-school disputes of the 1920s, which centred on the defence of community independence from missionary educational control, suggest that these had always been on the cards. Without the issue of clitoridectomy, full separation would only have been delayed. The larger grouping, the Kikuyu Independent Schools Association, soon accepted official inspection in return for small grants in aid. Wanting the same respectability as the missions from which they had broken, the independent groups started their own churches, but only after the CMS had turned down their plea for help with ordination. The *mbari* search for power needed a church connection that transmitted the ritual and belief of the new age. But KISA allowed private conscience to rule their members in the matter of clitoridectomy. Perhaps they had this indifference forced upon them from below; it would certainly have relieved *mbari* from the fear of any church threat to property.[462]

The whole issue soon lost heat. The CMS continued to permit local discretion. The AIM and the CSM stuck to their hard-won advances in women's emancipation, as they saw it. The AIM never recovered from the crisis but, then, its schools were weak. The CSM's rapid growth resumed after an interruption of only five or six years.[463] A sample survey more than 40 years later suggests that their determination was rewarded. In 1972, it seems, 41 per cent of Kikuyu secondary schoolgirls were still circumcised. But there was much denominational variation. Less than 10 per cent of Presbyterian girls had been operated on. Of the Anglicans, almost none were cut in Kiambu, where Leakey had stood by Arthur; 60 per cent were initiated in Murang'a, where Kahuhia had temporized. About 70 per cent of both Catholic and 'independent' schoolgirls were still circumcised.[464] Differences in church teaching had had a great effect on social practice; but individual conscience and social pressure meant that no church took a single view. Kikuyu were not defined by the unthinking practice of clitoridectomy but by their debates about its slow retreat.

The KCA was involved with independent schools and churches through its individual members, not as a party. Rapid growth, then repression and economic slump, dissipated what cohesion it had briefly known as a newspaper-reading group of bustling straddlers. Like Thuku, its members looked more and more to their property. Independent schools showed what was possible, the KCA what was not, in a politics increasingly divided by class and clan. The schools elicited *mbari* self-help for local progress and power. The KCA raised large sums to send Kenyatta to London but, given Kikuyu parochialism and the enmity of chiefs, never converted aspiration into a political machine. This failure is well shown by the KCA's role in marshalling evidence for the Kenya Land Commission, which toured Kikuyuland in late 1932 and early 1933. Kikuyu made great efforts to make their case heard; nearly 200 *mbari* submitted written claims to alienated land; more than 700 witnesses spoke. Their evidence is one of the richest deposits of oral tradition anywhere in Africa. But the KCA's internal rivalries produced three different statements; and *mbari* trustees, guarding an independence that was in a real sense their property, did not accept formal KCA aid. They founded a Kikuyu Land Board Association instead, attached to the KCA but in effect an autonomous committee of 30 *aramati*.[465] Dynastic theory was above political party; *mbari* trustees mistrusted *riika*. Equally, dynastic theory, as already noted, did not move the Commission. Too many *mbari* claimed the same land, bought for improbable numbers of goats from Ndorobo beekeepers. Even the bones of Koinange's grandfather, exhumed at such ghastly risk, failed to suspend disbelief. The Commission made little provision for compensation for *mbari* as *mbari*. In one particular case it recommended the eviction of a Kikuyu settlement at Tigoni, an area surrounded by white farms; they would be moved to a forested area claimed by another subclan and known, 20 years later all too well, as Lari.[466]

Men of the *irungu* generation had mobilized opinion to protect the good name of Kikuyu men from the giddiness of women, to defend *mbari* land from mission interference and then to claim its restitution from the Crown. But the challenges of clitoridectomy and the Land Commission had shown that the KCA could deal only in cash and opinion. It could not manage power and property. Its individual members could do so, but only as they gained in household virtue and status on local age-graded *kiama*, the councils which adjudicated within and between *mbari*. *Mbari* were now, still more clearly than before, the propertied foundations of elementary education. But the Land Commission's dismissal of their case showed that, even when strenuously coordinated, they could not deliver power on any but the lowest level. A disillusioned chief Koinange warned London: 'Although some definite line of peace is tried to be reached at, if the decision should be . . . that the White settlement retain their farms which were deprived off from the natives with the graves of their ancestors and their crops therein, there will be an infinite grievance amongst the natives so far.'[467] He did not say, he could not know, who or what – now that both *riika* and *mbari* had proven to be empty vessels – might authorize more forceful protest, should the line of peace fail to hold.

PROPHETS, TEACHERS AND POLITICIANS

The British, trying years later to explain Mau Mau, thought that Kikuyu had no proper authority for revolt. They were perhaps not far wrong, which is not to say that they understood Kikuyu perplexities. The British explained what seemed to be widespread joint Kikuyu action by the intimidatory manipulation of magical tribal sanctions or ecstatic messianic belief on the part of cynical modern men. Lumping together the mysteries of the tribal mind, many officials thought that Mau Mau had descended both from the independent schools and from the prophetic spirit churches, which also took their origin from the late 1920s.[468] This was to assume a connection that no Kikuyu would accept. Prophets were anathema to the independents; politicians despised them. But politicians also hated each other, contesting in court the proper relation between their own power and their supporters' wealth. It remains to show just how divided Kikuyu political thought and theology was in the late 1930s, how ill-prepared to meet the next crisis, after the Second World War. By reading the language of theology and education at the time one also gets closest to eavesdropping on a language of class. Divisions between churches were in part seen as contrasts between the lunatic poor and the progressive rich. Only the latter could try to reconstruct a joint politics of *mbari* and *riika* in the service of 'sharpening' the Kikuyu mind for political action. Whether they delivered a proper return on their supporters' investment was another matter.

Whites divided in response to the crisis of 1929. So did Kikuyu. By 1934 two fundamentally different strands of thought were visible, each complex. The division between *kirore* and *karing'a*, thumbprint and true, no longer looks as wide as once it did. It could certainly be bitter. But the conflicts were more factional than ideological. *Kirore* were within, *karing'a* without the parochial patronage networks of the state. Otherwise, each group was divided over clitoridectomy; both urged patriotic production and better schools; independents employed mission-trained teachers; their church liturgies were much the same; KCA members were in both camps; children found the independents' fees as steep as the missions' and spiralled up many school networks. *Kirore*, all mission church members and many chiefs, were no puppets. They assumed growing responsibilities. Kikuyu ministers and teachers multiplied; missionaries did not. Chiefs, like district commissioners, had to manage rising numbers of extension workers from government departments. The *karing'a* or *aregi*, the independents, split. The larger and more efficient

KISA spread through Nyeri and Murang'a. The Kikuyu Karing'a Educational Association was based on southern Kiambu. Each was linked to a church. KISA's African Independent Pentecostal Church was in fact staidly Anglican; KKEA's African Orthodox Church was said to be unorthodox. But their differences, also, were less important than their likenesses. Each was a loose federation of subclan schools, reliant on local initiative. Like the mission schools they attracted enthusiasm, effort and financial sacrifice. Stone classrooms were built and teachers paid not only out of fees but also from the proceeds of school bazaars, sports and soccer matches, circumcision ceremonies. A benefactor might assign to the school a stand of the wattle trees that increasingly fixed readers' property rights and deprived their tenants of the use of previously unused scraps of land. Independents even mounted huge sports meetings in the heart of the white highlands; teams travelled from over one hundred miles (160 km) away.[469] In one of their hymns they sang: 'Lord, forgive us, we are not rejecting you but the thumbprint.'[470] Theologically unadventurous, the aims of the *aregi* were those of the *kirore*, to progress in a productive and educational idiom at once British and Kikuyu. Moreover, they knew how to assemble the necessary resources, both the popular support that made suppression impossible[471] and, in the case of KISA, even grudging official approval.[472]

The second strand could scarcely be more different, woven by people known as *arathi*, prophets, or *aroti*, dreamers or, more recently, *akurinu*, the spirit-filled growlers. The British called them, in Swahili, *Watu wa Mungu*, the men of God, or just a *dini*, an ecstatic sect. The Holy Spirit taught them in dreams; their schools taught only scripture. Officials were wary of prophets, since 'the Holy Ghost would rarely appear to have seen eye to eye with [the] Authority' of government.[473] Nor did prophets enjoy popular support. Kenyatta thought them peculiar; property was to them a sin and money the root of evil. To outsiders they were 'simply a bunch of lunatics'.[474] The *akurinu* were in fact the only true Kikuyu revolutionaries; they committed their Christianity against conventional materialisms, traditional and modern. Their appearance was stimulated by the publication of the Kikuyu New Testament in 1926, not by the crisis over circumcision; by 1942 they were said to be entirely indifferent to female initiation.[475] Their founding myth tells how a young man, Joshua Ng'ang'a, barely literate, studied the gospels for two or three years in a cave. He realized that missionaries did not know real spiritual power. Called in dreams, some followers became ill if they resisted. They particularly valued texts that indicated that the gift of prophecy would come on all believers, not just the rich and the clergy. Prophecy was part of Kikuyu religious tradition. Visions did not make the *akurinu* odd. What was strange was their refusal to compromise. Even their ritual avoidances were extreme, more Levitical than Kikuyu.

They condemned all sacrifice, whether to *Ngai* or the ancestors; scorned sorcery and charms; refused European clothes and modern medicine and, in early days, relied on Jehovah to feed them. They carried arms, whether against the evil one or against wild animals while on pilgrimage through the bush was unclear. They changed in this and other respects after their three founders were killed, possibly by mistake, in a police ambush in 1934. But the various *akurinu* branches persisted in what can properly be called anti-social behaviour. They had no desire, until well after the Second World War, to be of the world. Their rigid rules against pollution made them avoid others; their refusal to pay bride-wealth condemned them to endogamy. It is difficult to resist the conclusion that they followed a Christianity of the poor. Many *akurinu* were sons of squatters; few had much schooling; they wanted not improvement but to be saved. Only one of their number is known to have been in the KCA. They had nothing in common with the *aregi*, although for a year or two there was some cooperation. *Aregi* informed on the growlers after the 1934 affray; independent churches also expelled prophets who became filled with the Spirit. The prophets felt profoundly Kikuyu. Other Kikuyu found that claim hard to take; it was mad to think that the spirit, not property, saved.[476]

Wealth certainly seemed to heal some of the divisions in Kikuyu politics by the end of the 1930s. His son Peter Mbiyu claimed that chief Koinange was the largest landowner in Kenya, with the most contented tenants.[477] The old chief, for his part, taught the younger Koinange on his return from overseas what it was to be *mundu wa tha*, a man of compassion; his American university degree would be worthless unless it delivered power to his compatriots. Perhaps he remembered his *muthirigu*-singing critics. Together, they aimed to meet the growing need of both sets of independent schools by founding, at Githunguri in Kiambu, the grandly named Kenya Teachers College. It opened in January 1939, with a sports meeting attended by a surprised and discomfited Chief Native Commissioner and Director of Education. The occasion was blessed by an elder with ritual leaves in one hand and a microphone in the other. The call of *atiriri Agikuyu* was always up to the minute, first in the press and now over a public address system. The Koinanges presided over a committee (with a senior CMS teacher as secretary) which brought together the two independent schools associations. The local *mbari* gave the land, as other *mbari* gave land to the feeder schools.[478] Chief Koinange had himself just stage-managed the production of the greatest work of Kikuyu dynastic theory, a celebration of *mbari* over *riika*, by organizing committees of elders to oversee the ethnographic work of his circumcision-son Louis Leakey.[479] Peter Mbiyu, on the other hand, saw the potential in *riika*. Perhaps drawing on his own schooldays at the missionary Alliance High School, where he had been age-mate and classmate to Obadiah Kariuki, now his brother-in-law and a leading *kirore*, he got age-sets to bureaucratize themselves with secretaries and committees and made each responsible for some aspect of his new college. One piped in water. Local lorry owners, whose main business was with the wattle and charcoal trade, supplied building stone from other supporters' quarries.[480]

Saying and doing had a focus it had had before only in the attempted rescue of Nairobi's fallen women. The Githunguri college, which never quite reached its teacher-training goal, overwhelmed as it was by unqualified students, was nicknamed 'the sharpener' or whetstone, *inoro*. To clear the forest of politics needed brains. Mau Mau forest fighters later named their units from Kiambu the Kenya Inoro Army in Githunguri's honour.[481] As there had been money in monarchy ten years before, so now there was profit in ethnic nationalism. The college's builders were Kikuyu; the contract to feed its 200 pupils, who numbered over 400 by 1940, went to Joseph Kang'ethe and the KCA. Education became a locomotive of rural capitalism. The mixture of virtue and profit which had built the college also had a trans-ethnic dimension. It welcomed students from elsewhere in Bantu-speaking Kenya. The KCA, with which Koinange made his peace in the aftermath of the Land Commission, was at the same time discussing with Luyia and Luo traders from Nyanza how to enlarge the African share of the maize trade.[482] The party also devised inter-ethnic oaths of loyalty, on printed forms, to stiffen resistance against cattle-culling and other soil conservation measures in Kamba and Teita country.[483] For men who combined the strengths of *mbari*, *riika*, good education and access to the state, the trans-ethnic politics of trade and production were as natural as they had been for the big men of the past.

But there was a shadow over all Kikuyu politics, to which there seemed to be no answer, cast by the question of political virtue. In stateless, fee-paying, forest-clearing society, the reciprocity between service and protection was personal, public, calculable. Successful patrons deserved to eat well; who herded goats ate meat. But under the state, direct, personal rewards were in the gift of its chiefs alone. We have seen how difficult they found it to wield power with virtue. Their opponents had no power, and still less prospect, therefore, of virtue. They could promise only collective rewards in the future, some change in the policy or structure of power. Both the state's agents and their opponents needed cash. Effective opposition needed a great deal, whether for travel or lawyers' fees. But it was difficult for politicians to deliver much in return, except for the symbolic goods of meetings and an enhanced language and sense of collective identity. *Muigwithania* was worth a great deal more than its purchase price. But, given the gap between private cash subscriptions and uncertain public goods delivered in return, no politician was free

of the grubby suspicion of harvesting other people's shillings, as chief
Koinange put it, when authority ought to come from harvesting one's
own maize. An arbitrary state bred unaccountable oppositions. They
were neither registered nor audited; probably nobody in the KCA knew
how much money was raised in its name. And there was almost no
opportunity to trump the doubters with the unanswerable magic of
success. Only successful big men can break rules. Reciprocity is not
altruism. Disputes over money tore the patently unsuccessful KCA
apart in the 1930s, setting Harry Thuku, elected its president after
his return, against his deputy, Jesse Kariuki, in a damaging court case,
accompanied by street brawls between their supporters. Many in the
KCA thought that Thuku's farm, *Paradise*, was built with their cash.[484]
Thuku thereupon founded his own Kikuyu Provincial Association,
claiming a virtue superior to that of the KCA because he, a rich farmer,
subscribed to good causes while KCA members, shiftless city-dwellers,
lived off their party.[485] Politicians never overcame this source of dispute
and suspicion. And authority was even more elusive after the Second
World War. The needs of the poor and the ambitions of the wealthy
had both increased. The pressures of the settlers and the state became
altogether more menacing. *Mbari* organization was once again found
inadequate; ideas of *riika* were contested. Education, as in the *muthirigu*,
was again seen as a temptation to treachery. It was now clear who were
Kikuyu. Decades of debate had seen to that. But it was increasingly difficult for the rising ranks of the poor to answer to the moral pull of self-
mastery. Their *wiathi* needed political action. Where Kikuyu could find
the requisite authority for that remained terrifyingly uncertain. It is time
to turn, finally, to the question of what Sam Thebere did not say.

Terror

Risings or revolutions have dynamics of their own, independent of the
social structure, economic grievance or political thought of the subject
peoples or lower orders who take part in them. Society divides people
as much as it unites them for a purpose, as Kikuyu knew all too well.
Hardships, as already argued, do not without question suggest formulae
for their redress. Political authority often lies with those who are only
half inclined to lead insubordinate action, since their relative wealth and
power make them as valuable to rulers as to rebels. For all these reasons most rebels are reluctant. Risings from below generally grow out
of resistance to change imposed from on high. Rulers are better able
to change social relations; external threat or internal rivalry may force
such changes on them. High-political crisis is a common cause of deep
upheaval. Rulers can unwittingly create revolutionary situations if they
try to tighten up the laxities of property and power that used to make

life tolerable for their subjects, or reform defective means of control and consultation or, more often, when they haltingly try to do both; when they then suppress moderate opponents who had hopes of reform; and when this reaction threatens ordinary people who turn, in despair, to sterner leaders.[486] Mounting danger then divides both rulers and rebels. Some, hawks, harden means and ends. Others, doves, look more urgently for compromise. Revolutionaries can be either. They rarely know they are on the way to revolution until they get there. Revolutions are rare and partial, the work of survivors. These, hawk or dove on either side, clutch at new allies in the crisis and end up by imposing a new order for their own safety.[487] All these remarks apply to Mau Mau.

It follows that we can fully explain Mau Mau only by a many-stranded narrative that shows men and women caught unawares by events as well as forewarned in thought. This essay is not that narrative;[488] it does not explain Mau Mau. It adds the missing thread of meaning that explanation needs, without which high politics remains intrigue, its rhetoric manipulation. The remaining pages will suggest how much, and how little, divided loyalists from nationalists; why, among the latter, conservatives like Kenyatta could inspire and yet disdain the men of violence; how difficult it was for conservatives and militants alike to organize support; and the social terror that this involved. My approach rests on my reading of the Kikuyu labour theory of value, a language of class. It informed constituencies of hope and fear and, to some extent, controlled their conflicts. What it was to be Kikuyu was debated throughout this period. Different imaginations of tribe shaped and were shaped by both social struggle and political event.

While a final answer cannot be looked for here what, nonetheless, was Mau Mau? My evidence suggests very different answers to those found in the earlier analyses that I have criticized. It was certainly not the tribal movement represented by its white opponents; it did not embody a 'tribal mind' maddened by modernity. There are four replies to this colonial view. Kikuyu had reason to resist British rule. They had different grievances as squatters, townsmen, small farmers or middle-class clerks and businessmen. Next, therefore, there was no one Mau Mau, a manipulated monolith. Kenyatta and his fellow defendants could not have 'managed' it, as charged at their trial. Several movements, none calling itself 'Mau Mau', became uneasily connected. Nor, then, did their underlying Kikuyu nationalism have one voice; while they still argued about one ideal, the civic virtue of self-mastery, some voices were alight with hope, others hoarse with despair. Lastly, their nationalism showed, in part, a principled refusal to fight other peoples' battles, which would have been to adopt their causes. *Ngai*, the dividing God to whom Kikuyu prayed, had not given Gikuyu and Muumbi all the lands of Kenya; others too owed an unassisted patriotic duty to him;[489] they had to close their own doors against the wilderness.[490] We now have less reason to be shocked by the lack (not absence) of Kenyan nationalism in Mau Mau than Barnett's readers did 25 years ago, when they were told that nationalism was led by a tribe.

Nor, secondly, can we today accept the first scholars' view, that Mau Mau was the hooligan child of the moderate politicians' lost 'control' over popular opinion. That was what Kenyatta called it, *kimaramari*.[491] We can no more use his partisan term than we can still call Mau Mau mad. Rather, there was a renewed battle for Kikuyu authority, even sharper than two decades before. The issue was civic virtue, achieved by one party but seemingly out of the other's reach. The struggle, it was said, ranged *wanyahoro*, men of business, peace and sexual calm, some of whom became 'loyalists', against *imaramari*, naughty children, and *mikora*, spivs and loafers.[492] Kenyatta and other conservative leaders, mainly from Kiambu, were *itonga*, 'men of means'. Their followers were also proven by household mastery, able to produce and reproduce. These virtuous actions entitled them to say, to demand political rights. They were divided, as always, by *mbari*; but many were creatively united, secretly on oath and publicly in age sets, as the Koinanges had developed them before the war. In another echo of the 1920s, their first radical opponents were youths from Nyeri and Murang'a who worked in Nairobi. They were time-bandits. They mixed up the sequence of personal moral growth, they repudiated ancestry. They shocked the elders because, like Sam Thebere, they seemed to have no idea how to win full adulthood, a household and a right to say. Kenyatta did not control the ambitions of such men, the Forty Group as they were called. Unable to meet his conservative expectations they turned convention upside down. But hooligans do not make the disciplined guerrillas that many young men became. Militant politicians came to control their imaginations to greater effect than Kenyatta, if largely by exploiting Kenyatta's weakness, his ideas and his name.

Next, against radical scholars who deny Mau Mau's ethnicity in order to stress its class, one may quote the proverb that 'those without previous dealings with each other have no cause to quarrel.'[493] We can read it in two ways, external and domestic, to show how ethnicity and class reinforced each other. Kikuyu had more cause than other Kenyans to quarrel with the state and settlers, in their reserves, on the white highlands and in Nairobi. Government saw Kikuyu hillsides as the African farmland most in need of hard labour, called communal but in fact socially divisive, against soil erosion. Most farm labour-tenants were Kikuyu. It mattered that the squatter resistance to new labour contracts was largely Kikuyu. Settlers rejected the squatters' Kikuyu construction of their rights; squatters had Kikuyu means of insistence; their sense of betrayal by other Kikuyu was another spur to the squatters' Mau Mau. And if the Forty Group were thugs in Nairobi they were time-bandits at home. Kikuyu pursuit of external claims was shaped by internal quarrel.

For class formation, like charity, began at home. It sharpened claims on ethnicity. As *mbari* arenas of patronage closed ranks against dependants, both rich and poor sought wider fields of unequal obligation. Sub-clan conflict fired the imagination of a polity that was not clannish. Land had once been people with generations of previous dealings; it was now subject to historical dispute about the different legal principles of descent, labour and affiliation; and all clannish history, like Harry Thuku's on return from exile, had become tribal. Struggle about class also embittered the language of disagreement over the twin obligations of fertile wealth and industrious poverty. External Kikuyu spokesmen, *athamaki*, were the most successful African rural capitalists. Land shortage forced them, more than the big men of other ethnic groups, to be expropriators. The quarrels of social closure that drove poor Kikuyu to town also made them the liveliest townsmen in Kenya. Workers and artisans faced the greatest gulf between their earnings and rising prices for the property which proper social dealings required. They were nearest to falling off the spiral stair of self-respect. They had to rethink, more than workers from elsewhere, both what 'tribe' could offer them and what other community there might be. They needed more than, say, Luo or Kamba workers, the propertied freedoms that made town life one of self-mastery, or more pay, to fend off the shame of proletarianization with rural investment. They were the first to go on strike. But industrial action had palpably failed them by 1951. Townsmen were split. Skilled workers had been bought off with industrial unions. Mass general unionism by unskilled workers and self-employed artisans, often the same people, was triumphant in Mombasa in 1947 but then smashed in the Nairobi general strike of May 1950.[494] Land-poor Kikuyu then had little option but to fight with renewed determination the agrarian quarrels they were currently losing to landowners both white and black.

But, to address the latest schools of historiography, struggles about class take many forms. As I have argued, they are not as neatly regimented as disputes between conservative and Marxist scholars may lead one to believe. Throup has named the purpose of the control which the early historians thought moderate politicians had lost. It was to use the peasantry as a 'battering ram' to break open the gates of state power for their middle-class expropriators, but not for peasants themselves, to enter.[495] Peasant and worker awareness of this class exploitation was what, for Njonjo, fired Mau Mau. Not merely impatient with the failures of open politics, they opposed all reform that might include the political class, but not its mass support, within a negotiated redistribution of property and power. But lived experience was less clear-cut than either view allows. The ideological reciprocities of civic virtue imagined a contract between rich and poor that many could not bring themselves to deny, whether as cynics or heroes. This moral tie caused political uncertainty and, hence, anxious social terror. But it may also have curbed, on both sides of the Mau Mau war, Kikuyu use of terrorism against each other, violence calculated to demoralize opponents by flouting accepted rules of killing.[496] It was a dirty war; it could have been dirtier still.

To sum up, there were several Mau Maus, a name coined by their enemies. Regionally distinct and socially varied, they recruited squatters, townsmen, farmers and traders. Some leaders hoped self-mastery would earn reform; most followers feared that class closure and state oppression had killed off their chances of civic virtue. No Mau Mau was united, split between *mbari*, right holders and *ahoi* within *mbari*, *mbari* and *riika*. The social contract of labour theory that weighed generous wealth against obedient sweat was also strained. In the nationalist crisis of 1947 to 1952 it almost snapped. Barren greed met idle vagrancy, intimate enemies. Both also faced the strange new language of worker syndicalism. This incipient break in Kikuyu thought was repaired by the Emergency. Conservative and dissident thinkers were jailed for up to ten years. Conservative thought, taught by grandparents as much as oaths, regained its inherited sway in the forest war. Discipline and delinquency were bitter but familiar foes. Repression failed to unify Mau Mau in either command or thought. Dissent continued with the struggle. Kenya's peasant revolution was the work not only of Mau Mau but of its parents and enemies too, doves as well as hawks.

CONTEXTS

The First World War and postwar slump generated a disunited Kikuyu nationalism. The Second World War and postwar boom divided it further. The two crises, apparently similar, were very different. Kenya's white settlers made gains in each; each time the state had to recognize African interests too. In the 1920s it could do so without bending white dominance; 20 years on, Africans could advance only at white expense. For the earlier Kenya was still a segmentary state, stitched together in an elastic patchwork of separate bargains with local notables, white and black. The later Kenya was more centralized. By however much its government pleased one set of racial interests it forfeited the freedom to appease another.

After the First World War the settlers, now enfranchised, got the state to redirect African men from domestic production towards wage labour by means of pass controls, taxes and coercion. Chiefs resented these burdens, Thuku denounced them. A sharp slump, London's displeasure and African anger forced the government to relax its pressure on black labour. Under the declared ideology of imperial trusteeship for African interests – with which the then Secretary of State for the Colonies, the

Duke of Devonshire, refuted the rival claims of Kenya's white and
Indian immigrants – the state even supported what Kikuyu and others
saw as patriotic production. African farming flourished in the well-
watered years of the later 1920s. Some settlers had cut wages in the
slump; all had to double them by the end of the decade to compete with
peasant earnings; for a time they also welcomed Kikuyu emigrants on
generous squatter terms.[497] The economic cycle stimulated the expansion and contraction of Kikuyu politics. The KCA came nearest to uni-
ting opinion in an alliance of progress with the state at the peak of
the late-1920s boom. Individual *mbari* fought hardest for their separate
school gateways to power, whether in pure *karing'a* or in *kirore* thumbprint
mode, at the bottom of the 1930s slump. One cannot suggest such gen-
eralizations for the 1940s; Kikuyu experience of both good and bad times
had become divided by class.

After 1944, like any *ancien régime* shocked by the audit of war,
the colonial state tried to expand production and broaden consent.
Whites seized the economic opportunity; they persuaded all but Africans that large farming was the best way to help the sterling area
recover in a dollar-dominated world and to increase Kenya's export
earnings and welfare budgets. Their strategic loyalty attracted a Britain facing the prospect of a Russian war. Settlers had previously needed
the state; now it seemed that the state needed them. This reversal of
settler–state relations fated the other half of reform, the expansion of
consent, to be little more than talk. Moderate African leaders were galvanized by hopes that were hard to sustain. Whites kept the legislative
sway they had seized after the earlier war; they won executive power in
several areas of policy, most provocatively over black as well as white
farming. Wanting security of property and capital investment, settlers
turned against their squatter farm families, black tribes that had infil-
trated the white highland pale. On the roads and in town Africans also
faced new movement controls as the number of work seekers overwhelmed job vacancies. Kenya's population had begun to outgrow its
stratified economy.

Africans had little to set against these defeats. Their first
representative on the Legislative Council was nominated in 1944, and
shortly more; but not being elected nor were they heard. Local Native
Councils became African District Councils but their greater power only
made them better servants of the state. Moreover, what older men
counted as gain, younger ones saw as loss. Wages, for instance, were
not cut this time but, almost worse, were depressed in real terms by
soaring food and housing prices. Black farmers, traders, landlords and
officials spiralled up; manual workers passed them, down the stair to
poverty. Soil conservation work was equally divisive at home. Some
big farmers had ploughed on the contour for years; their ridge-top

fields needed little other treatment. Poor peasants had to terrace their hillside plots two or three days a week, week after week, hoeing by hand. Cash-crop expansion was halted by these anti-erosion measures; it resumed in the late 1940s to divide farmers further. Kikuyu were angry that African-grown coffee, long needed for their civilizing mission, was allowed to others more distant from white estates in the 1930s but denied to them until 1951. And by 1948 they knew that coffee permits would be limited to men with enough legally secure land to feed a household too. The first proviso, security, excluded *ahoi*, however rich; the second, surplus land, kept from the poor the one crop that might have earned them enough to hang on to what little they had.[498] Far from bringing shared wellbeing, this veteran campaign sharpened the divide that drained civilizing male labour, with loose women, to town.

But political geography separated Kikuyu farmers most. Agricultural officers soon learnt how to raise farm income in the reserves. White farmers in those areas best suited to squatters took no time at all to decide that their Kikuyu should play no part in increasing production save as wage workers. Renewed white immigration, farm subdivision and mechanization threw back the peasant frontier in the Rift Valley. Squatters had to sign new contracts that cancelled almost all their rights to domestic production and failed entirely to compensate them with more pay, not that money ever could. Of all Kikuyu, squatters faced the steepest cliff of class formation. They looked to fall from a prosperous peasantry on what by right of clearance was their future property, to ill-paid labour on another's land.

Kikuyu politics, then, had two contexts in 1945. It was, first, harder to evade a revitalized white ascendancy. Africans feared that settlers would win more power, not least because white fears of future retreat made them defend more stoutly what they had. Next, class formation had removed all prospect of united Kikuyu political action. Cursed readers had made their peace with society between the wars; the KCA had assumed the duties of wealth as the league of compassion, *uiguano wa tha*. Two decades on, not all could agree that wealth was fertile. By 1952, political songs commonly referred to government's supporters, often the prosperous, as *ereriri*, the selfish ones, and *thaka*, handsome but barren.[499] If the rich refused to be fertile patrons the poor could not be obedient clients; they had little choice but idle delinquency. That was the terror of class formation; if the rich lost civic virtue the poor could not earn self-mastery. *Athomi* prodigals had been welcome to return because their literacy was fertile in power. The question now was whether and, if so, how, landless workers, spivs, thieves and prostitutes could also be Kikuyu, once hopes of reform were dashed and calls for discipline by moderate leaders were discredited with them.

CONSTITUENCIES

Self-conscious African political constituencies formed after the war. Some grasped hopes of reform, others were gripped by fear of oppression or social closure. There were three constituencies of high-political hope, the moderate pan-ethnic nationalists in the Kenya African Union, conservative ethnic nationalists of the KCA and urban, not yet militant, trades unionists. There were also three realms of low-political fear. They were mostly Kikuyu, squatter, peasant and townsman, class-based but ethnically defined. All these projects, high and low, failed between 1947 and 1950. It was not that politicians lost control; they had none to lose. Rather, all politics was plunged into a 'nationalist crisis'. In this ordeal, shared by many African colonies at the time, a rush of events drew hitherto distinct political visions together, exposed their contradictions and forced them to compete, with profound and unpredictable results. High-political competition forged a new deep politics. High hopes confronted low fears when competitive leaderships looked for and then had to satisfy popular supporters. Mass passions checked some leaders, encouraged others, and thereby changed the course of nationalism.[500] In West Africa the crisis ended uncertainty and launched the parties and coalitions that won independence. In Kenya the crisis separated territorial and ethnic nationalisms further; it was not resolved until after the Mau Mau war.

In Kenya, as elsewhere, the crisis forced territorial high politics into a deep encounter with the local, ethnic, concerns of the poor. Most ethnic nationalisms, as already noted, found room enough for power in local government at the district level. They disengaged from the centre as it became more dangerous. Kikuyu deep politics, focused on conditions not only in the reserves but also on the white highlands and in Nairobi, could not withdraw. Two Kikuyu leaderships, divided by generation, aim and method, had to compete in a wider political arena demarcated by conflict with settlers and the state. In a trial of strength, both appealed to popular constituencies of fear already formed. Aroused, revived or disciplined by this high-political competition, these then prepared for more concerted effort. Aims hardened, from resistance against the state to taking it over. Mass energy drove leaders further apart. Conservatives, who wanted progress but not social upheaval, were appalled that civil disobedience might invite popular violence. Militants, prepared to challenge elders' authority as well as British rule, were steeled. Their followings became more divided too, in the abstract by class struggle but in fact by kin dispute. Householders with land for posterity were conservative and could become loyalist. Fathers who could not endow

408

sons, or juniors who could not marry, were militant and likely to become Mau Mau. But how far the politics of external demand became internally violent under British pressure also depended largely on the Kikuyu social imagination. Fear of rivals' sorcery bred fiery retribution; it also fostered protective solidarities, on oath. The despair of ageing adolescents caused criminal abandon; hope of generation succession inspired insurgent discipline. The language of disagreement still served to classify and manage conflict. In the Mau Mau war this dynamic process may have further defined Kikuyu as an ethnic community of thought, mutually murderous but arguing still. But thought alone never governs behaviour. Tumultuous events, especially the white response to Mau Mau, helped to turn anti-colonial resistance into rebellion and then Kikuyu civil war. I cannot here recount the crisis. I can suggest how Kikuyu variously brought their political thought to bear upon it. Their ability to survive owed less to their political organization than to their moral imagination.

The Kenya African Union was the first new constituency of hope. Its early history plays a vital but in the end peripheral role in my story. The KAU neither owed nor added much to Kikuyu thought. But its emergence revived Kikuyu politics, by example and threat. Its failure then showed the limits of legal remonstrance by black subjects under a colonial regime mortgaged to its immigrant white citizens. Frustration fed the nationalist crisis and, with it, the tribalization of politics. Until then the KAU was, briefly, a coalition of modern elites from the coast, sons of freed slaves, and upcountry secondary-school graduates. Most were teachers and civil servants at ease with whites; earthier traders were few. Leaders of urban welfare associations, who policed middle-class rules of ethnicity, showed guarded sympathy. All were fired by the nomination of the first black legislative councillor, Eliud Mathu from Kiambu, for some their old teacher or colleague, and by prospects of office.[501] Their hopes rested on official recognition of their personal qualifications, not on the worth of all those they claimed to represent. True, they used the language of native rights and liberal reform. But they thought adult education an answer to urban crime; and in an early petition asked, in a chapter on education three times longer than that on land, for Kenyan schools to teach Latin, to help Africans continue their education overseas. Clinching that argument with a Shakespearean tag, they patronized the working poor.[502] Unsurprisingly, the KAU was not a mass party. In 1948, a year after Kenyatta's election to the party presidency had awakened popular interest, its newspaper complained that there were only 15,000 members, not all paid-up.[503] The paper then died. Until engulfed by crisis the KAU was a purely middle-class project. Most Kenyans mistrusted its white-collar aloofness. Non-Kikuyu thought it Kikuyu-led; old Kikuyu politicians feared that its elite youth was dangerously untried. Some KCA leaders had been detained and their party banned at the start of the war, on flimsy suspicion of trafficking with the Italian enemy.[504] They wanted to revive the KCA rather than join the KAU. But in a move that set the nationalist crisis in train from above, they nerved themselves to take over the intelligentsia's party when their 50-year-old but now academically distinguished leader Kenyatta returned from Britain at their expense in September 1946 and failed to lift the ban.[505] The KCA had to remain clandestine, but it was, after the KAU, the second realm of hope. Their hopes were very different. The contrast between the shallow roots of Kenyan liberalism – or, later, of syndicalism – and the moral depth of conservative ethnicity explains why the nationalist crisis, when it came, was so divisive.

The KCA remained wedded to the plutocratic theory that wealth, open to all who persevered, was the fount of civic virtue. It followed that political reform would spring from Kikuyu industry, not from elite education. The KCA expected more of the obedient poor than ever the KAU could inspire. Continuity of thought was matched by the KCA's divisions, district rivalry and mutual suspicion. But the party was also newly divided, by age and experience. That was a change. Both continuity and change can best be understood by comparing the thought of the returned Kenyatta with that of his press secretary Henry Muoria, a mere boy when many KCA elders had been initiated in the time of influenza. He had joined the party in 1938. In 1945 he founded the first and most influential new Kikuyu newspaper, *Mumenyereri*, the 'Guardian', *Muigwithania*'s spiritual heir.[506]

Kenyatta returned more a Kikuyu than a Kenyan leader. But on landing at Mombasa he spoke in Swahili, with Swahili proverbs. He warned that he brought no magic solutions from Europe; nor did he have an atomic bomb. African unity was in any case more powerful; progress was up to them. They were their own worst enemy; 'what bites you is under your own clothes.'[507] But on arrival in Kikuyuland he turned his back on the crowds that had cheered his train at every stop. He wanted a rural home. His exile's instincts were those of Harry Thuku 15 years before. He bought a 30-acre farm in four lots in his home *mbari*, built a stone house, and married into the most powerful family in southern Kikuyu, the Koinanges.[508] He was clearly *gitonga*, a man of means with, presumably, farmworkers or tenants. He could act. He was therefore *muthamaki*, one who could say.

Kenyatta's words showed the conservatism of exile; he had not kept abreast of the arguments. Deploring alienated labour and lost Kikuyu seed more than their causes, he condemned rickshaw boys and prostitutes. His people must show the pride they had earned by braving the circumciser's knife. In his book, which KCA leaders read and advertised in *Muigwithania* before the war,[509] he had called it the key to citizenship. Power came from knowing one's people and their mother, the soil, rather than from books, perhaps a jibe at the KAU's young men. Nonetheless, Kikuyu must still convert wealth into the Western progress that fought imported dangers, as his *athomi* friends had urged before. Foreigners did not get jiggers in their toes; Kikuyu must build clean stone houses too. Sweat won rights; 'a diligent child does not lack an adopter.'[510] He was still elaborating the lesson in political geography he had drawn in 1928. Kikuyu, he then warned, must follow the New Zealand Maoris, not native Australians. As the former were 'a very diligent people ... they are permitted to select four men to represent them in the Big Council'; since the latter 'were decreasing by reason of their sloth ... they got pushed to the bad parts of the land'. If Kikuyu were 'diligent and obedient, our Government here will surely listen to our cry.'[511] That was all he had then said about the state; he hoped it would be shamed into change rather than pressed. The little he said now distanced him further from the KAU.

In 1944, still in England, Kenyatta published a moderately worded pamphlet, *Kenya: The Land of Conflict*,[512] which Muoria brought out in Kikuyu early in 1947.[513] It told of theft and oppression but accepted that whites could only be expelled by a 'bloody insurrection' that nobody wanted. Kenyatta did not ask for the return of white farmland; but Africans, not new immigrants, must have first claim on its empty acres. Only self-government on a non-racial franchise could make Kenya tolerable for all, whites included. These were standard liberal arguments, if also more than the KAU yet dared to say. Back home, Kenyatta recognized that talk of stolen lands, poor black wages and schools was painful to whites. But he had painful things to say to his people, in a conservative Kikuyu critique far more radical than the then liberal imperial view. It was their own lack of self-mastery, he said, that allowed British oppression. Too many readers were greedy. Once in government pay they dared not speak; those who enslaved them knew their price. Chiefs had also become servile, unlike the gallant Waiyaki. The state could order Africans to hit each other; that was why whites despised them as savages, *acenji*.[514]

His radical conservatism persuaded Kenyatta that the pursuit of self-mastery by all, rich and poor, was the best means to secure reform. A strong civil society, as we might say today, would force the state to be responsible. The early KAU believed, to the contrary, in liberal imperial paternalism, a doctrine that charged colonial states with the task of raising backward peoples to the level of civil society, capable of self-rule. Its leaders hoped that their cooptation into responsible public office would allow them, the modern elite, to guide and control the uplift of the mass. They must 'put up an example'.[515] The KAU accepted the hegemony of the British civilizing mission. Kenyatta did not. Yet, despite this philosophical difference, he did not justify violence against the state. Rather, he called on his people to persevere in their own civilizing mission. This might well goad the state to violence, discrediting British rule and justifying them. History was his guide.

Kenyatta claimed to have been in the crowd shot down by the police in 1922 as they called for Harry Thuku's release. To a British audience he stressed the discipline of Thuku's protest. A civil servant himself, his leadership had been authorized by chiefs and backed by the most important men in every village; the Nairobi crowd had been 'quite unarmed and defenceless'. It was up to the British public to see that similar cries, if unheeded by local officials, were heard by the imperial government,[516] a plea he repeated several times.[517] Kenyata noted that the Devonshire declaration on the paramountcy of African interests, which he translated for *Muigwithania*, had followed Thuku's protest.[518] Returning home, he taught this history's lesson. Elected to the KAU presidency in June 1947, he warned his members, in an echo of Thomas Jefferson, that the tree of liberty would have to be watered by African blood. He had once used this image to praise warriors who protected the country they had liberated from tyranny in the first *ituika*.[519] Patriotic discipline could be costly. Muoria, to whom Kenyatta confided his belief that a rising number of political prisoners would herald freedom's dawn,[520] expounded the text in a pamphlet, *Our Victory does not Depend on Force of Arms but upon Truth*. The British had conquered the Kikuyu; they had killed the protesters of 1922. But they had also left India, Egypt and Palestine; they were leaving West Africa and the Sudan. Some of them even admitted 'that it was wrong to be motivated by such desires to conquer others'. Africans must show a courage that would shame them further. It might bring imprisonment and the sack, as Thuku had suffered, even death. But these would bring freedom; 'he who is expelled by force will return but he who is convinced by truth never comes back.' To fight was barbarous; it showed neither intelligence nor the justice of one's cause. As another proverb put it: 'Only an ignorant young bull risks getting gored by mounting a cow from the front.'[521]

Kenyatta had not been swayed by cosmopolitan thought, least of all by his notorious visits to Moscow. He knew the value of British public opinion; he had friends in the Labour Party, now the government.[522] But he had become a Kikuyu elder. He opened speeches with the saying: 'I speak openly; I am nobody's dependant.' His audiences understood him to be asserting independence from his father-in-law, Koinange. He built his house with subscriptions from his age-set. But he had married into the establishment and when, a few years later, Grace Koinange died in childbirth, Kenyatta married Ngina, daughter of yet another chief who had called for Thuku's detention, Muhoho Gatheca. He enjoyed wearing the cloak Emperor Haile Selassie gave him in 1936 and sported a heavy ebony stick, said to be from the Gold Coast chief Nana Sir Ofori

Atta; its carved head illustrated the proverb: 'An elephant is not defeated by its tusks', which is to say that leaders enjoy their burdens. He claimed to have been sustained in England by the wisdom of Kinyanjui and Wambugu, paramount chiefs of Kiambu and Nyeri, who had had harsh things to say about the KCA.[523]

Kenyatta's tribute to his old enemies is perhaps best explained by the fact that the KCA, in Kiambu at least, had meanwhile been captured by his father-in-law, the man it had once tormented. Chief Koinange also chaired the successor body to the Kikuyu Land Board Association, which the KCA had set up to coordinate response to the Kenya Land Commission in 1932. This committee of *aramati*, sub-clan trustees, was known, appropriately enough, as *Mbari*. Once distrustful of any organization not obviously under land elders' control, it was now the KCA fulfilled.[524] Some cursed readers, the best connected, elders by now, had not only come home like the prodigal, they ruled in their father's house. Without benefit of *ituika*, the *irungu* had matured into a ruling *Maina* generation, succeeding their *Mwangi* fathers who had 'sold land for office'. The KCA was now an elders' party. Among its leaders were men prepared to shoot in defence of property.[525] Their legislator, Mathu, advised on their motor insurance.[526] KCA leaders in Kiambu were different in one crucial respect from their colleagues elsewhere. Koinange's clandestine crossing of the floor had made them a factional part of the establishment. The Kiambu KCA was conservative not only socially but also politically. Although no less intent on keeping power in the hands of elders who were also improving farmers, the KCA elsewhere was politically more radical. In Murang'a and Nyeri it had failed to penetrate the official patronage structure, based as it was on chiefs' *mbari*. But in all districts *mbari* affiliation was the best channel of loan finance and commercial trust.[527] And the KCA represented big farmers who had won land disputes against juniors, perhaps now their employees; many were produce traders, shopkeepers, builders and lorry owners as well.

The visible focus of Kikuyu patriotism and Koinange family power remained Githunguri college. Fed by the independent school networks in the reserves and the Kikuyu colonies elsewhere, the *riika* or age-sets remained its main donors. These were Kenyatta's most demonstrative power base; he became the college's president on Peter Mbiyu Koinange's departure for further study in Britain in 1947. He delighted people by using the greetings peculiar to each set. He and chief Koinange, who retired in 1949, sponsored *riika* meetings as *athamaki*. *Riika* warriors had always been tools of their sponsors' power as much as the teeth of age-set solidarity. Kenyatta's ethnography had also praised *riika* enforcement of sexual discipline, and deplored its mission-inspired decay.[528] And now there was under-age drinking.[529] He clearly hoped that his politics, no less than Githunguri's funds, would be underpinned by a revival of corporate pride. *Riika* celebrated their rivalry with festivals in the college grounds.[530] More young people were getting initiated without due ceremony, by the roadside, *njiriani*, or in hospital. But they could also come together by road, by the truckload, to build the 'sharpener', the whetstone of independent knowledge at Githunguri. These age-set competitions of hope became increasingly confined to Kiambu.[531] Why this was so may be explained in my later consideration of the indisciplined time-banditry of fear, which was concentrated among townsmen who hailed from Murang'a and Nyeri. Meanwhile, Githunguri restored gender discipline too. The market women whom the KCA once feared joined up under Rebecca Njeri to build a girls' dormitory with their trading profits. They had to get their husbands' permission but any man who attended their meetings had to wear a skirt. To judge by a song in which their cheerleader Njoki wa Thuge many years later condemned the miniskirt, they would have been long: 'Where have all the sheep and goats gone? Lower the hemline all over Kenya.' She could as well have composed it for *Muigwithania* in 1928.[532]

Henry Muoria, however, was a man of the new age. Briefly on the KAU committee, he was secretary of his *riika*, the *ndege* or aeroplane age-set of 1927, mortified by his failure to hire a plane to impress a Githunguri fund-raising party. He was the first to build a stone house in his *mbari* and the first Kenyan to own a Citroën car, a *traction avant*. These were the rewards of political pamphleteering and popular journalism. He had read *Facing Mount Kenya* when a railway guard on the cold night run from the highest station in the Empire, Timboroa, to Eldoret, furthest point of the Afrikaner trek from the Cape. Learning journalism by correspondence, he wrote his first pamphlet, the 100-page *What Can We Do for Our Own Sake?* on the hottest sector of the line, down to the Magadi soda works. Published early in 1945, its sales encouraged him to leave the railway and found his paper, *Mumenyereri*. In editorials and further pamphlets Muoria, the KCA's first historian,[533] developed Kikuyu labour theory in four dimensions. Where Kenyatta had stuck to the theme of self-mastery, Muoria showed the compatibility of Christianity with Kikuyu materialism and the Kikuyu need for democracy; he also argued the rights of education and the duties of wage labour. It all added up to a formidable call for patriotic discipline.

As a CMS schoolboy, baptised by Canon Leakey, Muoria had signed the *kirore* petition for the protection of non-circumcisers. It is not then surprising that he became concerned to reconcile Kikuyu and Christian belief. The problem must have troubled many of his generation. He found his answer in two directions for which missionaries offered no guide, in Kikuyu moral thought and biblical criticism. Muoria started with the proposition that God wanted good things for his creatures. He had to rely on human hands. To use one's talents honoured God, idleness insulted him. To pray without action was to believe in magic. Faith was shown in works; God loved a hard worker. Kikuyu should not be deceived that poverty was saintly; Christ had condemned not wealth but greed. Muoria ended his first pamphlet with a chapter 'On being rich and its meaning'. Drawing on the Kikuyu obsession with clearing away the psychic and physical dangers of the wild, he concluded that: 'Wealth is like a big broom with which one sweeps away all the bad things so that the good things can be kept intact . . . All sorts of poverty and all needs are swept away. This enables the rich man to live in peace.' Light should stream through the rich man's windows. The ignorant built huts 'full of darkness and the smell of goats' and sheep urine and their droppings.' His readers must not be upset by this revelation of 'how things used to be before the advent of the white man'; there was no point in mourning the past.[534] Moreover, biblical criticism, to which the fundamentalist missionaries of his day were averse, might show that Africans were not inferior. Science had not disproved God; it merely enabled man to understand what God intended. Clever Europeans had proved that not everything in the Bible was true. Clever Africans ought to continue their work. They might then discover that what the Bible said of them was also false: 'Namely that the black men were cursed by their father who ordained that they should be forever the slaves of the white people.'[535]

A railway worker for 14 years, Muoria had become a businessman. The broom of capitalism was a tool of civic as much as private virtue. If England was a nation of shopkeepers, why not Kikuyu?[536] Business enterprise was as patriotic as farm production. Trade preserved a future for African children; white commerce encouraged further white immigration. But most African businesses failed. Traders were ignorant, thieves, jealous of partners.[537] They had to change. The state must make that possible. Enterprise caused dispute; discussion led to understanding; cooperation brought progress. Kikuyu must therefore be allowed freedom of assembly. Yet chiefs could prohibit meetings. This was oppression. Without discussion there would be no schools, no trade, no politics, no escape from slavery. Kikuyu were not proud but they had more schools and companies than other Kenyan peoples; they had more need of democracy too.[538] Nor should Kikuyu be dismayed by white learning. They should remember two points. First, while they could not write before the missionaries came, the wisdom of their preliterate intellectuals, coiners of proverbs, was second to none. Secondly, literacy had started in Africa, with the Egyptians. The British derived all their learning from them, through the medium of Greece. And Socratic method, as Muoria showed by quotation from Plato's *Republic*, was the same as the Kikuyu ideal of conciliar reasoning.[539] Nonetheless, even if no Kikuyu need be ashamed of their intellectual history, the wiser and better educated among them – perhaps another echo of Plato – were better able to see through the wall of ignorance that hid the future. Ignorance was the fruit of idleness, wisdom of work. Let the ignorant follow educated advice.[540]

Finally, it was from Plato that Muoria derived his ideas on wage workers. His own career was also an example. Just as men must work, he argued, so too must nations. The larger the nation the better it worked. It could divide its labour, as men had different limbs and organs. The more people did the tasks for which they were suited the more Kikuyu would prosper. Politics united the various limbs. An idler was 'an invalid as far as the affairs of his nation are concerned.'[541] Landlessness was no excuse. Not all Kikuyu could expect to farm their own land. But in working for others they must show the same sense of responsibility as herdsmen, love their labour and not hate their employer, whether white or black. If they were poor, Muoria urged in 1945, it was because they were lazy.[542] His first reaction to trades unionism was that of a labour officer; it was an essential discipline. Workers must obey leaders who negotiated their claims with government and ordered them back to work. Negotiation was not collaboration.[543]

Muoria was reacting to the 1947 Mombasa general strike. At this date trades unionism may still be counted among the constituencies of hope. It was of two kinds. There were staff unions, as with the largest East African employer, the railway, which had long had industrial and welfare policies far in advance of other companies. The railway union leader called the strike by unskilled and casual workers foolish. But his members enjoyed a relatively secure career structure and, many of them, tolerable family housing. The mass of Mombasa townsmen did not. They created another, general, kind of unionism. This emerged during the strike, more an exercise in direct city democracy than an instrument of wage bargaining. But 'disorganization' was itself a threat to the state. The strikers secured considerable improvements. Many of them also retained a measure of control over the alternative job and petty trade options that made them, in official eyes, a headless mass of casual workers but, in their own, the independent men their rural kin aspired to be. They gave the leadership of their African Workers Federation to the middle-class Chege Kibachia who, like Muoria, straddled the worlds of capitalist farming, trade and popular politics. Perhaps his chief credential for the strikers was his acquaintance with Eliud Mathu, his old teacher. Struggle about class was not yet class conflict. Kibachia was moved to help the strikers in order to prevent towns from so demoralizing the young that they were unfit to return to rural life. Mombasa workers, Kikuyu and people of other ethnic groups alike, struck for self-mastery. They were, in the short term, remarkably successful.[544]

The rural constituencies of fear were not. Since Mombasa's port workers could strangle Kenya's trade, the state had to loosen their grip. Within the kid gloves of concession it also held a firmer hand of trades union law. For large employers could hope to offset the cost of better pay and family welfare against the benefit of stable, skilled workers, fewer, less rowdy than migrants; and officials began to see that class and trades unions might be more controllable forms of social division than race and tribe.[545] This was partly because many workers were losing their agrarian rights to rural capitalists and, with them, the freedom to resist incorporation into the labour market. But the social relations of property in this agrarian Kenya were at the same time being built into ethnic identities by the external and internal architectures of recent history. The state reinforced this tribalization of property and power. Security for the rich bred fear in the poor; lacking control over land, they found themselves being denied the multiple, often trans-ethnic, rights to its usage by which they had survived and some had prospered.

The Mau Mau of the Kikuyu diaspora was a reply to this closure of the pliant frontiers of precolonial ethnicity.[546] Adoption of people had then matched trade in goods and services; it did so still. But emigrant Kikuyu rights now choked official dreams of proper Maasai ethnicity as well as settler farm planning. Officials in Maasailand and Rift Valley white farmers both decided to break the squatter grip. But both refused to grant the compensating rights of representation or residence that would weaken the tribal or racial defences of property. Each saw state patronage of Kikuyu colonization elsewhere as the answer, as in the new settlement area carved from the Mau forest at Olenguruone. Kikuyu squatters did not. The poor felt equally threatened in Kikuyuland. Rural capitalism squeezed their dependent land rights; the state forced them to labour against the soil erosion that menaced peasant and therefore settler Kenya. For erosion in the reserves raised the spectre of hordes of famished peasants trampling down the white highland fences in search of land. The generous laxity of patronage that the poor needed for a start in self-mastery was at all points under attack; some young men in Nairobi had scant hope of or interest in rural virtue at all.

After the shock of *kifagio*, both the Rift Valley and Maasailand and the forests between remained frontiers of opportunity for the Kikuyu diaspora. Squatters earned far more from stock and produce sales than from their waged farm labour. Polygyny rates were higher in the Rift than in the reserves; so were circumcisers' fees; independent schools flourished. If landlords became oppressive then a good living could be made as forest department squatters, who cleared ground for tree nurseries by growing their own crops for a season. Charcoal burners and pit sawyers found their niche. Maasai patrons welcomed farm tenants and access, through Kikuyu clients, to the Rift Valley stock trade. In some areas intermarriage made it immaterial who was Maasai, who Kikuyu. Kikuyu became partners with 'Maasai who ate potatoes' like Harry Nangurai, an early member of the KCA. By 1951 over 150 African shopkeepers were licensed in Nakuru district alone, mostly general retailers who bought from Indians but also butchers, carpenters, hoteliers, smiths and tailors. Turnover was as high as £600 per month. Outside official knowledge, the trans-ethnic trades in livestock, timber and charcoal boomed. Women thronged food markets. The state tried to police borders, to check the movement of people and stock. Such harassment kept squatter communities alert. They struck ritual roots into the soil and deterred strangers by denying them access to adjudication and dance. Traders carried political ideas; KCA membership fostered commercial trust.[547] But the doors of opportunity began to close, in Maasailand at the beginning of the Second World War and, on white farms, after the war had brought untold prosperity to settlers and squatters alike. The squatters' very success invited retaliation under the slogans of Maasailand for the Maasai and the Rift Valley for whites.

Olenguruone turned out to be a disaster for the state and a tragedy for Kikuyu, later hymned as martyrdom. The settlement was intended to meet British insistence that land be found for squatters displaced by the intensification of white farming. Most of the 4,000 Kikuyu who were sent there early in the war were squatters at one remove who had left the Rift Valley to negotiate easier conditions with Maasai. Privately profitable to Maasai patrons, immigrants in large numbers became publicly disquieting. Officials, imagining a pure Maasai ethnicity that had never existed, played on these fears to secure the expulsion of any Kikuyu whom their Maasai patrons no longer cared to protect. The resettled Kikuyu then found that they were up against another arm of policy, which saw them as a pilot scheme in the controlled smallholder husbandry – subject to rules of contour cropping, rotation, grazing and inheritance – that might in future save all peasant Kenya from soil erosion.[548] British and Kikuyu invoked different histories in a conflict of authority. Officials maintained that, as trespassers in Maasailand, the Kikuyu must, in gratitude to the state, be its obedient tenants, government *ahoi*. Led by Samuel Koina Gitebi, an old KCA man, independent schoolteacher and timber merchant, the Kikuyu espoused a history of property and freedom thrice denied. Their fathers had been expropriated from Kiambu before 1914; settlers then turned them off the Rift Valley land they had cleared by their sweat; even the taming of the Maasai wilderness was now held against them. But the state must, at last, compensate them for their sweat and loss of property; it must grant them Olenguruone to use as they chose. If they could no longer enjoy the transethnic contracts of protection under which they had made the Rift Valley and Maasailand flourish, then Kikuyu must insist on their *mbari* rights.

A long struggle between Kikuyu refusal to obey the rules and official threat of eviction ensued.[549]

Olenguruone Kikuyu are famous in Mau Mau historiography for inventing a new oath of resistance. The KCA oath of loyalty conformed to normal legal practice in being given to household heads, whose word implied the assent of the family they protected behind their *riigi*. The Olenguruone oath was given to all, men, women and children alike, a shocking dilution of responsibility. No participant seems to have explained why. My own answer is speculative. But household heads must have seen the rules of tenure as a subversion of self-mastery. If wives had to obey crop regulations and the official demand for impartible inheritance by primogeniture discriminated between sons, then dependants must also swear disobedience to the state. The householder's word was not enough; he could no longer, unaided, close his *riigi* against officialdom. But this loss of self-mastery was turned to advantage. The Olenguruone community stood solid against government threats; their oath was an inspiration to others.

At the end of the war settlers felt free to confront what they called the 'squatter menace' and cancel most of the cultivation and grazing entitlements of their farm labour.[550] Squatters resisted with strikes and sabotage. Some moved to easier employers; not all settlers could afford to intensify their farming. But many squatters were stripped of their illusion of *kuna*, land clearing rights to the future, 'when African labour began to be replaced by machines.'[551] Moved from their villages into labour lines, *laini*, many Kikuyu were reduced to the level of 'the poor', like Luo monthly workers; some even had dried fish in their rations, loved by Luo but hated by Kikuyu. Forced livestock sales destroyed accumulated capital; settlers were like rich men who seized the poor man's midden, as one Thiongo Kigotho complained. He lost his crops and cattle; 'all that wealth has turned into manure for the white man's fields.'[552] But non-compliance with the new terms risked total eviction.

Squatters adopted the Olenguruone oath of unity, hoping that mass refusal of the new contracts would make settlers relent. They swore solidarity farm by farm, encouraged by ex-squatter traders in touch with Olenguruone, KCA men in Nakuru town and rural markets.[553] This was a crisis far worse than the *kifagio* of 20 years before. As then, outsiders gave advice. When Joseph Kinyua, KAU's Nakuru branch secretary, told arrested squatters to obey the rules they became 'noisy and aggressive. They . . . did not know who Mr Kinyua was, neither did they know whom he represented.'[554] Chiefs again warned that there was no room in Kiambu. But squatters had now, as they had not had before, their own solidarities. From Olenguruone, Gitebi led a long march of 150 miles to consult Koinange; others later called on Kenyatta to help. Rift Valley KCA members organized

3,000 evicted squatters into the Kikuyu Highlands Squatters Landlords Association – a revealing self-description – to demand reinstatement in Kiambu. Some invaded the governor's residence. Chiefs and officials offered no help and little sympathy, advising only a return to what squatters now called the slavery of the highlands, *ukombo ya ruguru*.[555] Many capitulated early in 1947, but the demands of low politics were beginning to press on high, a first tremor of the nationalist crisis from below.

The deep politics of crisis loomed largest in the links between Nairobi and Kikuyuland. Rural capitalism and state pressure fanned three quarrels, between rich and poor, men and women, adults and young. They were more openly expressed in Nyeri and Murang'a than in Kiambu. Differences in the internal histories of *mbari* formation and *ahoi* alliance make inter-district contrasts dangerous. But the lawyer Arthur Phillips saw two distinctions between Kiambu and its neighbours. Outright sale of land was more common; Kiambu chiefs, still the most cohesive political machine, interfered more in land disputes.[556] There was a frantic scramble for property after the war; Kiambu courts took £13,000 in fees in 1949, £24,000 in 1951, not to mention bribes.[557] To extend the earlier argument about *mbari* redefinition under the goad of patriotic production, it seems that Kiambu peasants enjoyed less *mbari* solidarity than their northern counterparts. More exposed to political corruption, they must have been more divided by the need to buy protection, and less able to express open opposition to soil conservation work. Those aggrieved by Kiambu chiefs tended to file private law suits; mass civil disobedience was more common elsewhere.[558] Deceived by their imagination of egalitarian custom, officials had made contour-terracing a 'communal' task comparable, they thought, to neighbourly working parties or *ngwatio*. Peasants knew it as forced labour and called it *mitaro*, ditching.[559] Increasingly onerous after the war, the work was evaded by the rich and performed by the poor, as once in the days of conscript labour for settlers. Wealthy men ploughed flat hilltop farms. The poor had to hoe widely separated hillside fragments; their poverty demanded time and effort, mostly from women. And now they had to work even harder, digging *mitaro* that, without the manure they could not afford, made their land less fruitful still.[560]

Opposition to communal work obliged government to make *mitaro* a household responsibility. This brought no relief: the labour, enforced by fines, still fell largely on women whose men worked elsewhere. Helpers had to be paid; they were 'made tired by Government', not by friendly assistance. Men disliked paying for work on their wives' fields; and completed *mitaro* might awaken claims for redemption.[561] All this state invasion of self-mastery was seen as a threat to life. To work to order on land inherited from the heroic generations *Ndemi* and *Mathathi* was slavery; 'useless trenches' were no substitute for stolen land.[562] Kikuyu knew as never before that they had no control over chiefs whose severity, what district commissioners called keenness, was a condition for their continued enjoyment of an office of profit.[563] Men ran away to the slavery of the highlands, women to prostitution. Chiefs' wives were exempt from *mitaro*. Other men's worn-out wives miscarried; a district commissioner even told them to have fewer children, to save the land.[564] Olenguruone was coming home. And the decisive opposition to *mitaro* was as shocking as the Olenguruone oath. It was instigated by young townsmen whose kin lived mainly in Murang'a and Nyeri. The more senior of them had served overseas in the war. They lived on petty trade and artisanal services that the respectable thought a temptation to crime. They called themselves the *anake a forti*, the unmarried warriors[565] of 1940, the Forty Group.

The angry collapse of the communal terracing campaign in late 1947, what one might call the *mitaro* war, was, as has long been recognized, a key moment in the growth of British impatience with all African politics and in the latter's militant mobilization.[566] The African side bears further examination. In this first clash between conservative and militant Kikuyu nationalisms, hope and fear, the militants won. In British eyes, Kenyatta's strategy of using self-mastery as a legitimate pressure on the state was discredited. But that was because, in Kikuyu terms, it was outflanked by women who were effectively household heads and men without households of their own; these broke the rules of seniority in order to attack the state that menaced their civic virtue. Muoria's disciplines held no hope for them. As the new KAU president, Kenyatta addressed the Murang'a branch in July 1947. His old colleague, now chief, Parmenas Githendu Mukiri, opened the meeting by commending *mitaro*. The 10,000-strong crowd shouted him down. Kenyatta supported him; people must save their soil. Faced with another roar of dissent, he agreed that men, not women, should do the work.[567] Government saw this proviso as sabotage; there were few able-bodied men on the land. *Mitaro* work ceased. But the attack on the chiefs was pressed home from another quarter; women destroyed *mitaro*, men of the Forty Group roughed up officials. Eventually chief Ignatio Morai's police guard shot dead one of a mob who taunted authority by drunkenly lascivious dancing, European-style, like the *Muthirigu* dancers of an earlier generation.[568] Another of Kenyatta's old KCA friends, Jesse Kariuki, berated the young men for causing trouble between their political leaders and government. If they were 'worth calling men' they must stop complaining about women's oppression, 'give up pickpocketing in Nairobi' and dig ditches themselves.[569] Nor was he merely hoodwinking the police informer present. The generational conflict was far too serious.

Early in 1947 the Kiambu KCA had begun to extend a new oath of loyalty to members farther afield. As was proper, they recruited only trusted household heads. It was also politically necessary, for propertied self-mastery hid fears of envy that the KCA had to lay to rest. Initiates sipped a soup of vegetables and goat's blood, the threatened fruits of the land and the essence of social relations that must not be betrayed. Many also held a goat's thorax to their chest, a symbol on which suspected sorcerers swore their innocence.[570] Participants and scholars have, for different reasons, been reluctant to discuss the KCA's need to combat sorcery beliefs, but its spokesmen were carefully selected from *mihiriga* or clans believed to be sorcery-free; and Mau Mau recruits have confirmed an anti-sorcery purpose in later oaths.[571] Sorcery had long been feared as an adjunct to claims for redemption of improved land. Its dread must have dogged rural capitalists, like the leaders of the KCA, who were less and less able to show *tha*, compassion, towards their dependants. As recalled by James Beauttah, KCA veteran and KAU's militant Murang'a chairman, there was no social trust between Kikuyu at their hour of greatest political need.[572] Trust was normally sworn in two contexts, between *mbari* rightholders with propertied relations to lose and between circumcision age-mates. Dedan Mugo, head of the *riika* groups that funded Githunguri and embodied this second basis of trust, refused to give the KCA oath 'to children or to young men who did not understand what they were doing.'[573] The young men of the Forty Group understood very well; but they were doing different things.

The Forty Group look to have recognized Mugo's logic; they had no oath of their own.[574] But their slogan also turned tradition upside down by what I have called time-banditry. Kikuyu expected solidarity in annual initiation sets and, in the past, in the 'regiments' in which age-sets were serially grouped. They also saw alternate generations as ritually equivalent; one was reborn in a grandchild. The Forty Group challenged all three perceptions. They were not an age-set. One of their leaders was circumcised, mission-style, as early as 1937; any man initiated during the 1940s was eligible for membership.[575] Their name, the *anake* of 1940, suggests that they thought of themselves as a junior regiment; no elder could have seen them as such without the required rituals. Finally, the Forty Group asserted that their parents (*not* their grandparents) were born, initiated and married in 1940, the same year that they themselves underwent all these life crises.[576] It is hard to think of a more appalling affront to authority. It jumbled up the young men's own moral growth; it destroyed the generational basis of civic virtue, seniority and inheritance. Beauttah remembered it as 'a sort of joke'. Elders must have thought it a poor one, and he too was frightened by the 'Forty'.[577] Perhaps the Group mocked the basis of the rural property they did not have; they may also have embodied that nightmare for elders like Kenyatta, whose disciplined fundraising depended on competition between proudly distinct age-sets.[578] Fear of the Forty may also have stemmed from a sense that they were rejecting old authority in order to find a new basis of self-mastery in town. Repudiating ancestry, they would make their own way.

The urban middle class and the officials in whom they confided saw the Forty as a criminal gang who, when they were not extorting funds for the KAU or the African Workers Federation (AWF), acted as pimps, supplying Kikuyu girls to Indians.[579] But the Forty themselves were keen to repatriate prostitutes on behalf of the Kikuyu General Union, wanted all girls circumcised, and saw to it that 'no woman could leave their husbands for Nairobi or wear short dresses'.[580] They branded a rural headman with the insult that *athomi* a generation earlier had most resented: *mucenji*, a heathen savage.[581] It seems, unsurprisingly, that many were undecided between acting as migrant sons or townsmen.[582] They wanted to prove their rural civic virtue by rounding up loose women; they also raised funds for independent schools in Nyeri and Murang'a, to get even with Kiambu. Kahinga Wachanga, a Forty Group leader who was later a forest fighter, tried to organize on an explicitly anti-Kiambu basis.[583] But the ex-soldiers among them had skills that enabled them to survive in the informal economy of African Nairobi; respectable Africans called them spivs, *mikora* or even *imaramari*, hooligans or 'yahoos'.[584] Perhaps above all, they found it difficult to rise above the rank of *anake*, to marry and become 'worth calling men'. Rural land was increasingly beyond their reach; Nairobi had not yet agreed to what later became known as 'site and service' schemes, which might have enabled them to build their own housing in town.[585] It was not the first time that men deprived of the hope of full manhood had turned against a society that excluded them but, as in Elizabethan England, what made the Forty Group restive also deprived them of authority.[586] Some had urban, others had Kikuyu ambitions; all lacked Kikuyu resources. With neither householder nor age-mate rights to command sworn allegiance, they lacked cash and organization. The Forty seem to have dissolved in 1948, but not before they had shocked the KCA elders as much as the colonial state. The subsequent KCA attempt to control them was at the heart of the nationalist crisis.

CRISIS

By 1947 postwar Kenya's contradictions had erupted into conflict.[587] White settlers, thoroughly alarmed by the prospect of an African future, still had the power to hold it at bay. Their financial sway, whether in the legislature or in municipalities, baulked government attempts to better African conditions. Their highland district councils refused to accept official plans to grant squatters villager rights of residence and choice in the farm-labour market. For its part the state nursed both the white export economy and, so it thought, a sustainable peasant future in what I have called a second colonial occupation.[588] Pessimistic officials backed this agrarian police drive for soil conservation and peasant resettlement on unoccupied – that is, unsuitable – land until 1951. A new official generation had by then rediscovered the faith of the late 1930s in a radical reform of black land tenure and the rapid extension of white plantation crops to African growers. They pressed these improvements, too late, as an answer to rural poverty and then as a counter-revolution to Mau Mau. But in the interim a flinty administrative resolve to subdue African opposition had quashed the former official instinct for the craftier politics of African collaboration.[589]

The disappointed constituencies of hope turned sour. The KAU failed to bend the ear of central government; this was convinced that immigrant farm and business confidence, for which it saw no local substitute, could stand no more than a very slow admission of Africans into a multiracial partnership. African legislative councillors, dependent on chiefs' support and the governor's nomination, kept their distance from the politicians. In the rural districts, especially in Kikuyu, officials saw party politics as a selfish threat to their alliance with the chiefs in saving peasant farming from soil erosion. Non-Kikuyu leaders turned to their own district politics, away from a party that offered little save Kikuyu dominance. The authority of all political elites was then damaged by government's adoption of the Beecher report on educational reform, named after its missionary chairman. This promised an increase in state aid, subject to strict control over the age of pupils' entry to school.[590] This condition hit the independent schools, whose most valued community service was to admit the many 'over-age' children who delayed or interrupted their education to earn their school fees. In face of the flood of land litigation, it now looked as if the poor would never rid themselves of the handicap of illiteracy. After Beecher, elite claims that all could earn self-mastery if only they persevered became a mockery.[591] Eliud Mathu put his name to the reform. And many felt that Kenyatta had abused the independent schools' trust by misappropriating the huge sums raised for Githunguri.[592]

If the KAU and the KCA were compromised, the third constituency of hope, the AWF, collapsed. After its initial success in Mombasa in January 1947 the Federation failed to react to the arrest of Chege Kibachia and other leaders a few months later. It was hobbled by the official favour now shown to separate industrial unions and by hostility between Nairobi's mainly Kikuyu townsmen and migrant workers from elsewhere. These resented paying most of their wages to Nairobi's Kikuyu landlords and food suppliers; they feared Kikuyu-dominated crime. Retaining agrarian rights in their own less crowded and more distant districts they were also less committed to town. Kibachia's friendless fate was a salutary lesson. Kenyatta and the KAU broke from their previous cooperation with the AWF and opposed the plan to strike in his support. They argued that industrial unionism offered a new channel of legal pressure; the omnibus AWF, in any case a possible rival to KAU, did not.[593] Kenyatta thus failed to act on the precedent he had himself drawn from Harry Thuku; perhaps he feared that, with Nairobi now full of the sort of angry young men who formed the Forty Group, protest would be too ill-disciplined to command reform. His opponents thought otherwise. Some criticism was oblique. Demanding to know 'Where are our Gandhis and Nehrus in Kenya?', the newspaper *Radio Posta* thought the 'common man in the street was partially to blame when we do not produce strong fearless leaders'. In future, leaders must be able to rely on what Kibachia had lacked, 'a strong fortress behind them'.[594] But the common man blamed Kenyatta directly. At an AWF meeting in Nairobi noticeable for the number of 'unknown persons' who spoke, he was said to be in the government's pocket. Two weeks later, he and others like him were accused of using their overseas education for private gain rather than African benefit. Workers must 'look to their own class' for help.[595] By 1948 the constituencies of hope had been thwarted by state power and their own consequent divisions. The realms of fear, now overwhelmingly Kikuyu, expanded and pressed on high politics the deep anger of class and ethnic betrayal.

Contested authority caused nationalist crisis; it was also the crucible of terror. Political oaths reflected this terror; they did not create it. People faced, as always in crisis, uncontrollable events, conflict between interests and ideals, personal rivalry and frailty. But Kikuyu faced a further problem of their own. They had to wrestle with the contradiction between their parochial political culture of wealthy self-mastery, linked to land, and their pressing need for a wider power to shepherd the poor against the threefold threat of the slavery of the highlands, the shanties of Nairobi and an arbitrary state.[596] Conflict between the autonomy of *mbari* right-holders and organized power was a familiar, if now terrifying, dilemma. But a new argument emerged as well, between the ethnic demand for fertile patronage and the growing sense expressed by the 'unknown persons' of the AWF that workers should look not to their rural expropriators but to their own solidarity for salvation. The state's ability to divide and crush worker action in Nairobi, latent in the AWF's failure to defend Kibachia in 1947 but plain for all to see through the clouds of tear gas in the general strike of May 1950, helped the ethnic theory of political action to win supremacy. But the dissolution of the Forty Group had already shown how little young men could do on their own; it was not only state power that taught that tribe might have more leverage than class. If tribe was the answer, however, then wealth had to be more accountable to poverty than the closure of *mbari* against their dependants had hitherto shown it to be. By 1952 some rich men had become Mau Mau's bankers; others were burnt to death as its sorcerer foes. Out of class conflict Mau Mau became an internal ethnic war. Its thought was more moral than political, about personal reputation rather than structural relations. To understand the thought we need to appreciate how it was challenged by events. These unfolded in three overlapping phases, along three mutually observant axes, between Kiambu and the Rift Valley, Nairobi and Kiambu and, finally, between Nairobi and northern Kikuyu.

The struggle for control within the squatter resistance to Olenguruone's rules and settler restrictions taught three lessons, the incompatibility of local and tribal authority, the readiness of youth to outrun the old, and the high price of failure. Relations between the Kiambu KCA in Koinange's *Mbari* and the squatters had been uneasy ever since the long march from Olenguruone in early 1946. Squatters took their resistance into their own hands. Kenyatta and the Koinanges were impressed by their solidarity.[597] They may also have seen it as a threat. Squatters seem not to have known who was in charge of organizing them and taking their money in these years.[598] But their leadership was competed between local young militants, stiffened by knowledge of what life would be like in Nairobi's slums if they did not stand fast, and older KCA men, including the larger squatter traders, who still trusted in the patronage of Kenyatta and the *Mbari*.[599] Rival recruiting was costly for its targets. At a time when squatters were being forced to get rid of their stock, political fees of up to £5 – twenty times what the KAU charged – seemed to many to be a form of distraint and politics a trade in cheap livestock.[600] Some will have recalled an old complaint against the KCA between the wars: that it remembered them only at harvest, in order to collect their dues.[601] In retrospect, squatters saw the period between late 1947 and early 1948 as the start of '*Mau Mau*'. Government sources first heard the term in March 1948, in complaints about forced initiation at Ngata farm, near Nakuru, from which Wanjiru wa Kinyua had once bravely written that first woman's letter to *Muigwithania*. There is no agreed etymology. Some said it was a Swahili acronym, others a childish code-word, others a mishearing of *muma*, an oath.[602] But some squatters felt that they were being dunned, whether by local young men as in the 1890s, or by the emissaries of *Mbari*, at any rate by *kiama kia mau mau*, a 'council of greedy eaters' who demanded much and delivered little.[603] An epithet first used by its victims, the name was adopted by the movement's enemies, Kenyatta included. Rural squatters rejected both *Mbari* intrusion from Kiambu and the moderation of their own established KCA leaders. They formed their own Mau Mau of the diaspora. In Nakuru town Mau Mau similarly grew out of the KCA youth wing, who became impatient with their elders from around 1948. They were distinguished from their seniors in five respects; they were young, they had only recently come to town from the insecurity of the farms, their trades were still precarious, they had little schooling and they contemplated violence.[604] They did not call themselves the Forty Group; they must have seemed every bit as alarming to prosperous traders long established in Nakuru.

The young men's anger was reinforced by the fate of the nearby Olenguruone Kikuyu. After a legal battle the last were evicted in early 1950. Some took refuge with squatter friends, others with their Kiambu *mbari*. The remainder were sent to another settlement on the Yatta plains below Mount Kenya, as hot and dry as Olenguruone had been cold and wet. Crowds mobbed their resistance heroes as the prison convoy passed.[605] Kikuyu called the Yatta the land of black rocks, *mahiga mairu*. In their view, all 'the wealth and hopes' of their *mbari* rights had been smashed. Carried off in lorries, like logs, they were served on arrival with wormy maize porridge and then, naked, made to dig latrines. Josephine died after eating buffalo meat supplied by the police. Her fate brought home the full horror of expulsion to the wilderness from the sweated cultivation rights of Olenguruone. Kikuyu had acquired new martyrs. Kenyatta could only telephone and ask if the waifs were well.[606]

The second origin of Mau Mau lay on an axis of mutual failure between Kiambu and Nairobi. Its political thought was contested. Only one side has told its story, the militants of Nairobi.[607] The conservatives kept silent; their purposes have to be inferred. A decision to adopt mass initiation, inspired by Olenguruone, sealed the pact between town and country. Its chronology is uncertain, thanks to the secrecy and confusion of the time and the lack of documentary evidence. Many have dated the concordat to late 1948.[608] Others, including John Mungai, whose taxi drivers provided the political communications, have said February 1950.[609] It is probable that a coalition formed in 1948 was then galvanized two years later.[610] In 1948 an alliance was needed to resolve an internal competition to reconstruct political authority out of ruined hopes and formless fears. By early 1950 it had to respond to external threat. A settler manifesto of white supremacy, *The Kenya Plan*, seemed to be abetted by the state in the Olenguruone evictions and the grant of a royal charter of city status to Nairobi. Disagreement over strategy, between conservatives anxious to retain a broad African front and militants impatient for a vanguard to force the pace, caused the pact to break up almost immediately from within, even if each side still needed the other in public.

By 1948 the KAU was an empty shell.[611] Kenyatta was discredited by his failures to use the Githunguri building fund for the purpose intended, to halt *mitaro* and to support Kibachia. But the Accra riots in the Gold Coast suggested the strategic role of towns; Kenyatta's London friend, George Padmore, thought that they marked the beginning of the end of colonial slavery.[612] Chief Koinange then announced that he had been deceived by whites. The Kikuyu treaty with Lugard and his own agreement to supply squatters had been betrayed. He blamed the evicted squatters' plight on 'Lord Delamere to whom these people gave much wealth'.[613] Dynastic theory lay in ruins. If landlords could not tame colonial rule then they must, however reluctantly, follow the householders of Olenguruone and share that task with their juniors. But these must be disciplined, unlike the Forty's young men. Domenic Gatu and Kahinga Wachanga took the oath of unity from the Koinanges after the Forty Group had fallen apart. Welcomed at last to adulthood, Wachanga remembered it as 'the oath of understanding'.[614]

The townsmen of Nairobi were as much at a loss as the landowners of Kiambu. Despite angry talk, the AWF had done nothing; the Forty, if it had ever been a Group, was one no longer. Industrial unions were being registered for the fortunate few, skilled men who worked for the state, the railway or larger firms, and whose families lived in company housing, what Luo called a place of children, *ka jonyuol*.[615] New attempts to form a general union, launched in May 1949 as the East African Trades Union Congress, were hampered by suspicion between Indian and African workers; once in being, the EATUC mustered little organization and less income.[616] Kiambu and Nairobi needed each other. Rural landlords had to restore a leadership questioned by popular anger on the highlands, in the *mitaro* war and in slum Nairobi. Townsmen looked for an authority that was thwarted by the struggle between respectable ethnicity or legal trades unions and the survival of the self-employed poor. But, according to the militants, the conservatives needed their support and had to accept their terms. They imparted this self-interested view at a time when Kenyatta ruled Kenya. It reflects their complaint that their sacrifices were ignored by the independent government; perhaps also the universal instinct to invent tradition as sanction for any new departure.[617]

The truth is more complicated. Men changed their plans in face of crisis; what they intended did not always happen. The militants were first led by Fred Kubai and John Mungai. Neither was an old KCA hand. While Kubai's father came from Kiambu and had been a colleague of Thuku,[618] his mother was from the coast; he had no rural background. Mungai was from Murang'a. They led the transport workers, mainly taxi drivers, strategic heirs to the printers and clerks of Thuku's day. They are said to have imposed three terms on the KCA's *Mbari* elders. Trust must be extended to all reliable Kikuyu, not heads of household alone; initiation must be free for those unable to pay the existing fee of shillings 62/50, about twice the Nairobi monthly minimum wage; and political allegiance must be given a militant aim. The Kiambu KCA was slow to accept and, while the first two terms were carried out, their purpose was disputed.[619] After due preparation, mass recruiting started in 1950, in Nairobi and the northern reserves, but not in Kiambu. Here *Mbari* retained authority. Only about 20 per cent of Kiambu men were initiated before the Emergency; of the district's male expatriates in the Rift Valley and Nairobi, half were sworn.[620] Recruitment was more general in Murang'a and Nyeri if the police estimate of mid-1952 is correct, that a quarter of all Kikuyu were Mau Mau.[621] Entrance fees were also set on a sliding scale. The propertied and well-paid continued to subscribe shillings 62/50, if necessary by instalment.[622] Many paid little or nothing, especially when political tension and the pace of recruiting increased in 1952.[623] But what was Mau Mau's meaning? What were recruits like Wachanga given to understand?

Mau Mau conducted two debates, between conservative self-mastery and militant action, and between ethnicity and class. An initial distinction between ethnic pressure and working-class militancy was overturned. Plans for violence then divided Kikuyu still further and threatened non-Kikuyu survival in town. These phases were never clear cut, but the turning point came in 1950 and 1951. The debates can be followed in the clauses of the two main Mau Mau oaths and their attendant history lessons, in the slender record of working-class opinion, and in the little that is known of the Indian Marxist Makhan Singh's attempt to reconcile class and ethnicity; but more can be said of the similar project by the Kikuyu ex-soldier Gakaara wa Wanjau.

The new KCA oath of unity or first Mau Mau oath was both ritually stronger than the KCA loyalty oath and more demanding. Both used the banana-frond arch of circumcision – not found in normal political or judicial oaths. The new oath contained not only goat's meat and blood but also a wider array of Kikuyu vegetables and cow's milk, something for which Thuku had scorned the Europeans. The ordinary ritual separations of gender and circumcision guild were broken by mixed initiation. Men and women were admitted; *ukabi* and *karing'a* guilds were joined. All were *karing'a*, pure Kikuyu, now. Such shocking novelty required that recruits be tricked or forced into taking the oath, without time to object.[624] They had to give seven undertakings, on pain of death. They must be loyal, obedient, help each other and tell no tales; they must sell land neither to whites nor to hostile Kikuyu; and give to funds. By 1952 some recruits had to swear to no less than 21 clauses. Eight of these enjoined obedience, solidarity and secrecy; five promised economic support; five more swore gender discipline – to keep female initiation but to forswear prostitution, interracial marriage, desertion of a pregnant girl and divorce; two promoted education, one of them by rejecting the Beecher report. Only one promise was military, to hide ammunition.[625] All recruits were given a lesson in political history, of which some were woefully ignorant.[626] Its main theme was the dynastic complaint that the British had betrayed Waiyaki's blood-brotherhood with Lugard in 1890. Waiyaki was said to have left a dying curse on the land, *kirumi*: none must sell it to foreigners lest they die. As he was led away captive he had told his warriors not to fight; his prophetic advisor Chege wa Kibiru foresaw, instead, that whites would go when Githunguri was built.[627] The lesson, as Kenyatta said in *Kenya the Land of Conflict* – still on sale in Kikuyu in 1952 – was that new times needed new tactics; and Henry Muoria was glad to announce that the college extension was finally started in August 1949.[628] Recruits called themselves *karing'a*, circumcised, or *Gikuyu na Mumbi*; all but the sceptical Mohammed Mathu have recorded a thrilling sense of rebirth into a new community, *muingi*. As late as September 1952 Mau Mau demanded from most of its members, in what even the hostile *Corfield Report* called a 'comparatively innocuous oath of allegiance', no more than the earnest improvement expected of circumcised citizens and a readiness for self-sacrifice.[629]

Working-class Nairobi, from which militant impatience sprang, had a different sense of solidarity and mistrusted educated leadership. The police got whiffs of class warfare from informers, but no more than that; for all the settler panic, few officials took seriously the idea of a communist Mau Mau.[630] Muoria made sport of the whites' red scare. Kikuyu had no use for equality of rich and poor; anyway, communism was a European idea.[631] But the anonymous members of the AWF had wanted to pressure the unreliable Kenyatta into action. And their Luyia secretary had gone further: the Federation should be 'the leading party and be superior to the KAU', empowered to discipline delinquents of any tribe.[632] This scorn for party politics and desire for a self-governing general union, revived in the EATUC, was like the syndicalism of early working-class movements elsewhere, in Europe or the USA. It was still cross-cut, nonetheless, by continuing faith in the possibility of patriotic overseas education. Two leading militants, the clerical trade unionist Bildad Kaggia and the trader Eliud Mutonyi, both to become members of the Mau Mau central committee, worked for the further education of young men from their district, Murang'a. And their own collaboration in clandestine politics showed that there could still be ethnic trust between worker and capitalist.[633]

In retrospect, syndicalism had no chance of forcing radical change. African Nairobi was divided; the state was ready to be tough. The EATUC's failure in the 1950 general strike confirmed these lessons of the AWF's collapse. The strike was called amidst peculiarly Kikuyu fears – that Nairobi's new city status would allow it to expand at Kikuyu expense and that a fresh pass law against 'spivs and drones' would harass the largely Kikuyu self-employed. And it was crushed by a police force enlarged by a special constabulary of non-Kikuyu workers, angered by the violence of masterless townsmen and the low paid. Kenyatta had warned that hasty deeds would cause such schism; Muoria, often his mouthpiece, had explained why Nairobi would not in fact expand.[634] But to what other solidarity could townsmen turn? Kenyatta advocated mere trades unionism; the militants scorned that as a surrender to the state.[635] Nor have I found any socialism in their thought. Their leading intellectual, Bildad Kaggia, has recorded none;[636] Kubai has not talked of it. Perhaps that needed too much faith in the state; and neither Kaggia nor Kubai shared Kenyatta's respect for ordinary people.[637] Their mentor was Makhan Singh, an Indian Marxist and union organizer. What little can be inferred of his teaching suggests that he consciously spared workers the stark choice between class and ethnic allegiance. Sometime between his return from India in 1947 and his arrest at the outset of the strike, he was said to have written a paper proving that Kikuyu had always been communist.[638] Indirect – and later – evidence suggests that Singh had in mind an innocent communalism in which labour was not exploited for gain, 'help was willingly sought and gladly given [and] the community took care of everyone and his family.' Such 'tribal organization' resisted colonial forced labour, where necessary in 'secret tribal groups' opposed to 'stooge chiefs.'[639] This myth-making played into the hands of 'natural' leaders like the KCA. If it is not too much for the evidence to bear, Singh can be read as suggesting that the militants' quest for authority might well take the path of obedience to the ethnic self-mastery of Kiambu.

While Makhan Singh may have pointed a way out of the syndicalist blind alley, his communalism scarcely addressed the problem of militant mobilization. Gakaara wa Wanjau saw more clearly the difficulties in creating unity of effort out of social division. Son of an early Kikuyu presbyterian minister in Nyeri (later killed by Mau Mau),[640] Gakaara had been expelled from the leading black school, the Alliance, one of three boys who refused to apologize after almost all of them had gone on a food strike early in the war. He then served in Ethiopia as an army clerk.[641] In 1948, angered by the squatters' ordeal, he published in Swahili a pamphlet entitled *The Spirit of Manly Courage and Effort for the African*. His thought was quite different to that of Kenyatta and Muoria, more sensitive to the demoralizing impact of a racist state. Whites had given Africans new wants but denied them the equal pay, land and free trade that would satisfy them. He disagreed with Kenyatta that black weakness was the cause of white power; rather, the state had set Africans against each other. African officials, poorly paid, had to be corrupt to afford a modern life. Africans were not ignorant but exploited. To regain a proper self-esteem they must first understand the extent of white deceit. They could then learn from the spider and build, out of their own substance, schools, hotels and aeroplanes as splendid as whites'. All depended on unity between rich and poor. The rich must not be content with their own success. Nor must the poor stand idly by, waiting to enjoy the fruits of 'a labour of which you have refused to be part'.[642] Gakaara might still accuse the poor of being free riders, but wealth was not by itself patriotic; the rich must make sacrifices too. The contract of labour theory, between generous wealth and obedient poverty, which Kenyatta and Muoria took for granted, had to be renegotiated in order to get power. It may have been no co-incidence that Gakaara came from Nyeri. For it was on the third axis of Mau Mau growth, between Nairobi and the northern Kikuyu districts, that antagonism to the rich and their association with the state first led to violence.

Politics in Nyeri and Murang'a was different to that of Kiambu. I have already noted the greater imaginative power of *ituika* in the north, the faster dissolution of *mbari* authority in the south, the cohesion of Kiambu's chiefs. The Forty Group had highlighted such contrasts. Three more are also relevant, in geography, land and cattle owner-ship. Nyeri and Murang'a were farther from Nairobi; this made them more receptive to its influence. Many Kiambu workers went to Nairobi daily; those from the north had to endure its slums. Northern business-men seem also to have had more city property. Northern townsmen took urban politics home; Kiambu commuters did not.[643] The greater vola-tility of the north may also have reflected differences in landholding. In 1950 there were 100,000 smallholdings in Kikuyuland, evenly distri-buted between the three districts. But in Kiambu their acreage was very unequal. Forty per cent of its landed households had fewer than 2.5 acres each, squeezed into less than 10 per cent of the district's area; but a quarter of all holdings spread over half the land, each with 7.5 acres or more. Murang'a's pattern was very even by contrast; 80 per cent of its holdings, with fewer than 5 acres each, took up 54 per cent of the land; scarcely anybody had more than 15 acres. Nyeri lay between these extremes; more than 40 per cent of landed households had between 2.5 and 5 acres. Since household size grew with the size of holding, these figures indicate differentials in family power rather than in individual wealth. Before the wide introduction of tea and coffee in the Emergency, cattle were wealth's most divisive form. The only detailed figures date from 1960, after a planned drive to upgrade cattle. While this built on earlier trends, one cannot be precise about the years before 1952. None-theless, the northern districts had far more livestock. Murang'a had twice as much as Kiambu, but its cattle were 'unimproved'; Nyeri, on the other hand, had over twice as many upgraded cattle as Kiambu. While half Nyeri's cattle were owned by people with fewer than 5 acres, critically, a man with 10 or more acres was much more likely to own improved stock than one with 5 acres or less.[644]

It is dangerous to infer political inclination from economic data. Poverty breeds apathy as much as anger; the rich can fund generous patronage or unanswerable control as well as incite hostility. Nonetheless, agrarian contrasts do seem to have had political parallels. The many large landowners of Kiambu appear to have dominated their poor. This may be partly because the latter were too dependent on the Nairobi vegetable market to risk disrupting trade; the continuing flow of northern immigrants to Kiambu's dormitory suburbs may also have created a stranger population too reliant on local goodwill to cause trouble.[645] Many who might otherwise have been Kiambu's poor were absentee, as highland squatters. In Murang'a, by contrast, there was a largely equal 'middle peasantry' more amenable to *mbari* solidarity, a society better able to stand up to its chiefs. Nyeri's divisions, not so sharp as Kiambu's, were perhaps more readily expressed. The 40 per cent of its householders with between 2.5 and 5 acres may, again, be seen as that 'middle peasantry' that everywhere is most likely to resist what they see as threat, neither made powerless by poverty nor yet rich enough to rely on influence.[646]

The relationship between cattle, land and power in Nyeri stimulated the growth of what one may properly call social terror and its resistance. The menace of state or settler power likewise provoked civil disobedience at Olenguruone, in the Rift Valley, in the *mitaro* war and in the Nairobi strike. In all these cases leaders had to share responsibility with juniors or risk impatient repudiation by the young. But it was the Nyeri drama that marshalled the fullest array of threats to Kikuyu wealth and freedom, revealing a depth of mutual fear without which the violence of Mau Mau cannot be understood.

The issue focused on cattle, veterinary medicine and enclosure. In the 1930s some cursed readers had wanted yet another state intervention, to inoculate cattle against rinderpest. For some had bought high-grade cattle, which gave more milk than the local zebu breeds, from white ranchers who were glad of any market in the Depression. Their value outweighed the hostility of neighbours more interested in herd size than yield. The war then brought compulsory inoculation, to protect not African but settler stock. Some beasts died from the injection but rinderpest was eradicated from Nyeri. There was a new problem; grade cattle were more vulnerable than zebu to tick-borne fever. Dairy farmers, chiefs among them, had to protect them by dipping. State aid was conditional on dipping by all stockowners in 'progressive' areas; unimproved cattle, though immune, could still be hosts to ticks. And all had to share the cost. Veterinary officers looked to a general upgrading of stock as their part in saving African income while taking pressure off the land. Dipping would be matched by culling poor stock and artificial insemination. Dairy owners also fenced their relatively large holdings into paddocks, doubtless at the expense of *ahoi*.[647] Nyeri's middle peasants found themselves threatened by the powerful few. The scheme also revived prewar fears of a general destocking campaign. This was all too easily seen as a ruse to maintain the settler labour supply by robbing Africans of their domestic income, not least because it was devised by a South African expert, Dr Pole-Evans.[648] Africans were still more alarmed – as was government – to learn that a senior agriculturalist, Norman Humphrey, felt that Nyeri's soil could be saved only if half its population were removed. Government cleared new settlements in empty lowlands. Even the moderate KAU called, instead, for the white highlands to be opened to Africans. Otherwise, to move Kikuyu from their malaria-free hills to mosquito-infested plains looked like 'a gentle process of extermination'.[649]

A popular anti-dipping campaign started in 1946. Ex-soldiers took the lead, as in the *mitaro* war. Some had had cattle culled in their absence; their Nyeri District Ex-Soldiers African Friendly Association, NDESAFA or, in a nice play on words, 'Deserver', was forbidden to trade cattle between clean and dirty, tick-free and tick-infested, areas; it was also prevented from taking over a wartime dried-vegetable factory, which had given thousands of smallholders a new income but which, the governor judged, stood no chance of competing with the freeze-drying method being introduced in America. Ex-soldiers' gratuities were also eaten up by purchase of war-surplus lorries, soon wrecked on country roads. Denied prosperity by the state, so they thought, they refused to subsidize its African friends' investments. The Forty Group joined in, fighting chiefs and scaring cattle-owners away from dips. The state withdrew from general compulsion to local option; cattle-cleansing was enforced only where chiefs persuaded a majority of their people to dip.[650] The conflict between Nyeri dairymen and their neighbours was a home-grown version of the struggle between settlers and squatters. Like that other war, its skirmishes continued into the Emergency. In late 1952 some grade cattle were poisoned. When the Kikuyu 'home guard' was then formed to fight Mau Mau, its loyalist members were recruited largely from the ranks of dairymen, among them one of Nyeri's staunchest chiefs, the former KCA man Muhoya Kagumba. Conversely, hundreds of unimproved cattle were confiscated in reprisal for Mau Mau attacks.[651]

What was this dairy war about, this conflict of dipping tanks, fences and poison? The obvious explanation may be enough; a middle peasantry refused to pay for their big men's advance, whether by cash subsidy or by losing to fenced enclosure their own multiple rights in land. Mixed farming was a domestic fifth column, allied to the external threat of destocking and population removal. But there was perhaps a darker side. There were rumours of extermination. KCA leaders were protecting themselves against each other's sorcery. What if the instruments of the state were another form of this malign power, in league with rural capitalism? The needles of rinderpest inoculation had killed many stock; artificial insemination implied the castration of bulls – just as some Kikuyu had feared that the Land Commission had emasculation in mind for human beings.[652] One may also imagine that cattle crushes and dips were a concrete sign of state control over African capital, just as *mitaro* or Olenguruone's crop rotation rules broke down the *riigi* of the household domain. Further, the Forty Group wanted to ban injections of children born in hospital and the chiefs' 'sale' of girls as farm labour. Their leader Wachanga was amazed to meet a friend he had last seen 20 years ago; he had supposed that the Nairobi fire brigade had drained his blood to give to anaemic whites.[653] There were similar rumours all over colonial East Africa.[654] A few years later James Beauttah was convinced that rinderpest inoculations in Murang'a were poisoning Kikuyu cattle; and thousands of women, now the main rural householders, 'sang and danced' in protest outside the district commissioner's office.[655] Some were jailed, new heroines who faced uncleanness, *thahu*, from drinking prison porridge from broken pots, and whose children's lives, in an echo of the *muthirigu*, were threatened by lack of milk.[656] Africans had earlier seen literacy as European magic.[657] Many now accepted scientific medicine as an alternative to their own healing practices; but there was no reason why others should not still see the apparatus of medicine and veterinary science as sorcerous invasions of the blood stream. It was another terrifying aspect of an arbitrary state. Violence was a legitimate defence.

It appears that violence was first seen as a political necessity by the former KCA, now KAU, leadership in Murang'a and Nyeri. James Beauttah claimed to have formed a Sabotage Committee in 1948, with members from Nyeri and the white-settled district to the north, Nanyuki. They intended to cut farm telephones and to starve settler cattle by burning off pasture. Then in 1950 he subverted the new alliance between Kiambu and Nairobi by enlisting the city's taxi drivers in an Action Group, to murder Governor Sir Philip Mitchell.[658] The plot, if such it was, misfired. For the alliance between Kiambu and the Nairobi militants was blown apart, not only by conflict between syndicalist action and ethnic self-discipline, but also by sudden death. Early in 1950, around the time of the Nairobi city charter celebrations, one of ex-chief Koinange's sons, Gathiomi, was killed. By most accounts it was an accident; but it may have been an execution for refusal to take the oath, or on suspicion of informing to government.[659] More conservatives were alienated when Domenic Gatu, lately of the Forty Group and recently recruited to Mau Mau, tried to kill Muchohi Gikonyo, city councillor and Murang'a trader, as punishment for his support of Nairobi's charter.[660] KCA elders must also have resented the militants' demand that Nairobi's prostitutes and thieves be recruited; it is possible that the militants were themselves yielding to pressure from the people who controlled much of Nairobi's rented accommodation and domestic services.[661] Mau Mau was banned a few months after urban syndicalism was destroyed in the general strike. All that was left to the militants was to take over, for secret purposes, the open but moribund structures of the KAU. This they did in 1951, first its Nairobi branch and then the national executive committee. By their own account, Kenyatta opposed them, just as he was slow to support Beauttah, then on trial for his part in Murang'a's resistance to cattle inoculation.[662] Mau Mau recruitment was now, unambiguously, in the hands of Nairobi, based at Kiburi house. Once the headquarters of the wattle and charcoal trade, it now housed *Muhimu*, the 'very important' Mau Mau central committee, later known as the *kiama kia wiathi* or freedom council.[663] By the end of 1951, therefore, the various strands of Mau Mau appear to have come together. Working-class militancy had divided Kikuyu townsmen from the rest. Olenguruone and the squatters had shown the power and the limitations of mass ethnic pressure. Fred Kubai and Bildad Kaggia had won the competition with the KCA of Kiambu for its control. Rural violence in Murang'a and Nyeri had come in from the cattle dips and *mitaro* ditches to lend political purpose to the crime of town.

As if to concede the field to the men of violence, government now rained four fatal blows on the constituencies of hope. It adopted the Beecher report on education; dropped plans for a non-racial identity card; revoked a promise to add more African members to the legislature.[664] And London ignored a KAU petition for the restoration of lost land, Kenyatta's attempt to use his British political connections. The KAU had secured 67,000 signatures; the futility of this constitutional effort was the militants' authority for violence.[665] Yet Kenyatta and the KCA *Mbari* retained their faith in legal pressure; and they now had, as Kibachia had not, a 'strong fortress' of sworn mass loyalty behind them. The militants began a new recruiting drive; they were prepared to push matters to a violent crisis, seemingly the only way to get Britain to intervene against white settler power. Kenyatta stormed the country, perhaps to compete with them; he addressed meeting after KAU meeting, demanding self-mastery in the cause of reform. The militants travelled on his bandwagon, recruiting for Mau Mau after dark, once the

formal proceedings had closed.[666] But the more the militants prepared
for violence, the more their authority came in question.

KIRIRA

In precolonial times *mbari* elders had controlled secret knowledge or
customary lore, *kirira*, in order to suppress disputes. Between the wars
chiefs, *mbari* trustees and the KCA had been careful not to press their
disagreements over land titles to the point of open conflict in front of
British commissions of enquiry. It was too dangerous to give strangers
such knowledge; they might be able to use a divided past to divide
Kikuyu still further in future. By 1952 the defence of existing rights was
no longer the issue; Kikuyu had to have an external power, both to win
back the border lands alienated from 'their own fields', *mashambaini*, and
to convert squatter rights into ownership in the Rift Valley, *ruguruini*.
The Mau Mau movement, let alone Kikuyu as a whole, never agreed
on the moral economy of the power they needed. There were four insolu-
ble conflicts over its distribution which Mau Mau regarded as threats
to security and therefore tried to suppress. They involved right-holders
and *ahoi*, squatters and other landless Kikuyu, rich and poor, and young
and old. Simply to enlist in the *muingi*, the community of Gikuyu and
Muumbi, to become a sworn 'Kikuyu', solved neither of the underlying
issues. These were the growing inconsistencies between ethnic parochialism and tribal power, and between stateless labour theory and the
critical role of the state in deciding personal fortune. Elders by now
insisted that people were land only where they still had *mbari* rights; Mau
Mau 'circumcision' might confirm that connection but could scarcely
override it on behalf of, say, *ahoi*. Farm squatters, on the other hand,
could not be sure that their rights of clearance would give them first claim
on white settler land; Mau Mau might prove to be a more powerful
estate agent, answerable not just to them but to all its subscribers. Rich
men enjoyed the authority of saying and doing; but they could not be
trusted on that score alone. They might be generous men of means; they
could as well be sorcerers or Christian 'hypocrites'. The landless poor,
'people of no consequence,'[667] were poor claimants to land; nor did
they, except at some local levels, control Mau Mau. As for the young
men who did most of the fighting, it was not clear if they were a new
generation to whom power was due or merely the servants of elders who
might reward them with land. On all these matters Sam Thebere had
nothing to say; they constituted a terror of unknowing. The need for
secrecy – the *kirira* of Mau Mau – amid all this confusion, led to mutual
fear, deliberate terror and, just as deliberately, to principled efforts to
keep the peace.

The contradiction between parochialism and power was at its most
severe in the reserves; while the political needs of all Kikuyu expanded,

eligibility to land had contracted on to the core lineages of the hundreds of *mbari*, almost certainly, as later figures were to prove, a minority of the population. *Mbari* trustees enjoyed an authority over land recognized by all. They may not have exercised it with compassion; they may have turned off their *ahoi*; but abuse of authority did not destroy its basis. Their rivals or the dispossessed appealed against past wrongs, not against *mbari* right in general. The political problem lay in the fact that *aramati* controlled only the land their ancestors had bought or cleared, knowledge of whose history was their title to property. This often embraced the settler farms – 1 per cent of the white highlands – that Kikuyu knew to be theirs, *mashambaini*. There might be dispute about the *mbari* to which it belonged, but it was best to keep such quarrels local. As we have seen, some *mbari* asserted their rights by beating their bounds, between the rows of settler coffee, before the Land Commission arrived in 1932. The equation that *aramati* drew between their own autonomy and *mbari* property meant that they could not accept the KCA as their collective spokesman. And this parochialism of property had increased by 1952, as descent took legal precedence over clientage and affiliation. Since land disputes were local, some thought it folly to fight a general war to recover *mashambaini* property. This consideration could turn nationalists into 'loyalists'. The elder Josephat Wandimbe, for instance, had been an independent schools leader since 1931 and became KAU branch chairman in the north Tetu area of Nyeri in 1947. This was to be one of the toughest centres of rural Mau Mau, the home of Dedan Kimathi. But Wandimbe could not sanction violence. He supported 'those who favoured constitutional means because if the land, freedom and the country were theirs, why did they have to fight if it belonged to them?'[668] Wandimbe had, I think, two objections to war. First, legal pressure should be enough to deliver lost land to its rightful owners, the *mbari* seniors and, in so doing, keep power in proper hands. Secondly, only those without land and power wanted to fight; but their war would reopen a mass of disputed history that had already been decided in the courts. Thousands like him were just as anxious as the militants to be rid of colonial rule. But, as elders who had proved both their own self-mastery and the legal superiority of their lineage history, they wanted to inherit its power. His was the conservative politics of Kenyatta and the KCA *Mbari* of Kiambu. The so-called loyalists took the same view.

There were similar divisions among the Rift Valley squatters. They experienced two levels of conflict between autonomy and power: between their diaspora and Kikuyu as a whole, and between farm communities and their local leaders. Kikuyu labour theory promised rights in the farms they had cleared. It did not deliver the power to assert them. Squatters had to ally with others, the elders said with Kiambu, the younger with Nairobi. But either alliance compromised their autonomy and risked their exclusive right to the Rift. This fear, no less than continuing settler efforts to enforce the new labour contracts, made squatters noticeably more impatient than farmers in the reserves. Some squatters had complained that Mau Mau was 'greedy'. The same suspicion of alliance may have spurred them to plan the first steps to violence, so as not to surrender that initiative to others. Sometime in late 1951, it seems, some squatters formed a *kiama kia bara* or war council. Squatters have also claimed that their leaders invented a specifically warrior oath for Mau Mau, the *batuni* or 'platoon' oath.[669] This is not certain. One former squatter has claimed that there was no such oath in the Rift before the Emergency; some say it originated in a leaders' oath devised in 1948, probably on the Kiambu–Nairobi axis; and Mutonyi, chairman of *Muhimu*, said it was under Nairobi's control.[670] This discrepancy in the evidence is a good example of Mau Mau's inability to resolve the opposition between parochialism and power. The second level of conflict showed how this general problem affected squatters locally. The two main students of the squatters, Kanogo and Furedi, dispute the sociology of their recruitment to Mau Mau. Kanogo believes that decision lay with the separate farm communities, *mbari* of sweat as it were. Furedi stresses the strategic network of knowledge controlled by traders and farm foremen.[671] How far this tension caused difference over policy is unclear. Both levels of uncertainty came together on the declaration of the Emergency. Confusion hinged on the unknowable answer to the question whether continued employment for settlers confirmed or forfeited a right to inherit their land. Did farm labour still earn *kuna* rights of clearance; or had it become 'slavery', now that sweat was devalued by machines? There were rumours that Kenyatta would issue land titles to all who joined the KCA or perhaps Mau Mau.[672] Squatters hedged their bets. Many returned to Kikuyuland, lest their continued highlands slavery disqualify them from land distribution; but they also left some kin behind on the farms, to preserve their *kuna* claims.[673]

The dilemmas of the diaspora reflected the presumption of free moral choice at the heart of Kikuyu labour theory. The need for power raised awkward questions about the value of squatter sweat. The continued worth of wealth was still more open to debate. Muoria had praised it as the broom that swept away the dirt of poverty and promoted peace. Wa Wanjau – who in 1952 published his *Spirit of Manly Courage* in Kikuyu, now entitled *Where There's a Will, There's a Way* – called for the contract between rich and poor to be re-examined. He did not say how. Nor did he condemn wealth; he too thought it a liberation.[674] Kikuyu could not escape the moral tyranny of *wiathi*. Their organic intellectuals were rich, as were their heroes, past and present. The memory of Waiyaki, generous landlord and patriot, permeated the *nyimbo*, the songs that roused public meetings and were published in pamphlets. One of these prayed that 'King' Kenyatta might be wealthy; another promised the corollary: he would pity the landless.[675] Even the militants claimed to be *athamaki* by adopting their slogan, 'say and act', *kuuga na gwika*, as their own. Mutonyi, their chairman, tried to ensure that wealth continued to direct the new project of direct action against whites. Rich lorry owners hosted the 'tea parties' at which Mau Mau swore in new recruits on the *thenge* or goat oath, as it was often called. Mutonyi had it in mind that *mbari* elders had used this oath, a form of ordeal, to defend the social order; it forced one to hand over a sorcerer, murderer or thief to justice. In another show of wealth, Mau Mau staged elaborate funerals for its dead.[676] And *nyimbo* extolled entirely conventional words and deeds, without which Kikuyu would fall 'by the roadside' like the idle poor. Cultivators, civilizers, must have no dealings with animals or ogres, creatures of the wild, in other words, the British.[677] Mutonyi was a trader; in an allegedly typical notice, Mau Mau cursed 'those who try to stop us selling our goods where and when we want'.[678] All who could invest in politics, one imagines, were as keen as Mutonyi to remove from trade the political constraints of race and chieftainly faction. He estimated Mau Mau income to be around £500,000. The movement entrusted these funds to men rich enough to be honest; who could afford to be patriotic.[679] From its base at Kiburi house, the centre of urban commerce, Mau Mau appeared to bank, literally and metaphorically, on the civic virtue of rural capitalism.

But Mau Mau did not trust all capitalists. Some rich Kikuyu, far from being banked upon, were burned to death in their huts, first in Nyeri, then in Murang'a, but rarely in Kiambu. Twenty-four chiefs and headmen were attacked in early 1952. Their kin commonly had to assent to their execution, as was normal in Kikuyu proceedings against supposed sorcerers, to prevent claims for compensation.[680] Mau Mau was trying to eradicate sorcery in its own ranks; the *batuni* oath advanced this purpose. Some militants now ascribed sorcery to their enemies. The *mitaro* and dairy wars, which threatened life, were reaching a horrible climax. The British called the arson terrorism. Many Kikuyu apparently saw it as counter-terror, a healing fire against rich *eriri*, 'who thought only of their own stomachs', or *thaka*, the handsome but barren ones who had an envious motive for destroying their victims' fertility.[681] The seeming rise in fears of sorcery was another effect of the conflict between the collective militant drive for power and the establishment's personal enjoyment of it. Kikuyu labour theory was premised on personal responsibility and reciprocal obligation. Virtuous wealth was encumbered with public debt; immoral wealth had no known social ties. The state had vastly increased the realm of immoral action. Stateless thought had not had to distinguish private and public spheres of responsibility; lack of Kikuyu control over the state made its office holders peculiarly vulnerable to suspicion of personal evil. *Nyimbo* condemned all who sold land for office, a general charge against chiefs. It was councillor Gikonyo's supposed sin; chief Luka of Lari was a prime example.[682] Wealth derived from the state rather than sweat lacked obligation to others' labour. 'Office land', *migunda wa wabici*, flouted such reciprocity by its owners' privileged evasion of the knowing tribunal of local law.[683] But all Kikuyu were competing for scarce land. Enmities multiplied. Terrifyingly partisan judgments of personal integrity could decide the difference between laborious civic virtue and barren sorcery among men of means.

Fiercely divided on the worth of wealth, what could Mau Mau offer to the poor? Its quest for power had to find what Kibachia lacked, a 'strong fortress' of common men. The Forty Group had had no time for political leaders. *Mbari* elders would not share power with the landless. Squatters wanted to hoard their sweat. Self-interest decided if rich men were patriotic bankers or traitorous sorcerers. No fortress could be built on such foundations. It required consensus on whether or not men of means in general, *itonga*, could offer hope to the anonymous poor. Inherited labour theory provided no answer; it judged the terms of patronage and clientage between persons. A diligent child might find an adopter; equally, he who herded goats expected to eat meat. But by 1950 more and more Kikuyu were excluded from the means of production and self-mastery by inequality rather than idleness. Their poverty was not delinquent but structural. Land was now scarcer than labour. Rich men failed to adopt the poor but ate more meat. Kikuyu were engaged in a struggle about class. They asked class questions. Some continued to give conservative answers, like Kenyatta and Muoria. Some posed radical criticisms, like the AWF and Gakaara wa Wanjau. Makhan Singh tried to mediate between them. Nobody provided class answers; rules for the allocation of settler land were in dispute and had to be consigned to the realm of *kirira*, secret knowledge. If labour theory did not meet the case, the question was whether any other system of belief did any better. By 1950 all Kikuyu leaders were literate, acquainted with Christian doctrine. The British charged Mau Mau with anti-Christian belief. Two questions arise. The first is whether the idea of religious war stands up to scrutiny, stripped of its propaganda. And secondly, did the conflict, if such it was, hinge on the nature of poverty and its remedy? The answer to both is no. The new religions, like the old, were not systematic but heterodox. They were not systematically opposed. They overlapped; they also addressed different problems in the human condition. Nor did the three main Kikuyu Christianities or the eclecticism of Mau Mau possess a concept of structural sin that might have demanded justice rather than patronage for the poor. The violence of Mau Mau shocked liberal reforms of property and labour law into motion, and the easing of racial restriction on markets and political rights. But doves in the state pushed the reforms ahead for reasons of state; churchmen applauded them but did not inspire.

Mau Mau's relations with the three Christianities were governed by the churches' views on the contract of civic virtue between rich and poor. The first Christianity was that of the Kikuyu establishment, largely Anglican and Presbyterian. It was worldly in belief and practice, conventionally Kikuyu in its estimate of wealth. Its sensibilities, as the Anglican Muoria's pamphlets showed, were closer to the Old Testament than the New. Jehovah, I believe but cannot prove, made *Ngai* a more instrumental God. Membership of a mission church gave entry to well-paid employment and, to judge by the growing number of Christian chiefs, to political office. Missionaries complained that 'the greatest problem that the Church had to face was that of its own popularity;'[684] if so, their own status was at fault. They preached salvation; but they encouraged improvement, including the stone houses that symbolized progress; their schools enjoyed state subsidy; from 1924 to 1947 one of their number had spoken for Africans in the legislature. They taught the power of the Word but were men of power in the World, 'teaching Christianity while practising imperialism' as the journalist Kingsley Martin put it.[685] Apart from the Salvation Army no established mission cared for outcast Nairobi until the 1950s.[686] Missionary judgment on both the worldliness of their followers and the evil of Mau Mau was misplaced; it measured both against an ideal faith, not the one they had to live themselves. It was natural for establishment Christianity to be as materialist as the old religion. The two enjoyed an easy syncretism that missionaries deplored, expecting of their adherents a purer dependence on Grace than their own. Mutonyi, soon to be Mau Mau chairman, had his shop blessed both by a church pastor and a traditional elder.[687] Its eclecticism is the key to understanding Mau Mau belief.

However vigorously missionaries would deny it, Mau Mau owed much to this first Christianity. The movement grappled with the church's failures and widened its popular appeal. Kaggia, unconsciously echoing the missionaries, has implied that Mau Mau broke from the KCA because the latter remained Christian.[688] That is to suggest for both bodies a systematic theology that neither they nor the missionaries possessed. The missions' chief failure was their inability to enter the peasant world of personal misfortune. Prayer might secure God's mercy; it was no answer to the personal evil willed by other men on earth. The KCA, as we have seen, took precautions against sorcery additional to prayer. Missionaries found Mau Mau oaths disgusting because, with their generalized belief in original sin and a scientific attitude to bodily disease or the caprices of nature, they did not grasp the full horror of the occult power, even if it was as mundanely material as poison, that

Kikuyu knew to be available to their personal enemies. Both KCA and
Mau Mau oaths seem therefore to have been not so much opposed to
Christianity as alternatives to it in a magical field that missionaries
would not enter. Furthermore, they committed recruits to a cause that
Christians could agree was just, some of them angry that their faith was
abused by its association with racial oppression. All nationalisms have
this power to unite people of otherwise divergent beliefs. Christian members of Mau Mau have in any case noted that no recruiting oath directly
repudiated Christianity, only missionary attacks on such customs as clitoridectomy, and the Beecher report. They also feared less the magical
consequences of breaking the oath than the anger of those whom they
would thereby betray.[689] A major element in Mau Mau belief, therefore, seems to have been non-Christian rather than anti-Christian.

Mau Mau also gave some Christian ideas a wider audience. Many
of its members had never been to school; they may still have seen literates
as cursed readers. But politics came to them now in hymn tunes. Mau
Mau's theology seems to have come from the independent churches.
These also believed, with the missions and the old religion, in justification by works. Their teaching has been little explored.[690] The political
nyimbo of the 1950s would seem to be the best source. The British called
these 'Mau Mau hymns'. They were really those of the independent
church militant; I have been unable to detect in them a divided tradition,
part religious, part secular. If Kubai and Kaggia wanted to teach political theory they ought to have put it in song. The *nyimbo* popularized images not found in the old religion. Belief in the old God,
Ngai, the Jehovah of the Old Testament and a political Christ, anger
against sorcery, all played a part, coloured by the civic religion of ethnic
nationalism. The *nyimbo* were no more anti-Christian than those of any
national church that enlists God on its side at time of war. They compared Kikuyu with the children of Israel and the British with the Egyptians. These echoes of an Exodus by a tribe *already* knowing God were
made the more resonant by the publication of the Kikuyu Old Testament
in 1951.[691] Kenyatta was generally compared with the prophet Moses
or called a king, leading to freedom and wealth, not to salvation. In only
one hymn was he also a Messiah: 'he gave his life to save us'.[692] It thus
seems that Mau Mau hopes were couched in a purposive, historical,
tradition that owed much to mission Christianity. It was primarily a
political faith; Kenyatta's grace was arguable rather than universally
believed. Many *nyimbo* had hymn tunes. Whites thought that blasphe-
mous in itself. But hymns were now a popular song form;[693] and no
missionary, so far as I am aware, condemned the scabrous march-
ing song of white settlers in the Kenya Regiment set to the tune of
'Onward Christian Soldiers'.[694] The *nyimbo* were also full of biblical –
but Kikuyu – calls to good behaviour: men were known by their

fruits, the prodigal must return to his people.[695] More often they taught unadorned Kikuyu labour theory. This could conform to folk Christianity, as in the saying: 'God helps those who help themselves.' They warned, with withering Kikuyu reproof, that the lazy could expect no freedom, nor wastrels 'free things', certainly not cattle. Only toil gave right to land.[696] In all, therefore, this-worldly religion, Christian or nationalist, was little more than a theological prop to the KCA's plutocratic political theory. It was of small comfort to the structural poor.

However, just as there was a Kikuyu discourse of disagreement, so too there was dissident religious belief. Two Kikuyu Christianities scorned wealth. Both were hostile to Mau Mau. Neither was politically helpful to the poor. We have met one in the prophetic, growling churches of the *akurinu*; whites called them *dini* or sects. Some whites thought Mau Mau sprang from this pentecostal Christianity.[697] Nothing could be further from the truth.[698] *Akurinu* trust in the Holy Ghost rather than wealth had brought their founders' expulsion from the independent *karing'a*, true Kikuyu church. But in 1947, when Kikuyu politics entered the nationalist crisis, one sect – and outside opinion, African and British, tended to lump them together – showed every appearance of political activism. Within weeks of the police killing of strikers at the Uplands bacon factory and a dancer in the *mitaro* skirmish between chief Ignatio and the Forty Group, both Kikuyu and whites were shaken by the 'Gatundu affray' near Kenyatta's home. Members of the *dini ya Jesu Kristo*, a millenarian squatter sect expelled by their white landlord, cut up a tailor who refused to make them a flag free of charge; of the police who came to arrest them two Africans and their white inspector were killed. The *dini* said that government had fallen; the police were the devil's soldiers. Whites accused the skin-clad sect of 'rabid Kikuyuism'; respectable Kikuyu thought them animals or lunatics, neither Kikuyu nor Christian. Moreover, their leader's brother was one of the governor's gardeners; the *dini* looked like an official ruse to give Kikuyu a bad name. Both Kenyatta and chief Waruhiu wanted it banned.[699] But the *dini ya Jesu Kristo* was quite unlike the other *akurinu* churches. These continued to separate themselves from normal life. Unlike the missions, they actively opposed sorcery and were obsessed with ritual cleanliness. They refused to drink blood or to mix 'godliness with politics'. Indeed, one of their prophets heard in prayer that only those of his adherents who found it too hard to obey God should turn to Kenyatta. Some dreamers got into trouble for refusing to join an unknown *kiama* or party, which may or may not have been Mau Mau.[700] If any *akurinu* did join the movement, which is uncertain, it was as individuals.[701] The *akurinu* brought consolation and community to the poor; they did not preach political action on their behalf.

Some missionaries explained Mau Mau as the politicians' reply to
the emergence of a third form of Christianity. This was the revival
movement that swept through the protestant mission churches of East
Africa from the late 1930s. Revival deepened personal faith, convert-
ing those who had previously been Christian adherents only. It often
touched those who had enjoyed worldly success. Revivalists demanded
public confession of sin; their deadly sins included worldliness, anger and
envy; they saw themselves washed in the blood of Christ as other Kikuyu
were cleansed by the blood of a ram.[702] It looks as if the *akurinu*, revival
and Mau Mau all had different answers to sorcery. Nationalists were
said to fear that their worldly Christianity was being subverted into political quietism. Missionaries saw Mau Mau as a counter-revival to keep
religion in this world.[703] But revival also challenged clerical white control; the 'saved' or 'the brethren' as they called themselves, trusted only
the inward authority of spiritual rebirth.[704] Not all missionaries were
similarly 'broken' in spirit; some despaired, inconsistently, that their
finest Christians had become so otherworldly that they despised politics as a 'dirty game'.[705] Indeed, Mau Mau and missionary criticism of
revival was, from opposite sides, remarkably similar. If, one pamphlet
demanded, Christians 'do not like the wealth of this earth let those who
are not Christians, or those who like wealth, ask for what they want'.
Christians had clean bodies because they had good jobs; it was hypocrisy
to say that they were uninterested in wealth.[706] Evidently it was felt that
revival destroyed the political cause of all Kikuyu, both rich and poor.
Missionaries were probably right to believe that both the KCA and Mau
Mau were shocked by revival's threat to distance Christian leaders, for
the first time, from nationalism. For, once missionaries and indeed some
settlers were saved, revived Christianity lost its racial colouring. Revival
in the established churches, like the spirit churches outside them, led to
a pacifism in the Mau Mau war deeply distrusted by both sides. In the
mounting conflict both missionaries and district commissioners resented
the revivalists' abdication from defence of the colonial order. The need
to have religious truth on one's own side and to attribute heresy to the
other became all the more urgent in 1952 as Kikuyuland was consumed
by political violence.[707]

Some Mau Mau leaders prepared for war. The *batuni* oath, also called
the *muma wa ngero* or oath of evil crime, showed that they meant business;
its initiates undertook to kill on order, whether whites or hostile Kikuyu,
even their own kin.[708] Central Kenya was full of rumours from as
early as 1947, that all whites would be massacred in a 'night of the long
knives'.[709] Nor was this just settler panic, as Whitehall was inclined to
believe. The informants were Kikuyu; and Kikuyu then and since have
said that this was Mau Mau's long-term aim.[710] Mau Mau had up
to 800 precision weapons at the start of the Emergency and Africans,

assumed to be Kikuyu, had stolen nearly 300,000 rounds of ammunition from the army's main arms depot; many of these were of small calibre, perhaps to be used in hunting.[711] Nonetheless, the British declared the Emergency; the Kikuyu did not rise in revolt. The state was reacting to two crises. One was on the white highlands. Here a fitful agrarian war had been simmering since the introduction of new squatter contracts in 1945. Settler and police pressure by way of evictions, movement control and local curfews matched squatter strikes, machine-breaking and arson. Grass fires to destroy pasture in the area north of Nyeri – perhaps as planned by Beauttah – and cattle-maiming gave a new intensity to this squatter jacquerie in 1952. Angry settlers called for firm measures; equally angry squatters elbowed their way on to existing but hesitant farmworker committees.[712] But it was the murder of one of the most senior Kikuyu chiefs, Waruhiu, in early October, that decided the new governor, Sir Evelyn Baring, to declare the Emergency for which settlers had pressed. For the second crisis, much the more murderous, divided Kikuyu against each other.

It is difficult to chart the Kikuyu conflicts. There were so many. Most violence probably stemmed from land disputes, between and within *mbari*, perhaps particularly in Murang'a and Nyeri. Mau Mau groups and their local oppositions fought out a myriad of contested histories, as I think Josephat Wandimbe had feared. Mobilization to resist oppression, to refer to an earlier argument, roused others to cling to its inequalities or simply to evade its costs.[713] Decision to take action met equally brave and principled refusal to be intimidated. Informers against Mau Mau oath ceremonies were murdered before they could become court witnesses. All sections of Kikuyu opinion were ignorant and confused about Mau Mau's aims. All wanted reform. All wanted self-mastery. Many believed that that required self-government, that *wiathi* needed *uhuru*. Few wished to pursue that goal by force. Even Mau Mau members were at odds. Some still trusted in petition; others relied on the civil disobedience that fought the *mitaro* and dairy wars; but some wanted to rush to arms.[714] Even chiefs joined Mau Mau; other chiefs decided to cleanse its initiates by a new *thenge* oath. Private Kikuyu enmities were thus generalized in two equally intimidatory anti-sorcery campaigns.[715] Both the main groups of independent churches and schools divided internally on the issue of violence.[716] But continued enmity between these *aregi* or refusers of 1929 and their *kirore* mother churches produced the fiercest conflicts of all, especially in Murang'a where the *kirore* too had recently seceded from the African Inland Mission.[717] Mau Mau revived the school property disputes of 1929; conflicts over the Beecher report repeated those of clitoridectomy. Some *mbari* wanted to retain control over their children's schooling, no matter what their age or examination failures; others accepted the rules applied by the missions, to get state aid; opposing *mbari* might share the same school. Parents' committees argued the issue out; the sharp decline in church congregations in late 1952 possibly owed as much to this renewed struggle for *mbari* autonomy as to the spread of Mau Mau.[718]

But the missions saw resistance to Mau Mau as religious war. It is difficult to know if Mau Mau took the same view. Some local groups did. In at least one case a dead goat, a *thenge*, desecrated a church altar.[719] Many mission-school teachers were killed, and one or two African pastors, wa Wanjau's father included. The police had no idea how many Kikuyu were murdered by Mau Mau before the Emergency, since their bodies were generally hidden. But the missions would have known if their employees went missing. They probably constituted a majority of the 34 known murder victims in the months before the Emergency; then in 1953, the war's first year, over 60 teachers were attacked, nearly half of them being killed.[720] This was a small minority of the hundreds of teachers employed, but many of them will have been protected by taking the oath of unity. Revivalists felt especially threatened; some were martyred for refusing to drink the blood of goats when they had been saved by 'the blood of the Lamb'. Two Anglican revivalists were killed for giving tea to thirsty policemen; others were spared precisely because they could be trusted not to help the police; Catholics were at risk because Mau Mau feared the power of the confessional.[721] A senior Anglican missionary thought that Kenyatta had launched a cultural onslaught on Christianity, comparing it to 'the weevils that spoil the corn'. Kenyatta certainly loathed denominational division. He wanted the *dini ya Jesu Kristo* banned. But he was glad to have a church pastor open a political meeting with prayer.[722] It seems likely that his attacks on sectarianism were misinterpreted as hostility to Christianity as a whole. I do not have the data to tell if the murder of Christians was prompted or accelerated by the churches' decision to excommunicate Mau Mau members in August 1952.[723] One feels that had Mau Mau leaders ordered a general attack on the churches, there would have been many more martyrs; after all, they had no defence. Virtually all African clergymen survived, very possibly because most refused to bear arms. Those who died were probably killed not so much because they were Christian but because their refusal to take the oath was a breach of secrecy; parochial *mbari* disputes about church property must also have taken their toll.

Mau Mau faced the same parochial problems within. Its members' memories have encouraged scholars to draw elaborate organizational charts of a pyramid of *Muhimu* authority, descending from its apex in Nairobi through district, location and *mbari* committees.[724] Doubtless that was the intention. But Kikuyu politics was not like that. The pyramid was an imagined political tribe; real moral ethnicity remained 'local government run mad'.[725] Parochialism and power were still at odds. Private entrepreneurial oathing mocked organization; some Mau Mau bankers betrayed their trust.[726] Leaders had to face still greater suspicion of harvesting other men's shillings for their own greedy eating, now that they demanded so much more cash. The need for secrecy, no less than the large scale on which politics now had to operate meant that leaders had to trust strangers. When the first detainees, the presumed leaders of Mau Mau, arrived behind barbed wire at the outset of the Emergency, they found that many of their company were quite unknown. Despite the fact that they were nearly all *itonga*, men of means, all prominent in trade, independent education or politics, they did not know each other, and were filled with mutual suspicion.[727] It is striking too, in reading interview transcripts from the early 1970s, how few of these veterans kept in touch; they had no idea where many former associates lived.[728] Kikuyu high politics was ignorant; the deep politics of relations between leaders and followers had no regular means of communication at all. It had to be negotiated at the decreasing number of KAU meetings that government permitted in 1952. These exposed not mutual understanding but bitter cross-purposes. The best documented is that of 26 July 1952 in an open field outside Nyeri. There were 25,000 people at the meeting, many of them young men from Nairobi, bussed in by the militants. The police restricted the length of the meeting. Kenyatta was the main speaker; he had to spend much of the time silencing the young men. They reacted violently when senior chief Nderi – whom Kenyatta once praised as Wang'ombe's son – and an African district officer, both at Kenyatta's invitation, spoke up for law and order. Nor did Kenyatta himself say what the young men wanted to hear. Murder would not bring freedom; KAU was not a fighting union; they must await the findings of the forthcoming Royal Commission; whites could stay in Kenya under black self-government; even African rule would need police. Mau Mau was theft and drunkenness. Criminality, *umaramari*, the indiscipline of the naughty child, could never bring *wiathi*, adult self-mastery and, by extension, independence. The police were not impressed by Kenyatta's moderation, they never were, but it needed great moral and physical courage; he left the meeting a shaken man.[729] Yet when KAU meetings were further restricted, Kenyatta asked the district commissioner for Kiambu how government could expect him, as it constantly demanded, to 'bring these young "forty" types to heel' – a revealing illustration of his views on Mau Mau's insolence.[730] It is normal for men of power to disqualify their political opponents by calling them morally delinquent. But Kenyatta had no power; he wanted it. Yet he was deliberately dividing his supposed supporters; the risks were enormous; it is hard to believe he did not mean what he said. Mau Mau leaders faced the same problem.

Mutonyi thought that poverty, unlike wealth, knew no patriotism. The impatience of Nairobi's angry young men put even the lives of militant leaders at risk.[731] Yet *Muhimu* also threatened to kill Kenyatta if he did not stop criticizing Mau Mau.[732] It is no wonder that his London friend, the black South African writer Peter Abrahams, found him in August 1952 plunged in friendless gloom. He was caught in the cleft of the colour bar, 'victim both of tribalism and of westernism gone sick.'[733] Mau Mau was scarcely a tribal movement; its hooliganism seemed about to destroy the chief inventor of a disciplined tribe.

Nevertheless, it is difficult to place much weight on the militants' claim that they were even then embarking on cross-ethnic recruitment by inventing other tribal oaths.[734] The British certainly feared that that was on the cards.[735] And many non-Kikuyu did join Mau Mau, especially from the Embu, Meru, Kamba and Maasai peoples, with a few Luyia and still fewer Luo. But there are several objections to the idea of an organized alliance, a broader pyramid of command. First, the methods of Kikuyu recruitment presupposed that recruiting officers had close personal knowledge of their initiates. Second, there is good evidence that Kikuyu leaders were divided on the question whether others were worthy of trust.[736] Third, Mau Mau had grown out of external grievances and internal conflicts that other peoples experienced to a far lesser degree. What brought others into Mau Mau was, rather, what one might call mundane trans-ethnicity, private livelihoods on the mutable old frontiers that administrative and political tribalism never fenced off. A common life with Kikuyu in Nairobi was the recruiting sergeant among the Kamba; Embu and Meru shared much the same language and had many Kikuyu immigrants; the 'half-breed' Maasai whom British despised were the same potato-eaters who had always prospered on the Kikuyu–Maasai margins, essential brokers of trans-ethnic trade; Dorobo forest-dwellers, some of whom could as well have been called Kikuyu, Maasai or Kalenjin, occupied another closely associated economic niche; Luo migrant fishermen on the rivers south of Mount Kenya had dealings with Kikuyu cultivators; Boran arms smugglers from the north exported ivory from the Mount Kenya forests in return. Membership of Mau Mau for all such people was in large part a condition of getting on with their daily lives.[737]

The most cogent objection to the notion of an organized pan-tribal Mau Mau, as distinct from one that spread by an easy trans-ethnicity, lies in the particularity of the Kikuyu political vision of the future. While *mbari* narrowed it seems that the image of generation succession by *ituika* expanded. The KCA *irungu* still thought of themselves as a frustrated *Maina* generation, to judge by their complaints about their banned *ituika*; some Kikuyu called Mau Mau *Maina*'s war. Some also thought its oaths as revolutionary as the spirit of the first *iregi* generation; they have called the supposed 'night of the long knives' the 'great *ituika*'. Squatters saw resistance to the postwar 'slave' contracts as a younger generation's battle for their parents' comfortable old age.[738] I have found only two references to *ndamathia* in post-war Kikuyu writing. One is in Njoroge's folklore; Muoria's wife Nuno also brought the dragon to the rescue of little sister Kikuyu, despised by her brother the whites.[739] Perhaps too many thought the dragon had been cast into hell. Kenyatta's enemies accused him of planning Mau Mau as a re-enactment of *ituika*, portrayed as revolution in his book.[740] Mutonyi thought of Kenyatta as a 'fire-stick elder'. This term is not found in formal Kikuyu ethnography, perhaps because of the *kirira* that cloaked *ituika* ceremonial. If the role was akin to that found among the pastoral peoples with whom Kikuyu shared their past, and a version of the *muthirigu* song suggests that it was, then Mutonyi had in mind a senior elder who initiated generation succession.[741] The Mau Mau fighting oath, *batuni*, included *ituika* symbols. It is true that most of those who took this second oath were of warrior age, below 30 years; they lacked the elder status that entitled them to enjoy the ritual advantages of a 'ruling' generation.[742] But this was a period of crisis, as I have suggested was always the case at *ituika*; the Forty Group had shown how to upset moral time; scarcely anybody living had witnessed a 'real' *ituika*; it was no longer a rule-bound institution, if it ever was. It was an idea; and a strikingly apt one at that. An *ituika* would 'redeem the country' from the *Mwangi* elders who had 'sold' it and whom the *nyimbo* urged to keep silent. It would have imparted an awesome sense of disciplined duty to young men whom many elders, Kenyatta included, thought to be hooligans. Waruhiu Itote, one of the first to enter the forest to prepare for war, in August 1952, called his base *thingira ya iregi*, the house of revolution.[743]

But Mau Mau had another historical analogy in mind for its fighters. Their most common appellation was *itungati* (sing: *gitungati*) or rear-guard. They could have called themselves *ngerewani*, the vanguard. The choice of name may have indicated an intention to fight a defensive war; it also connoted expectant service. When at school Karari Njama, later a senior Mau Mau commander, had joined a club called *Gikuyu Gitungati Ngerewenwa Thingiraini*: 'Kikuyu Servants – or Rearguards – Receive Rewards at the Elder's Hut'.[744] The inference must be that the young insurgents did not feel eligible for power as a new generation. Rather, they were guarding their political elders.[745] Even in its plans for war Mau Mau seems to have been internally divided. Dashing young *ngerewani* might have been expected to lead the 'night of the long knives'; experienced *itungati* were the 'strong fortress' that civil leaders needed behind them. Some were doubtful that young men deserved even that degree of respect. Kaggia simply called them 'our boys'; they were also known as *ihii*, a grossly insulting term for an uncircumcised youth.[746]

Divided strategy and uncertain esteem reflected the many voices of popular support. While *nyimbo* exhorted mothers to ululate their support for 'courageous sons', some sons flouted the oaths that forbad recruits to consort with prostitutes. Some oath parties were entertained with the hymn tunes of the *nyimbo*. Other sponsors advertised the jazz guitars of the pop-star Shinda Gikombe's band.[747] But the image of *ituika* was perhaps able to encompass diversity; in the past it had been an expensive means of removing conflict and suspicions of sorcery. *Ndamathia* had once brought rain; *ituika* had cleansed the land. Mau Mau might end the drought of oppression and restore the lost acres. One *nyimbo* drew that parallel: 'Wake up all of you, . . . we have found the beast we have been looking for . . . When you hear a thunderous noise you should know it is not rain or thunder clouds. It is the guerillas heading towards Nyandarwa to fight for our freedom.'[748]

WAR AND PEACE

The Mau Mau war transformed both Kenya and Mau Mau. It defeated two sets of hawks, the settlers and the forest fighters. It installed two sets of doves in power, the departmental officers of the state and the constitutional politicians of the KAU. The first prepared the agrarian ground on which the latter negotiated independence; Mau Mau had shown that majority African rule was the only form of freedom possible. But the peace had first been made by those who had no direct interest in its outcome, the British army who had reinforced the fight and the imperial government which had paid most of its costs. They had to take account, especially, of the men who had been at the forefront of the civil war, the so-called 'loyalists' of the Kikuyu Guard. Those who had most wanted war, settlers and Kikuyu militants, were the ones who lost it. Kenyatta had not wanted war; a few months before its outbreak a pamphlet, *The Prayers of Waiyaki*, issued in his interest if not in his name, had declared him to be the old dynast's reincarnation; it had reminded Kikuyu, as if to mobilize the teachings of the oath of unity against the promises of the *batuni* oath, that Waiyaki had ordered his warriors not to fight.[749] And some who had helped to plan violence were not prepared to face its costs. The militants of Nairobi had warning of their arrest. They did not take to the forests with their 'boys'. Nairobi continued to supply these with arms and men until the British cleared Kikuyu townsmen out of the slums in early 1954. Otherwise the *itungati* were left to their own devices. Few of them had had much education, although they managed to find 63 camp clerks from among their number.[750] They had to argue out their own reasons for suffering deprivation, danger and death. Mau Mau had started as a collection of rural movements that came to town. In town the militants tried to give it a sense of direction. But the arguments between violence and discipline, generation succession and client service, continued. The movement then flowed back to the rural areas whence it came, its purposes never finally agreed. In October 1952 the British effectively decapitated Mau Mau. They removed Kenyatta, its inspiration. They also detained its strategists, Kubai and Kaggia. And they made it difficult for its executive management, the remaining members of *Muhimu*, to keep in touch with their servant *itungati*. These last increasingly fell back on their ethnic roots of disillusioned but determined rural labour theory, to continue the debate on the future that their civil leaders had left unresolved. Kaggia, like other leaders, waited for the police to pick him up. He left no instructions for the conduct of the war. But he found the time to ensure that his printer, laundry and tailor would be paid.[751]

This is not a military history. The Emergency deserves a study of its own.[752] This essay can only make brief reference to four aspects of the Mau Mau war which take up earlier themes. These are the social control of violence, the discipline and division of command, the difficulties of adult gender and, finally, the religious traditions and political theory that inspired the forest fighters' endurance. Kikuyu continued to be at war with each other and continued to seek peace.

First, then, Mau Mau was on both sides a dirty war. As in all wars the need to stress the atrocious behaviour of the enemy and the chivalry of one's own champions made truth about either the first casualty. But on the British side stern operational orders and a succession of court cases leave little doubt that the security forces regarded Mau Mau fighters, and at times all Kikuyu, as scarcely human.[753] Equally, Mau Mau knew the value of terrorizing its enemies, although its methods of killing were not always as horrific as propaganda made out.[754] But on both sides Kikuyu tried to maintain a social control over violence. One can illustrate this contention in four instructive ways. They delayed fighting, as Waiyaki and then Kenyatta commanded; Mau Mau tried to apply the maxims of civic virtue to war; the loyalist Kikuyu Guard was often neutral; Mau Mau did not set out to destroy the Christian suppliers of education. First, there was little fighting for the initial five months of the Emergency. It was a time for both the British and Mau Mau to build up their forces, but it was more than that. The British, remembering 1939, called it the 'phoney war'. Kikuyu seem, rather, to have hoped it was the last chance for peace. Many of them were awaiting the outcome of Kenyatta's trial on the charge of managing Mau Mau. Two consequences followed. It might help his case if Kikuyu showed how strongly he was supported. In Kiambu, at least, many who had refused to join a hooligan Mau Mau now decided that, if Kenyatta had indeed been in charge, it was a political cause that even the respectable could join. Further, if he won his case, there might after all be no need to fight.[755] There continued to be, in short, a preference for disciplined ethnicity over militant action, despite the indiscriminate violence that large numbers of Kikuyu, Mau Mau and loyalist alike, were suffering at the hands of ignorant and angry security forces.

Both Mau Mau units and the government-sponsored Kikuyu Guard seem to have taken the same view. Mau Mau could not afford to alienate popular support by illegitimate killing, particularly of women and children; its fighters needed supplies, food, shelter and information from the rural communities from which they came. Violence was, where possible, made subject to the moral audit of labour theory. People were not killed just because they were rich. Wealthy men were respected if they were also people of compassion, *andu a tha*. Men like Josephat Wandimbe survived to recall their opposition to Mau Mau. If their trading stocks had to be raided for supplies, then forest gangs made a strict record, to allow future compensation. Local elders were consulted over reputations to ensure that execution was justified.[756] Mau Mau was not class but moral war. That was partly what made it so terrifying to its Kikuyu opponents. Victims were not structurally knowable; morally negotiated reputation was what counted – and who, in the bitter parochial conflicts over land, could predict that?

That unknowability seems in many areas to have been a motive for chiefs and others to form self-protection groups that the British later turned into an irregular force, under white command, the Kikuyu Guard. Most Guard units, not, I think, by accident, had a large number of Mau Mau members. Guard units intended to keep the peace rather than to prosecute a war, even that led by the dairy farmer, chief Muhoya, whom the British held up as one of Nyeri's loyalist heroes.[757] The British, clearer in their mind about the evil of Mau Mau than many loyalist Kikuyu, would have none of that. 'The mere avoidance of getting involved with either side, in other words, neutrality, was intolerable.' The British were as angry as insurgents from Nyeri and Murang'a, at Kiambu's preference for intrigue rather than war.[758] In the northern districts, however, an increasingly violent war erupted in mid-1953. By the end of 1956 the Kikuyu Guard were reckoned to have killed 4,500 Mau Mau, not far off half the total insurgent dead, and to have lost 730 men of their own. But it was a discriminate war. Mau Mau attacked guard posts rather than villages.[759] In Murang'a, Mau Mau and loyalists were divided either by *mbari*, or by *kirore* and *karing'a* church allegiance. Where both divisions coincided, as up on the forest edge, the war was at its bloodiest. Mau Mau thought of the headquarters of the independent but *kirore* African Christian Church there, Kinyona, as 'Berlin'.[760] Local hostilities sustained the general war.

That is why the Lari massacre of March 1953, the worst of the war, cannot be considered, as the first historians suggested, a tragedy separate from Mau Mau as a whole.[761] Chief Luka of Lari and his kin had 'sold land for office'; he was made chief after his *mbari*, with much reluctance, accepted land that was claimed – but not cultivated – by others, in return for their own eviction from land that was surrounded by white farms. Here was an extreme example of a general problem. A geographical mosaic of historical claims on the future was always at risk of arbitrary realignment by the state. At Lari many women and children were burnt in their huts, as well as chief Luka. Mau Mau seems to have been determined that such an atrocity should not recur. But Kikuyu Guard units were hardened to fight. Wars enlarge their appetite on such atrocity, just as Mau Mau feared.[762]

Nevertheless, the final example of Mau Mau's control of violence seems to have been fairly well applied throughout the war. This relates to the fate of missions and schools. Mau Mau and the African Christian Church fought a long but local war. As already noted Mau Mau attacked other teachers too; they also attacked missions. But they attacked very few. One motive was to get medical supplies. When they ransacked the Catholic mission on the forest edge at Tutho the insurgents took care not to hurt its nuns. Many Christians gathered at mission stations for protection; but they did not wire themselves in nor mount much of a guard. Attendance at schools soon picked up; church congregations revived. Few missionaries carried arms; none, it appears, was killed. Perhaps still more remarkably, mission-school supervisors, who travelled hundreds of miles a month with their teachers' pay packets, either with one or two police guards or none at all, were not ambushed on the way. The Anglican supervisor in Murang'a, Cyril Hooper, son of the missionary whose typewriter had produced the KCA's first petition 20 years before, had an unmuffled exhaust on his car so that Mau Mau, hearing him coming, would let him pass unharmed.[763]

Early in the war, to turn to the second of my overall themes, the insurgents realized that it could only be one of defence.[764] If some had intended to massacre all Europeans, that ceased to be possible once British troops arrived and the local battalions of the King's African Rifles were deployed against Mau Mau. Most forest fighters thought that, as *itungati*, they could do no more than give their political leaders a stronger negotiating hand,[765] even if some began to think in terms of future Mau Mau rule.[766] Defensive war needed popular support; support in the reserves was essential for supplies; only discipline could ensure that supply was willing. That needed authority; forest leaders had to have the prestige of high military rank and a unified command. Three factors in particular worked against them. First, their soldiers came from many different sources. The Nairobi central committee, which remained in existence until the end of 1953, supplied, on Mutonyi's account, comparatively few.[767] When young men entered the forests from the reserves they did so as members of particular *mbari* or chiefs' locations.

And many were ex-squatters with little local knowledge or connection, dumped in the reserves en masse by settlers who wanted to get rid of this fifth column from their farms. In the forests, therefore, the old Kikuyu contradiction between parochialism and power continued.[768] It was overlaid by a second, much more serious division, between ex-squatter fighters and those from Nairobi or the reserves. The commanders of the Rift Valley men wanted to keep that area of action, and therefore its promised land, for themselves; but squatters who remained on the farms were reluctant to permit raids on settlers who would in reprisal evict them from employment.[769] Mau Mau was thus forced to direct most of its aggressive energy to the reserves, to uproot the tree stumps of loyalist resistance, as the name of the reserves' military command indicated, the Kenya Levellation Army.[770]

This strategic straitjacket reinforced the need for leaders to insist on the disciplined obedience that Kikuyu seniors had always demanded of juniors. Forest meetings enacted rules of behaviour, principally to control violence, including rape; penalties for infraction were severe, often death.[771] Mau Mau memoirs, accordingly, hold particular scorn for insurgent units that were mere bandits, *komerera*. The term refers to concealment, idleness, or bending low (in Nairobi it was a nickname for the drop-handlebar sports bicycles used by Mau Mau patrols).[772] How far *komerera* gangs existed, how far the were the standardized nightmare of all forest commanders, is hard to say. They were said to steal indiscriminately from peasant stores and flocks; to abduct girls; and to be too cowardly to attack an armed enemy. These external military failings stemmed from internal indiscipline. *Komerera* were vagabonds, 'masters of themselves'; they refused to have communal camp stores. Their worst recorded offence, for which the penalty was death by strangulation, was to administer 'a strange oath' to compel *itungati* to desert any leader 'who did not participate in fetching food and firewood, building his hut and carrying his own luggage.'[773] Insurgent songs resisted the slackness of indiscipline by recalling Kenyatta's message to the mass meeting at Nyeri in July 1952: 'Vagrancy and idleness do not produce benefits for our country.'[774]

Mau Mau's worst nightmare was a splinter group, the Kikuyu Musical Society, sometimes corrupted as 'Moscow', possibly the source of the 'strange oath'. The society seems to have originally been a dance band. It was taken over by young urban insurgents who felt that the central committee was too cautious. It clashed a number of times with authorized insurgent units. In 1954 Field Marshal Dedan Kimathi even complained to the governor about the behaviour of this musical Moscow gang. Disciplined insurgents feared that it would disgrace all Kikuyu. The musicians were said to take drugs, drink heavily, dance in their offices and to want to abolish private property and turn all women, even wives, into 'communal sources of pleasure'.[775] There was none of this primitive communism in Mau Mau.

But the third, and perhaps fatal, problem for the forest leadership was the growing conflict between the educated and unlettered. The educated Kimathi had usurped the overall leadership of the unlettered Mathenge, who, unlike Kimathi, had military experience. Their rivalry became generalized. The educated dominated Kimathi's 'Kenya Parliament'. Less-educated men supported Mathenge's 'Kenya *riigi*'. The title implied a responsibility for all the Kenya household that Kimathi may have thought insolent in men who lacked education; he also accused them of being inspired by no more than local and personal jealousies.[776] The members of the *riigi* thought the parliamentary group, on the other hand, to be too much enslaved by the European and Christian ideas of their superior education; Kimathi's official photograph pictured him with three pens clipped to his pocket and a pile of exercise books in his hand.[777] The division widened to a chasm when government opened surrender negotiations in 1955. Kimathi resisted the offer; members of the *riigi* decided to explore it, partly to defy what they saw as Kimathi's growing dictatorship. It was the end of any semblance of united resistance, already eroded by the appalling toll of battle and privation.[778] Literacy had helped to invent a tribe; allied now to the gun it seemed to threaten its ethnic parochial virtues.

The third overall theme of the Mau Mau war was the role of household and gender. The British were horrified by the active part played by women on behalf of Mau Mau and detained thousands of them. One of their most perspicacious young officials thought Mau Mau attracted women by giving them back the honoured status from which they had been deprived by social change. They had little education or salaried power. But Mau Mau offered them full membership of a political movement; they could be warriors, spies or food suppliers who, in the absence of their men, now controlled 'the means of production'.[779] And women did sustain the forest war as mothers, wives and sisters. They helped to organize the food supply for the men in the forests.[780] They sang and prayed for their sons as they did so.[781] But they also had to survive. They were forced to engage in the communal labour of building Guard posts and strategic trenches along the forest edge. Many women feared that the state would destroy their reproductive fertility by this labour, as in the *mitaro* war, as well as by punishment for refusal.[782] Waruhiu Itote, as General China the commander of Mau Mau forces on Mount Kenya, presided over a heated debate on the proper attitude for the insurgents to take to this double female role. What decided the issue was the women's part in reproduction; even loyalist wives were mothers of the future and must not, in the aftermath of the Lari massacre, be wantonly killed.[783] But the female responsibility for posterity also helped to end the war. As the fighting dragged on and the British in 1954 herded the scattered population into villages, known by the hated name of *laini*, to separate the insurgents from their suppliers, so women came to feel that freedom was not worth famine. Their support for Mau Mau fell away. This, no less than unequal combat and dissension in command, brought the fight to a finish.[784]

The women's part in the forest war itself was just as ambiguous and hotly contested, between women and men and, rather better recorded, between men themselves. Kikuyu men were facing an unprecedented crisis. Their own rules of war assumed that they would be away on raids for a few days at most. Sexual intercourse was thought to weaken their prowess and their warrior oath of loyalty; warriors' rations on raids must be cooked by mothers and wives but not by unmarried girls; there was the general prohibition on sex in the bush.[785] But the Mau Mau war dragged on for years. Many young women fought to be more than mothers and wives; perhaps 5 per cent of the forest fighters were women.[786] Many men were frankly terrified at what this would mean for gender discipline.[787] They appreciated the women's skill and courage as spies and sometimes as seductresses of the enemy.[788] Men also welcomed their conventional household services of cooking, cleaning and carrying.[789] But even here men were worried; it took manpower to guard women. And wifely chores could be a security risk, as the great laundry disaster showed; British planes bombed a Mau Mau camp at which the girls had left clothes out to dry.[790] But what disturbed men most was, first, the old taboo against wartime sex and then, when that became impossible to sustain, that sexual competition would wreck comradeship and discipline.[791] Two solutions were adopted. Early in 1954 the insurgents in the Nyandarwa forests decided that sexual liaisons should be registered as marriages, with prohibitions on adultery and divorce. And both in the Nyandarwa and, more formally, in the Mount Kenya forests, officer status conferred sexual privilege, an enforcement of hierarchy but also another threat to discipline.[792] Nor were these real marriages. The insurgents did not discuss whether bridewealth should be paid, although the columns of the pre-Emergency vernacular press were full of such debate. The only two forest *nyimbo* to raise marital questions saw failure to pay bridewealth as fatal to relationships.[793] The impossibility of sustaining proper adult gender roles in the forest must have been for many fighters the hardest privation to endure.[794] A number of Mau Mau memoirs reserve their most deeply felt remembrances to the start or resumption of proper marital relations at the end of the war or the culmination of detention.[795] The war itself had conferred no such civic virtue.

Finally, Mau Mau fighters were both sustained and divided by religious faith and political theory. As in all wars religious belief was deepened. But the insurgents had three different sets of beliefs, those of the old religion, the same worldly faith reinforced by the Old Testament, and political messianism. Gikoyo is the only representative we have of the unlettered whom other memoir-writers tend to scorn. He had faith in diviners, the *andu ago*. He also thought more deeply about Kikuyu belief in the afterworld. In his travels he passed a 'hill of cattle' under which he could hear the lowing of cows and bleating of sheep. Those who were executed for indiscipline were said to be sent to herd Kimathi's cattle.[796] The place of the living dead and their possessions may well have sustained some insurgents' hopes for their posterity. But for other fighters the forest war was another echo of Exodus. Karari Njama, Kahinga Wachanga and Dedan Kimathi all had their Bibles with them.[797] Njama reflected that the Israelites had had to endure similar hardship; Kimathi was compared with Moses; in his surrender talks Wachanga accused the British of breaking the Ten Commandments.[798] The British were also cast in the role of the Philistines, sending an iron-clad giant Goliath against them, whom some said might also have been General Smuts from Australia.[799] But the New Testament and mission hymns continued to be adapted too, to provide hope for the future. Both Kimathi and Kenyatta were Messiahs; and like their enemies in the Kenya Regiment, the insurgents marched to their own words for 'Onward Christian Soldiers'.[800]

All three religious traditions pointed to a promised land. Mau Mau gave thought to how it should be ruled. Kimathi volunteered his support to rescue 'two great kings', Seretse Khama of the Ngwato and Kabaka Muteesa II of Buganda from their British exile.[801] But Mau Mau no longer hoped that the British monarchy would save them from the settlers who had betrayed the intentions of Queen Victoria. The state still made much of royal symbols of loyalty. The new Queen had acceded to the throne while on holiday in Kenya. Her coronation was celebrated with much festivity in the midst of the Mau Mau war.[802] Mau Mau was not impressed. They stepped up attacks on the day of the coronation and buried coins with the Queen's head upside down.[803] They had their own Queen; Kimathi's girlfriend Wanjiru was made to marry him when he became the equivalent of a senior elder as prime minister of the Kenya Parliament.[804] They had also acquired a sense of the populist possibilities of monarchy. After a fight in Murang'a the British picked up a Mau Mau notebook in which the dead owner had written his own version of British history. Who taught him I do not know. Perhaps it was the sort of teaching to which government objected in the independent schools. But it was a rebellious tribute to the liberating traditions of the colonial oppressor and perhaps an indication of hopes for Kenya's future. The English, after all, were admirable. They had fought the Romans in their own forest for 120 years, strengthened by an oath. They began to pay a poll tax 'among themselves' in 1378. Two centuries later they again bound themselves by oath to resist foreign enemies. In 1629 they had sworn that the King should levy taxes only as 'agreed by the common people'. Finally, after their civil war and the restoration of the monarchy, the English agreed to obey their rulers 'so that they can rule well'.[805] Mau Mau members were determined to record their own history for the instruction of posterity.[806] But it was by searching other men's history that they began to think about the nature of the state. The Kikuyu Association of chiefs had long before tried to reconstruct colonial rule by dynastic theory from above. Mau Mau was contemplating independence by means of a dynastic theory from below. And 'King' Kenyatta, as the *nyimbo* called him, was restored to his people once the Emergency, Kenya's own civil war, was over. Kikuyu and other Kenyans would now be able to put this populist theory of political legitimacy to the test.

The peasant revolution of the peace was lost by the white settler hawks at independence. That does not mean that it was won by the hawks of Mau Mau. They had lost the war, and could not dictate the terms of peace. The peace was won, instead, by a natural coalition of doves and hawks on both sides of the war. Kenyatta and his conservative Kikuyu colleagues were its leaders, doves who had inspired Mau Mau with hope. Their chief allies were Mau Mau's most hawkish wartime enemies, the men of the Kikuyu Guard. Both had hedged their bets throughout. Nationalist crisis and the narrow factions of the colonial state had separated them in 1952, not interest nor ideology. Majority rule and the expansion of the state made room for them both in power. Their alliance was underpinned by the professional doves of the state, district commissioners glad to turn from government by civil war to managing the agrarian revolution devised by departmental experts in the agriculture and veterinary departments. Under the name of the Swynnerton Plan the state intensified the spread of cash crops and dairy cattle in the African reserves, on the startling new basis of generalized private, freehold, property. For Kikuyu, land registration and consolidation during the Emergency was the final, bitter, codification of *mbari* history. But it was also the means whereby the sorcery of the rich expanded to become the titled property of middle peasants. In some places land registration excluded their unruly children, the *imaramari*. Some of the tens of thousands of Mau Mau detainees – about whom I have had nothing to say and whose experience was perhaps the chief legacy of the war – returned home to find that the politics of consolidation had punitively robbed them of land. But again, the war was not carried to its logical limits; most of them received back what was agreed to be theirs.[807] Nevertheless, dynastic landlord theory, as the Kikuyu Association had earlier demanded, was finally marked out on the ground. In the 1920s *mbari* seniors and chiefs had distinguished a minority of right-holders from a tenant majority. Figures of Kikuyu landlessness and emigration at independence, 40 years on, finally proved them right.

Land-poor forest fighters had failed to reconstruct labour theory or gender in a manner that gave them new rights to land. About a quarter of Kikuyu households in their home districts were landless in 1963. In addition, 38 per cent of women lived outside their home districts, barely less than men. Moreover the age-sex pyramids, as demographers call them, of Kikuyu in the former white highlands were those of long-established communities or, if recent immigrants, then of people who came as complete households.[808] It seems then that 60 per cent of Kikuyu no longer had access to land within their own *mbari* or that of a local patron. Symbolic initiation by Mau Mau circumcision had not determined how land would be allocated to such land-poor or landless people. In any case Mau Mau had not won the war. In the Kikuyu home districts, the fertile hills where the fig tree grew, and where the state now supported smallholder farming, former 'loyalists' retained the levers of power.

In the Rift Valley, the promised land, the peace was equally bitter. Many squatters returned to their former employment before the end of the Emergency; the settlers, as the legend of the squatter Wamugumo told, could not do without them. That did not mean that they all inherited the land as the settlers departed. Indeed, their agrarian war resumed as the military one came to an end and independence loomed. It was more complicated now. The state fought to retain as many large farms as possible, convinced that the Rift was no place for smallholder farming. Other peoples had longer historical claims than Kikuyu to the land, the Maasai and Kalenjin. African politicians fancied the life of gentlemen farmers. Chiefs in the overcrowded Kikuyu reserves also wanted to settle both clients and enemies in the Rift, as before the First War. Squatters thus faced many hostile claimants for the land they had nourished with their sweat. Some, as when they had founded the *kiama kia bara*, took the law into their own hands by occupying deserted farms. Some submitted to the clientage of state-sponsored settlement schemes. Still others felt shamefully ignored. Yet, for all their bitterness, squatters did not entirely lose the peace. The balanced composition of the Rift Valley Kikuyu population at the 1962 census suggests that Mau Mau had given many of them enough menacing power to assert their *kuna* right to *ithaka* there, after all. Nellie Grant's squatters, who bought her out on her departure, will not have been the only ones who were entitled to call their new property *Mataguri*, 'we have been here a long time'.[809] Mau Mau had divided Kikuyu. But Kikuyu politicians, with Kenyatta at their head, were winning control of the state. They wanted a strong constituency of support. Political tribalism provided it.

Squatters were a minority of Kikuyu. They used Mau Mau's recent memory to intimidate politicians; while politicians responded, not all their constituency had been squatters. As in the years before the Emergency and in the military demarcation dispute in the forest, squatter clearance rights still conflicted with tribal power.

Mau Mau *itungati*, subject to the collective discipline of their movement's circumcision, had entered the forests in groups, not to seek their fortune but to serve their elders in hope of future reward. Kenyatta needed their help in banging his head against the tree of power, so that Gikuyu's children could eat the fruit that fell to the ground.[810] At independence he was able to shake its topmost branches with a word. Government waived repayment of the loans it had made to the widows of Dedan Kimathi and Stanley Mathenge to enable them to buy land.[811] Many former fighters were now endowed with household property; all of them had earned the new right of *wiathi*, the vote. They were free to fly up separately. But most remained poor. The future would decide whether this new mark of citizenship gave the poor more rights than the old, not just against the wealthy but against the holders of state office. In the past poor clients had worked for self-mastery. State clientage had now allowed many of the poor to establish a household; the question was whether it would also confer *wiathi*. A similar query hung over the rich and powerful. Kikuyu thought was still a moral rather than political theory; it distinguished hard-earned civic virtue from the evil sway attained through the dark power of sorcery or by alliance with strangers. It remained a theory of persons and reputation rather than of institutions or classes. Wealthy men in the past had always had their eye on the poor man's midden; but they had also had to work, and reward with goats the work of others, in the public eye of small communities. Big men could now get state loans, nobody quite knew how, in the private corridors of power. Harry Thuku, his enemies said, had harvested other men's shillings to build his *Paradise*; Mau Mau accused chiefs of selling land, which was people, for office; at independence the people's representatives used office to buy land.[812] Could they also buy the people?

Past, present and future

We can now return, with Kenya's own scholars, to the relations between past, present and future. Mazrui long ago thought historical debate was essential to a future free society, the responsible political culture that we call nationhood. Ogot has also called for dialogue between past and present.[813] This essay is an entry in that debate. It is written from outside Kenya, with a stranger's blind grasp on the evidence. But it may help to give voice to a hitherto muffled past, in which the ethnic arguments that alarm new states and their students turn out to have been as much about class and citizenship as about tribal division.

I have tried to study real people arguing, and failing to resolve, the issues of their day. Kikuyu nationalism provided a comfortable vehicle for uncomfortable arguments, as nationalisms do. Its thought generated a tribe out of dynastic division; learnt its own history in the imported lessons of the Bible; called for the civilizing sweat of labour to be freed from the slavery of settler capital, to serve patriotic Kikuyu production instead; praised the educational privilege that sharpened the political awareness of all; defended male-ruled households against the feminine treachery of towns; crowned wealth's private virtue with the civic right to lead a reinvented people; but also gave poor clients the ideas with which to hold their rich patrons to public account.

Kikuyu nationalism, like others, was a search for solidarity in face of class formation and intrusive state power. But its moral languages of class, conservative or militant, failed to wrestle with the deepest contradictions of capitalism and the state. Structural wealth and poverty were known but little understood. Like Kenyatta in the 1920s, so Henry Muoria in the 1940s, guerrillas in the 1950s and rural women in the 1980s all repeated the proverbial truth that wealth proved virtue, poverty delinquence.[814] Only the Forty Group and, more systematically, Gakaara wa Wanjau, began to think otherwise. Meanwhile, time robbed the poor of much of their opportunity and relieved the rich of some of their cares. Social mobility ran up against class closure; state office was not accountable; land became property and ceased to be people. Sorcery was a more common explanation of injustice than the inequality of state power. How *wiathi* could be earned by poor men without *ithaka* nobody – not even Kubai or Kaggia, let alone Sam Thebere – could say. The anonymous syndicalists of Nairobi may have had an answer but the industrial trades unionists showed the wisdom of dependence. How fathers could remain men if they had no land for their sons, or sons become men without marriage, nobody knew. Women could scarcely marry men of no property, even when both had proved their adulthood in the forests. At the top of the social scale the demands of civic virtue, disputatious but slow to change, could not bridle wealthy men who built dissident coalitions wider than *mbari* or who enjoyed state power, first as chiefs and later as ministers of state. *Ndamathia*, a power to which wealth had been subject, was either dead or the devil.[815] No rules of political accountability replaced the rituals of *ituika*. Generation succession passed into history, political succession was in colonial hands. Cash did not acquire the moral linkage that goats had had with people. Abrupt rejection of clients' claims during famine had given way to persistent pressure against tenants' rights in land. The harvest of other men's shillings was too often stored in private granaries. Under the threat of class closure, as previously in dearth, Kikuyu faced social terror. However much Mau Mau militants believed 'the creed of Gikuyu and Muumbi', the solidarity of the *Mwangi* and *Irungu* generations which it invoked was not unbreakable, nor were the 'nine clans' one.[816]

Britain imposed a State of Emergency on Kikuyu; Kikuyu faced one of their own. But if there is any lesson to be learnt from this history, it is that those who faced the terror of not knowing how civic virtue could be achieved in social practice, how to allocate and control authority, continued to argue these questions out. They were neither mad nor bewildered but divided. Ageing boys fought against class closure to become men. Some women fought to be more than mothers and wives. Mau Mau fighters called themselves *itungati*, rearguards of a defensive political war. They distinguished disciplined insurgency from idle banditry accordingly; resisted the arrogance of Kimathi's power; and spared men of compassion however wealthy, *andu a tha*. When the war was over squatters' rights of clearance remained at odds with the patronage of men with political power. All these were the dilemmas of a querulous moral ethnicity. This was the reverse of the political tribalism which, too much modern analysis suggests, is the sole stuff of contemporary African politics, with uncritical clients grateful for any crumbs from their rulers' factional feast.

In their attempts to control violence, Kikuyu insurgents weighed class injustice against imagined ethnic reciprocity. They were well aware of wider, inter-ethnic relations. Kenyatta used Swahili proverbs; by 1952 a Kikuyu crowd cheered rather than jeered when the Luo leader Achieng Oneko said he might marry a Kikuyu.[817] *Muhimu* took steps to build a pan-ethnic alliance; Kimathi's Parliament and Mathenge's *riigi* both claimed to be Kenyan. But a militant pan-ethnic alliance would have imposed on all its parties unacceptable costs, for five reasons. First, and in general, once one drops the dogma that ethnicity must fade in the light of modernization, there was no reason why other peoples should volunteer for a war which in any case divided the Kikuyu who were mainly involved. They would need much persuasion to risk their lives; but, secondly, the intensity of Kikuyu politics repelled rather than persuaded them. Kikuyu faced sharper class division than others. Acting on their saying that 'those without previous dealings with each other have no cause to quarrel', they quarrelled between themselves about class. Other groups, not so divided socially, were less obsessed by dreams of tribal unity; nor were their nationalisms in such need of alliance. Thirdly, Kikuyu had fewer close dealings with other groups; because they had less cause to quarrel with them neither did they have to seek out compromise. It was too late to do so once the purpose risked violent death. Political scientists used to argue the cultural case that rising market transactions widened identity by wearing down old ethnic barriers.[818] Kikuyu history makes the political point that the need to settle disputes added contractual bargains to the newly enlarged identity of tribe. This reflection is reinforced, fourthly, by the old wisdom about the tribal corollaries of uneven regional development. Rich Kikuyu came to scorn the idle backwardness of ethnic others;[819] in outcast Nairobi Kikuyu townsmen made others suffer by the entrepreneurial drive of their own ambition or despair. Other nationalisms were not merely parallel projects to subject change to the moral audit of ethnicity and to oppose the British; they were also, in part, defensive agianst Kikuyu. Yet the trans-ethnicity of daily survival brought Mau Mau many willing non-Kikuyu allies.

Finally, the British offered Africans no arena of debate wider than their invented tribes. The rulers of late-colonial states found it hard to escape the causal circle that still rings multicultural states today. In the late 1940s the British in Africa tacitly accepted that they lacked ideological coherence and, therefore, any claim to hegemony, legitimacy. But that did not make them more willing to transfer power. Swinging between nostalgia for tribal order and dreams of cooperative progress, the British had to have an agreed sense of direction themselves before they would permit Africans to organize their own. If Africans were allowed to enjoy political freedoms as wide as the state, they would, it was feared, only add British political incoherence to their own ethnic division. The imperial problem with African nationalism was not that it would eventually take over but that it might very soon destroy already fragile colonial states. Anarchy was more likely than revolution. So colonial governments allowed Africans power only over those local political communities which they had themselves created and whose rules they were thought to respect. The illegitimacy of the state bred deep political crisis. From above, an incoherent state feared popular mobilization; from below, Africans invented small political loyalties, defensive against the state. Around these tribal imaginations, in 1952, the Kenyan government drew boundaries of blood. Subsequent liberal reforms did little more than give them open political expression.

In that last respect independent Kenya has done better than both its colonial predecessor and many of its African contemporaries. Its government has in general kept the peace; its 'hegemonic project' or search for legitimacy has scarcely been totalitarian, if often brutal. The state has also worked well in those areas which matter most to most people. There have been recurrent food crises but, in a fast rising population, almost no Kenyans have starved;[820] an increase in the sum of human welfare – the poorest always excepted – is undeniable. Nonetheless, the state has periodically resorted to force, openly with firearms and police batons, secretly behind cell doors. Restrictions on political rights and the ministerial use of public shillings for private profit are common knowledge. Political tribalism is blamed for both failings. The state sees its malignant force behind the popular unrest which now and again must be repressed; its critics attribute tribal faction to official corruption. The question, then, is whether any dialogue with history can offer a way out of this contemporary contradiction between parochialism and the accountability of wider power.

This essay cannot analyse modern Kenyan politics. But it may perhaps, as with Mau Mau, suggest a deeper understanding of its contested moral economy. In any country, under the lash of global markets which no one state can control, the productivity or futility of politics is governed by the relations between the state and its civil society. States are knots of self-interested, rival, bureaucracies with varying capacities to extract loyalty and revenue from their subjects and to give service in return; they are to some degree obedient to variously cohesive political teams called governments. Governments respond in different ways to their civil society, made up of social interests which are more or less free to form their own representative bodies outside the state and, therefore, to demand some reciprocity in the political bargains that deliver obedience and income in return for state favour. The connections between states, governments and civil society exist largely in the mind; they are very unevenly legitimate. At the worst, states are protection rackets; their people have to invest more in protection than in production; capital has to be a political pimp. Conversely, the more the inequalities of power are negotiated, the more efficient their productive outcomes are likely to be. Equally, efficiency can be its own legitimacy. For all its manifest failings the Kenyan state has been comparatively efficient and for most of its people, therefore, legitimate. The reasons are not immediately clear, nor have they been adequately explained. Reference to deep historical memory may help to do so.

Kenya's public ideology, like that of other African states, is an elder's dream. Social order is said to follow from obedience to leaders who release communal energies.[821] It sounds, and is meant to sound, like stateless plutocratic theory. Wamugumo could even be a national hero. But Kenya's leaders, like others, look to be recruited more by high-political intrigue than by the transparent exercise of popular will. That is not entirely certain, since the high politics of patronage can mould civil society and thus its ambitions. Competition for public goods fosters political tribalism. This, now the main institution of civil society, sets client communities against similar external rivals. Patronage is undoubtedly an effective means of identifying political constituencies, the modern external architecture of tribe. But, in contradiction to the official ideology of productive order, the effects of political tribalism can all too easily be destructive, for some countries fatally so. Patronage feeds on the political redistribution of state revenue. This may further enrich already wealthy regions, perhaps to the benefit of the national product but at the risk of intolerable political strain; or it may subsidize economically weaker but factionally importunate areas at the expense of investment, without which revenue fails.[822] The former tendency characterized Kenyatta's rule, the latter arap Moi's, reflecting their different ethnic origins.[823] But they were and are only tendencies, not self-destructive obsessions. There are two observable reasons for this political moderation which go some way to differentiate Kenya from other African states; but they are not a full explanation.

The first is simply the ruthless skill of Kenya's high politics; ethnic bias has rarely overruled cool calculation. It may be that the divisions of anti-colonial nationalism, of which Tom Mboya was so aware, have been the cautious tutor here. Skill in managing political tribalism is the art of knowing one's own creation. The second factor is the ironic legacy of Kenya's white farmers. Always quicker than other tribes to protect their sectional interests, their once racial cartels now serve the interests of class. The settler past lingers in a civil society unusually well founded in producer organizations, professional associations and, at intervals, a free press, all checks on political tribalism. But there is another historical legacy, partly derived from African resistance to the settlers, which has been less noticed by scholars. It lies deep in popular memory and in the unstated assumptions of high politics. This is the moral ethnicity that has been my quarry and which, when flouted, raised up the terrors of Mau Mau.

Political tribalism flows down from high-political intrigue; it constitutes communities through external competition. Moral ethnicity creates communities from within through domestic controversy over civic virtue. It ascends from deep antagonism to the very forces on which political tribalism thrives, class closure and overbearing state power. Its Kikuyu history is not entirely one of failure; it is the only language of accountability that most Africans have; it is the most intimate critic of the state's ideology of order. But moral ethnicity is not given its due in analyses of modern Africa; political tribalism, often called clientelism, is accorded too much explanatory sway, perhaps because it makes fewer demands on the evidence. Sceptical moral ethnicity is of course vulnerable to political tribalism's calls for solidarity. Behaviour that fails the test of civic virtue becomes heroic when it wins state favour for a client group or defends it from the all-too readily imagined nightmare of communal exclusion from power. But any analysis of Kenya's politics that neglects the deep politics of moral ethnicity must be shallow and misleading, like the colonial and indeed many scholarly explanations of Mau Mau that saw minority manipulation of mass opinion rather than a dynamic process.

Wealth, Poverty & Civic Virtue in Kikuyu Political Thought

In modern Kenya the language of moral ethnicity has to be oblique; it demands an argued accountability of power that the ideology of order will not accept. But the language is heard, as in the *muthirigu* of 1929 or the *nyimbo* of 1952,[824] in popular song, with audio cassettes taking the place of the press and the microphone; in scurrilous rumour about big men's unmanly failings; in the political gossip of the 'peoples' republics of the *matatus*';[825] or from pulpits. In recent times intellectuals have not found Kenya a free society. The indiscreet have been detained or forced into exile; or, if student demonstrators, rusticated home. There these modern *athomi*, only a generation or two removed from the first cursed readers, have had to justify their liberal or socialist criticisms of the state to often unsympathetic seniors who judge politics by the conservative criteria of moral ethnicity. Threatened by a youthful delinquency which recalls Mau Mau, they nonetheless have their own critique of a state that separates power from virtue, ruled by men who are suspected of harvesting other men's shillings, not their own maize. Folk memories of a time when poor men and women were goaded beyond endurance by such grievance must make today's rulers uneasily aware of the potential of popular censure. Moral ethnicity may not be an institutionalized force; but it is the nearest Kenya has to a national memory and a watchful political culture. Because native, it is a more trenchant critic of the abuse of power than any Western political thought; it imagines freedom in laborious idioms of self-mastery which intellectuals too easily dismiss. High-political awareness of the vigilance of moral ethnicity may be, as much as canny political tribalism and a lively civil society, what keeps Kenya at peace.

Neither political tribalism nor moral ethnicity will disappear. They are two sides of the worldwide politics of cultural pluralism.[826] Tribalism remains the reserve currency in our markets of power, ethnicity our most critical community of thought. Ethnic nationalism has been mobilized rather than disarmed by modern states, no matter whether liberal or authoritarian. The universal question becomes, then, how to save multicultural politics from the fearful minority domination or barren factional bargains that suppress productively principled argument. External architectures of control have stimulated the rival solidarities of political tribalism; interior architectures of civic virtue have prompted the awkward questions of moral ethnicity. If we are all condemned to live with the first we need to enlarge the languages of the second. If states cannot eradicate tribalism, the arguments within ethnicity must somehow infuse states. That is easy enough to say. How difficult its politics might be will be governed, as always, by the interplay between political practice and public opinion. Political practice is easily swayed by political tribalism. Public opinion can be bought or intimidated. But, if only one listens, there are sterner opinions to be heard from the past. The ancestors did not know about the state; they had scant sympathy for the poor. But they knew the difference between fertile self-mastery in leaders and barren greed; they had a keen regard for the personal autonomies which, under the law, give citizenship a chance of self-mastery. Commenting on a draft of this essay, two Kalenjin teachers from western Kenya remarked that their own thought argued the same issues as the Kikuyu, if with different metaphors.[827] That is not surprising, but it seemed to be so to them. Inside every united tribe a debated ethnicity is struggling to get out. More public awareness of common ethnic predicaments might sometimes deter high-political resort to the auction room of tribalism. It would no doubt be a small step, but the ethnic arguments of gender and household, class and generation need to get into the history books. Mazrui and Ogot were right. Deep debates are suppressed by high faction. They could, if heard, lead to argument on the accountability of state power. To give them voice one must, at the least, lend an ear to alternative pasts.

Notes

1. Tom Mboya, *Freedom and After* (London, 1963), pp. 61–5.
2. As Mboya implied: *ibid.*, pp. 68–9. It is symptomatic that while he said almost nothing about the connection between politics and gender in nationalism, it was the first thing he turned to in illustrating the positive aspects of tribalism.
3. The evocative concept of Benedict Anderson, *Imagined Communities: Reflections on the Origin and Spread of Nationalism* (London, 1983).
4. *Ibid.*; a remarkable conclusion from a Marxist analyst.
5. Kenyans close this gap every day. But the recent 'S.M.' Otieno burial litigation shows how easily a crude distinction between a Christian, golf-playing, Shakespeare-quoting modern Kenyan nationality and barbaric tribalism can still be constructed, each unsympathetic to women's rights; see Sean Egan (ed.), *S.M. Otieno: Kenya's Unique Burial Saga* (Nairobi, 1987), J.B. Ojwang and J.N.K. Mugambi (eds), *The S.M. Otieno Case: Death and Burial in Modern Kenya* (Nairobi, 1989) and, forthcoming, David W. Cohen and E.S. Atieno Odhiambo, *Burying SM: The Politics of Knowledge and the Sociology of Power in Africa*.
6. See, more generally, Chapter 9 above.
7. My ethnographic guides include L.S.B. Leakey, *The Southern Kikuyu before 1903* (3 vols, London and New York, 1977); his rival, Jomo Kenyatta, *Facing Mount Kenya* (London, 1938); and ex-district commissioner H.E. Lambert, whose *Kikuyu Social and Political Institutions* (London, 1956) was closer to Kenyatta than Leakey. The earliest work was the most sympathetic: W.S. and K. Routledge, *With a Prehistoric People: The Akikuyu of British East Africa* (London [1910] 1968). Closest to my interests are Greet Kershaw, 'The land is the people: a study of social organization in historical perspective' (Chicago University Ph.D thesis, 1972) and Carolyn M. Clark, 'Land and food, women and power, in nineteenth-century Kikuyu', *Africa* 50(4) (1980), pp. 357–70. The driest are John Middleton and Greet Kershaw, *The Kikuyu and Kamba*

of Kenya (London, 1965), the most patronizing C. Cagnolo, *The Akikuyu* (Torino, 1933), the most schematic A.H.J. Prins, *East African Age-class Systems* (Groningen, 1953). Kikuyu autobiographers have a simpler view of their society than the ethnographers and, probably, their own grandparents.

8. Among the important official sources are minutes of the three Kikuyu Local Native Councils (as they were termed from 1925 to 1949); these I have skimmed rather than studied since they record policy-related argument rather than the social metaphors by which argument gained point and colour. The key Kikuyu evidence printed by the state is in *Kenya Land Commission Evidence*, Vol i (Nairobi, 1933) [cited henceforth as *KLCE* i]. It fills 214 pages of directly reported speech or written memoranda. Of 960 pages of 'non-native evidence' much is Kikuyu in origin, reported at second hand.

9. The only remaining copies (it appears) are those filed in KNA, DC/MKS. 10B/13/1.

10. Edmondo Cavicchi (ed.), *Problems of Change in Kikuyu Tribal Society* (Bologna, 1977).

11. Police translations of *Mumenyereri* for 1947–50 are in KNA, MAA. 8/106; I am indebted to David Throup, whose notes allowed my perusal to be rapid. I have seen one original issue, 20 September 1952, which the editor H.M. Mwaniki had with him when he flew to London for what has become nearly 40 years of exile. Thanks to Revd John K. Karanja for a translation.

12. R. Mugo Gatheru, *Child of Two Worlds* (London, 1964); Rebmann Wambaa and Kenneth King, 'The political economy of the Rift valley: a squatter perspective', ch. 9 in B.A. Ogot (ed.), *Hadith 5: Economic and Social History of East Africa* (Nairobi, 1975); Peter Beard (ed.), *Longing for Darkness: Kamante's Tales from Out of Africa* (New York and London, 1975).

13. John Spencer, *James Beauttah, Freedom Fighter* (Nairobi, 1983); Bildad Kaggia, *Roots of Freedom 1921–1963* (Nairobi, 1975); Eliud Mutonyi, 'Mau Mau chairman' (typescript); Henry Muoria Mwaniki, *I, the Kikuyu Tribe and the White Fury* (Nairobi, forthcoming) with the author's pamphlets and Kenyatta's speeches from the 1940s; Harry Thuku, with Kenneth King, *An Autobiography* (Nairobi, 1970).

14. Josiah Mwangi Kariuki, *'Mau Mau' Detainee* (London, 1963); Gakaara wa Wanjau, *Mau Mau Author in Detention* (Nairobi, 1988).

15. Donald Barnett and Karari Njama, *Mau Mau From Within* (London, 1966), for Karari Njama's forest memoirs; Waruhiu Itote (General China), *'Mau Mau' General* (Nairobi, 1967); and H.K. Wachanga, ed. Robert Whittier, *The Swords of Kirinyaga: The Fight for Land and Freedom* (Nairobi, 1975) are officers' accounts. For other ranks see, Gucu G. Gikoyo, *We Fought for Freedom* (Nairobi, 1979); Ngugi Kabiro, ed. Don Barnett, *Man in the Middle* (Richmond, BC, 1973); Mohammed Mathu, ed. D. Barnett, *The Urban Guerrilla* (Richmond, BC, 1974); Karigo Muchai, ed. D. Barnett, *The Hard Core* (Richmond, BC, 1973); Joram Wamweya, ed. Ciira Cerere, *Freedom Fighter* (Nairobi, 1971).

16. Obadiah Kariuki, *A Bishop Facing Mount Kenya: An Autobiography, 1902–1978* (Nairobi, 1985); E.N. Wanyoike, *An African Pastor, the Life and Work of Rev. Wanyoike Kamawe 1888–1970* (Nairobi, 1974).

17. Mathew Njoroge Kabetu, *Kirira kia Ugikuyu* (Nairobi [1947], 1966); Daniel Kinuthia Mugia, *Urathi wa Cege wa Kibiru* (Nairobi, 1979); Ngumbu Njururi, *Tales from Mount Kenya* (Nairobi [1966], 1975); Wanjiku M. Kabira and Karega wa Mutahi, *Gikuyu Oral Literature* (Nairobi, 1988); Jean Davison (ed.), *Voices from Mutira: Learning and Change in the Lives of Rural Gikuyu Women* (Stanford University, 1986). My thanks to John Karanja for translations from Kabetu and Mugia.

18. G. Barra (ed.), *1,000 Kikuyu Proverbs* (Nairobi [1939], 1960); Ngumbu Njururi (ed.), *Gikuyu Proverbs* (Nairobi [1968], 1983).

19. Bethwell A. Ogot, 'History, ideology and contemporary Africa', presidential address to the Historical Association of Kenya, mimeographed, Nairobi, 27 August 1981.

20. C.R. Cheney, *Medieval Texts and Studies* (Oxford, 1973), p. 8; I owe the reference to Rosamond McKitterick.

21. Ludwig von Hohnel, *Discovery of Lakes Rudolf and Stefanie*, vol. i (London and New York, 1894), pp. 300-1, where Waiyaki is Uatahaj Uajaki; F.D. Lugard, *The Rise of our East African Empire* (Edinburgh and London, 1893), pp. 325-33, where he is Eiyaki – to cite the earliest of many sources for Waiyaki, whose role in Kikuyu thought I intend to discuss elsewhere.

22. See Chapter 2 above, for more comment on Kinyanjui.

23. C.W.L. Bulpett (ed.), *John Boyes, King of the Wa-Kikuyu* (London, 1911).

24. Leakey, *Southern Kikuyu*, vol. i, p. 480; Godfrey Muriuki, 'Virginia Edith Wambui Otieno: a genealogy', in Ojwang and Mugambi, *S.M. Otieno Case*, pp. 186-8.

25. For the place of all three in Kikuyu history, see Godfrey Muriuki, *A History of the Kikuyu 1500-1900* (Nairobi, 1974), pp. 143-53, 158-63, 174-5.

26. A highly appropriate term from the work of Anthony Giddens.

27. For the most complete dependence on the elders see, Leakey, *Southern Kikuyu*, vol. I, pp. xii-xv. Kenyatta (*Facing Mount Kenya*, p. xviii) learned much from his own elders; as district commissioner, Lambert was sympathetic to the elders' view. Prins (*Age-class Systems*, pp. 8, 47, 50, 109, 112) deferred to Peter Mbiyu Koinange, who claimed the status of ruling elder. For accounts more sceptical of authority, see the Routledges' *Prehistoric People* and Kershaw's 'Land is people'; both works give unusual attention to women's views.

28. David M. Feldman, 'Christians and politics: the origins of the Kikuyu Central Association in northern Murang'a 1890-1930' (Cambridge University Ph.D., 1978) first argued this case.

29. On the assumption that the 198 Kikuyu subclans claiming to have suffered land alienation in *KLCE*, i, pp. 261-5, gave their *aramati*, or young men qualified by lineage standing to become such, as their 'representatives'. One-third of these were Christians by 1932.

30. The position has scarcely changed from that given by Terence Ranger in 'Personal reminiscence and the experience of the people in East Central Africa', ch. 7 in B. Bernardi *et al.* (eds), *Fonti orali: antropologia e storia* (Milano, 1978), but Gikoyo, *We Fought*, published a year later, is the story of an unschooled man.

31. Muthoni Likimani's fictionalized accounts, in her *Passbook Number F. 47927* (Basingstoke, 1985) are not *by* a poor woman. For lives of 'ordinary' rural women see, Davison, *Mutira*; for rural activists, Cora Presley, 'Kikuyu women and their nationalism' (Stanford University Ph.D, 1986); for women (many of them Kikuyu) who lived out a contradiction of rural society while deferring to some of its values, Luise White, *The Comforts of Home: Prostitution in Colonial Nairobi* (Chicago and London, 1990).

32. Wanjiru wa Kinyua to editor, *Muigwithania* 1, xii (May 1929), p. 7; Wanjiru was a squatter at Ngata farm, Njoro, where, 20 years later, government first stumbled on Mau Mau: CO, *Historical Survey of the Origins and Growth of Mau Mau.* (Cmd 1030, 1960), cited henceforth as *Corfield Report*.

33. Barra *Proverbs*, no. 811.

34. Kershaw, 'Land is people', p. 335.

35. Tabitha Kanogo, *Squatters and the Roots of Mau Mau 1905-63*, (London, 1987) pp. 22-3.

36. Quoted as a common saying by Henry Mwangi Gichuiri in *Muigwithania* 1: vi (Oct 1928), p. 7.

37. M.W.H. Beech, '*The* Kikuyu point of view', 12 December 1912: KNA, PC/CP. 1/4/2: Kiambu Political Record Book, part ii; reproduced in G.H. Mungeam (ed.), *Kenya: Select Historical Documents 1884-1923* (Nairobi, 1978), pp. 477-9 (my emphasis in title).

38. T.G. Benson (ed.), *Kikuyu–English Dictionary* (Oxford, 1964); *English–Kikuyu Dictionary*, compiled by A. Ruffell Barlow, ed. by Benson (Oxford, 1975); cited hereafter as Benson (1964) and Benson (1975).

39. I am grateful to Tabitha Kanogo, John K. Karanja, Mungai Mbayah, Karega Munene, Henry Muoria Mwaniki, Godfrey Muriuki and George K. Waruhiu but exonerate them from responsibility for the errors that remain.

40. I am suggesting that Kikuyu thought, however serviceable to a dominant minority, was socially negotiated like other hegemonic political theories, for which, see Antonio Gramsci, *Selections from the Prison Notebooks* (London, 1971).

41. My predicament mirrors that of the Kikuyu Central Association, who prefaced their statement to the Land Commission with the complaint that they had 'to borrow means and methods and ape the manner in which the case may appeal to you from your point of view and according to your standards of measuring the requirements of a people who from the alien point of view are a species of living being which was hardly known to them about fifty years ago.' Memorandum of 1 Dec 1932, *KLCE*, i, p. 191.

42. Njururi, *Proverbs*, no. 60.

43. As in Chapters 2, 3, 4 and 9, above.

44. See Chapter 7 above.

45. Colonial Kenya had a submerged civil society. The chief critics were professional men retired from colonial service, the doctor Norman Leys, in *Kenya* (London, 1924) or the engineer W. McGregor Ross, in *Kenya from Within* (London, 1927); or an academic like L.S.B. Leakey, in *Kenya Contrasts and Problems* (London, 1936). Missionaries could champion African interests: see Roland Oliver, *The Missionary Factor in East Africa* (London, 1952), esp. ch. 5, and Leon P. Spencer, 'Christian missions and African interests in Kenya, 1905–1924' (Syracuse University PhD, 1975). There was also the 'protest voice' among field officers, for which see T.H.R. Cashmore, 'Studies in district administration in the East Africa Protectorate 1895–1918' (Cambridge University PhD, 1965), pp. 7, 48, 62–3, 78–89, 102–6, 109–12, 118–19; and Bruce Berman, *Control and Crisis in Colonial Kenya: The Dialectics of Domination* (London, 1990), pp. 110, 138, 152–4, 161. Indian and British lawyers were keen critics of executive decision. When Africans first reached professional status in the 1940s and enjoyed some of the respect officially conceded to certificated knowledge, they were difficult to silence.

46. Zolberg, *Creating Political Order*, pp. 128–34; this discussion of postcolonial Africa applied equally to the colonial era.

47. Generally, J.M. Lee, *Colonial Rule and Good Government: A Study of the Ideas Expressed by the British Official Classes in Planning Decolonization 1939–1964* (Oxford, 1967). For Kenya, Berman, *Control and Crisis*, esp. chs 3, 5 and 6.

48. Ronald Hyam, *Empire and Sexuality: the British Experience* (Manchester and New York, 1990).

49. For despair, John Dunn and A.F. Robertson, *Dependence and Opportunity, Political Change in Ahafo* (Cambridge, 1973), p. 168; and desire, Luise White, 'Separating the men from the boys: constructions of gender, sexuality and terrorism in central Kenya, 1939–1959', *International Journal of African Historical Studies* 25(1) (1990), pp. 4–6.

50. For the goat bag, Charles Chenevix Trench, *The Desert's Dusty Face* (Edinburgh, 1964), pp. 4–5; the first British rulers in India 'shook the pagoda tree' of public power for private profit.

51. For a withering attack on this core weakness of colonial rule in Kenya, where whites were not noted for Christian forbearance, see J.C. Carothers, *The Psychology of Mau Mau* (Government Printer, Nairobi, 1954), pp. 26–7. For some Africans' very Anglican association of state and religion see F.B. Welbourn and B.A. Ogot, *A Place to Feel at Home: A Study of Two Independent Churches in Western Kenya* (London and

Nairobi, 1966), p. 19; and for the spiritual unease of both Africans and British officials, Karen E. Fields, *Revival and Rebellion in Colonial Central Africa* (Princeton, 1985).

52. H.E. Lambert, 'Foreword' to Norman Humphrey, *The Liguru and the Land* (Nairobi, 1947), pp. i–ii; David Throup, *Economic and Social Origins of Mau Mau* (London, 1987), pp. 72–7.

53. For which see Berman, *Control and Crisis*, ch. 3.

54. The classic study is J. Gus Liebenow, *Colonial Rule and Political Development in Tanzania: The Case of the Makonde* (Evanston, 1971), pp. 138–50; for Kikuyu, Leakey, *Mau Mau and the Kikuyu*, p. 63; Graham Greene, *Ways of Escape* (London, 1980), pp. 200–1.

55. Arthur Phillips, *Report on Native Tribunals* (Nairobi, 1945).

56. For which, see note 116, p. 310 above.

57. See Chapters 4 and 5, above.

58. See Chapter 10, above; and Berman, *Control and Crisis*, chs 6 and 7; F. Cooper, 'Mau Mau and the discourses of decolonization' *Journal of African History* 29 (1988), pp. 313–20; Throup, *Origins*, chs 4, 7 and 9.

59. Berman, *Control and Crisis*, pp. 314–22; compare Richard Crook, 'Legitimacy, authority and the transfer of power in Ghana', *Political Studies* vol. 35 (1987), pp. 552–72.

60. For official guilt over the squatters' plight, see Anthony Clayton and Donald C. Savage, *Government and Labour in Kenya 1895–1963* (London, 1974), pp. 305–11, 336, 356–7, 360–3; Throup, *Origins*, pp. 99–110. For magistrates' concern for dependent lineage rights threatened by seniors, Phillips, *Native Tribunals*, pp. 49, 52, 59, 64–5; Gordon Wilson, *Luo Customary Law and Marriage Laws Customs* (Nairobi, 1961).

61. Robert M. Maxon, *Conflict and Accommodation in Western Kenya: The Gusii and the British, 1907–1963* (London and Toronto, 1990) shows how comfortable relations between state and ethnicity could be.

62. For eyewitness evidence, see 1903–4 mission diary entries in Cavicchi, *Problems*, pp. 112–13, and E. May Crawford, *By the Equator's Snowy Peak* (London, 1913), pp. 36–7; for analysis, Feldman, 'Christians and politics', p. 85.

63. Cavicchi, *Problems*, pp. 108–10: quoting a school essay of 1946. I do not know when this version was born; it was alive 20 years later when Muriuki conducted his research: see his *History*, p. 133. For Kabira and wa Mutahi, *Gikuyu Oral Literature*, p. 7, the story serves male domination.

64. L.J. Beecher, 'The stories of the Kikuyu', *Africa* 11 (1938), pp. 80–1. By 1970 some thought Wangu had herself been one of the legendary matriarchs: Taban lo Liyong (ed.), *Popular Culture of East Africa* (Nairobi, 1972), pp. 83–4.

65. *Mumenyereri*, 20 September 1952, p. 4.

66. Wamweya, *Freedom Fighter*, p. 57; Wachanga, *Kirinyaga*, p. 192.

67. Cavicchi, *Problems*, pp. 114–15, quoting a priest who taught in Kikuyu from 1952 to 1964.

68. Chang Hwan Kim, 'Africanization and the rise of a managerial class in Kenya: an empirical study' (Oxford University D.Phil, 1986), pp. 280, 284–8.

69. J. Irungu and J. Shimanyula, *Treachery in Fort-Hall* (Nairobi, 1984).

70. In 'No Easy Walk: Kenya'; Acacia Productions for Channel Four Television, broadcast 5 September 1987.

71. See discussion in John Lonsdale, 'Mau Maus of the mind', *Journal of African History* 31(3) (1990), pp. 416–19; for *wiathi*, Benson (1964), pp. 18, 194.

72. Renison M. Githige, 'The religious factor in Mau Mau, with particular reference to Mau Mau oaths' (Nairobi University MA thesis, 1978), p. 61. For *athuuri*, Cavicchi, *Problems*, p. 17; Benson (1964), pp. 532–3; missionaries used another derivative of the verb *thuura* (to choose) for the biblical last judgment.

73. Kenyatta, *Facing Mount Kenya*, pp. 8–11.

74. Clark, 'Land and food'.

Wealth, Poverty & Civic Virtue in Kikuyu Political Thought

75. *Corfield Report*, p. 200. Kenyatta was perhaps heard as expounding the proverb *Muregi gwathwo ndangihota gwathana*, 'he who refuses to obey cannot command': Barra, *Proverbs*, no. 526.

76. As proudly claimed by the women whom Davison recorded in *Mutira*. 'No gain without pain' is the moral of no less than 88 (9 per cent) of Barra's *Proverbs*, as perhaps one would find in any culture.

77. Kenyatta, *Facing Mount Kenya*, pp. 141-2, 188, 193.

78. Githige, 'Religious factor', pp. 164-5, believes that the use of *kurua* (circumcision) for 'oath' reflected a need for secrecy, not moral analogy. For contrary evidence, Rob Buijtenhuijs, *Essays on Mau Mau: Contributions to Mau Mau Historiography* (Leiden, 1982), pp. 82-4.

79. Another synonym for Mau Mau.

80. Barra, *Proverbs*, no. 23; Njururi, *Proverbs*, no. 28; neither gives my gloss, which I owe to H.M. Mwaniki; compare the proverb quoted as an epigraph at the beginning of the previous chapter and Prins, *Age-Class Systems*, p. 52.

81. See, especially, Ernest Gellner, *Nations and Nationalism* (Oxford, 1983).

82. 'Left' modernization theory was as much deceived as 'right'. Leroy Vail would not now, as he did in *The Creation of Tribalism in Southern Africa* (London & Los Angeles, 1989), p. 2, illustrate its hopes for pan-ethnic class consciousness with the thought that Africa 'would be a continent of new Yugoslavias'.

83. Thomas Hodgkin, *African Political Parties* (Harmondsworth, 1961), p. 36-7.

84. Edward Shils, *Political Development in the New States* (The Hague & Paris, 1964), p. 31.

85. Leakey, *Southern Kikuyu*, i, pp. 90-105, 485-91.

86. See Chapter 2, above, and the sources cited in its notes 9 and 17, to which should be added Charles H. Ambler, *Kenyan Communities in the Age of Imperialism: the Central Region in the Late Nineteenth Century* (New Haven and London, 1988).

87. Vail, 'Introduction' to *Creation of Tribalism*, p. 15.

88. Eugen Weber, *Peasants into Frenchmen: The Modernization of Rural France 1870-1914* (London, 1977).

89. David W. Cohen, 'Doing social history from Pim's doorway', ch. 4 in O. Zunz (ed.), *Reliving the Past: The Worlds of Social History* (Chapel Hill, NC, 1985).

90. For a recent literature review see, Terence Ranger, 'Ethnicity and nationality in southern Africa: eastern European resonances', paper presented to Moscow Institute of African Studies, 1990.

91. Arguing generally as I am here, 'clan' is a permissible imprecision, meaning a small, to varying degrees fictive, kin segment. For Kikuyu the appropriate term would be *mbari*, subclan. The 'nine clans' of Kikuyu, the *mihiriga*, had almost no political presence.

92. These three paragraphs have developed the contrasts between the conscious building of state power and its vulgar formation introduced in Chapter 2, above.

93. As hoped for in Mugo Gatheru, *Child of Two Worlds*, p. v.

94. For speculation that Kenyatta used this axiom to point a political moral, see note 75 above.

95. Gikoyo, *We Fought*, p. 289.

96. Gakaara wa Wanjau, in interview for John Spencer, 30 April 1972; I am much indebted to Prefessor Spencer for copies of the interview transcripts, which provide much of the data for his *KAU*.

97. Barnett and Njama, *Within*, p. 246.

98. Evidence of chief Koinange and Canon Leakey, *KLCE*, i, pp. 167, 865.

99. Barra, *Proverbs*, no. 282; see also nos 43 and 722.

100. Benson (1964), p. 229; Routledge, *Prehistoric People*, pp. 243-4; Leakey, *Southern Kikuyu*, iii, pp. 1105.

101. He employed it in two articles in one issue of *Muigwithania*, i, 7 (Nov 1928), 'Let

us agree among ourselves' and 'Bearing up the Kikuyu nation'; his brother James Muigai used it in the next issue, writing to the editor (Kenyatta).

102. British scepticism about the seriousness of the curse featured in Kenyatta's trial: Montagu Slater, *The Trial of Jomo Kenyatta* (London, 1955), pp. 156-7, 167, 175-6, 186, 238. In the 1970s Kaggia (*Roots*, pp. 113- 14), appeared to agree that Kenyatta was evasive but his thoughts were censored; since Kenyatta's death, Kaggia has taken the opposite view: Granada Television, 'End of Empire: Kenya', screened 1 July 1985. My argument about his title is an interpretation that I have not tried to confirm with the author.

103. Eric Sherbrooke Walker, *Treetops Hotel* (London, 1962), pp. 111-12, 128, 138. Kikuyu attitudes to monarchy are discussed below.

104. Carl C. Rosberg and John Nottingham, *The Myth of 'Mau Mau': Nationalism in Kenya* (New York & London, 1966) pp. 181, 370; Ian Henderson, with Philip Goodhart, *The Hunt for Dedan Kimathi* (London, 1958), p. 267.

105. East Africa Command, *A Handbook on Anti-Mau Mau Operations* (Nairobi, 1954), pp. 99-104, 3-5.

106. Leakey, *Southern Kikuyu* i, pp. 168-9; Professor Kershaw, in personal communication.

107. Carothers, *Psychology*, pp. 4-5.

108. Ngugi wa Thiong'o, *Petals of Blood* (London, 1977), p. 68.

109. Muriuki, *History*, pp. 52-4.

110. Charles Dundas, 'The organization and laws of some Bantu tribes in East Africa', *Journal of the Royal Anthropological Institute*, vol. 45, NS vol. 18 (1915), 297; Kenyatta, *Facing Mount Kenya*, p. 27.

111. lo Liyong, *Popular Culture*, p. 83.

112. Njururi, *Proverbs*, no. 386.

113. The literature on Kikuyu land tenure is large and contentious. Most accessible are Gavin Kitching, *Class and Economic Change in Kenya: The Making of an African Petite Bourgeoisie* (New Haven, 1980), pp. 280-3; Middleton and Kershaw, *Kikuyu and Kamba*, pp. 48-52; Muriuki, *History*, pp. 73-82; and M.P.K. Sorrenson, *Land Reform in the Kikuyu Country* (Nairobi & London, 1967), ch. 1, but I have learned most from Kershaw, 'Land is people' and personal communication, especially on the subject of the *mbari* oath.

114. Cavicchi, *Problems*, pp. 31-3, quoting the press of 1929 and oral statements of 1947. The Yoruba of Nigeria say the same: Sara S. Berry, *Fathers Work for Their Sons* (Berkeley and Los Angeles, 1984).

115. Cavicchi, *Problems*, p. 11; Benson (1964), p. 189.

116. Barra, *Proverbs*, has 37 proverbs with these meanings.

117. *Ibid.*, no. 104; Benson (1964), p. 84.

118. Barra, *Proverbs*, nos. 964, 978. President Kenyatta used such sayings to argue against socialism; see, Robert Buijtenhuijs, *Mau Mau Twenty Years After: The Myth and the Survivors* (The Hague, 1973), p. 32. Samuel L. Popkin, *The Rational Peasant: The Political Economy of Rural Society in Vietnam* (Berkeley and Los Angeles, 1979), pp. 24-7, discusses this 'free rider' problem.

119. Barra, *Proverbs*, no. 33 (and 19 others of similar meaning).

120. Dundas, 'Organization and laws', p. 303.

121. Kenyatta, *Facing Mount Kenya*, p. 257; see also A.W. McGregor, 'Kikuyu and its people', *Church Missionary Review* 60 (1909), p. 30; Leakey, *Southern Kikuyu* i, p. 48; H.E. Lambert, *The Systems of Land Tenure in the Kikuyu Land Unit* (University of Cape Town [1949] 1963), p. 20.

122. Muriuki, *History*, pp. 32-3.

123. Benson (1964), p. 18, but my exegesis.

124. von Hohnel, *Lakes Rudolf and Stefanie* i, pp. 310, 314.

125. B.E. Kipkorir, 'The Alliance high school and the origins of the Kenya African elite

1926-1962' (Cambridge University PhD, 1969), pp. 343-6.

126. For the general cultural conditions of colonization, see Igor Kopytoff (ed.), *The African Frontier: The Reproduction of Traditional African Societies* (Bloomington, 1987), ch. 1.

127. For uphill migration to Kikuyu, see R.D. Waller, 'The lords of East Africa: the Maasai in the mid-nineteenth century' (Cambridge University PhD, 1978), pp. 320-6, 339-44 and Ambler, *Kenyan Communities*, although the Kikuyu case is at the periphery of Ambler's historical vision.

128. Muriuki, *History*, pp. 37-61, 113-15.

129. *Ibid.*, p. 133.

130. For the rarity of both strong lineage systems and corporate age organizations in common, see Jack Glazier, *Land and the Uses of Tradition among the Mbeere of Kenya* (Lanham, Md, and London, 1985), pp. 71-2; for a comparative approach baffled by the peculiarity of the Kikuyu, see Bernardo Bernardi, *Age Class Systems: Social Institutions and Polities Based on Age* (Cambridge, 1985).

131. Annual age (or circumcision) sets were periodically grouped as regimental sets, with a few years of 'closure' of male – but not female – circumcision during the period of regiment formation. The clearest, perhaps too clear, account is in Prins, *Age-class Systems*. The *ituika* process of generational succession is discussed below.

132. Cowen, 'Differentiation', p. 4.

133. Kershaw, 'Land is people', pp. 112-22; Samuel Kibicho, 'The continuity of the African conception of God into and through Christianity: a Kikuyu case study', in E. Fashole-Luke *et al.* (eds), *Christianity in Independent Africa* (London, 1978), p. 386; Valeer Neckebrouck, *Le peuple affligé: les déterminants de la fissiparité dans un nouveau mouvement religieux au Kenya central* (Immensee, 1983), pp. 257, 280-1; Leakey, *Southern Kikuyu*, ii, pp. 551-65, 588-701, 938, 967, 975, 986, details the differences between the guilds without explaining them.

134. Brian G. McIntosh, 'The Scottish Mission in Kenya, 1891-1923' (Edinburgh University PhD thesis, 1969), pp. 302-7, tells how Kikuyu catechists from southern *mbari* were ridiculed further north.

135. Peter Marris and Anthony Somerset, *African Businessmen: A Study of Entrepreneurship and Development in Kenya* (London, 1971), pp. 30-2; Barra, *Proverbs*, nos. 983, 984; Njururi, *Proverbs*, nos. 575, 576.

136. Leakey, *Southern Kikuyu*, i, pp. 461, 494.

137. Benson (1964), pp. 108, 253, 308; one derivative of the verb *gera*, to measure, was an 'examiner' or 'tempter', which missionaries used for the biblical Satan. Both *ngero* and *umaramari* were later applied by senior and successful Kikuyu, including Kenyatta, to the delinquency of Mau Mau; see Lonsdale, 'Mau Maus of the mind', pp. 419-20; I owe the comparative dimension to Richard Waller.

138. Buijtenhuijs, *Mau Mau Twenty Years After*, p. 25; *idem*, *Le Mouvement 'Mau-Mau'*, (Paris, 1971), pp. 42-8.

139. One is reminded of another forest-clearing people, the Asante (who were driven also by the lure of gold), for whom see, especially, Ivor Wilks, 'The golden stool and the elephant tail: an essay on wealth in Asante', *Research in Economic Anthropology* 2 (1979), pp. 1-36; and T.C.McCaskie, 'Accumulation, wealth and belief in Asante history I: to the close of the nineteenth century', *Africa* 53(1) (1983), pp. 23-43.

140. Compare Kershaw, 'Land is people', pp. 1, 39.

141. Benson (1964), p. 284; Kenyatta, *Facing Mount Kenya*, p. 328.

142. Benson (1964), p. 459; for equatorial Africa, see Jan Vansina, *Paths in the Rain-forests: Towards a History of Political Tradition in Equatorial Africa* (Madison, 1990), pp. 73-4.

143. J. Kenyatta, 'Igai muhuthia thi twiteithie', *Muigwithania* i, 8 (Dec 1928 - Jan 1929), pp. 1-2.

144. Mutonyi, 'Mau Mau chairman', ch. 4; 'Interrogation of Waruhiu s/o Itote, alias "General China" ' (Kenya Police Special Branch, Nairobi, 26 January 1954), para. 253 (privately held).

145. For the political role of Kiburi house see, Kaggia, *Roots*, pp. 67–8, 80, 97, 103–8, 116; Mutonyi, 'Mau Mau chairman', p. 49.

146. Kim, 'Africanization', p. 284.

147. Geoff Lamb, *Peasant Politics: Conflict and Development in Murang'a* (Lewes, 1974), p. 34.

148. As cautioned by both James C. Scott, *The Moral Economy of the Peasant: Rebellion and Subsistence in Southeast Asia* (New Haven and London, 1976) and his critic Popkin, *Rational Peasant*.

149. Content analysis of proverbs is a crude tool of interpretation but the only one I have for the precolonial period. See Barra, *Proverbs*; the three proverbs critical of the wealthy are nos. 4, 66, 676. The sentiments of Njururi's nearly 600 proverbs were proportionately similar.

150. Kershaw, 'Land is people', p. 17.

151. Benson (1964), p. 330; Michael Cowen, 'Differentiation in a Kenya location', (University of East Africa Social Science Council conference paper, Nairobi, 1972) p. 4.

152. Middleton and Kershaw, *Kikuyu and Kamba*, pp. 50–1; Kershaw, 'Land is people', pp. 54, 60, 73, 91, 216–17, 302–5. Kenyatta, in *Facing Mount Kenya*, chs 2 and 3, said scarcely anything on dependent relations. For a comparative perspective see, John Iliffe, *The African Poor, a History* (Cambridge, 1987), pp. 69–70.

153. All calculations are from Barra, *Proverbs*. For scornful attitudes to poverty, see nos. 27, 81, 125, 131, 171, 229, 234, 360, 466, 495, 538, 569, 718, 811, 846, 917, 938, 943; for a man of compassion, no. 178; for commendation of generosity, nos. 18, 19, 342; for love and economics, nos. 619, 621. See Routledge, *Prehistoric People*, pp. 246–7, for social differentiation in hospitality; and Cagnolo, *Akikuyu*, p. 212, for missionary strictures on the same.

154. The early analyses of gender relations in Routledge, *Prehistoric People*, pp. 120–46 and Dundas, 'Organization and laws', pp. 284–91, 295, 300–3 are strikingly similar to the recent discussions by Clark, 'Land and food' and Greet Kershaw, 'The changing roles of men and women in the Kikuyu family by economic strata', *Rural Africana* 29 (1975–6), pp. 173–93.

155. For the fullest account see, Jocelyn Murray. 'The Kikuyu female circumcision controversy, with special reference to the Church Missionary Society's sphere of influence' (University of California, Los Angeles PhD thesis, 1974). From a large bibliography see also, Marshall Clough, *Fighting Two Sides: Kenyan Chiefs and Politicians 1918–1940* (Niwot, 1990), ch. 7; Feldman, 'Christians and politics', ch. 5; Hyam, *Empire and Sexuality*, pp. 189–97; David P. Sandgren, *Christianity and the Kikuyu: Religious Divisions and Social Conflict* (New York, 1989), ch. 4; Robert W. Strayer, *The Making of Mission Communities in East Africa* (London, 1978), ch. 8; Robert L. Tignor, *The Colonial Transformation of Kenya: the Kamba, Kikuyu, and Maasai from 1900 to 1939* (Princeton, 1976), pp. 235–50.

156. Davison, *Mutira*.

157. Clark, 'Land and food'; Kershaw, 'Changing roles'.

158. Barra, *Proverbs*. See nos. 261, 773, 982 for condemnation of women's uncontrolled sexuality (there is no comparable disapproval of men); for respect for mothers, nos. 70, 71, 112, 145, 185, 419, 488, 497, 507; and criticism of fathers, no. 228.

159. Leakey, *Southern Kikuyu*, i, pp. 502, 508; Njururi, *Tales*, pp. 1–14; Kabira and wa Mutahi, *Oral Literature*, pp. 49–53, 68–78, 81–2.

160. Barra, *Proverbs*, no. 782.

161. Kenyatta, *Facing Mount Kenya*, p. 203; Kershaw, 'Land is people', pp. 79, 175 fn; Benson (1964), pp. 163–4.

162. Routledge, *Prehistoric People*, p. 195.
163. Kenyatta, *Facing Mount Kenya*, is the only authority to suggest a Kikuyu tribal governing structure, but then he was a cultural nationalist to whom the functional anthropology of the interwar years was ideally suited, with its premise of social structures working in close harmony; he was also general secretary of the Kikuyu Central Association, claiming to represent all Kikuyu.
164. Kenyatta, *Facing Mount Kenya*, p. 186, argues that same point, if in more dramatic terms.
165. Barra, *Proverbs*. Over one per cent (nos. 55, 77, 113, 169, 180, 262, 668, 903, 904, 905, 972, 976) said the elderly were a burden; four in a thousand (nos. 144, 224, 278, 754) nonetheless called for their weakness to be respected; only six (nos. 188, 193, 244, 396, 496, 946) indicated that age had positive value because of its wisdom.
166. For structural and conjunctural poverty in land-rich economies such as precolonial Kikuyuland see, Iliffe, *African Poor*, p. 4.
167. Buijtenhuijs, *Essays*, pp. 173-4.
168. For the political economy of conquest see Chapter 2 above.
169. Barra, *Proverbs*, no. 380; see also nos. 9, 46, 150, 151, 265, 266, 267, 268, 483, 654, 739, 786, 870.
170. Cagnolo, *Akikuyu*, pp. 199-202.
171. For a general discussion, see Amartya Sen, *Poverty and Famines: An Essay on Entitlement and Deprivation* (Oxford, 1981).
172. Canon Leakey, *KLCE*, i, p. 865.
173. C.W. Hobley, *Kenya from Chartered Company to Crown Colony* (London, 1929), p. 160.
174. Wachanga, *Kirinyaga*, p. 145.
175. Kershaw, 'Land is people', pp. 177-9; compare Ambler, *Kenyan Communities*, pp. 144-5.
176. Benson (1964), pp. 340-1 (*munyamari*), 522 (*thirimai*), 521 (*muthini*), and 186 (*muimwo*) respectively. These terms do not exhaust the varieties of poverty: see Benson (1975), p. 219.
177. L.S.B. Leakey, 'The economics of Kikuyu tribal life' *East African Economics Review* 3(1) (1956), p. 169.
178. Kershaw, 'Land is people', p. 81.
179. Lambert, *Kikuyu Institutions*, p. 104.
180. Kershaw, 'Land is people', p. 164.
181. Barra, *Proverbs*, nos. 771, 66; Njururi, *Proverbs*, p. 63.
182. A proverb found in neither Barra nor Njururi, which I owe to Henry Muoria Mwaniki.
183. Leakey, *Southern Kikuyu*, ii, p. 735; Kershaw, 'Land is people', p. 161.
184. Kershaw, 'Land is people', p. 80.
185. Kenyatta, *Facing Mount Kenya*, pp. 235-6; Kibicho, 'Continuity of African conception of God', p. 372; Njururi, *Proverbs*, no. 415.
186. Barra, *Proverbs*, nos. 93, 94, 109, 127, 260, 445, 539, 579, 603, 636, 691, 741, 755, 921; Njururi, *Proverbs*, no. 549.
187. Routledge, *Prehistoric People*, p. 231.
188. Leakey, *Southern Kikuyu*, iii, pp. 1211-31; Kenyatta, *Facing Mount Kenya*, pp. 299-308; Routledge, *Prehistoric People*, pp. 272-7.
189. Leakey, *Southern Kikuyu*, iii, pp. 1104-17; Kenyatta, *Facing Mount Kenya*, pp. 263-8; Routledge, *Prehistoric People*, pp. 239-44.
190. C.W. Hobley, *Bantu Beliefs and Magic, with Particular Reference to the Kikuyu and Kamba Tribes of Kenya Colony* (London [1922], 1938), pp. 103-27; see also, Leakey, *Southern Kikuyu*, iii, pp. 1232-77. Kenyatta, *Facing Mount Kenya*, has almost nothing to say about *thahu*, which he translates as 'defilement'. Mary Douglas, *Purity and Danger: An Analysis of Pollution and Taboo* (London, 1966) makes no mention of the Kikuyu

but could have been written with them in mind; and compare Randall Packard, 'Social change and the history of misfortune among the Bashu of eastern Zaire', pp. 237-67 in Ivan Karp and Charles Bird (eds), *Explorations in African Systems of Thought* (Bloomington, 1980).

191. Kenyatta, *Facing Mount Kenya*, pp. 280-99; Leakey, *Southern Kikuyu*, iii, pp. 1120-210 (p. 1141 for the poor novice); Routledge, *Prehistoric People*, pp. 249-68.

192. Routledge, *Prehistoric People*, p. 118.

193. Barra, *Proverbs*, no. 945; Kabira and wa Mutahi, *Gikuyu Oral Literature*, pp. 68-73; Cavicchi, *Problems*, pp. 51, 53. See also Ngugi, *Petals*, p. 6, for playground defecation as a curse on a new school.

194. Cagnolo, *Agikuyu*, pp. 139-46; Hobley, *Bantu Beliefs*, pp. 27-31, 97-101; Leakey, *Southern Kikuyu*, ii, pp. 938-91, iii, pp. 1103-19; Routledge, *Prehistoric People*, pp. 168-73, 239-44. Kenyatta, *Facing Mount Kenya*, pp. 13-14, 263-8, writes of communion with ancestors without mentioning disposal of the dead.

195. The first Scots missionaries in Kikuyu were kept awake by hyenas cracking the bones of the recently dead nearby, while 50 years later British soldiers were told that the howl of a hyena might indicate a Mau Mau raid: McIntosh, 'Scottish mission', p. 164; East Africa Command, *Handbook*, p. 39.

196. In chronological order, my authorities on *ituika* are: McGregor, 'Kikuyu and its people', pp. 32-3; Routledge, *Prehistoric People* (1911), pp. 237-8, 307-14; Dundas, 'Organization and laws' (1915), pp. 244-7; Hobley, *Bantu Beliefs* (pre-1914 information), pp. 92-6; DC Fort Hall to PC Nyeri, 8 August 1919, KNA: PC/CP. 1/7/1; Lambert, *Kikuyu Social and Political Institutions* (information from early 1930s), pp. 58-65; Cagnolo, *Akikuyu* (1933), pp. 120-5; Parmenas Githendu Mockerie, *An African Speaks for His People* (London, 1934), pp. 36-41; Kenyatta, *Facing Mount Kenya* (1938), pp. 186-94; Leakey, *Southern Kikuyu*, iii (research thwarted, 1937-8), pp. 1278-84; Prins, *Age-class Systems* (1953), pp. 41-57, 116-18; Muriuki, *History* (1974), pp. 21-4, 109; see also Benson (1964), pp. 248, 463-5, 467.

197. Leakey, *Southern Kikuyu*, iii, p. 1279.

198. Cavicchi, *Problems*, p. 19; see also Benson (1964), pp. 12-13.

199. In addition to the sources cited for *ituika*, see Benson (1964), pp. 245, 289; Gerhard Lindblom, *The Akamba, an Ethnological Monograph* (Uppsala, 1920), p. 274; Njururi, *Tales from Mount Kenya*, pp. 74-83: 'The story of moon and sun'. *Ndamathia* is clearly related to other devouring yet life-giving dragons found in other human imaginations. For other African examples see, T.O. Beidelman, *Moral Imagination in Kaguru Modes of Thought* (Bloomington, 1986), pp. 173-7; Luc de Heusch, *The Drunken King, or the Origin of the State* (Bloomington, 1982), ch. 2; Gwyn Prins, *The Hidden Hippopotamus* (Cambridge, 1980), pp. 19, 121; Thomas Q. Reefe, *The Rainbow and the Kings: A History of the Luba Empire to 1891* (Berkeley and Los Angeles, 1981), ch. 3; Alice Werner, *Myths and Legends of the Bantu* (London, 1933), chs 14 and 15.

200. Prins, *Age-class Systems*, p. 43, summarizes the contending proposals.

201. Compare Muriuki, *History*, p. 21 (generations and *ituika*) and Cagnolo, *Akikuyu*, pp. 199-202 (famines).

202. Kershaw, 'Land is people', pp. 153-69, 177-85.

203. *Ibid.*; Peter Rogers, 'The British and the Kikuyu 1890-1905: a reassessment', *Journal of African History* 20 (1979), pp. 261-4, quoting as part of his evidence the oral tradition collected by Muriuki.

204. According to Cagnolo, *Akikuyu*, p. 202, there was a 'famine of sweeping the courtyard' in 1840, shortly after a possible *ituika*, which may indicate how the new generation sought to impress its authority and avert calamity.

205. For what might be done see, Patrick Harries, 'Exclusion, classification and internal colonialism: the emergence of ethnicity among the Tsonga-speakers of South Africa' and Terence Ranger, 'Missionaries, migrants and the Manyika: the invention of

ethnicity in Zimbabwe', chs 3 and 4 in Vail (ed.), *Creation of Tribalism*. Kikuyu and Embu share the same Bible; their early scriptures seem also to have been used for some years in Meru, judging by the relative delay in Meru translations: David B. Barrett *et al.* (eds), *Kenya Churches Handbook* (Kisumu, 1973), p. 99.

206. For Meru, see B. Bernardi, *The Mugwe, a Failing Prophet* (London, 1959), pp. 116–18.

207. Bernadi, *Mugwe*, pp. 22–4, 90–7; J. Glazier, 'Generation classes among the Mbeere of central Kenya', *Africa* 46 (1976), pp. 313–26; Lambert, *Kikuyu Social and Political Institutions*, pp. 62–5; H.S.K. Mwaniki, *The Living History of Embu and Mbeere to 1906* (Nairobi, 1973), pp. 53–5; Satish Saberwal, *The Traditional Political System of the Embu of Central Kenya* (Nairobi, 1970), pp. 47–68.

208. See, for example, Gideon Mugo Kagika to editor, 'Unity in the common ancestor', *Muigwithania* i, 3 (July 1928), p. 10; and 'tea party' advertisements at the back of *Mumenyereri*, 20 Sept 1952.

209. Muriuki, *History*, pp. 88–97, 145–70; Rogers, 'British and Kikuyu'.

210. Kershaw, 'Land is people', pp. 88–90.

211. Muriuki, pp. 94–5; Kershaw, 'Land is people', pp. 90–4, 173–7 and (for *mbari* and *riika* oaths) personal communication; Benson (1964), p. 254; Church of Scotland foreign missions committee, *Mau Mau and the Church* (Edinburgh, 1953), p. 5.

212. Kershaw, 'Land is people', pp. 17–24.

213. To adopt the concepts of Anthony Giddens, *Central Problems in Social Theory* (London, 1979).

214. Compare Scott, *Moral Economy*, pp. 157–60; Prins, *Hidden Hippopotamus*, pp. 13–14.

215. Karl Marx, *Capital*, i, (Harmondsworth, 1976), pp. 701–6, 1067–71; *idem, The Eighteenth Brumaire of Louis Bonaparte* (Moscow, 1954), p. 10.

216. See Chapter 4, above.

217. Compare E.P. Thompson, *The Making of the English Working Class* (London, 1965), p. 194.

218. Compare Keith Hart, 'Swindler or public benefactor? The entrepreneur in his community', pp. 1–35 in Jack Goody (ed.), *Changing Social Structure in Ghana* (London, 1975).

219. Asked by George K. Ndegwa and indirectly answered by Petro Kigondu, both KCA leaders: *Muigwithania* i, 4 (August 1928), p. 10; *ibid.* i, 7 (November 1928), p. 7.

220. See pp. 33–9 and Chapter 4, above.

221. Arguments against migrant labour are discussed below. For chief Koinange's criticisms of Maasai and settlers: *KLCE*, i, pp. 130, 167.

222. Kenyatta's confusion between these named generations in *ibid.*, pp. 423–4. For their possible place in history, Muriuki, *History*, p. 21, and in constructing nationalism, below.

223. Kibicho, 'Continuity', pp. 370–88, for a contrary view.

224. M.P.K. Sorrenson, *Origins of European Settlement in Kenya* (Nairobi, 1968), pp. 176–89; now revised by John Overton, 'The origins of the Kikuyu land problem: land alienation and land use in Kiambu, 1895–1920', *African Studies Review* 31 (2) (1988), pp. 109–26.

225. For the political history not given here see, in published sequence: *Corfield Report*; Rosberg and Nottingham, *Myth*; Sorrenson, *Land Reform*; Buijtenhuijs, *Mouvement 'Mau-Mau'*; Murray-Brown, *Kenyatta*; Tignor, *Colonial Transformation*; Spencer, *KAU*; Throup, *Origins*; Kanogo, *Squatters*; Furedi, *Mau Mau War*; Clough, *Two Sides*. And three theses: Feldman, 'Christians and politics'; Presley, 'Kikuyu women'; E.N. Wamagatta, 'A biography of senior chief Waruhiu wa Kung'u of Githunguri' (Nairobi University MA, 1988).

226. See Chapter 6, above.

227. Cowen, 'Differentiation'; Kitching, *Class and Economic Change*, esp. pp. 244–6; John Iliffe, *The Emergence of African Capitalism* (London, 1983), ch. 2.

228. White, *Comforts*, pp. 31-42, and, for differing views, Janet M. Bujra, 'Women "entrepreneurs" of early Nairobi', *Canadian Journal of African Studies* 9 (2) (1975), pp. 216-20.

229. Sorrenson, *Land Reform*; Cowen 'Differentiation', 'Capital and household production', and 'Commodity production in Kenya's Central Province', ch. 5 in Judith Heyer *et al.* (eds), *Rural Development in Tropical Africa* (London, 1981); Kitching, *Class and Economic Change*, pp. 29-39, 62-73, 110-30; David Anderson and David Throup, 'The agrarian economy of Central Province, Kenya, 1918-1939', ch. 1 in Ian Brown (ed.), *The Economies of Africa and Asia in the Inter-war Depression* (London, 1989).

230. *Native Labour Commission 1912-13*, pp. 130, 183, 232-7: witnesses Mwangi, Kinyanjui, Wambura, Gatororo, Kori, Kamao wa Kabiam, Kamao wa Mushiri, Mbatia, Makumi, and Njeroge.

231. Marion W. Forrester, *Kenya To-day: Social Prerequisites for Economic Development* (The Hague, 1962), pp. 75-6, 116-29.

232. Compare Joan Vincent, *African Elite, the Big Men of a Small Town* (New York, 1971).

233. In sequence: Beech, 'The Kikuyu point of view'; sworn statement (against Thuku) by Wamarema Kimani, 16 February 1922, in Northey to Churchill, 21 July 1922: PRO, CO533/280; Kenyatta, 'Let us agree among ourselves and exalt the Kikuyu', *Muigwithania* i, 7 (November 1928), pp. 2-3; Leakey, *Defeating Mau Mau*, p. 64; Mutonyi, 'Mau Mau chairman', p. 79; wa Kinyatti, *Thunder*, p. 31; for my gloss on *thaka*: Leakey, *Southern Kikuyu*, iii, p. 1368 and Gatheru, *Child of Two Worlds*, p. 42.

234. Bujra, 'Women entrepreneurs', pp. 225-34; White, *Comforts*, ch. 6.

235. Frederick Cooper, *On the African Waterfront* (New Haven and London, 1987).

236. Mary Parker, 'Political and social aspects of the development of municipal government in Kenya with special reference to Nairobi' (report to Colonial Office, 1948), pp. 196-7 and Appendix 5.

237. Mathu, *Urban Guerrilla*, pp. 28-9; J.M. Bujra, 'Ethnicity and religion: a case-study from Pumwani, Nairobi' (Institute of African Studies, Nairobi, 1970), pp. 10-11; White, *Comforts*, p. 209. The relation of Islam to Mau Mau needs research; in rural Embu, Nairobi Muslims were strong supporters: David Throup, 'Mau Mau in Embu' (Cambridge workshop on 'Constructing Terror', 1991).

238. White, *Comforts*, p. 191.

239. For Mau Mau views on Nairobi's thieves and prostitutes see: *ibid.*, pp. 204-20; Spencer, *KAU*, p. 208, quoting Fred Kubai; *idem*, *James Beauttah*, p. 97; Kariuki, *'Mau Mau' Detainee*, p. 23; Kaggia, *Roots*, pp. 96-7; Mutonyi, 'Mau Mau chairman', pp. 48, 68, 106-7, 114-15.

240. Mathu, *Urban Guerrilla*, pp. 12, 18, 23; Mathu's nickname, Mohamed, implied no adherence to Islam.

241. White, *Comforts*, pp. 190-3; Mutonyi, 'Mau Mau chairman', pp. 51-2.

242. Kaggia, *Roots*, p. 57.

243. Kitching, *Class and Economic Change*, pp. 220-33; Press Office summary of African press opinions, 1946-51: KNA, PC/RVP.2/27/34.

244. M.P. Cowen and J.R. Newman, 'Real wages in central Kenya 1924-74', (mimeo, nd).

245. Kitching, *Class and Economic Change*, pp. 280-97; Robert H. Bates, *Beyond the Miracle of the Market: the Political Economy of Agrarian Development in Kenya* (Cambridge, 1989), pp. 27-31.

246. Kershaw, 'Changing roles of men and women', pp. 185-91; for 1950, see Jeanne M. Fisher, *The Anatomy of Kikuyu Domesticity and Husbandry* (Department of Technical Co-operation, London, 1955).

247. Compare Bill Bravman, 'Struggle over the terms of society: a social history of the Wataita 1883-1951' (Stanford University PhD thesis, 1991).

248. G. Kershaw, 'Land, employment and income in the development of inequality' (Ms, 1986), pp. 3-4.

249. Mwangi Waide and paramount chief Wambugu, to *Native Labour Commission*, pp. 130, 201; I infer the high status of skins from photographs in Routledge, *Prehistoric People*, and discussion of stock ownership in Kershaw, 'Land is people', pp. 77-81, 208-38. For the politics of deference: James C. Scott, *Weapons of the Weak: Everyday Forms of Peasant Resistance* (New Haven and London, 1985).

250. M.W. Beech (quoting Kiambu elders) and chief Wambugu: *Native Labour Commission*, pp. 72, 201. For the lexicon of work: Benson (1964), pp. 413, 535, 561; Benson (1975), p. 328; Cowen, 'Differentiation', pp. 3-4; Leakey, *Southern Kikuyu*, iii, p. 1368; Wanyoike, *African Pastor*, p. 15.

251. W. Caine, Dr Horace Philp and Dr Norman Leys, *Native Labour Commission*, pp. 13, 206, 272.

252. *Ibid.*, pp. 236, 238.

253. Clough, *Two Sides*, pp. 50, 195.

254. Compare Vail, Preface to *Creation of Tribalism*, p. ix.

255. For which see Cowen, 'Capital and household production'.

256. Kershaw, 'Land is people', pp. 102-7, 309.

257. Overton, 'Kikuyu land problem', pp. 118-20; Kitching, *Class and Economic Change*, pp. 212-26.

258. Roger van Zwanenberg, *Colonial Capitalism and Labour in Kenya 1919-1939* (Nairobi, 1975), pp. 210-74; Kanogo, *Squatters*, pp. 8-95; Furedi, *Mau Mau War*, pp. 22-74.

259. Wambaa and King, 'Squatter perspective', pp. 195-7.

260. To compare squatter migration to precolonial land settlement; see above, p. 14.

261. Wambaa and King, 'Squatter perspective', pp. 197-9; *Native Labour Commission*, pp. 214-16, 229-31.

262. For Nyeri, see *Report of Committee on Native Land Tenure in Kikuyu Province* (Nairobi, 1929), p. 44; Muriuki, *History*, p. 176; Cowen, 'Differentiation' and 'Patterns of cattle ownership and dairy production 1900-1965' (IDS Nairobi, 1965).

263. Compare *Committee on Native Land Tenure*, pp. 15, 22-7; Kenyatta, *Facing Mount Kenya*, pp. 22, 30, 34-5, 44; Leakey, *Southern Kikuyu*, i, pp. 115-22; Fisher, *Kikuyu Domesticity*, pp. 207-13; Middleton and Kershaw, *Kikuyu and Kamba*, pp. 50-1, with: Thuku, *Autobiography*, p. 57; and Wanyoike, *African Pastor*, pp. 1, 7-9, 18, 23, 175 (a good source for the coarsening terms of clientage).

264. Kikuyu Association to Governor Sir Edward Grigg, 25 November 1925: KNA, PC/CP. 8/5/1.

265. Frank Furedi, 'The development of organized politics among the Kikuyu' (School of Oriental and African Studies, University of London, MA thesis, 1970); Feldman, 'Christians and politics', pp. 129-224; Tignor, *Colonial Transformation*, pp. 226-35; Spencer, *KAU*, pp. 25-79; and Clough, *Two Sides*, pp. 41-136 give full accounts. Key sources are in Mungeam, *Kenya: Documents*, pp. 484-522.

266. Sorrenson, *Land Reform* coined the term 'Kikuyu gentry'.

267. For example, D.A. Low, 'British East Africa: the establishment of British rule, 1895-1912', and John Middleton, 'Kenya: administration and changes in African life, 1912-45', in Vincent Harlow and E.M. Chilver (eds), *History of East Africa*, ii (Oxford, 1965), pp. 44-50 and 350 respectively; Muriuki, *History*, pp. 167-9, 175; Tignor, *Transformation*, pp. 45-59; Throup, *Origins*, pp. 144-51. For revisionist accounts, William Ochieng, 'Colonial African chiefs: were they primarily self-seeking scoundrels?' ch. 3 in Ogot, *Hadith*, 4; Clough, *Two Sides*; and above, pp. 34, 36-7, 55, 71, 87, 92.

268. Wamagatta, 'Waruhiu', p. 133.

269. See political record and chiefs' characters books: KNA, PC/CP. 1/1/1-2; PC/CP. 1/4/1-3; PC/CP. 2/1/1; DC/NYI. 9; DC/FH. 4/1-6; DC/KBU. 3/8 and DC/KBU.

11/1. For Kinyanjui's 'heavily contested' 16,000 acres: *KLCE*, i, pp. 273–86; also Wanyoike, *African Pastor*, pp. 9, 34–5, 94–6.

270. Routledge, *Prehistoric People*, p. 207.

271. Narrated by Henry Muoria Mwaniki.

272. DC Fort Hall to PC Kenia, 8 April 1919: KNA, PC/CP. 1/7/1; Fort Hall Annual Reports 1925–27: DC/FH. 5–7; Tignor, *Colonial Transformation*, pp. 68–72 and Throup, *Origins*, pp. 146–7 for chiefs; Kenyatta, *Facing Mount Kenya*, pp. 196–7 and Prins, *Age-class Systems*, pp. 47–8 (with Peter Mbiyu Koinange's view) for the 'ban'; for theology, see below. Compare Charles Ambler, 'The renovation of custom in colonial Kenya: the 1932 generation succession ceremonies in Embu', *Journal of African History* 30 (1989), pp. 139–56.

273. C.W.L. Bulpett (ed.), *John Boyes, King of the Wa-Kikuyu* (London, 1911), an important source for Low, 'British East Africa', pp. 24–5; and Muriuki, *History*, pp. 157–61.

274. A metaphor derived from Scott, *Weapons of the Weak*, p. 333, and a universal phenomenon.

275. See *Muigwithania* i, 3 (July 1928), p. 9 and i, 4 (August 1928), p. 6 for KCA tributes to the Karuri and Waiyaki dynasties; Cavicchi, *Problems*, pp. 215–43, for Kikuyu speculation in the 1930s and 1940s on 'aristocracy', including Karuri; and Kenyatta, *My People of Kikuyu* (London, 1942), p. 64. The Nairobi reprint (1966), p. 59, put the eulogy to Nderi in the past tense but made no mention of Mau Mau's contrary view.

276. Evidence of chief Nderi (of his father Wang'ombe's dying wish), Waiganjo Ndotono, Andrew Gathea, Kikuyu Loyal Patriots and KCA in *KLCE* i, pp. 92–4, 153, 165–6, 171–3, 192–8; of chief Koinange, before the Joint Select Committee on Closer Union in East Africa (amongst whom was Lord Lugard): see Committee's *Report*, vol ii (House of Lords Paper 184, 1931: cited hereafter as *JSCCUEA*), p. 401; and of Joseph Kang'ethe (former president, KCA), in oral testimony to John Spencer, 30 September 1972; White, *Comforts*, p. 132. Kikuyu were right about the history of land policy, for which see, Sorrenson, *European Settlement*, ch. 3.

277. See chief Koinange and KCA: *KLCE* i: pp. 130, 198; Elspeth Huxley and Margery Perham, *Race and Politics in Kenya* (London, 1944, 1956).

278. Chief Koinange, 'Memorandum on Njunu land', January 1934: PRO, CO533/441/9.

279. A.F. Holford-Walker (District Commissioner, Nanyuki) to Provincial Commissioner, Central Province, 27 July 1954; Chairman, Mweiga-Ngobit Emergency Committee to Nanyuki District Emergency Committee, 15 September 1954: KNA, DC/NYK. 3/1/19.

280. Kenyatta, *Facing Mount Kenya*, p. 322.

281. Clough, *Two Sides*, p. 66.

282. F.W. Isaac, memorandum, *Native Labour Commission*, p. 300.

283. McIntosh, 'Scottish mission', pp. 148–9.

284. Mungeam, *Kenya: Documents*, p. 484; Clough, *Two Sides*, pp. 39–40.

285. S.H. Fazan, 'An economic survey of the Kikuyu Reserves', ch. 1 in *KLCE* i, pp. 972–6.

286. The view of both the 1929 *Native Land Tenure Committee* and Phillips' *Native Tribunals* (1945).

287. Compare views of chief Koinange, Waiganjo Ndotono, Kikuyu Loyal Patriots, Kenyatta and Dr Arthur in *KLCE* i, pp. 129, 153, 171–2, 424, 459, 470, with Kenyatta, *Facing Mount Kenya*, pp. 41–52.

288. Report of the *Kenya Land Commission* (Cmd 4556, 1934), pp. 78–114, refutes Kikuyu landlord theory. Koinange displayed a portrait of Queen Victoria at his home, seen by Mrs Richard Frost.

289. Thomas Hodgkin, *Nationalism in Colonial Africa* (London, 1956), ch. 3, reviews the

Wealth, Poverty & Civic Virtue in Kikuyu Political Thought

then literature. Rosberg and Nottingham, *Myth* and F.B. Welbourn, *East African Rebels: A Study of Some Independent Churches* (London, 1961) were the first studies of Kikuyu religion and politics, criticized in Sandgren, *Christianity and the Kikuyu*, pp. 5–6.

290. For the most remarkable see Gatheru, *Child of Two Worlds*, pp. 35–50, 65–70.
291. Wanyoike, *African Pastor*, pp. 48–50; Thuku, *Autobiography*, p. 59.
292. In addition to sources cited below, see Kibicho, 'Continuity'; Silvana Bottignole, *Kikuyu Traditional Culture and Christianity* (Nairobi, 1984); Neckebrouck, *Peuple Affligé*; Murray, 'Female circumcision'. For the desire for spiritual conflict, compare Wanyoike, *Pastor*, p. 25, and Parmenas G. Mockerie, *An African Speaks for His People* (London, 1934), p. 27, with John Iliffe, *A Modern History of Tanganyika* (Cambridge, 1979), p. 220.
293. Strayer, *Mission Communities*, p. 60; McIntosh, 'Scottish Mission', pp. 244–6; Kevin Ward, 'The development of Protestant Christianity in Kenya, 1910–1940' (Cambridge University PhD thesis, 1976), pp. 115, 117–18; Kariuki, *A Bishop Facing Mount Kenya*, p. 17.
294. McIntosh, 'Scottish mission', pp. 267–70; Feldman, 'Christians and politics', pp. 74–9.
295. Wanyoike, *Pastor*, p. 57; Thuku, *Autobiography*, p. 8.
296. Sandgren, *Christianity*, pp. 38, 51–2; Feldman, 'Christians and politics', p. 84.
297. Sandgren, *Christianity*, pp. 37–40.
298. Thuku, *Autobiography*, p. 8; Jeremy Murray-Brown, *Kenyatta* (London, 1972), pp. 50–2; Kenyatta, *Facing Mount Kenya*, pp. 156, 327, for *ngwiko ya gecomba*, which I have rendered as 'foreign fondling'.
299. Sandgren, *Christianity*, p. 42; Ward, 'Protestant Christianity', p. 114; Wanyoike, *Pastor*, pp. 29–30, 50, 75, 83–5; Beard, *Longing for Darkness: Kamante's Tales*, ch. 2.
300. Sandgren, *Christianity*, pp. 41, 61; Strayer, *Mission Communities*, p. 80; Feldman, 'Christians and politics', pp. 87–93. Wanyoike, *Pastor*, pp. 67–78; Gatheru, *Child of Two Worlds*, pp. 58–9.
301. John V. Taylor, *The Growth of the Church in Buganda* (London, 1958), pp. 181–2.
302. Cowen, 'Differentiation'; Mungeam, *Kenya: Documents*, pp. 509–10; Kenyatta, *Facing Mount Kenya*, p. 20; Murray-Brown, *Kenyatta*, p. 80; Sandgren, *Christianity*, pp. 51–3, 61–5.
303. Kershaw, 'Land is people', pp. 116, 122.
304. Professor Kershaw, fieldnotes; Wamagatta 'Waruhiu', p. 449; Muriuki, *History*, pp. 20–2.
305. J.F. Raynor, 'The words of God: native zeal to preach and hear', *Inland Africa* 3 (8) (New York, August 1919), p. 12.
306. Geoffrey Hodges, *The Carrier Corps* (New York, 1986), pp. 111, 178, 182; see also, McIntosh, 'Scottish mission', pp. 331–8; Feldman, 'Christians and politics', pp. 96–115; Wanyoike, *Pastor*, p. 39.
307. Thuku, *Autobiography*, pp. 28–9; Mungeam, *Kenya: Documents*, pp. 509–10; enclosures in Northey to Churchill, 12 April 1922: affidavits by Waruhiu Kungu, Karunja Kungu, chief Waweru Kanja, Makimei Mogoi and W.F.G. Campbell: PRO, CO533/276. Thuku was pressing dynastic theory 40 years later: see Rosberg and Nottingham, *Myth*, p. 37. For the postwar context, see Chapter 5 above.
308. Thuku, cables to London, 18 July and 7 August 1921: PRO, CO533/272; manifestoes in Mungeam, *Kenya: Documents*, pp. 506–7.
309. *Papers Relating to Native Disturbances in Kenya* (Cmd 1961, 1922), pp. 5–6 (emphasis added); for David's appeal to a shepherd nation, Gatheru, *Child*, p. 18.
310. Statements in Northey to Churchill, 21 July 1922 by Waruhiu, Wamarema, chiefs Kibathi, Muhoho and Koinange (the latter two to be Kenyatta's fathers-in-law): PRO, CO533/280. 'Judas' became a common epithet for colonial chiefs: Muga

483

Gicaru, *Land of Sunshine* (London, 1958), pp. 17, 119.

311. Kariuki, *Bishop*, p. 22.

312. Joseph Kang'ethe and Gideon Mugo, talking to John Spencer, 30 September 1972 and 21 December 1973; Thuku, *Autobiography*, pp. 25-7; Spencer, *KAU*, p. 41; Rosberg and Nottingham, *Myth*, p. 47. None mentions *ndamathia*; the secondary accounts are nervous of drowning.

313. *Native Disturbances*, p. 5.

314. Only Welbourn, *Rebels*, p. 236, has commented on this passage: 'i.e. snake in the grass', which he found without 'anthropological significance'. I do not know Thuku's term for 'snake', a serious ignorance as discussion below will show. Kenyatta notes that *ituika* celebrants wore skin bracelets dipped in goats' blood, not that they must not drink milk: *Facing Mount Kenya*, p. 192.

315. A deliberately descriptive term which avoids the misleading analytic precision of 'bourgeoisie' or 'petit bourgeoisie' and the implied teleology of 'proto-capitalist'.

316. Sandgren, *Christianity*, pp. 56-7; Spencer, *KAU*, pp. 43-4, for another, not necessarily contrary, view.

317. As always, *Muigwithania* correspondents expected readers to know their Bibles, citing Luke 15 rather than telling the story: letters in issues i, 4 (Aug 1928), p. 11; i, 10 (February–March 1929), p. 16; and i, 11 (April 1929), p. 9.

318. Henry Mwangi Gichuiri (*Muigwithania*'s second editor and to whose memory Kenyatta dedicated his pamphlet *My People of Kikuyu*) in *Muigwithania* i, 10 (February–March 1929), p. 2.

319. Spencer, *KAU*, pp. 35, 57, 60, 62-3; Feldman, 'Christians and politics', pp. 221-8; Sandgren, *Christianity*, pp. 51-66.

320. Gavin Kitching, *Land, Livestock and Leadership: The Rise of an African Petit-bourgeoisie in Kenya, 1905-1918* (Nairobi, 1981); Kim, 'Africanization', pp. 40-9.

321. Godfrey Muriuki's suggestion; also Kariuki, *Bishop*, p. 23.

322. For the class-forming role of LNCs see Kitching, *Class and Economic Change*, ch. 7 and Kim, 'Africanization', ch. 2.

323. Kershaw, 'Land is people', p. 202; Benson (1964), p. 438.

324. Church of Scotland, *Memorandum Prepared by the Kikuyu Mission Council on Female Circumcision* (Kikuyu, 1 Dec 1931), appendix iii [cited henceforth as CSM, *Memorandum*]; Kariuki, *Bishop*, pp. 28-30; Spencer, *KAU*, pp. 57-8; Clough, *Two Sides*, pp. 119-22.

325. McIntosh, 'Scottish mission', p. 408; Strayer, *Mission Communities*, p. 80; Ward 'Protestant Christianity', p. 129; *Native Affairs Department Annual Report 1925* (Nairobi, 1926), p. 3. I infer the theology of abundance behind the Christian fee payments. It reflects a common missionary complaint but not one I have seen in this precise context.

326. McGregor, 'Kikuyu and its people', p. 33; Crawford, *Equator's Snowy Peak*, pp. 55-6; anon, 'Where ancient cults prevail', *Inland Africa* 3 (3) (1919), pp. 10-13; Cagnolo, *Akikuyu*, pp. 122-3.

327. Benson (1964), p. 248 for *mukuuri* and *kuura bururi*.

328. Eve's serpent (Genesis 3 : 1) was a simple snake in both Bibles: *nyoka* and *nyamuyathi*. The distinction between the Swahili 'large snake' and *ndamathia* in Revelation 12 : 7 (and elsewhere) was deliberate.

329. Spencer, *KAU*, p. 46.

330. Mathew Njoroge Kabetu discussed *ndamathia* dispassionately later in his *Kirira kia Ugikuyu* (Nairobi 1947), pp. 92-3. (Thanks to Revd John Karanja, Mr Mungai Mbaya and Mr Karega Munene.)

331. Kenyatta, *Facing Mount Kenya*, p. 326.

332. *Ibid.*, p. 196; also *Muigwithania* i, 4 (August 1928), p. 10; i, 6 (October 1928), p. 9; i, 7 (November 1928), p. 1; i, 8 (December 1928-January 1929), p. 7.

333. *Muigwithania* ii, 1 (June 1929), inside front cover.
334. Richard St Barbe Baker, *Men of the Trees* (London, 1932), pp. 139–44; Baker was in Kenya 1920–23. Compare Genesis 11 : 1-9 and Luc de Heusch, *The Drunken King or the Origin of the State* (Bloomington, 1982), pp. 56–61, 201, 229–32, 245.
335. Mockerie, *An African Speaks*, pp. 36–42.
336. Kenyatta, *Facing Mount Kenya*, pp. 186–97.
337. District Commissioner Fort Hall to Provincial Commissioner Central Province, 9 September 1931: KNA, PC/CP. 8/5/5; Strayer, *Mission Communities*, pp. 129–32; Feldman, 'Christians and politics', pp. 221–5; Spencer, *Beauttah*, p. 23.
338. See complaints by editor Gichuiri and translator Barlow that contributors had not mastered standard Kikuyu: *Muigwithania* ii, 1 (June 1929), pp. 15–17. Cf Isabel Hofmeyr, 'Building a nation from words: Afrikaans language, literature and ethnic identity, 1902-1924', ch. 3 in Shula Marks and Stanley Trapido (eds), *The Politics of Race, Class and Nationalism in Twentieth Century South Africa* (London, 1987).
339. Mockerie, *An African Speaks*, pp. 64–5; *Muigwithania* i, 7 (November 1928), p. 4; i, 8 (December 1928–January 1929), p. 15.
340. In addition to Mukiri and Kenyatta there were Justin Itotia's two books on proverbs and ancestors (Kenneth J. King, *Pan-Africanism and Education: A Study of Race, Philanthropy and Education in the Southern States of America and East Africa* [Oxford, 1971], p. 169) and Stanley Kiama Gathigira, *Miikariire ya Agikuyu* (London [1934], 1959).
341. A.R. Barlow, note to his translation of *Muigwithania* ii, 3 (September 1929), p. 10; in the first published account of the Kikuyu myth of genesis, God endowed an anonymous couple with Kikuyuland: Routledge, *Prehistoric People*, p. 283.
342. *KLCE* i, p. 425. Kenyatta, *Facing Mount Kenya*, ch. 2, esp. pp. 22, 35.
343. *Report of Native Land Tenure Committee*, pp. 9–13, 35–50; Sorrenson, *Land Reform*, pp. 29–30.
344. Report of joint KCA and chiefs' meeting at Nyeri, 20 April 1928, in *Muigwithania* i, 8 (December 1928–January 1929), pp. 5, 12 and *ibid.*, i, 9 (Feb 1929), pp. 8–14; and of KA and KCA meeting at Kiambu, *ibid.*, i, 11 (April 1929), pp. 1–3, 15–16.
345. KCA to Secretary of State, 14 February 1929, in *Correspondence between the Kikuyu Central Association and the Colonial Office 1929–1930* (Nairobi, 1930), p. 7: KNA, PC/CP. 8/5/5; KCA to Sir Samuel Wilson, 30 May 1929: PC/CP. 8/5/3; KCA memorandum and Kenyatta's evidence in *KLCE* i, pp. 203, 429.
346. *Report of Native Land Tenure Committee*, pp. 51–62.
347. KLP Memorandum, 1 June 1932, *KLCE* i, p. 177.
348. KCA Memorandum, 1 December 1932 and Kenyatta, more coolly, in London, *ibid.*, pp. 196–7, 425.
349. KCA to Sir Edward Grigg, 31 December 1925: KNA, PC/CP. 8/5/2; Tignor, *Colonial Transformation*, p. 239; Feldman, 'Christians and politics', pp. 191–201; Sandgren, *Christianity*, pp. 61–5; McIntosh, 'Scottish mission', pp. 408–9; K.J. King, 'The politics of agricultural education for Africans in Kenya', ch. 9 in B.A. Ogot (ed.), *Hadith 3* (Nairobi, 1971), pp. 145–9.
350. Spencer, *Beauttah*, pp. 5–6, 29–30; Stanley Kiama and Job Muchuchu in *KLCE* i, pp. 105, 115.
351. Dagoretti Political Record Book i (1908–1912), p. 35: KNA, PC/CP. 1/4/1; Kiambu Handing over Report (23 February 1920): DC/KBU/13; KCA to Grigg, 31 December 1935 and KCA meeting with District Commissioner Fort Hall, 25 July 1927: PC/CP. 8/5/2. Historians have been as reticent about burial as about Thuku and the dragon.
352. Wanyoike, *Pastor*, p. 22; Father Lammer: *KLCE* i, p. 904; McIntosh, 'Scottish missions', p. 149.
353. Wanyoike, *Pastor*, pp. 82–5.

354. Senior chief Koinange wa Mbiyu, 'Memorandum on Njunu Land', January 1934: PRO, CO 533/441/9.

355. *Ibid.*; and heated argument in *KLCE* i, pp. 630-9.

356. As was questioned earlier, p. 320 above.

357. Joshua Mbeti to *Muigwithania* ii, 2 (July-August 1929), pp. 3-4.

358. Kenyatta, editorial in *ibid.*, i, 4 (August 1928), pp. 2-3; *idem* (?) 'Christmas sports, Kabete', i, 8 (December 1928-January 1929), p. 3; Gideon Mugo Kagika, 'Showing forth that which is right', ii, 1 (June 1929), pp. 7-8.

359. Kenyatta, editorials in *ibid.*, i, 3 (July 1928); i, 4 (August 1928); i, 6 (October 1928); i, 8 (December 1928-January 1929).

360. Koinange to *Muigwithania* i, 10 (February-March 1929), p. 14; Leakey, *Mau Mau and the Kikuyu*, pp. 68-71. See also: Bruce Berman and John Lonsdale, 'Louis Leakey's Mau Mau: a study in the politics of knowledge', *History and Anthropology* 5 (2) (1991).

361. KCA petition to Secretary of State, 14 February 1929, in *Correspondence between the KCA and the Colonial Office*; memoranda by KCA and Parmenas Mockerie in *KLCE* i, pp. 203, 442.

362. Chief Waruhiu, oral evidence, 14 November 1932, *KLCE* i, p. 132.

363. See Feldman, 'Christians and politics', pp. 202-24, for the 'politics of prosperity'.

364. Which Justin Itotia first published in 1928: see p. 303, n. 3, above.

365. KCA memorandum to Hilton Young Commission (on Closer Union in East Africa), *East African Standard* (Nairobi), 4 February 1928.

366. After having undertaken not to engage in subversion: Governor Sir Edward Grigg to W.C. Bottomley, 13 June 1929 (PRO, CO533/388/9), as Kikuyu suspected: Spencer, *Beauttah*, p. 21.

367. Thuku, *Autobiography*, pp. 50-1, 54, 57-8, 95-6.

368. Again, I echo Anderson, *Imagined Communities*. But for the Kenyatta quotation see the beginning of Chapter 11, above.

369. Benson (1964), p. 54; from the Swahili *ushenzi*: upcountry heathendom.

370. 'Song of the Field' in *Muigwithania* ii, 3 (Sept 1929), back cover.

371. KCA to Grigg, 31 December 1925 and comments thereon by R.G. Stone, 2 January 1926: KNA, PC/CP 8/5/2.

372. Job Muchuchu, 'Syphilis comes from friendship', *Muigwithania* i, 7 (November 1928), pp. 6-7; H.M. Gichuiri, 'Profit from the field', *ibid.*, i, 8 (December 1928-January 1929), p. 6. The KCA message echoed the Colony's Medical Department: Margery Perham, *East African Journey: Kenya and Tanganyika 1929-30* (London, 1976), p. 188.

373. Koinange, evidence in 1931 before *JSCCUEA* ii, p. 417; L.S.B. Leakey, *Kenya Contrasts and Problems* (London, 1936), p. 13.

374. Joseph Kang'ethe, 'Voice of the chairman', *Muigwithania* i, 3 (July 1928), p. 12.

375. Kenyatta, 'Message from *Muigwithania*', *ibid.*, i, 4 (August 1928), p. 3; *idem*, 'Have done with trifling', *ibid.*, i, 8 (December 1928-January 1929), p. 1; Alessandro Maimba and J.N. Gachuere to *Wathiomo Mukinyu* (May 1932; June 1948): Cavicchi, *Problems*, pp. 90-6.

376. Feldman, 'Christians and politics', pp. 246-52; Clough, *Two Sides*, p. 82.

377. Gichuiri to *Muigwithania* i, 4 (August 1928), pp. 7-8.

378. Job Muchuchu, *ibid.*, i, 6 (October 1928), pp. 15-16.

379. Kenyatta, *ibid.*, i, 7 (November 1928), p. 14.

380. Muchuchu, *ibid.*, p. 7; Mockerie, *An African Speaks*, pp. 66-7.

381. Kenyatta to *Muigwithania* i, 12 (May 1929), pp. 8-10 and *idem* (as editor), 'Let us agree among ourselves and exalt the Kikuyu', *ibid.*, i, 7 (November 1928), pp. 1-3, citing Hebrews 11 : 24-5. Dane Kennedy, *Islands of White: Settler Society and Culture in Kenya and Southern Rhodesia, 1890-1939* (Durham, NC., 1987), pp. 168-73, for 'poor whites'.

382. Alessandro Maimba to *Wathiomo Mukinyu* (October 1930): Cavicchi, *Problems*, p. 85.
383. Koinange, evidence before *JSCCUEA* ii, p. 413.
384. All LNC debates repeated the argument that African traders ought to be assisted against Indians, to prevent the expatriation of profit; see also Mukarura (pseud.) to *Muigwithania* i, 4 (August 1928). p. 12.
385. Kenyatta, evidence in London, 16 June 1932: *KLCE* i, p. 430.
386. Gakaara Wanjau, *Agikuyu, maumau na wiyathi* (Karatina, 1971), p. 50; thanks to Ann Biersteker for the reference.
387. Senior chief Koinange to *Mumenyereri* (12 July 1948): KNA, MAA. 8/106; Wambaa and King, 'Squatter perspective', p. 197.
388. Gatheru (squatter-born), *Child of Two Worlds*, p. 8.
389. Kanogo, *Squatters*, p. 172, reporting the squatter view; also Furedi, *Mau Mau War*, p. 53.
390. Kabira and wa Mutahi, *Gikuyu Oral Literature*, pp. 107–9; see above, p. 334.
391. The distinction is made by (squatter-born) Gicaru, *Land of Sunshine*, p. 58.
392. G. Kershaw, 'The Rift Valley and Mau Mau' (typescript, 1987).
393. Kanogo, *Squatters*, p. 19; Elspeth Huxley, *Out in the Midday Sun: My Kenya* (London, 1985), p. 33. *Laini* seem inseparable from oppression in modern Kikuyu thought: their reserve boundaries, the Nairobi police lines in which Thuku was held, and the emergency villages in which the population was corralled in the 1950s to deny support to Mau Mau, were all *laini*.
394. Gicaru, *Land of Sunshine*, p. 32.
395. Wanyoike, *Pastor*, p. 26.
396. Benson (1964), p. 130; I am grateful to Mungai Mbayah for his etymological cautions here.
397. Wambaa and King, 'Squatter perspective', p. 199.
398. Benson (1964), pp. 37, 205.
399. Michael Walzer, *Exodus and Revolution* (New York, 1984) for Exodus' inspirational role; and V. Neckebrouck, *L'onzieme commandement: étiologie d'une église independante au pied du mont Kenya* (Immensee, 1978), pp. 279–86 for the Bible as popular oral literature.
400. Nakuru Police to Comissioner, 19 May 1934: KNA, PC/CP. 8/7/4; P. Thiong'o to *Mumenyereri*, 9 February 1948: MAA. 8/106; Jocelyn Murray, 'The Kikuyu spirit churches', *Journal of Religion in Africa* 5 (1974), pp. 198–234; Philomena Njeri, 'The Akurinu churches: the history and basic beliefs of the Holy Ghost Church of East Africa 1926–1980' (Nairobi University MA thesis, 1984), pp. 84, 110.
401. Koinange, in evidence before *JSCCUEA* ii, p. 402.
402. 'Meeting at Kiambu' *Muigwithania* i, 11 (April 1929), p. 15; Chiefs Koinange, Njonjo, Waruhiu and Karanja to *East African Standard* (unpublished, 17 December 1930), in CSM, *Memorandum*, Appendix IV. 3.
403. Wambaa and King, 'Squatter perspective', p. 203; CSM, *Memorandum*, Appendix 3.
404. Secondary accounts of *kifagio* offer little help; see Tignor, *Colonial Transformation*, p. 177; Spencer, *KAU*, p. 76; Kanogo, *Squatters*, pp. 46–55; Furedi, *Mau Mau War*, pp. 76–7.
405. A.R. Barlow, memorandum in *KLCE* iii, p. 3024.
406. See above, pp. 340–1.
407. See above, pp. 15, 36–9 for the 'vulgarization of power'. For Kenya there is no study of the consequent construction of law to match Martin Chanock, *Law, Custom and Social Order: the Colonial Experience in Malawi and Zambia* (Cambridge, 1985); or Sally Falk Moore, *Social Facts and Fabrications: 'Customary' Law on Kilimanjaro, 1880–1980* (Cambridge ,1986).
408. See letters and reports in *Muigwithania* i, 6 (October 1928); a few years later the young

Bildad Kaggia, to become an intellectual leader of Mau Mau, was nicknamed Prince of Wales for being the best boy at school: *Roots of Freedom*, p. 11.

409. Feldman, 'Christians and politics', pp. 219–20; Kigondu was later one of the first Mau Mau detainees.

410. The legend was told to Henry Muoria Mwaniki by George Kirongothi Ndegwa, KCA secretary in the late 1930s. From London Kenyatta wrote excitedly about 'Seeing the King and his Lady with one's own eyes', compared guardsmen to lines of sorghum and drew the moral that tradition worked. *Muigwithania* ii, 2 (July–August 1929), pp. 6–8.

411. G.K. Ndegwa and D.C. Waihenya, 'Trading by girls and women in Nairobi: the beginnings of insubordination', *Muigwithania* i, 8 (December 1928–January 1929), pp. 7, 9.

412. White, *Comforts of Home*, pp. 95–6, 107–9.

413. Benson (1964), p. 152.

414. Kenyatta, 'Let us agree among ourselves and exalt Kikuyu'; *idem*, 'Bearing up the Kikuyu nation'; H.M. Gichuiri, 'Enfeebling the Kikuyu': *Muigwithania* i, 7 (November 1928), pp. 2–3, 11, 12.

415. P.K. Mugo to *Muigwithania* i, 11 (April 1929), p. 3.

416. Muchuchu to *Muigwithania* i, 6 (October 1928), p. 15; 'The story of Parmenas Mockerie of the Kikuyu Tribe, Kenya', ch. 7 in Margery Perham (ed.), *Ten Africans* (London [1936], 1963), p. 162; Kiongo wa Kahiti, 'Original names', *Muigwithania* i, 10 (February–March 1929), pp. 15–16.

417. F. Gechohi and Modeste Kamuto to *Wathiomo Mukinyu* (1930 and 1936): Cavicchi, *Problems*, pp. 29–30, 101–3.

418. Presley, 'Kikuyu women' pp. 224–6.

419. Editor, 'Stir up the soil so you may find precious things', *Muigwithania* i, 7 (November 1928), p. 13.

420. Mukarura to *Muigwithania* i, 4 (August 1928), p. 12.

421. Kenyatta, 'Bearing up the Kikuyu nation', *Muigwithania* i, 7 (November 1928), p. 11; report of Kinyanjui's death and burial in *ibid.*, i, 10 (February–March 1929), pp. 3–6.

422. Gideon M. Kagika to *Muigwithania* i, 7 (November 1928), p. 1; K. Kirobi to *ibid.*, i, 8 (January 1929), p. 14: Kirobi's actual words warned that a man might 'lose his body' and 'cut himself'.

423. Reuben Muteria to *Muigwithania* i, 6 (October 1928); Kenyatta, 'Bearing up the Kikuyu nation', *ibid.*, i, 7 (November 1928), p. 11; 'Song of the field', *ibid.*, ii, 3 (September 1929), back cover.

424. First seen by Feldman, 'Christians and politics', pp. 252–5.

425. Kenyatta especially, after the event: *Facing Mount Kenya*, pp. 130–54; p. 135 for the quotations.

426. To simplify the scheme in Karen E. Paige and Jeffery M. Paige, *The Politics of Reproductive Ritual* (Berkeley and Los Angeles, 1981).

427. Sandgren, *Christianity and the Kikuyu*, p. 73; Hyam, *Empire and Sexuality*, pp. 75–8.

428. This is the main thesis of Murray, 'Female circumcision controversy', on which I chiefly rely.

429. Sandgren, *Christianity*, pp. 91–3, 175–82; CSM, *Memorandum*, p. 3.

430. Sandgren, *Christianity*, p. 91; S.G. Kuria to *Muigwithania* i, 10 (February–March 1929), p. 11; Tabitha Wangui to *ibid.*, ii, 1 (June, 1929). Schoolgirl pregnancies today are blamed on the abandonment of initiation rites: Davison, *Mutira*, pp. 43–4, 102–3.

431. Cecil Bewes, Diary, 19 June 1929, quoted in Murray, 'Female circumcision controversy', p. 169.

432. For Gathigira, see Murray, 'Female circumcision controversy', pp. 19–25;

Kenyatta, *Facing Mount Kenya*, ch. 6.

433. Davison, *Mutira*, pp. 42, 99, 102, 144, 188, 228.

434. Kenyatta, *Facing Mount Kenya*, p. 134.

435. *Ibid.*, pp. 146, 135.

436. Wanjiru wa Kinyua to *Muigwithania* (May 1929), pp. 7-8, apparently referring to Galatians 5 : 6; compare Ng'ang'a Ngoro's recollection in Rosberg and Nottingham, *Myth*, p. 119.

437. L.S.B. Leakey, 'The Kikuyu problem of the initiation of girls', *Journal of the Royal Anthropological Institute* 61 (1931), p. 279.

438. Davison, *Mutira*, pp. 195, 282, for expectations that husbands beat wives.

439. CSM, *Memorandum*, pp. 63-76.

440. *Ibid.*, pp. 7, 30-3.

441. Reproduced in *ibid.*, p. 42. For the view, with which I agree, that Kang'ethe genuinely believed that the CSM wanted to abolish clitoridectomy, see Murray, 'Female circumcision controversy', pp. 135-6. For the uses made of Kang'ethe's question, see Rosberg and Nottingham, *Myth*, p. 118; Tignor, *Colonial Transformation*, p. 242; Spencer, *KAU*, p. 76.

442. CSM, *Memorandum*, p. 41.

443. For the invention of Embu and Meru tribal authorities in this period, see Ambler, 'Renovation of custom'; Lambert, *Kikuyu Social and Political Institutions*, chs 5 and 9; Bernardi, *The Mugwe*.

444. I here follow Tignor, *Colonial Transformation*, pp. 267-71; Feldman, 'Christians and politics', pp. 288-93; Sandgren, *Christianity*, pp. 76-81.

445. CSM, *Memorandum*, p. 45.

446. D.R. Crampton, Acting Provincial Commissioner, Central Province, to Chief Native Commissioner, 27 May 1920: KNA, PC/CP 7/1/2; Murray, 'Female circumcision controversy', pp. 110-13; Clough, *Two Sides*, pp. 139-41.

447. See, for example, S. Kuria to *Muigwithania* i, 10 (February-March 1929), p. 11.

448. Clough, *Two Sides*, p. 142, citing C. Waruiri's Nairobi University BA thesis, 1971.

449. Ward, 'Protestant Christianity', pp. 151, 161.

450. CSM, *Memorandum*, pp. 35-40; also, for resentment at the curtailment of debate in Embu, see H.E. Lambert to Provincial Commissioner Central Province, 14 October 1929: KNA, PC/CP. 8/1/1.

451. For various versions of *muthirigu*, see CSM, *Memorandum*, Appendix V; Murray, 'Female circumcision controversy', p. 162; Spencer, *KAU*, p. 105; Sandgren, *Christianity*, pp. 175-82; Wamagatta, 'Waruhiu', p. 197.

452. S.H. La Fontaine to E.B. Horne, 31 December 1928 and minutes of meeting at Kahuhia, 16 March 1928: KNA, PC/CP. 8/5/3.

453. *Muigwithania* i, 8 (December 1928-January 1929) and i, 9 (February 1929): reports by Henry Mwangi Gichuiri of joint meeting of chiefs and KCA at Nyeri, 20 April 1928.

454. Sandgren, *Christianity*, pp. 76-9; compare Ambler, 'Renovation of custom', pp. 149-50.

455. *Kirore* petition of 12 September 1929, in CSM, *Memorandum*, Appendix IV.

456. Greet Kershaw, field notes.

457. Clough, *Two Sides*, pp. 150-1; Spencer, *KAU*, p. 79.

458. I exclude the notorious circumcision and murder of the AIM missionary Dr Hulda Stumpf, since it appears to be peripheral to the crisis narrative. See Hyam, *Empire and Sexuality*, p. 193, for a recent account, but a full discussion awaits the findings of Dr David Anderson's research.

459. Ward, 'Protestant Christianity', pp. 179-81; Sandgren, *Christianity*, pp. 88-90, 99.

460. As in agreement between Revd W.P. Knapp and District Commissioner Fort Hall, February–March 1930: KNA, PC/CP. 8/1/1.

461. H.S. Scott (Director of Education), to Colonial Secretary, 18 January 1930: *ibid.*

462. For the independent churches and schools, see J.B. Ndungu, 'Gituamba and Kikuyu independency in church and school', ch. 7 in B.G. McIntosh (ed.), *Ngano* (Nairobi, 1969); John Anderson, *The Struggle for the School* (Nairobi, 1970), pp. 115–29; Welbourn, *Rebels*, ch. 8; Tignor, *Colonial Transformation*, pp. 267–72; Sandgren, *Christianity*, ch. 6; Neckebrouck, *L'onzieme commandement*, ch. 15; Clough, *Two Sides*, pp. 147–50.

463. R. Macpherson, *The Presbyterian Church in Kenya* (Nairobi, 1970), table on p. 115.

464. Murray, 'Female circumcision controversy', ch. 13.

465. For the Kikuyu collection of land evidence, see Rosberg and Nottingham, *Myth*, p. 145; Spencer, *KAU*, pp. 85–6; and, most helpfully, Ng'ang'a Ngoro's interview for Spencer, 1 August 1973.

466. For the Commission's thoughts on Tigoni and Lari, see *Kenya Land Commission Report*, pp. 36–8, 42–5, 83, 115–18, 153.

467. Koinange, 'Memorandum on Njunu Land': PRO, CO533/441/9.

468. See, in particular, the well-informed D.H. Rawcliffe, *The Struggle for Kenya* (London, 1954), pp. 32–5; also, Rosberg and Nottingham, *Myth*, pp. 324–31.

469. Sandgren, *Christianity*, ch. 6, is the best account of funding and organization; see also Elspeth Huxley (ed.), *Nellie: Letters from Africa* (London, 1980), pp. 130–2, and L.S.B. Leakey, 'Native Affairs: Kikuyu squatters on farms', November 1939: KNA, NM. 1/857 for the independents in the Rift Valley.

470. Njeri, 'Akurinu', p. 39.

471. Provincial Commissioner Central Province to Colonial Secretary, 7 August 1934: KNA, SR 1/175.

472. For education department relations with the independents, see Anderson, *Struggle for the School*, pp. 125–8; Tignor, *Colonial Transformation*, pp. 271–2; Sandgren, *Christianity*, pp. 110–13.

473. H.E. Lambert (District Commissioner Kiambu) to Provincial Commissioner Central Province, 15 June 1942: KNA, PC/CP. 8/7/4.

474. Kenyatta, *Facing Mount Kenya*, pp. 273–7. The quoted opinion was widely held by Kikuyu; Kenyatta appears to attribute it to the British alone.

475. Lambert to Provincial Commissioner Central Province, 15 June 1942, as above; the main secondary authorities on the *akurinu* are silent on the issue.

476. This paragraph is based on Murray, 'Kikuyu spirit churches'; Njeri, 'Akurinu'; and Sandgren, *Christianity*, Ch. 7.

477. Mbiyu Koinange, *The People of Kenya Speak for Themselves* (Detroit, 1955), p. 64; see also, *idem*, 'The Agrarian problem in Kenya', enclosed in Koinange to Prime Minister J. Ramsay Macdonald, 12 June 1933: PRO, CO533/437/16.

478. E.L.B. Anderson (District Commissioner Kiambu) to Provincial Commissioner Central Province, 26 January 1939; R.H. Wisdom (acting Director of Education) to Chief Secretary, 10 March 1939: both in Kiambu district education file in 1962 (courtesy of Greet Kershaw); Koinange, *People of Kenya*, ch. 4.

479. See the acknowledgment in Leakey, *Southern Kikuyu* i, pp. xi–xiv.

480. L.S.B. Leakey, 'Meetings of Kikuyu age groups', October 1939: KNA, NM. 1/857; idem, *Kenya Contrasts and Problems*, pp. 10–11; Koinange, *People*, p. 32.

481. Barnett and Njama, *Mau Mau from Within*, p. 245.

482. L.S.B. Leakey, 'Memorandum on the KCA' (December 1939): KNA, NM. 1/857; Director of Civil Intelligence to Provincial Commissioner Nyanza, 22 December 1939: PC/NZA. 2/554.

483. Governor Henry Moore to Secretary of State, 4 August 1940: PRO, CO533/523/38481.

484. Spencer, *KAU*, pp. 83-8; Clough, *Two Sides*, pp. 168-71.
485. Thuku's case was put by his friend Louis Leakey in Special Branch memorandum on the KPA, 31 October 1939: KNA, PC/CP. 8/5/6.
486. For the British part in making Mau Mau see Chapter 10, above.
487. From the comparative literature see, especially, Theda Skocpol, *States and Social Revolutions* (Cambridge, 1979).
488. But see Rosberg and Nottingham, *Myth*, chs 6-8; Spencer, *KAU*, chs 4-7; Throup, *Origins*; W.R. Ochieng' (ed.), *A Modern History of Kenya 1895-1980* (Nairobi, 1989) chs 5 and 6 by T. Zeleza and W. Maloba; Berman, *Control and Crisis*, chs 6 and 7.
489. An insight I owe to Greet Kershaw.
490. A Luo proverb as much as a Kikuyu one, I am told by Atieno Odhiambo.
491. Lonsdale, 'Mau Maus of the mind', p. 419; see also p. 336, above.
492. For *wanyahoro*, see p. 341, above and, as loyalists, wa Wanjau, *Mau Mau Author*, pp. 226, 227; *mikora* I owe to Tom Askwith (Municipal African Affairs Officer, Nairobi, 1945-9), quoting his Kikuyu assistant, Dedan Githegi; *imaramari* is the plural form.
493. Henry Muoria, 'The British and my Kikuyu tribe' (typescript, 1982), p. 96.
494. Clayton and Savage, *Government and Labour*, pp. 313-37; Cooper, *African Waterfront*, pp. 78-113; Throup, *Origins*, pp. 194-6.
495. Throup, *Origins*, p. 240; *idem*, 'Construction and Destruction of Kenyatta state', pp. 37-8.
496. Following Paul Wilkinson, *Political Terrorism* (London, 1973) and *Terrorism and the Liberal State* (London, 1977).
497. See Chapter 5, above.
498. Greet Kershaw, *Mau Mau from Below* (forthcoming).
499. Leakey, *Defeating Mau Mau*, pp. 60, 64.
500. I owe the model to Elie Kedourie, 'Saad Zaghlul and the British', in A. Hourani (ed.), *Middle East Papers No 2* (London, 1961), pp. 139-60; Clement H. Moore, *Tunisia since Independence* (Berkeley, 1965), pp. 26-40; and John Iliffe.
501. Rosberg and Nottingham, *Myth*, ch. 6; Kipkorir, 'Alliance High School', chs 5-7; Spencer, *KAU*, chs 4 and 5; Throup, *Origins*, pp. 175-8; Berman, *Control and Crisis*, pp. 322-38; Jack Roelker, *Mathu of Kenya* (Stanford, 1976); Joseph E. Harris, *Repatriates and Refugees in a Colonial Society: The Case of Kenya* (Washington, DC, 1987).
502. Mathu's speech to KAU meeting, 23 May 1948, in Kikuyu newspaper *Hindi ya Mwafrika*, 27 May 1948: KNA, MAA. 8/102 (courtesy of David Throup's notes on this file); KAU, 'The Economical, Political, Educational and Social Aspects of the African in Kenya Colony', August 1946: PRO, CO533/537/38672. For Shakespeare's importance to the identity of modern Kenyans see Cohen and Atieno Odhiambo, *Burying SM*.
503. *Sauti ya Mwafrika*, 15 April 1948: KNA, MAA. 8/102.
504. Berman and Lonsdale, 'Louis Leakey's Mau Mau', pp. 174-6.
505. Spencer, *KAU*, pp. 160-5, 192; Muoria, 'British and Kikuyu', p. 88 (informed by George Ndegwa, KCA general secretary); I follow David Throup, 'Moderates, militants and Mau Mau: African politics in Kenya 1944-1952' (Northeastern University, Boston, 1987), p. 4, rather than Spencer, in thinking that Kenyatta's return encouraged the KCA to dominate KAU.
506. Press circulation figures in Fay Gadsden, 'The African press in Kenya, 1945-1952', *Journal of African History* 21 (1980), pp. 533-5.
507. H. Muoria, *Guka kwa Njamba iitu Nene (The coming of our Great Warrior)* (Nairobi, October 1946), Muoria's first collection of Kenyatta's speeches, quoted in Muoria, 'British and Kikuyu', pp. 153-6.
508. Mbiyu Koinange, 'Jomo: colleague in the struggle for freedom and independence',

in Ambu H. Patel (ed.), *Struggle for 'Release Jomo and his Colleagues'* (Nairobi, 1963), p. 27; Sorrenson, *Land Reform*, p. 104; Murray-Brown, *Kenyatta*, pp. 229–30.

509. 'Third Report of the Advisory Committee appointed under Regulation 24 of the Defence Regulations' (26 August 1940), Transcript of evidence, p. 79, evidence of Charles Wambaa: PRO, CO533/523/38481; and Henry Muoria's recollection.

510. Muoria, *Guka kwa Njamba* and *Kenyatta ni muigwithania witu (Kenyatta is our reconciler)*, the second edition of Kenyatta's speeches (Nairobi, February 1947), in Muoria, 'British and Kikuyu', pp. 157–84.

511. Kenyatta, 'Conditions in other countries', *Muigwithania* i, 3 (July 1928), p. 8.

512. International African Service Bureau Pamphlet No. 3 (ed. George Padmore).

513. As *Muruguri wa 'Kenya Bururi wa Ngoe'*, copy in Muoria's possession.

514. Muoria, 'British and Kikuyu', pp. 172, 180–1; Kenyatta, *Kenya: The Land of Conflict*, pp. 9–10. Kenyatta's criticism is perhaps echoed in the contemporary Kikuyu term for civil servant, *ndungata*.

515. KAU, 'Economical, Political, Educational and Social Aspects', p. 18: PRO, CO533/537/38672.

516. Johnstone Kenyatta, 'An African People rise in Revolt: the story of the Kenya massacre: how Harry Thuku led the great struggle against imperialism', *Daily Worker* (London), 20, 21 January 1930. This paper was the organ of the British Communist Party, an odd readership to which to stress Kikuyu respect for duly constituted authority.

517. In letters to *Manchester Guardian*, 31 March 1932, 1 May 1934; *New Statesman and Nation*, 27 June 1935; *Time and Tide* 24, June 1938.

518. *Kenya: Land of Conflict*, pp. 10–12; *Muigwithania* i, 9 (February 1929), p. 1; Muoria, 'British and Kikuyu', p. 36.

519. Director of Intelligence to Chief Native Commissioner, 1 and 3 June 1947: KNA, MAA. 8/8 (again, I am grateful to David Throup for his notes on this file); Kenyatta, *My People of Kikuyu*, p. 25. Muoria invoked the Devonshire declaration in a *Mumenyereri* editorial as late as 1 August 1949: KNA, PC/RVP. 2/27/34.

520. Muoria, 'British and Kikuyu', p. 160.

521. Henry Muoria, *Uhotani witu tiwa hinya wa mbara no ni wakihoto* (Flash Printing Works, Nairobi, 1948).

522. I am glad of John Hatch's memory for this point. Labour's Commonwealth officer in the 1950s, now Lord Hatch of Lusby, he was struck by Kenyatta's insistence on the responsibility of the oppressed to help themselves.

523. Muoria, *Kenyatta ni Muigwithania witu*; *idem*, 'British and Kikuyu', pp. 169–72, 182; and reminiscence. Central Province intelligence report, March 1947: KNA, Secretariat 1/12/8 (courtesy of David Throup's notes); for Kinyanjui, Wambugu and the KCA, *Muigwithania*, i, 9 (February 1929), pp. 8–14.

524. This statement elides much detailed political history, for which see Rosberg and Nottingham, *Myth*, pp. 262–5; Spencer, *KAU*, pp. 203–6.

525. Spencer, *James Beauttah*, p. 95.

526. Notice in *Mumenyereri*, 9 February 1948: KNA, MAA. 8/106.

527. Mutonyi, 'Mau Mau Chairman', pp. 49–50.

528. Kenyatta, *Facing Mount Kenya*, p. 156; for his greetings: Kariuki, *Mau Mau Detainee*, p. 11.

529. Letter in *Mumenyereri*, 20 June 1949: KNA, PC/RVP. 2/27/34.

530. Muoria, reports in *Mumenyereri* 17 November 1947, 19 January 1948, 16 February 1948: KNA, MAA. 8/106.

531. Letter of complaint in *Mumenyereri*, 1 August 1949: KNA, PC/RVP. 2/27/34; *Corfield Report*, p. 11.

532. Mbiyu Koinange, *People of Kenya*, ch. 6; Rebecca Njau and Gideon Mulaki, *Kenya Women Heroes and their Mystical Power* (Nairobi, 1984), p. 45.

533. In *Ngoro ya Ugikuyu ni ya Gutoria* (*The Kikuyu spirit of patriotism is for victory*), 1947.

534. Henry Muoria, *What Can We Do For Our Own Sake?* (1945).

535. Henry Muoria, *Our Mother Is The Soil, Our Father Is Knowledge* (1948).

536. Henry Muoria, *Our Victory Does Not Depend on Force of Arms.*

537. Muoria, *What Can We Do?*; idem, editorial, *Mumenyereri*, 21 June 1948: KNA, MAA. 8/106.

538. Muoria, 'The goodness and help of meetings: meetings are more important to us than to other African tribes', *Mumenyereri*, 26 January 1948.

539. Henry Muoria, *Life is War by Action, to Win or Lose* (Nairobi, 1949); idem, *Some Greek Old Giants of Knowledge and Great Thinkers* (Nairobi, 1948).

540. Muoria, *What Can We Do?*

541. Muoria, *Life is War by Action.*

542. Muoria, *What Can We do?*

543. Editorial, *Mumenyereri*, 1 February 1947. KNA, PC/RVP. 2/27/34.

544. Cooper, *African Waterfront*, pp. 78-113 (p. 105 for Kibachia's motive); for Kibachia's place in Mau Mau historiography see above, p. 289.

545. Alice H. Amsden, *International Firms and Labour in Kenya, 1945-70* (London, 1971); Clayton and Savage, *Government and Labour*, chs 9, 11; Sharon Stichter, *Migrant Labour in Kenya: Capitalism and African Response 1895-1975* (Harlow, 1982), ch. 5; Cooper, *African Waterfront*, ch. 6; Berman, *Control and Crisis*, pp. 385-95.

546. I owe this insight to Richard Waller; see his forthcoming 'Acceptees and aliens: Kikuyu settlement in Maasailand' in Tom Spear and R. Waller (eds), *Becoming Maasai* (London, 1992).

547. For squatter social and economic conditions, see P. Wyn Harris (Labour Commissioner), 'The Problem of the Squatter', draft memorandum, 21 February 1946: KNA, LAB. 9/1040; District Commissioner Nakuru to Commissioner for Community Development, 29 January 1952: Min C & I. 6/783; J.H. Martin, 'The problem of the squatter: economic survey of resident labour in Kenya' (mimeo, February 1947: privately held); also, Gicaru, *Land of Sunshine*; Gatheru, *Child of Two Worlds*, chs 2-4; Kariuki, *Mau Mau Detainee*, ch. 1; Barnett and Njama, *Within*, ch. 3; Wambaa and King, 'Squatter perspective'; Kanogo, *Squatters*, chs 2, 3; Throup, *Origins*, pp. 103-4; Furedi, *Mau Mau War*, ch. 2; Kershaw, 'The Rift Valley and Mau Mau' (typescript, 1986).

548. D.M. Anderson, 'Depression, dust bowl, demography and drought: the colonial state and soil conservation in East Africa during the 1930s', *African Affairs* 83 (1984), pp. 321-43; Throup, *Origins*, pp. 63-9; also, Chapter 10, above.

549. Waller, 'Acceptees and aliens'; Sorrenson, *Land Reform*, pp. 82-5; Rosberg and Nottingham, *Myth*, pp. 248-55; Throup, *Origins*, ch. 6; Kanogo, *Squatters*, pp. 105-16; Furedi, *Mau Mau War*, pp. 80-3.

550. Settlers held different views on squatter rights to stockholding, depending on whether they were wheat, maize, or dairy farmers or beef ranchers; at high altitudes or low. For full discussion see, Throup, *Origins*, pp. 95-100.

551. Karari Njama, in Barnett and Njama, *Within*, p. 84.

552. Muoria, *Our Victory*; idem, *Our Mother is the Soil*; Wambaa and King, 'Squatter perspective', p. 201; H. Thiongo Kigotho to *Mumenyereri*, 9 August 1948: KNA, MAA. 8/106.

553. For the disputed sociology of squatter resistance, see Kanogo, *Squatters*, pp. 129-36; Furedi, *Mau Mau War*, pp. 92-9; M. Tamarkin, 'Mau Mau in Nakuru', *Journal of African History* 17 (1976), pp. 119-34.

554. A.T. Wise to E.M. Hyde-Clarke, 25 July 1945: KNA, LAB. 3/41.

555. Labour Commissioner to Chief Secretary, 17 September 1946; Notes of Sir Philip Mitchell's meeting with Kikuyu squatters at Government House, 1 February 1947;

Mitchell to Creech Jones, 19 February 1947: all in *ibid*. See also Clayton and Savage, *Government and Labour*, pp. 305–9; Throup, *Origins*, pp. 110–13, 129; Furedi, *Mau Mau War*, pp. 88–90.

556. Phillips, *Report on Native Tribunals* (1945), pp. 36–77; Phillips went on to become a distinguished law professor at the University of Southampton.

557. Sorrenson, *Land Reform*, p. 79.

558. Throup, *Origins*, pp. 159–61.

559. Throup, *Origins*, uses the official term *ngwatio*; it was not used by Kikuyu.

560. Spencer, *KAU*, p. 175; Kershaw, 'Closing doors of opportunity', pp. 17–18.

561. Jeanne Fisher, *The Anatomy of Kikuyu Domesticity and Husbandry* (Department of Technical Cooperation, London, mimeo, 1953), pp. 282–4; for changing policy, Anne Thurston, *Smallholder Agriculture in Colonial Kenya: The Official Mind and the Swynnerton Plan* (Cambridge, 1987), pp. 25–30; Throup, *Origins*, p. 152, ch. 9.

562. Political songs in wa Kinyatti, *Thunder from the Mountains*, pp. 36, 39.

563. Throup, *Origins*, pp. 146, 156.

564. Mumenyereri, 29 September, 6 October, 1 December 1947: KNA, MAA. 8/106.

565. Benson (1964), p. 10; of leaders for whom data is available, Wachanga was probably married by 1947 (*Swords of Kirinyaga*, pp. xxii–xxiii); Gatu seems to have married after the Emergency (*ibid*., appendix III); Mutonyi married in his mid-twenties but did not get land from his father until some time later ('Mau Mau chairman', pp. 37, 42).

566. *Corfield Report*, pp. 67–72; Rosberg and Nottingham, *Myth*, pp. 237–8; Spencer, *KAU*, pp. 175–8; Throup, *Origins*, pp. 151–64; and above, p. 186.

567. Intelligence report, 22 July 1947: KNA, Secretariat 1/12/8.

568. *Radio Posta*, 31 October 1947, quoting chief Ignatio at the trial of his assailants: KNA, MAA. 8/105 (courtesy of David Throup's notes on this file); Wachanga, *Swords of Kirinyaga*, pp. xxxiii–xxxv for subversive dancing in Nyeri.

569. Director of Intelligence to Chief Native Commissioner, 15 June 1948: KNA, MAA. 8/102.

570. Spencer, *Beauttah*, p. 103; Githige, 'Religious factor', pp. 95–8, 136–40.

571. *Ibid*., p. 119; Kariuki, *Detainee*, p. 31; Wachanga, *Swords of Kirinyaga*, p. 1.

572. Quoted in Rosberg and Nottingham, *Myth*, p. 243.

573. Quoted in *ibid*., p. 247.

574. Itote (a Forty Group member), *General China*, p. 38.

575. Mutonyi, 'Mau Mau chairman', p. 35; see also Itote, *General China*, p. 20; neither Wachanga (born 1923) nor Gatu (born 1924) mention their own circumcision but see the former's *Swords of Kirinyaga*, p. xxiv for eligibility.

576. Wachanga, *Swords*, p. xxxii; Mutonyi, 'Mau Mau chairman', p. 41.

577. Spencer, *Beauttah*, pp. 74–5.

578. Negley Farson, *Last Chance in Africa* (New York, 1950), pp. 113–15, gives a journalist's view of Kenyatta's relations with the Forty Group in late 1947.

579. Superintendent of African Locations to Nairobi police, 28 October 1947: KNA, MAA. 8/22.

580. Domenic Gatu, interviewed by John Spencer, 4 September 1972.

581. Wachanga, *Swords*, pp. xxxiv–xxxv: inadequately rendered as 'bastard'.

582. The disputed historiography of the Forty Group has reflected its subject; see White, *Comforts of Home*, p. 189.

583. Reports in *Radio Posta*, 24, 26 October 1947: KNA, MAA. 8/105.

584. Information from T.G. Askwith, Nairobi's African Affairs Officer after the war, quoting his Kikuyu assistant Dedan Githegi; excerpt from *Muthamaki* newspaper, 7 June 1951: Press office précis of opinion no. 11/1951.

585. T.G. Askwith (Commissioner for Community Development), memoranda on 'African vagrancy', 12 January 1950; 'Some observations on the growth of unrest

in Kenya', 24 October 1952; and 'Remedies for unrest', 30 October 1952 (courtesy of the author).
586. John Walter, 'A "rising of the people"? The Oxfordshire rising of 1596', *Past & Present* 107 (1985), pp. 90–143.
587. Throup, *Origins*, p. 248 and *passim*, is right to call 1947 the year of crisis; for other narratives of the crisis see Rosberg and Nottingham, *Myth*, ch. 7; Spencer, *KAU*, chs 5, 6; Berman, *Control and Crisis*, pp. 322–38.
588. D.A. Low and J.M. Lonsdale, 'Introduction: towards the new order, 1945-1963' in D.A. Low and Alison Smith (eds), *History of East Africa iii* (Oxford, 1976), esp. pp. 12–16, 40–8; reprinted as ch. 7 in D.A. Low, *Eclipse of Empire* (Cambridge, 1991); Throup, *Origins*, has recently re-emphasized its causal importance.
589. These agrarian policy changes have attracted a large literature. See Sorrenson, *Land Reform*; Michael Cowen, 'Commodity production in Kenya's Central Province', ch. 5 in Judith Heyer et al. (eds), *Rural Development in Tropical Africa* (London, 1981); Kitching, *Class and Economic Change*, chs 4, 7, 9; Lonsdale, 'Depression and the Second World War'; D.M. Anderson and D.W. Throup, 'Africans and agricultural production in Kenya: the myth of the War as a watershed', *Journal of African History* 26 (1985), pp. 327–45; Throup, *Origins*, chs 4, 9; Thurston, *Smallholder Agriculture*; above, Chapter 10.
590. *African Education in Kenya: Report of a Committee* . . . (Nairobi, 1949), esp. pp. 39–40.
591. I owe these insights to Greet Kershaw.
592. *Corfield Report*, pp. 183–9; D.W. Throup, 'The origins of Mau Mau', *African Affairs* 84 (1985), p. 430, is the first scholar to document criticism of Kenyatta on this score.
593. For Kenyatta's 'mere trades unionism': Makhan Singh, *History of Kenya's Trade Union Movement to 1952* (Nairobi, 1969), p. 158; Spencer, *KAU*, p. 172.
594. *Radio Posta*, 20 February 1948: KNA, MAA. 8/105.
595. Intelligence reports, 25 September and 10 October 1947: KNA, Secretariat 1/12/8.
596. For the continuing image of politicians as shepherds, see chief Koinange's complaint to the governor in *East African Standard*, 2 July 1948; and the praise song 'They sat at Kaloleni' (*c.* 1951) in Kabira and Mutahi (eds) *Gikuyu Oral Literature*, p. 151.
597. Rosberg and Nottingham, *Myth*, p. 243.
598. See the vagueness of Kanogo on this point, in her *Squatters*, pp. 126–9, where her data is, unusually, derived mostly from secondary sources; Kershaw, 'Rift Valley and Mau Mau' pp. 89–90, stresses this squatter ignorance.
599. Spencer, *KAU*, pp. 206–7; Furedi, *Mau Mau War*, pp. 103–6.
600. Kershaw, 'Rift Valley and Mau Mau' pp. 90, 96–7, and personal discussion.
601. Wambaa and King, 'Squatter perspective', p. 203.
602. Buijtenhuijs, *Mouvement 'Mau Mau'*, pp. 180–3, summarizes the alternatives; and see my 'Mau Maus of the mind', p. 393 n. 2.
603. An insight I owe to Greet Kershaw; see also, Electors' Union memorandum (undated, November 1952) in Margery Perham papers, Rhodes House: MP. 467/3; Karigo Muchai, *The Man in the Middle* (Richmond, BC, 1973), pp. 32–3. For the precedent, above, p. 349.
604. Tamarkin, 'Mau Mau in Nakuru'.
605. Throup, *Origins*, pp. 133–4.
606. Laments from the songs collected in wa Kinyatti, *Thunder from the Mountains*, pp. 53–8; Wachanga, *Swords of Kirinyagga*, pp. 6–8.
607. Pointed out by Buijtenhuijs, *Essays on Mau Mau*, p. 14.
608. *Corfield Report*, p. 165, citing detainees' 'confessions'; Spencer, *KAU*, p. 208, from interviews in 1972-3.
609. Rosberg and Nottingham, *Myth*, p. 259; also Barnett and Njama, *Within*, p. 41, both from interviews in 1962-3; 'Classification Report no. 3468: John Michael Mungai', 17 May 1956: Rhodes House Mss. Afr.s. 1534.

610. Also Leakey's view in *Mau Mau and the Kikuyu*, pp. 95-6.

611. Spencer, *KAU*, pp. 178-84; Gadsden, 'African press', p. 523, for African comment.

612. *Mumenyereri*, 15 March 1948: KNA, MAA. 8/106.

613. Koinange to *Mumenyereri*, 12 July 1948.

614. Gatu, interviewed by Spencer, 4 September 1972; Wachanga, *Swords of Kirinyaga*, p. xxxvi.

615. Edith Miguda, 'Mau Mau in Nairobi 1946-1956: the Luo experience' (Nairobi University MA thesis, 1987), p. 35; Sharon Stichter, 'Workers, trade unions and the Mau Mau rebellion', *Canadian Journal of African Studies* 9 (1975), pp. 259-75.

616. Clayton and Savage, *Government and Labour*, pp. 325-8; Makhan Singh, EATUC secretary, gives a formal account of meetings and memoranda in *Kenya's Trade Union Movement*, chs 16, 17, a cover for inaction.

617. See the origin myth of the Forty Group in Wachanga, *Swords*, pp. xxiii-xxiv; generally: Eric Hobsbawm and Terence Ranger (eds), *The Invention of Tradition* (Cambridge, 1983).

618. Spencer, *KAU*, p. 33.

619. Rosberg and Nottingham, *Myth*, pp. 247-8, 259; Spencer, *KAU*, p. 208; Githige, 'Religious factor', pp. 171, 177-8. I do not know how the sum of shillings 62/50 was arrived at.

620. Rosberg and Nottingham, *Myth*, p. 247; Kershaw, *Mau Mau from Below*.

621. *Corfield Report*, p. 31.

622. For example, Mungai ('Classification report'); Ngugi Kabiro, who earned shillings 200 per month: *Man in the Middle* (Richmond, BC, 1973), p. 27; Kariuki (a trader who had redeemed his father's land in Nyeri and turned friends into *ahoi*): *Mau Mau Detainee*, pp. 12, 26-7.

623. Barnett and Njama, *Within*, p. 119; Waruhiu Itote, *'Mau Mau' General* (Nairobi, 1967), pp. 40, 50; Joram Wamweya, *Freedom Fighter* (Nairobi, 1971), p. 45; Mohammed Mathu, *The Urban Guerrilla* (Richmond, BC, 1974), p. 10; neither Kanogo, *Squatters*, nor Furedi, *Mau Mau War*, have information on squatter fee payments.

624. Githige, 'Religious factor', pp. 140-1, 149-50, 164-5, 173, 186-7, 194.

625. *Ibid.*, pp. 190-1; Leakey, *Defeating Mau Mau*, p. 81; Barnett and Njama, *Within*, pp. 118-19; also, Kariuki, *Mau Mau Detainee*, p. 26; Kabiro, *Man in Middle*, p. 26; Mathu, *Urban Guerrilla*, p. 11; Muchai, *Hard Core*, p. 16.

626. Gikoyo, *We Fought for Freedom*, p. 35.

627. For the pacific myth of Waiyaki in 1938: Leakey, *Southern Kikuyu*, i, p. 31; in political education: Rosberg and Nottingham, *Myth*, pp. 180-1; Mbugua Njama, *Mahoya ma Waiyaki* (Nairobi, 1952); Kabira and wa Mutahi, *Gikuyu Oral Literature*, pp. 151-3; wa Kinyatti, *Thunder from the Mountains*, pp. 15, 25, 29; Kariuki, *Detainee*, p. 21. For *kirumi*: Kenyatta, *Facing Mount Kenya*, p. 114; Hobley, *Bantu Beliefs*, pp. 145-53.

628. *Mumenyereri*, 8 July 1949: KNA, PC/RVP. 2/27/34; and 22 September 1952, p. 4 (privately held).

629. *Corfield Report*, pp. 163, 166; and, more recently, Maia Green, 'Mau Mau oathing rituals and political ideology in Kenya: a re-analysis', *Africa* 60 (1990), pp. 69-87.

630. Anthony Cleary, 'The myth of Mau Mau in its international context', *African Affairs* 89 (1990), pp. 227-45.

631. *Mumenyereri*, 22 March, 10 May 1948: KNA, MAA. 8/106.

632. Director of Intelligence, reports of 25 September and 10 October 1947: KNA, Secretariat 1/12/8.

633. Kaggia, *Roots*, pp. 89-92 and Mutonyi, 'Chairman', pp. 46-7; generally: B.E. Kipkorir, 'The educated elite and local society: the basis for mass representation', ch. 12 in B.A. Ogot (ed.), *Politics and Nationalism in Colonial Kenya: Hadith 4* (Nairobi, 1972).

Wealth, Poverty & Civic Virtue in Kikuyu Political Thought

634. Rosberg and Nottingham, *Myth*, pp. 266–7; Clayton and Savage, *Government and Labour*, pp. 328–37; Spencer, *KAU*, pp. 214–15; *idem, Beauttah*, p. 84; Throup, *Origins*, pp. 193–5; *Mumenyereri*, 12 April 1950: KNA, MAA. 8/106.

635. Kubai, far from complying with official rules, led his taxi drivers against Nairobi's byelaws; Kaggia formed his clerical union in order to gain entry to the EATUC.

636. In his *Roots of Freedom*, where his main enthusiasms are for a Christianity stripped of white phariseeism and a retranslation of the Kikuyu Bible.

637. *Ibid.*, p. 63; *idem*, interview with Spencer (13 April 1972), p. 3; and Kubai in 'End of Empire' (screened 1 July 1985): 'we tried to exploit the ignorance of our people'.

638. For his influence, Kaggia, *Roots*, p. 78; for the paper, Classification report: John Mungai, pp. 9–10: Rhodes House, Mss. Afr.s. 1534.

639. Singh, *Kenya's Trade Union Movement*, pp. 1–2, 4 (written in the 1960s, this is an admittedly poor guide to what he may have written *c.* 1950); Dana A. Seidenberg, *Uhuru and the Kenya Indians: The Role of a Minority Community in Kenya Politics* (New Delhi, 1983) tells of programmes, not ideas; Iliffe's *African Poor* refutes the communalist myth.

640. R. Macpherson, *The Presbyterian Church in Kenya* (Nairobi, 1970), p. 122.

641. Wa Wanjau, *Mau Mau Author*, pp. x–xi for a brief autobiography; Kipkorir, 'Alliance High School', pp. 187–93 for the 1940 strike.

642. Wa Wanjau, *Roho ya Kiume na Bidii kwa Mwafrika*, in *idem, Mau Mau Author*, pp. 221–43; for his sales to squatters: Wambaa and King, 'Squatter perspective', p. 210.

643. Compare Rosberg and Nottingham, *Myth*, pp. 73–80.

644. *Kenya African Agricultural Sample Census 1960/61 Part I* (Nairobi, 1961), pp. 20–1; *Part II* (Nairobi, 1961), pp. 10, 29.

645. Kitching, *Class and Economic Change*, pp. 110–13, 120.

646. Eric R. Wolf, *Peasant Wars of the Twentieth Century* (London, 1971), pp. 289–92.

647. For the veterinary story, Michael Cowen, 'Patterns of cattle ownership and dairy production' (Nairobi University, mimeo, 1974), pp. 14–37; for paddocking, Sorrenson, *Land Reform*, pp. 135–6.

648. I.B. Pole-Evans, *Report on a Visit to Kenya* (Nairobi, 1939); in March 1940 the KCA circulated a condemnation of this report, entitled 'Notice re. the extermination of Goats, Sheep and Cattle': see 'Third report of advisory committee', 26 August 1940, in Governor Moore to Secretary of State, 28 September 1940: PRO, CO533/523/38481. For postwar memories of Pole-Evans: Johnson Maina to *Mumenyereri*, 29 September 1947; Spencer, *Beauttah*, p. 108; Henry Wambugu, interview for Spencer, 30 March 1972.

649. N. Humphrey, 'The relationship of population to the land in South Nyeri', p. 10 in Humphrey *et al.*, *The Kikuyu Lands* (Nairobi, 1945); KAU memo (August 1946), p. 2: PRO, CO 533/537/38672.

650. Cowen, 'Patterns of cattle ownership', pp. 35–9; Koinange, *The People of Kenya Speak for Themselves*, pp. 17–23; Mitchell to Creech Jones, August 1946: PRO, CO533/535/38516; Wachanga, *Swords of Kirinyaga*, pp. xxxii–xxxiii; interviews for Spencer with Gachuuru wa Ngorano (29 March 1972) and Henry Wambugu (30 March, 27 May 1972); Spencer, *KAU*, pp. 166–8; Throup, *Origins*, pp. 157–8.

651. Wachanga, *Swords*, pp. 16–17; Cowen, 'Patterns', pp. 41–2; in Murang'a the Emergency was also, in part, a dairy war: D. Mukaru Ng'ang'a, 'Mau Mau, loyalists and politics in Murang'a, 1952–1970'. *Kenya Historical Review* 5 (2)(1977), pp. 368, 372–3.

652. Evidence of Thinguri wa Kuria, 15 November 1932: *KLCE* i, p. 163.

653. Wachanga, *Swords*, pp. xxv, 9.

654. I owe this insight to Luise White, whose planned *Blood and Fire* may make better sense

of the phenomenon than I can. Jean-Francois Bayart, *L'Etat en Afrique: la politique du ventre* (Paris, 1989) is another encouragement to speculation.

655. Spencer, *Beauttah*, pp. 108–9; Governor Mitchell to Secretary of State, 12 November 1951: PRO, CO822/429.
656. Wa Kinyatti, *Thunder from the Mountains*, pp. 60–1, 'Women of Murang'a' ballad.
657. As recollected by Kenyatta, for example; Murray-Brown, *Kenyatta*, pp. 39, 341.
658. Spencer, *Beauttah*, pp. 80, 96–7.
659. For the view that Gathiomi's death was an accident: *ibid.*, p. 97; Classification report, John Mungai, pp. 6–9: Rhodes House, Mss. Afr.s.1534; Spencer, *KAU*, p. 234. For the view that it was a Mau Mau execution, interview for Spencer, 15 September 1972, by a senior Kiambu KCA elder; Gathiomi's death may be that described by Kaggia, *Roots of Freedom*, p. 110, an account with some resemblance to Mungai's; also Throup, 'Moderates, militants and Mau Mau', p. 17.
660. Domenic Gatu, interviewed in Wachanga, *Swords of Kirinyaga*, pp. 174–6; and for Spencer, 4 September 1972.
661. Spencer, *KAU*, p. 208; White, *Comforts of Home*, pp. 205–8.
662. Spencer, *Beauttah*, p. 90.
663. I have nothing to add to the accounts in Rosberg and Nottingham, *Myth*, pp. 269–72; Spencer, *KAU*, pp. 221–8; Kaggia, *Roots*, pp. 79–82.
664. Rosberg and Nottingham, *Myth*, p. 233, saw this last as 'a turning point'; see also, Spencer, *KAU*, pp. 216–21.
665. Rosberg and Nottingham, *Myth*, pp. 223–5; Spencer, *KAU*, pp. 225–6; Kaggia, *Roots*, pp. 114–15.
666. Again, I am unable to add to the accounts in Rosberg and Nottingham, *Myth*, pp. 270–6; modified by Spencer, *KAU*, pp. 228–32; modified further by Throup, 'Moderates, militants and Mau Mau', pp. 18–19. Governor Baring cited Kenyatta's campaign first among his justifications for declaring an Emergency, to Lyttelton, 10 October 1952: PRO, CO822/443.
667. The opinion of KCA elders in Nakuru: Tamarkin, 'Mau Mau in Nakuru', p. 131.
668. Interview for John Spencer, 28 March 1972; for a fictional comparison, see Mbugua's complaint in Ngugi wa Thiong'o, *A Grain of Wheat* (London, 1968), p. 117; I am grateful for Greet Kershaw's insights on this problem.
669. Tamarkin, 'Mau Mau in Nakuru', pp. 127, 130; Furedi, *Mau Mau War*, pp. 111, 113; see also Rosberg and Nottingham, *Myth*, p. 248.
670. Kariuki, *Mau Mau Detainee*, p. 33; Githige, 'Religious factor', p. 212; Mutonyi, 'Mau Mau chairman', p. 59.
671. Kanogo, *Squatters*, pp. 129–36; Furedi, *Mau Mau War*, pp. 92–9.
672. *Corfield Report*, pp. 77, 97.
673. Baring to Lyttelton, 24 February 1953: PRO, CO822/440; Kershaw, 'Rural stratification in Kiambu' (1986 typescript), p. 23.
674. Wa Wanjau, *Mau Mau Author*, p. 235.
675. Leakey, *Defeating Mau Mau*, pp. 73, 59.
676. Mutonyi, 'Mau Mau chairman', pp. 64, 71–2.
677. Leakey, *Defeating Mau Mau*, p. 68; wa Kinyatti, *Thunder from the Mountains*, p. 25.
678. *Corfield Report*, p. 164.
679. Mutonyi, 'Mau Mau chairman', pp. 67, 109–12; Henry Wambugu, interview for Spencer, 9 December 1972.
680. Member for African Affairs, *Legislative Council Debates*, vol. 50 (20 September 1952), cols 250–1; Kandara division handing-over report, 1 March 1955: Rhodes House, Mss. Afr. s. 839(1); compare Kenyatta, *Facing Mount Kenya*, p. 304.
681. For *eriiri*, *thaka* and fire in the *nyimbo*, see Leakey, *Defeating Mau Mau*, pp. 59, 60, 62, 64, 66 (the fate of Sodom), 70, 72; wa Kinyatti, *Thunder from the Mountains*, pp. 18, 24, 26, 36, 49, 61, 70, 91; Githige, 'Religious factor', p. 288.

682. For the general accusation in *nyimbo*: Leakey, *Defeating Mau Mau*, pp. 66, 70; wa Kinyatti, *Thunder*, pp. 40, 41, 43, 46, 91. For chief Luka: *Mumenyereri*, 10 May 1948.

683. Mukaru Ng'ang'a, 'Mau Mau in Murang'a', p. 372.

684. T.F.C. Bewes, *Kikuyu Conflict: Mau Mau and the Christian Witness* (London, 1953), p. 46.

685. Kingsley Martin, 'Report on Kenya ii: the African point of view', *New Statesman and Nation* (London, 6 December 1952).

686. See Andrew Hake, *African Metropolis: Nairobi's Self-help City* (London, 1977) for a study by the man most responsible.

687. Mutonyi, 'Mau Mau chairman', p. 50.

688. Kaggia, *Roots of Freedom*, p. 194.

689. Githige, 'Religious factor', p. 272; Barnett and Njama, *Within*, pp. 121–3 and Kariuki, *Detainee*, pp. 31–6, for Christian reaction to Mau Mau oaths; for Christianity and sorcery, Iliffe, *Modern History of Tanganyika*, pp. 236–7.

690. But see Welbourn, *East African Rebels*, ch. 8.

691. Leakey, *Defeating Mau Mau*, pp. 57, 63, 71; wa Kinyatti, *Thunder*, pp. 18, 39, 40.

692. Leakey, *Defeating Mau Mau*, p. 69; for other references to Kenyatta see pp. 57, 59, 66–8, 70–3; wa Kinyatti, *Thunder*, pp. 47, 56–7; Barnett and Njama, *Within*, p. 347; Githige, 'Religious factor', p. 284; Wanyoike, *African Pastor*, pp. 180–5.

693. As Kenyatta later pointed out to clerical critics: Agnes Chepkwony, *The Role of Non-Governmental Organisations in Development: A Study of the National Christian Council of Kenya 1963–78* (Uppsala, 1987), p. 86.

694. Guy Campbell, *The Charging Buffalo: A History of the Kenya Regiment, 1937–1963* (London, 1986), pp. 168–9.

695. Leakey, *Defeating Mau Mau*, p. 68; wa Kinyatti, *Thunder*, pp. 26, 38.

696. Leakey, *Defeating Mau Mau*, pp. 60, 67; wa Kinyatti, *Thunder*, pp. 18, 19, 31, 45, 90; for earlier analysis of the *nyimbo*, see B.A. Ogot, 'Politics, culture and music in Central Kenya: a study of Mau Mau hymns 1951–1956', *Kenya Historical Review* 5(2) (1977), pp. 275–86. Some have been reissued in D. Kinuthia Mugia, *Urathi wa Cege wa Kibiru* (Nairobi, 1979), pp. 58–73, and Gakaara wa Wanjau, *Nyimbo cia Mau Mau* (Karatina, ?1988).

697. D.H. Rawcliffe, *The Struggle for Kenya* (London, 1954), pp. 32–5; Rosberg and Nottingham, *Myth*, p. 324–31; Furedi, *Mau Mau War*, p. 109.

698. As the *Corfield Report*, p. 72, acknowledged in the case of the sect discussed below.

699. Reports and correspondence in *Mumenyereri*, 29 December 1947, 5, 12 January and 9 February 1948: KNA, MAA. 8/106; Rawcliffe, *Struggle*, p. 30; Muoria, 'British and Kikuyu', p. 223; Wamagatta, 'Biography of senior chief Waruhiu', pp. 265–7.

700. Joseph Ng'ang'a Kimani, 'Rules written on 3 March 1950' and 'Things to be observed by all Godly people', in Sandgren, *Christianity and the Kikuyu*, pp. 161–74.

701. Murray, 'Kikuyu spirit churches'; Njeri, 'Akurinu', pp. 73–8.

702. Wanyoike, *African Pastor*, pp. 165, 167.

703. Church Missionary Society [CMS], *Mau Mau* (London, 1952), p. 12; Church of Scotland Mission [CSM], *Mau Mau and the Church* (Edinburgh, 1953), p. 5; Welbourn, *Rebels*, p. 133; W.B. Anderson, *The Church in East Africa, 1840–1974* (Dodoma, 1977), p. 129.

704. Wanyoike, *African Pastor*, pp. 151–68; Ward, 'Protestant Christianity', pp. 353, 361; discussions with Jocelyn Murray, now writing the history of the Kenyan revival.

705. Bewes, *Kikuyu Conflict*, p. 41.

706. Mbugua Njama, *Mahoya ma Waiyaki* (Nairobi, 1952), translated as 'The prayers of Waiyaki' in 1968 by the then James Ngugi: appendix 4 in McIntosh, 'Scottish mission'.

707. It must have given whites reassurance to be able to quote Father Trevor Huddleston, white hero of black resistance to apartheid in South Africa, to the effect that Mau

Mau was 'a reversion to primitive superstition, . . . avowedly anti-Christian, . . . wholly evil, . . . the worst enemy of African progress in Kenya': *Johannesburg Star*, 12 December 1952, quoted in *Corfield Report*, p. 162.

708. For the *batuni* vows see: Barnett and Njama, *Within*, pp. 67–9, 131–2; *Corfield Report*, p. 167; Gikoyo, *We Fought for Freedom*, pp. 49–50; Githige, 'Religious factor', pp. 222–3; Itote, *Mau Mau General*, pp. 275–6; Kariuki, *Detainee*, pp. 29–30; Muchai, *Hard Core*, pp. 19–20; Wamweya, *Freedom Fighter*, pp. 52–3.

709. *Corfield Report*, pp. 72, 81, 141, 149, 151, 155n.

710. Barnett and Njama, *Within*, pp. 133–4; Githige, 'Religious factor', pp. 49–50; Thuku, *Autobiography*, p. 68; Wamagatta, 'Waruhiu', p. 362; Wanyoike, *African Pastor*, p. 189.

711. *Corfield Report*, pp. 225–9, 283; the police recovered much of the ammunition.

712. *Ibid.*, pp. 126, 138–40, 144, 156; Kanogo, *Squatters*, pp. 136–8; Furedi, *Mau Mau War*, pp. 112–18.

713. See above, p. 293.

714. Wanyoike, *African Pastor*, p. 186; this is much the best of the Kikuyu, indeed of any, accounts of the build-up to the Emergency.

715. *Ibid.*, pp. 180, 192–4; *Corfield Report*, pp. 134–6; Leakey (who claimed to have instigated the cleansing campaign), *Mau Mau and the Kikuyu*, pp. 100–3; Berman and Lonsdale, 'Louis Leakey's Mau Mau', p. 182; *East African Standard*, 1 August 1952.

716. Welbourn, *Rebels*, pp. 153, 155–6, 160–1, 198.

717. Sandgren, *Christianity and the Kikuyu*, pp. 157–9.

718. Correspondence in KNA, DC/MUR. 3/4/1, 'Education: CMS schools and African Anglican Church'; CSM, *Mau Mau and the Church*, p. 6.

719. *East African Standard*, 8 August 1952.

720. S.H. Fazan, *History of the Loyalists* (Nairobi, 1960), pp. 9, 80.

721. Githige, 'Religious factor', pp. 52, 182–3; Wanyoike, *African Pastor*, pp. 193–6; E.M. Wiseman, *Kikuyu Martyrs* (London, 1958), pp. 15–17.

722. Martin Capon, 'Kikuyu, 1948: a working answer', September 1948: KNA, DC/MUR. 3/4/21; Kenyatta in *KLCE* i, p. 422; *Corfield Report*, p. 301.

723. *East African Standard*, 22 August 1952.

724. Rosberg and Nottingham, *Myth*, pp. 271–3; Barnett and Njama, *Within*, pp. 61–6; Buijtenhuijs, *Essays*, pp. 61–5.

725. Routledge, *Prehistoric People*, p. 195.

726. Mutonyi, 'Chairman', pp. 110–12.

727. wa Wanjau, *Mau Mau Author*, pp. 2–3.

728. An impression gained from Professor Spencer's interview transcripts.

729. *Corfield Report*, pp. 301–8; and the memory of Godfrey Muriuki, present as a schoolboy.

730. *Corfield Report*, p. 153.

731. Mutonyi, 'Chairman', pp. 48, 105–7.

732. *Ibid.*, pp. 78–85; Kaggia, *Roots*, p. 114; Kubai, with a sinister chuckle in 'End of Empire'.

733. Peter Abrahams, 'The Blacks' [1959] reprinted in Langston Hughes (ed.), *An African Treasury* (New York, 1960), pp. 50–62; it is interesting that Abrahams' account of 'tribal man', immediately following his description of Kenyatta, started with the 'smelling out' of a sorcerer.

734. Kaggia, *Roots*, pp. 193–4; Kariuki, *Detainee*, pp. 31–2; Rosberg and Nottingham, *Myth*, p. 261; Barnett and Njama, *Within*, pp. 63, 66.

735. *Corfield Report*, p. 273, 202–18.

736. Mathu, *Urban Guerilla*, p. 23; Githige, 'Religious factor', pp. 183–4.

737. *Corfield Report*, ch. 9; Miguda, 'Mau Mau in Nairobi'; Embu Special Branch

Handing-Over Report, January 1956, Appendix A (privately held).
738. Githige, 'Religious factor', pp. 49-50, 53-6, 175; Gicaru, *Land of Sunshine*, p. 161.
739. Njoroge Kabetu, *Kiriria kia Ugikuyu*, pp. 92-3; *Mumeyereri*, 14 June 1948.
740. 'Report on the sociological causes underlying Mau Mau, with some proposals on the means of ending it' (secret), 21 April 1954: Appendix II (privately held).
741. Mutonyi, 'Chairman', p. 68; Kabira and wa Mutahi, *Gikuyu Oral Literature*, p. 23; Bernardi, *Age Class Systems*, pp. 48-50, 60.
742. Buijtenhuijs, *Essays*, pp. 92, 127-33.
743. Itote, *Mau Mau General*, p. 55, where the phrase is innocently translated as 'the cottage of our ancestors'.
744. Barnett and Njama, *Within*, p. 100.
745. As General Kaleba explicitly stated on his capture in 1954; see Lonsdale, 'Mau Maus of the mind', p. 416.
746. Kaggia, *Roots*, p. 107; Kabira and wa Mutahi, *Gikuyu Oral Literature*, p. 160; Githige, 'Religious factor', pp. 46-7.
747. wa Kinyatti, *Thunder from the Mountains*, p. 34; Mathu, *Urban Guerrilla*, pp. 13-14; *Mumenyereri*, 20 September 1952, p. 4.
748. Wa Kinyatti, *Thunder*, p. 45; Nyandarwa used to be known as the Aberdare Mountains.
749. Mbugua Njama, *Mahoya ma Waiyaki*.
750. Barnett and Njama, *Within*, p. 257.
751. Kaggia, *Roots*, pp. 116-17.
752. For some beginnings, see Anthony Clayton, *Counter-insurgency in Kenya 1952-60* (Nairobi, 1976); Basil Davidson, *The People's Cause: A History of Guerrillas in Africa* (Harlow, 1981), ch. 8; Robert B. Edgerton, *Mau Mau: An African Crucible* (New York, 1989), ch. 4; Randall Heather, 'Intelligence and counter-insurgency in Kenya, 1952-56', *Intelligence and National Security* 5(3) (1990), pp. 57-83.
753. And see Edgerton, *An African Crucible*, ch. 5.
754. Lonsdale, 'Mau Maus of the mind', pp. 397-9.
755. Kershaw, *Mau Mau from Below*.
756. Barnett and Njama, *Within*, pp. 141, 154-5, 177, 192-5, 222, 319, 324, 345, 349, 351; Gikoyo, *We Fought for Freedom*, pp. 36-7; Interrogation of Waruhiu Itote, alias 'General China' (Kenya Police Special Branch, Nairobi, 26 January 1954, p. 38 (privately held); Itote, *Mau Mau General*, p. 150; Muchai, *Hard Core*, p. 22; Mutonyi, 'Chairman', p. 108; Wachanga, *Swords*, pp. 23-4, 38-9, 46-7; Maina wa Kinyatti (ed.), *Kenya's Freedom Struggle: The Dedan Kimathi Papers* (London, 1987), pp. 39, 68; Buijtenhuijs, *Essays*, pp. 62-5, 67.
757. Barnett and Njama, *Within*, pp. 139-42; Kariuki, *Detainee*, p. 35; Koinange, *People of Kenya*, p. 65; Wanyoike, *African Pastor*, p. 194; Kinyatti, *Kenya's Freedom Struggle*, p. 62.
758. John Pinney (ed.), 'History of the [Fort Hall] Kikuyu Guard', 1957: Rhodes House, Mss. Afr.s: 1915(2); Fazan, *History of the Loyalists*, pp. 34, 48.
759. Pinney's 'History' is a dramatic account; Fazan, *History*, p. 78, for casualty figures.
760. Anonymous Mau Mau document, translated as 'A book of forest history or war in the forest and attacks here and there', captured by Willoughby Thompson in December 1953: Rhodes House. Mss. Afr.s. 1534.
761. Dedan Kimathi seems to have admitted it to have been a Mau Mau action: wa Kinyatti, *Kenya's Freedom Struggle*, p. 61.
762. Fazan, *History of the Loyalists*, pp. 29-33; Rosberg and Nottingham, *Myth*, pp. 286-92; Itote, *Mau Mau General*, ch. 18; Wanyoike, *African Pastor*, pp. 196-200.
763. Pinney, 'History of the Kikuyu Guard', pp. 5-6, 24, 34; information from Jocelyn Murray, Cyril Hooper and John Karanja.
764. Mutonyi, 'Chairman', p. 94; Kimathi, open letter to the British, August 1953: wa Kinyatti, *Kenya's Freedom Struggle*, pp. 57-8.

765. Kimathi, circular to field commanders, early 1954: in *ibid.*, p. 25; Interrogation of Kaleba, 28 October 1954: KNA, DC/NYK. 3/13/34.

766. Commander Ndiritu wa Thuita at session of the 'Kenya Parliament' February 1954; and Colonel Wamugunda to Kimathi, mid-1954: wa Kinyatti, *Kenya's Freedom Struggle*, pp. 36, 91.

767. Mutonyi, 'Chairman', pp. 100-1.

768. Minutes of the Kenya Parliament, chaired by Dedan Kimathi, February 1954: Maina wa Kinyatti, *Kenya's Freedom Struggle*.

769. Barnett and Njama, *Within*, pp. 275-83, 374 (for the ex-squatter general Kimbo of Thorpe's farm fame), 402-3, 410-11, 415.

770. *Ibid.*, pp. 149-58, 171, 245-6 (for Mau Mau order of battle), pp. 314-15.

771. Barnett and Njama, *Within*, pp. 164-6, 168, 194-5; Itote, *Mau Mau General*, p. 285-91; Wachanga, *Swords*, pp. 37-9; wa Kinyatti, *Kenya's Freedom Struggle*, pp. 21-2, 33-4, 41, 93.

772. Benson (1964), p. 226; Gikoyo, *We Fought for Freedom*, p. 306.

773. Barnett and Njama, *Within*, p. 479; for other accounts of *komerera* see *ibid.*, pp. 213, 221, 293-5, 376, 390, 397, 498; Itote, *Mau Mau General*, pp. 139-41; Kariuki, *Detainee*, p. 96; Mathu, *Urban Guerrilla*, p. 26.

774. Barnett and Njama, *Within*, p. 180.

775. Director of Intelligence and Security: 'The Kikuyu Musical Society and the "Moscow" oath', 12 July 1954: KNA, DC/NYK. 3/12/33 (courtesy of Randall Heather); Barnett and Njama, *Within*, pp. 341-3; Gikoyo, *We Fought for Freedom*, pp. 308-15; Mutonyi, 'Chairman', pp. 113-14; wa Kinyatti, *Kenya's Freedom Struggle*, p. 47.

776. Wa Kinyatti, *Kenya's Freedom Struggle*, p. 113; also Barnett and Njama, *Within*, p. 396.

777. Barnett and Njama, *Within*, pp. 265, 397-401, 413, 455-6, 471.

778. *Ibid.*, chs 18-20; Wachanga, *Swords*, ch. 7.

779. Peter Marris (District Information Officer) to District Commissioner Nyeri, 25 May 1954 (copy by courtesy of Greet Kershaw); Marris went on to a distinguished career in academic sociology.

780. Barnett and Njama, *Within*, p. 143; Gikoyo, *We Fought for Freedom*, pp. 46, 147, 164; Itote, *Mau Mau General*, pp. 63, 90-1; Presley, 'Kikuyu women', pp. 236-52.

781. Gikoyo, *We Fought*, pp. 50-1; Kabira and wa Mutahi, *Gikuyu Oral Literature*, p. 157.

782. Kariuki, *Mau Mau Detainee*, pp. 35-6; Wachanga, *Swords*, p. 93; Likimani, *Passbook Number F. 47927*, pp. 72, 74-81, 94-5, 115, 130, 156, 175 – fictional accounts said to be based on fact.

783. Itote, *Mau Mau General*, ch. 18.

784. Barnett and Njama, *Within*, p. 434.

785. Leakey, *Southern Kikuyu* i, pp. 502, 508; iii, pp. 1049-52.

786. Barnett and Njama, *Within*, p. 226.

787. Kanogo, *Squatters*, p. 148.

788. Gikoyo, *We Fought*, pp. 55, 71, 105-7, 145; Itote, *Mau Mau General*, pp. 57, 78, 115, 117; Kariuki, *Detainee*, p. 34.

789. Barnett and Njama, *Within*, pp. 153, 161, 166, 235; Gikoyo, *We Fought*, pp. 60, 92-3, 124-6, 152.

790. Barnett and Njama, *Within*, p. 291.

791. Barnett and Njama, *Within*, pp. 165, 187, 194, 215, 244, 248; Gikoyo, *We Fought*, pp. 60, 64-6, 110, 113-14; Itote, *Mau Mau General*, pp. 289-90; Wachanga, *Swords*, p. 37.

792. Barnett and Njama, pp. 219, 221-3, 248-9, 295-6; Itote, *Mau Mau General*, pp. 78, 281-2, 289-90.

793. Wa Kinyatti, *Thunder from the Mountains*, pp. 93-6.

794. For accounts similar to my own see, Kathy Santilli, 'Kikuyu Women in the Mau Mau Revolt: a closer look', *Ufahamu* 8(1) (1977-78), pp. 143-59; Jean O'Barr, 'Introductory essay', pp. 1-37 in Likimani, *Passbook*; Buijtenhuis, *Essays*, pp. 183-9; Kanogo, *Squatters*, pp. 143-9. For an orginal approach see, White, 'Separating the Men from the Boys', pp. 10-15.

795. Itote, *Mau Mau General*, pp. 223-7; Kariuki, *Detainee*, pp. 148, 172-7; Wachanga, *Swords*, pp. 151-2; Wamweya, *Freedom Fighter*, p. 199.

796. Gikoyo, *We Fought*, pp. 184, 192-4; Wachanga, *Swords*, p. xxi.

797. Barnett and Njama, *Within*, p. 184; Wachanga, *Swords*, p. 88; Ian Henderson, with Philip Goodhart, *The Hunt for Kimathi* (London, 1958), p. 254.

798. Barnett and Njama, *Within*, pp. 185, 440; wa Kinyatti, *Thunder from the Mountains*. p. 81; Wachanga, *Swords*, pp. 42, 77, 117, 120-1.

799. Gikoyo, *We Fought*, pp. 86-8; Wachanga, *Swords*, p. 75.

800. Barnett and Njama, *Within*, pp. 180-2; Wachanga, *Swords*, pp. 87-8.

801. Kimathi to Dr Mugwanji, 23 May 1954: wa Kinyatti, *Kenya's Freedom Struggle*, p. 20.

802. Official cinema vans each carried a 'loyalty and royalty' film; 10,000 pictures of the royal family were issued to Africans in 1950-1: Governor Mitchell to Major-General Hawkins, 10 December 1951: KNA, MAA. 7/573; for a Kenya press report of local coronation celebrations: Sir Philip Mitchell, *African Afterthoughts* (London, 1954), pp. 269-70.

803. Wachanga, *Swords*, p. 443.

804. Barnett and Njama, *Within*, p. 63.

805. 'A book of forest history': Rhodes House, Mss. Afr.s. 1534. The oath of obedience to enable rulers to rule well sounds much like the political theory of the Shambaa, who believed that tributary obedience was the best guarantee of fertility; see Steven Feierman, *Peasant Intellectuals, Anthropology and History in Tanzania* (Madison and London, 1990).

806. wa Kinyatti, *Kenya's Freedom Struggle*, pp. 24-8, 39, 86.

807. Sorrenson, *Land Reform*, ch. 14; Lamb, *Peasant Politics*, pp. 10-16; Mukaru Ng'ang'a, 'Mau Mau in Murang'a', pp. 371-3.

808. Paul Collier and Deepak Lal, *Labour and Poverty in Kenya 1900-1980* (Oxford, 1986), p. 147; S.H. Ominde, *Land and Population Movements in Kenya* (London, 1968), pp. 136, 151-5.

809. Huxley (ed.), *Nellie*, p. 270; for differing views on the fate of the squatters in the politics of the Rift Valley settlement schemes which sealed the independence deal see, John W. Harbeson, *Nation-building in Kenya: The Politics of Land Reform* (Evanston, 1973); Colin Leys, *Underdevelopment in Kenya: The Political Economy of Neo-colonialism* (London, 1975), pp. 73-98; Christopher Leo, *Land and Class in Kenya* (Toronto, 1985); Kanogo, *Squatters*, ch. 6; Furedi, *Mau Mau War*, chs 7, 8; Njonjo, 'Africanization of the "White Highlands" '.

810. To adapt a forest fighter's song: Barnett and Njama, *Within*, p. 347.

811. P.D. Abrams, *Kenya's Land Resettlement Story* (Nairobi, 1979), p. 65.

812. For a fictional account of the contrast between meritorious rural capitalism and the illegitimate use of state loans to buy land see, James Ngugi (wa Thiong'o), *A Grain of Wheat* (London [1967], 1968), pp. 67-70, 191-2.

813. Ali A. Mazrui, *Violence and Thought* (London, 1969), chs 5, 13; Ogot, 'History and ideology', p. 1.

814. For the last, see Davison, *Mutira*, pp. 178, 193, 206, 242, 256, 446.

815. For an echo of *ndamathia*'s role in deterring the abuse of power, *ibid.*, p. 97.

816. Contrary to wa Wanjau's 'Creed of Gikuyu and Muumbi': *Mau Mau Author*, p. 250.

817. *Corfield Report*, p. 307.

818. For an early exception see, Walker Connor, 'Nation-building or nation-destroying,' *World Politics* 24 (1972), pp. 319-55.

819. For an instructive example see, Oginga Odinga, *Not Yet Uhuru* (London, 1967), p. 81.

820. Robert H. Bates, *Beyond the Miracle of the Market: The Political Economy of Agrarian Development in Kenya* (Cambridge, 1989).

821. Daniel T. arap Moi, *Kenya African Nationalism: Nyayo Philosophy and Principles* (London, 1986); E.S. Atieno-Odhiambo, 'Democracy and the ideology of order in Kenya', ch. 7 in M. Schatzberg (ed.), *The Political Economy of Kenya* (New York, 1987).

822. Chris Allen, 'Staying put: handy hints for heads of state' (Paper for ASAUK symposium on Authority and Legitimacy in Africa, Stirling, 1986).

823. Bates, *Beyond the Miracle*; David Throup, 'The construction and destruction of the Kenyatta state', ch. 3 in Schatzberg (ed.), *Political Economy of Kenya*.

824. The latter of which were on sale on audio cassettes in 1990.

825. Atieno-Odhiambo, 'Democracy and the ideology of order', p. 200; *matatus* are Kenya's ubiquitous mini-buses.

826. To which Crawford Young's *Politics of Cultural Pluralism* remains a most useful guide.

827. At Stirling University, 1988, by courtesy of John McCracken.

Index

i

Index

Index

ethnicity, 199, 207–11, 303 n.10, 268–9, 277–8, 328–30, 350–3; construction of, 13, 38, 353–4, 360, 371, 404; inter-ethnic relations, 14, 25, 329; Kikuyu, 326–30, 336, 346–7, 392, 437; *karing'a*, 327, 336, 393, 397, 406, 429; *kirore*, 384, 393, 397, 406; tribalism, 267–8, 277, 279, 315; tribalism as a metaphor, 330–2; tribal identity, 268, 353; of Mau Mau, 315–7; and politics, 327–30, 330–2; precolonial, 348
ethnographies, in Kenya, 320, 468 n.7
explorers, European, in Kenya, 319

Fabianism, 209
false consciousness (*see also* ideology *and* class conflict
famine, famines, 14, 23, 30, 342, 346, 349, 364, 372
Fazan, Sidney, 376
fiscal policies, for colonies, 155, 166
Fonds d'investissement et du developpement economique et social des territoires d'Outre Mer (FIDES), 166, 176 n.100
Foreign Office, 16, 32, 85
'formal subsumption of labour', 129
forms of production, pre-capitalist, 129; domestic, 131, indigenous, 145
Fort Hall (Murang'a) District, 251, 395, 421, 433
Fort Smith, 25, 26
Forty Group, *see under: anake a forti*
Frank, Gunder, 179–80
French Colonial Africa, 145, 146–7, 148–9, 151, 153, 154–6, 157, 159, 160–3, 164, 165, 166–8
frontiers: African hunting, 17; farming, 90; Kikuyu frontier, 85, 342; Swahili trading, 21, 22; settlers, 47
Furedi, Frank, 297–8, 302

Ganda, 67
Gatu, Domenic, 428, 436
'Gatundu affray', 444
gender (*see also* circumcision), and ethnicity, 213, 329, 340; and labour, 359; and land, 359; and Mau Mau, 456, 457; and morality, 316–7; and Nairobi; sexual morality and, 316–7, 325, 386, 414; relations, 6, 340, 386–7, 390–91, 457
Gem, 52, 55
generation sets *riika, iregi*, among Kikuyu, 326–7, 336; succession, handover (*ituika, ndamathia*), 344–6, 475 n.131; 360, 364, 367, 370–1, 373–6; generational conflict, 56; over labour; Mau Mau as *ituika*, 450–1
German East Africa, *see* Tanzania
Getutu, 64
Ghai, Y.P., 83
Ghana (Gold Coast), 146–7, 170 n.24, 427
Gikonyo, Muchohi, 436
Giriama, 94
Girouard, Sir Percy (governor 1909–12), 88, 156
Grant, Nellie, 460
Griffiths, James (Sec. of State for the Colonies), 251
Grigg, Sir Edward (governor 1925–30), 112
Grogan, Ewart, 106
guns, firepower, 57

Gurr, Ted, 229
Gusii, 20, 32, 48, 49, 50, 51, 53, 58, 60–61, 62, 64, 66

Hailey, Lord, 164
Hardinge, Sir Arthur (consul-general, commissioner 1895–1900), 19, 33
Hay, Margaret Jean, 182
hegemony, 205–6
Heussler, Robert, 152, 159, 233, 237
historical analysis, 7
historical methodology, 2–3
historiography, 315; Africa generally, 204–212; colonial Kenya, 82–4; of Kikuyu ethnography, 320; of Mau Mau, *see* Mau Mau; projective and retrospective
Hobley, Charles (Uganda and E.A. administration 1894–1921), 26, 30, 53, 54, 56, 57, 65, 67, 71
Hodgkin, Thomas, 277, 281
Hooper, Cyril, 454
Hooper, Canon Handley, 454
Hountondji, Paulin, 210
Hyden, Goran, 27

ideology: of colonial states ('civilising mission'), 95, 235, 238–9, 323, 354; dynastic theory among Kikuyu, 428, 459; of Christianity, 274, 414–6; 'free things'; landlord theory: *see* dynastic theory; of Kikuyu, 315–6, 334, 353–5, 361–3, 410, 438–42; of Mau Mau; of multiracialism, 272–3, 283, 424; of nationalism, 275–6; of settlers, 354; of dominationaccumulation, 80; segregationist, 95
Igbo (Nigeria), 277
Imperial British East African Company (IBEAC), 16, 18, 22, 53, 85
imperialism, 322–6
Indians (Asians), settlement, 34; traders, 37, 38, 64; troops, use of, 17, 30, 34, 71, 87, 88
'indirect rule', myth and reality, 160–1
initiation, (*see also* circumcision), 388–9
Islam, 22; Muslims (Kikuyu), 53, 390
ituika, see, generation succession
ivory hunting, 51, 58, 78; trading: 21, 22, 26, 66, 85

Jackson, Frederick (IBEACO 1889–94; Uganda and E.A. administration 1894–1911), 69
jiggers (sandfleas), 23, 25, 381
Johnston, Sir Harry, 66, 68

Kabetu wa Waweru, 14
Kabras, 56, 70
'Kaffir farming' *see* squatters
Kaggia, Bildad, 333, 430, 436, 451, 462
Kagumba, Muhoya, 434
Kahinga Wachanga, 458
Kahuhia (Murang'a), 388, 393, 395
Kakamega, 70
Kakelelelwa, 56, 62, 67
Kakungulu, 69
Kalenjin-speaking peoples, 20, 23, 29–30, 51, 52, 66

Index

Index

Lancaster House Conference, 1960, 257
Land Commission, Kenya, (Carter) 1927, 115, 381
laini (Kik., means 'lines'), 88-9
land, 88-9; alienation of African, 2, 15, 35, 37, 228, 355, 361, 362, 365, 366; allocation of, by Mau Mau; competition for, 440-2, 459; consolidation, 254; cost of African, 358-9, 361; and ethnicity, 331-2; Kenya Land Commission ('Carter'), 381, 396, 400; 'reserves', African, 113-4; security of Kikuyu, 242, 362; 'stolen lands', demands for, 273, 365, 379, 396; struggles over, 137, 283, 361-2, 420, 'black', 424; terms for grants to settlers, 85-6; tenure, Kikuyu, 245, 339-40; title deeds, demands for, 378-9
landlessness, 229, 288, 425, 437, 460
Lari Massacre, *see under* Mau Mau
law, in Kenya, 324
Leakey, Canon Harry, 379, 389, 414
Leakey, Louis, 379, 399
Legislative Council (LegCo), 38, 90, 247, 251
legitimacy, state (*see also* state), 103, 142
Leys, Colin, 181
Leys, Dr Norman: 83
literacy, importance of, 294, 347
Local Native Councils (LNCs), African District Councils (ADCs), 162, 247, 372, 377, 381, 382, 392-3, 406
loyalists, among Kikuyu, 266, 291, 298
Low, D.A., 68, 83, 165
Lugard, Lord, 33, 160, 428
Luka, chief, 441, 453-4
Luo, 20, 21, 31, 39, 49, 50-1, 52, 53, 56, 57, 60-61, 63, 66, 67, 69, 110, 428
Luyia, 20, 21, 25, 26, 31, 50, 51, 55, 56, 60-1, 62, 63, 67
Luxemburg, Rosa, 134

McAuslan, J.P.W.M., 83
Macleod, Ian, 257
Maasai, 19-20, 21, 22-5, 26-7, 35-6, 39, 56, 67, 85, 460; ethnicity, 417; Maasai reserve, ('Maasailand'), 116, 417; relations with Kikuyu, 336-7, 348-9, 362, 383, 418
Machakos, 25, 26
Makhan Singh, 429, 431, 441
Mamdani, M., 102, 140
'man on the spot' dictum, 153, 154-5, 156
Marx, Karl, 104, 130, 277
Marx generational theory of history, 7
Marxism, structuralist, 6
Marxist analysis, 3-4, 136, 140-1, 182-3, 184-5, 187, 275; theory 5-6; critique of dependency theory, 129-30, 186, 199-200; formulations
Masters and Servants Ordinances (Kenya), 147-8; of 1906, 1910, 112; of 1916, 112, 113-4; rights of 'squatters' under, 114; offences ('desertion') under, 125 n.49; *kipande*, 170 n.29
Mathenge, Stanley, 456, 461
Mathu, Eliud, 247, 409, 413, 416, 424

Mathu, Mohammed, 430
Mau Mau, meaning of name, 426; 199-200, 217, 426-30, 437-51; British views of, 8, 274-5, 283, 328; 451-61; Corfield Report on, 275, 291, 301; deaths in, statistics, 295, 453; Detention Camps, 285, 448; ethnicity and, 315-7, 430; freedom council (*kiama kia wiathi*), 436; historiography of, 227-8, 258, notes 2-5, 270, 315-6; an internal ethnic war, 295, 426; interpretations of, 227-8, 229, 250; '*ithaka na wiathi*', 384; Kikuyu views on, 275, 286-314, 409; Lari massacre, 291, 441, 453-4; leaders, 338; metaphors of, 332-3; 'of the mind', 267; *nyimbo*, anthems of, 296, 358, 443-4; oaths, 227-63, 280, 425, 428-30, 445, 450; oaths, use of, 228, 250, 289-90; origins of, 9-10, 227-63, 280, 426-7; recruitment for, 357-8, 436-7, 449; religion and, 280, 441-8, 453-4; studies of, 8, 9-10; and violence, 252-5
Mazrui, Ali, 266-7, 287, 461, 468
mbari see 'clan'
Mbiu wa Koinange, Peter, *see under* Koinange
Mbona cult, 216, 217
Mbotela, Tom, 296
Mboya, Tom, 181, 191, 227, 316, 324, 328
Meillassoux, Claude, 130, 133
Meru, people and district, 19, 347-8, 449
missionaries, missionary societies, *see under* religion
military operations, British, 28-9, 54-5, 59-62
Mitchell, Sir Philip (Governor 1944-52), 197, 250, 252, 255, 260 n.44, 289, 435
modernization, 3; theory, 315, 316-7, 323, 329
modes of production (*see also* articulation), 129, 140, 352; domestic or household, 79, 132; estate, 102, 122; peasant commodity, 102, 129, 131; indigenous, 103, 117, 122; subordinated, 130; capitalist, 129-32
Moi, President Daniel arap, 218
Mombasa general strike, 1947, 416-7
Morai, Chief Ignatio, 421
monetary economy, in Kenya, 242-3
monopolies and monopsonies, 146
moral economies, 352
Mouzelis, Nicos, 132
Muchuchu, Job, 377, 382, 387
Mugo, Dedan, 422
Mugo, Gideon Kahika, 388
Muhimu, *see under* Mau Mau freedom council
Muhuho Gatheca, Chief, 412
Muhoya, chief, 453
Muigwithania, 318, 469 n.9, 320, 322, 374, 375, 381, 385, 388, 390, 400, 410, 414
Mukiri, *see* Parmenas
Mumenyereri, 318, 469 n.11, 410, 414
Mumia, Nabongo, 55, 56, 58, 64, 67, 69, 70
Mumias (place), 25, 26, 51, 52, 53, 55, 65
Mungai, James, 275
Mungai, John, 427, 428
Mungeam, G., 83
Munyua wa Waiyaki, 365
Munro, J. Forbes, 83, 182

Index

Index

and ethnicity, 215-7; Kikuyu, 343-4, 354, 367, 373, 458; Kikuyu Bible, 318, 330, 354, 360; Kikuyu Christians, 290, 331; and Mau Mau, 441-5, 447; missionaries, 15, 37-8, 111, 119-20, 228, 241, 369, 442, 445, 447; mission converts; 37-8; missionary societies: 393, 394-5, Africa Inland Mission (AIM), 367, 377, 392, 446; Church Missionary Society (CMS), 367-8, 370, 373, 386, 389, 393; Church of Scotland Mission (CSM), 367-8, 377, 392-3; religion and politics, Kikuyu, 273, 367; Salvation Army, 442

Renan, Ernest, 265, 266, 267, 269

reproduction (see also accumulation), 142-3

Registration of Natives Ordinance 1915, and 1919-20, 112

Resident Native Labourers' Ordinance 1918 (see also squatters), 114

resistance to colonial rule, 62-4

revival, see under East African Revival movement

Rey, Phillipe, 130, 135

riika, see under age sets and generation sets

rinderpest, 23, 25, 41, n.23, 63, 65

ritual uncleanness (thahu) among Kikuyu, 344

Rosberg, Carl, 228, 253, 287, 288, 290, 297, 315

Ross, McGregor, 83

Routledge, Mrs. K., 344

Royal Navy, 16, 17

Savage, D.C., 83

Sayre, Derek, 187

Sclater's Road, 52

Selznick, Philip, 233

Senegal, 163

settlers, European, in Kenya, 1, 6, 34-6, 37, 38, 47-8, 84, 88-9, 92-3, 105-7, 108, 118-9, 195-7, 235-7, 239, 242, 283-4, 324, 405-6, 407

Senteu, 25

sex, see gender

slave trade, 78; Arab/Swahili, 16, 17, 26, 51, 146

social engineering, colonial see development

social services, in African colonies, 149

Sociétés indigènes de prévoyance, see Cooperative societies, French

societies, capitalist, 138; indigenous, 137, 140-1, 238-9; precapitalist, 138; restructuring of, 149-50

soil erosion and conservation, 151, 245, 285

Somali, 17, 28

sorcery, sorcerers, 344, 346, 367, 409, 426

Sorrenson, M.P.K., 83

Sotik Kipsigis, 66

South Africa, 205-6, 215-6, 219

Southern African, settlement in, 47-8

Soyinka, Wole, 211

squatters ('Kaffir farmers'), 36, 37, 89, 90, 108-9, 114, 194; Kikuyu, 90, 355, 379, 383-5, 399, 403, 407, 417, 419-20, 427; and Mau Mau, 274, 284, 426, 432, 433, 460

spiralists (see also straddlers), 357, 380, 386

state, capitalist, 79, 142-3; colonial, 2, 22, 79-80, 83-4, 101-4, 122, 131, 133, 135-6, 138, 140-175, 151-63, 166-7, 180, 185-88, 192-3, 432; state building, control, 31-6; conquest, 5, 21-2, 205-6, 211; formation, 5, 15, 31-6, 36-9, 43, n.70; legitimation of, 142-3, 158-9; relative autonomy of, 5, 122, 142, 188, 195-6; theories of, structuralist, 7, 132, 182-3, 184-5, 186-7; instrumentalist, 187; derivationist, historical, 141

state building, control, 31-6

Stichter, Sharon, 182

straddling, straddlers (see also spiralists), 104, 182, 198, 324, 340, 355-6, 357, 372, 416

structuralism (see also state), structuralist origins of articulation, 130; role of state, 149

Sudanese soldiers, 17, 30, 62, 69, 70

Swahili language, 33; people 17, 21, 22, 51, 52, 53, 57, 63, 70

Swainson, Nicole, 201

Swazi, Swaziland, 47, 49

Swynnerton Plan, 459

Tanzania (Tanganyika, German East Africa), 47, 147, 148, 163, 164, 173 n.65, n.66, 209

Tate, H.R., 119

taxes, taxation, 14, 38-9, 57, 62, 71, 81, 110-11, 114-5, 121, 125-6, n.56 131, 137, 147, 149, 155-6, 157-6, 157-8, 173 n.65, n.66, 187; hut tax, 32, 58, 69, 87, 88, 92, 106; tax collectors, 37; poll tax, 92, 106

Teso, 51

thabari, 30, 349

thahu, 344, 367

Thebere, Sam, 326-7, 334, 359, 380, 401, 403, 437, 462

Thompson, E.P., 182

Throup, David, 299, 315

Thuku, Harry, 368, 370-1, 373, 374, 380, 400-1, 405, 410, 412, 425, 428-9, 461

Tignor, R., 83

Tilly, Charles, 183

trade, traders (see also capital, commercial), 169 n.19, n.20; Swahili, 21-2, 26, 65, 66; Kikuyu caravan, 22, 25, 26; East Asian (Indian), 33, 37, 38, 64, 71, 87, 170, n.24; African, 22, 64, 65, 66; Somali stock, 38; white, 33; French colonial, 169, n.18

trades union, 428, 430-1

'tribalism', tribe formation, see ethnicity

tsetse fly, 23, 25

Tugen, 20

ucenji ('heathendom'), mucenji, acenji, 381, 390, 411, 423

Uganda (Protectorate), 16, 26, 48

Uganda Railway, 16, 64; economics of, 83-4

Ugenya Luo, 51, 52, 57, 67, 69

Uiguano wa Muingi ('the Unity of the Community'), 228

underdevelopment, 179; theory of, 138, 140

Van Vollenhoven, Jan, 157

'villagization', 254

violence, in Kenya, African, 62; British, 13, 15,

Index